Taxing Women

Taxing
Women

Edward J. McCaffery

The University of Chicago Press
Chicago and London

EDWARD J. MCCAFFERY is professor of law at the University of
Southern California and the California Institute of Technology.

The University of Chicago Press, Chicago 60637
The University of Chicago Press, Ltd., London
© 1997 by the University of Chicago
All rights reserved. Published 1997
Printed in the United States of America

06   05   04   03   02   01   00   99   98   97   1   2   3   4   5

ISBN: 0-226-55557-7 (cloth)

Library of Congress Cataloging-in-Publication Data

McCaffery, Edward J.
    Taxing women / Edward J. McCaffery.
      p. cm.
    Includes bibliographical references and index.
    ISBN 0-226-55557-7 (cloth : alk. paper)
      1. Women—Taxation—Law and legislation—United States.
    2. Women—Taxation—United States. I. Title.
KF6289.8.W6M38   1997
336.2′0082—dc20   96-30188
                                    CIP

To Cruz

Contents

Tables and Figures

Acknowledgments

I could not have written this book without a good deal of help from my friends. It grew, rather remotely by the time I had finished it, out of two law review articles I mention in the bibliography. Many generous individuals and institutions helped me in those projects, and I thank them in the initial footnote of each; I here incorporate them all by reference. Scott Altman deserves a special mention of thanks, for his patient, ever thoughtful advice throughout the life of this project. Judith Resnik was a source of inspiration and many good research leads.

I thank Bruce Ackerman for encouraging me to do this book in the first place. I benefited from many discussions and workshops as I wrote. Nancy Staudt organized a conference on Critical Tax Theory at SUNY-Buffalo Law School; Jack Bogdanski organized one on Taxation and the Family at Lewis and Clark Law School, where I had the immense pleasure of meeting and sharing ideas with Marjorie Kornhauser and Larry Zelenak, whose work in the area I had long admired. Michael McIntyre kindly invited me to participate in a roundtable discussion at the National Tax Association's annual meeting, where I had the good fortune to meet Gene Steuerle. A brown-bag seminar at the California Institute of Technology allowed me to share ideas with many gifted individuals. A symposium on Institutional Barriers Facing Women in the Workplace sponsored by the UCLA *Women's Law Journal* allowed me to develop many of the concepts expressed in part 4 with greater precision and care, as did a faculty workshop at the University of San Diego Law School.

Other individuals were of particular help with the text. Boris Bittker, always the gentleman and scholar, kindly shared much of the intellectual history of tax with me. Carolyn Jones, whose work I much admire and use generously, especially in chapter 2, kindly read all of part 1 and gave me invaluable advice. Joni Hersch, whom I have yet to meet in person, but with whom I have shared many phone conversations, e-mail exchanges, and written correspondence over the years, was saintly in her patience in reading through the entire manuscript and giving me much-needed advice about labor-market economics. Grace Ganz Blumberg, who started the whole field of gender theory and tax, was a wonderful inspira-

tion, a source of background information, and, ultimately, a reader of
the entire manuscript, with excellent support, detailed comments, and
advice throughout.

As I wrote away, I was fortunate to have an excellent companion at my
side. Cindy Benton was more than a research assistant; she was a partner
throughout. Cindy patiently read every page nearly as I wrote it, and is
much responsible for the progress of the manuscript into its present form.
Cindy also organized a group of liberal arts student readers, whose input
was extremely valuable: Rhiannon Evans, Trevor Fear, Hannah Fearnley,
Helen Franks, Mark Masterson, Ellen Mulligan, and Alex Watts-Tobin. Of
this group, Sylvia Brainin deserves special mention and thanks for her
wonderful editorial comments on the whole manuscript. Jacqueline
Hough was an indispensable help with bibliographic materials. Laura Fry
and Kelley Poleynard greatly assisted in copyediting and page proofs.
Rosemary Hendrix helped in countless ways.

The library at the University of Southern California Law School never
ceases to amaze and impress me. Under the direction of Albert Brecht, the
librarians at this magnificent institution met every request I tossed to
them. Pauline Afuso, David Burch, Laura Cadra, Darin Fox, Hazel Lord,
and Brian Raphael deserve particular thanks for their ever-diligent help.

Other institutions have made major contributions. Some of the work
on the book transpired during a very productive year visiting at the Yale
Law School, under the tutelage of Dean Guido Calabresi. Many of the final
stages were done while I was spending part of my time at the California
Institute of Technology, with special thanks due to John Ledyard, Chairperson of the Division of Humanities and Social Sciences. Most of all, I
need to thank USC. Some portion of this gratitude goes to the Economics
Department, especially to Michael Magill, who tolerated an always distracted and distracting part-time student trying to learn some economics.
Some portion also goes to the Program in the Study of Women and Men
in Society, and to Judith Grant and Amy Richlin, who were a source of
inspiration and support. Another portion goes to the Philosophy Department, especially Sharon Lloyd, who generously allowed me to audit her
fine classes in political theory. But the lion's share goes to the Law School,
its faculty, and its ever-supportive dean, Scott Bice. A research leave from
teaching responsibilities in the fall of 1995 was especially critical in helping me to get the work done.

At the University of Chicago Press, Geoff Huck was a wonderfully patient and optimistic editor, who believed in the project even when its
written incarnation gave little reason to do so. Wilma Ebbitt worked wonders with the manuscript, and Leslie Keros was also most helpful. I am
grateful to several anonymous reviewers of both an initial proposal and a
later manuscript, arranged by both the University of Chicago Press and
other presses along the way.

Finally, there is the matter of my own family. My wonderful daughters, Cathleen and Allegra, never cease to bring joy to their tired and distracted daddy. Most of all, though, I owe thanks to my wife, Cruz-Elena Sundquist. Many authors write at this point that, without their spouse, there would be no book. While that is certainly true in my case, it might be better and more truly written that, without my spouse, there would be no author. Thanks, for everything.

Introduction

THE BASIC STORY

This book consists of one large story and many smaller ones. The large story has to do with the tax system of the United States and its effects on women. In a nutshell, it runs as follows: Major elements of tax were put in place in the 1930s, 1940s, and 1950s. This was a time when the traditional family—in which the man as father and husband worked outside the home and the woman as mother and wife worked inside it—was dominant. Tax law changes were put in place to foster and reward this single-earner household. These changes were left in place, all but unexamined, as the system kept growing. The tax system's strong bias in favor of single-earner families now sits uneasily under modern conditions. It pushes against stable families at the lower-income levels, against working wives at the upper-income ones, and, by limiting satisfactory options, against the many families in between. Everywhere women, especially working wives and mothers, are left stressed and unhappy.

Meanwhile, this political/historical tale merged into an intellectual/ historical one. The mainstream tax policy academy legitimated the structure of tax with a rhetoric of fairness, neutrality, and common sense. An emergent feminist voice was barely heard, even when its cries were consistent with basic economic principles. Changes in the workforce, such as the rising participation rate of married women, masked the need to reexamine first principles that had become obscured from view. But these changes have taken place in the face of lingering barriers to a richer, deeper equality. The result is the paradox that has objective measures of women's success, like the narrowing of the gender wage gap, accompanied by subjective measures of their frustration. All the while men have experienced surprisingly, even shockingly little pressure to change or to bear much of the burden of remodeled images of work and family. More dynamic, creative, and flexible ways of combining work and family have failed to emerge to help working wives and mothers deal with the contemporary facts of life.

1

SMALLER STORIES

Several smaller stories illustrate that one large story. The most extended are the true stories of Elizabeth and Susan, who make their first appearance at the start of chapter 1. These women decide to abandon the workforce after bearing children and witnessing firsthand the interaction of taxes and labor market forces on their lives and careers. There are also the stories of actual couples like Connie and David, each a successful young lawyer, who both work but who jointly decide that David's career must come first when trade-offs have to be made, as they inevitably do. To highlight the important class dimensions of the general story, there are stories of families, like the hypothetical Lowers, Middles, and Uppers, who play prominent roles in chapter 6. We will come to see the potentially severe impacts of tax rates in excess of 50 percent on wives in the lowest income classes; particular burdens on part-time labor; dramatic incentives for wives to stay home and for husbands to work more.

All of these and more are the stories of the tax system in context. While it is not always narrowly the case that the tax system "causes" these problems—and, to be clear, I am not claiming that tax is the sole or even the major cause of gender bias in America—the tax system does work together with other features of contemporary life to generate these effects, and never to alleviate them. Contexts matter. Tax laws do not operate in a vacuum, on a blackboard, or in a computer. They play a role as both cause and effect in the dynamics of daily life.

The bigger themes of the book become most clear in these smaller personal stories. The tax system, in itself and when combined with the rest of our social, political, and economic life, can have dramatic effects on fundamental decisions such as whether to marry or stay married, to work or not, to work part time or full. Political, economic, and legal systems, illustrated by the tangled web of tax laws, arise out of particular times and perspectives. Wittingly or not, these systems come to embody and then to entrench certain views of society and mundane, practical life. After their initial appearance, these systems take root and serve as anchors against greater social change. The brunt of the anchor's weight, at least in the case of the tax system, has fallen on women.

NOT JUST MARRIED WITH CHILDREN

This book will discuss how the tax laws treat married women with children. But it is not concerned solely with that category. Married mothers do, of course, form a large and vitally important class of persons. Even today, with falling marriage and fertility rates, statistics suggest that nearly 90 percent of women will get married, and at least 85 percent will bear one or more children. Indeed, the category of married women with children is so large that we can expect employers to consider all women in their relation to it, that is, as potentially or actually married, as parents or potential parents, and so on. That presumption turns out to have large effects in the labor market.

But all mothers, married or not, are affected by how the law treats married women with children. In 1992, 24 percent of all children in the United States lived in female-headed households, with no father present. A stunning 46 percent of these families lived below the official poverty line; many others were just above it. In 1993, 31 percent of all births in this country were to unwed women. The tax system's bias against two-earner families plays a role in these patterns, because it is seldom financially feasible to have a stable, two-worker family among the lower-income classes. Since a large percentage of African American and other minority group families are poor, these class biases take on a racial and ethnic cast. The same system set up with wealthy white families in mind, which still pushes wives in upper-income families to stay home, also pushes against stable families among the poor.

There is of course much that is offensive in reducing women to categories like "single mother" or "married with children," and I don't want to contribute to that effect. But the tax law has done so, and we will miss much of the story if we fail to concentrate on working wives and mothers. It was with the more or less conscious idea of this category of women as being essentially and ideally domestic, as stay-at-home mothers, that major elements of the tax law were created.

How society taxes married women with children has an impact on basic decisions about work, careers, and family. But our tale of taxing women is also simply illustrative of many other tales that could be told. The tax laws affect all of us, individually and as members of various groups. Once we have come to see that tax is unavoidably and pervasively political, and has in fact been used consciously and unconsciously in the service of particular political causes all along, we will be well on our way toward a better, deeper understanding of the life we are living. Many books could follow: about taxing men, single-parent households, racial and ethnic groups, same-sex couples, the elderly, nonresidents, and so on. Tax is political in spades. It is time we faced up to this fact.

EXPANDING THE STORY

With the one central theme in mind of the tax system and its effects on women, others emerge. The tax system becomes a major reason why real-world labor markets do not function as ideal economic theory would have them function. Once we have seen how tax has a dramatic impact on women and on the structure of work and family, the next step is to see how these effects interact with other features of our lives. Part 4 develops the story of how rational individuals in "free" markets, operating against the backdrop of significant market failures, including especially the tax laws, can generate a highly restrictive and gendered labor market. The story I shall tell is one among many labor market stories that could be told. I use it to illustrate the important point that the biases of the tax system cannot plausibly be confined to tax alone.

Another insight in this expansion of the tax tale is that the "gender gap," or the difference between women's and men's wages, is an incomplete measure of what truly matters. Many women seem to have accepted an ultimatum. The gender wage gap is closing in part because those women who work do so the way men have always worked and continue to work. Working women continue to educate themselves, work full time, persist in their career choices, marry later, have fewer children and have them later in life. In the face of these trends, the narrowing of the gender gap is neither surprising nor cause for automatic joy. If women act as men have always acted and continue to act, they should be paid like men. That's an important element of equality, to be sure, but it hardly begets gender justice, all by itself.

This gets complicated. Some women want to work exactly the way they are working, and there need not be anything essentially gendered about patterns of work, career, or ambition—full-time work is not "male" any more than housework is "female." What I mean to point to is an idea that has gotten lost in the process: the erstwhile promise, or hope, that the liberation of women would bring fundamental constructive change to the social structures of work and family. This has not happened, by and large, because markets have not changed—women have. Women have had to alter and even contort their behavior to fit traditional male patterns, while men, families, and the workplace have changed little, if any. Women are learning how to work within a structure laid down in a prior era of entrenched patriarchy, an era that created barriers against its own possible dismantlement.

The gender wage gap is not a complete measure of equality because meaningful, respectful equality can come only when we allow women and men to make diverse choices in their life plans and projects. I mean to restore a focus on the individual side of labor markets, to talk about individuals, their freedom and their choices. Many who care about gender discrimination have abandoned this individualistic focus because it appears too difficult to navigate twin dangers. On the one hand is a Scylla of free market, laissez-faire ideology, which would obligate us to accept every individual's choices and preferences as they stand. Under this view, we can advocate no change, as if this were the best of all possible worlds. The other hand features a Charybdis of "social engineering" that would have us throw out all reflections of individual choice, substituting some arbitrarily chosen and centrally mandated plan for betterment in their stead. Under this view, it seems as if some culturally elite vanguard presumes to know what is best for all of us.

It is possible to steer clear of these perils. The institutional rigidity in our models of work, career, and family, and the signs of psychic stress and unhappiness disproportionately manifest in women, point to something that is still deeply wrong. A close study of our tax laws shows that individual choices are being burdened and shaped by social structures that are unfair along gendered lines. Some progressive critics would reject markets and liberalism altogether; some conservative ones would abandon the project of social theory and conscious reform altogether. I believe that we can have better markets, and a better liberalism.

SOME ANSWERS

This book is mainly a description and criticism of modern tax structures, with a sustained focus on their gendered dimensions. The gendered structure of contemporary life is deep, and my project is mainly to help expose a little more of it. I imagine myself to be a therapist, aiming to help his client, here society at large, to better understand itself. I have lived with the ideas in this book for a long time, and I have come to appreciate their depth and complexity. I have no magic solutions, and I do not feel drawn to pretend that I do, even for purposes of writing a catchier book. The problems I will be describing are our problems, and we—I hope, a better informed, more inclusive and empowered "we," committed to equal concern and respect for all of our fellow citizens—will have to come to terms with them. I am especially worried that a focus on any particular solution, all of which can be controversial, complex, and particular, might distract from the greater and more permanent task of self-understanding.

Still, I will be offering at least tentative proposed solutions. I do so for several reasons: to offer some hope for a way out of the binds confronting women today; to show that solutions are possible; to further the intellectual history by demonstrating that particular, and particularly gendered, answers have been chosen all along, to the exclusion of other less gendered but equally available answers; to help come to a better understanding of the problems. My answers, such as they are, fall into three broad categories.

One is a series of practical recommendations, arising out of parts 1 and 2: moving to separate filing under the income tax and a second-earner exemption or a sharing of earnings under the social security system; putting in place more generous allowances for child-care expenses; restructuring the fringe benefit system. Two is an ideal legislative change, drawn from the theory of optimal tax, to be looked at in part 3: tax married women less; tax married men more. Three is more process-oriented and theoretical: it is simply that we should think about tax more, and differently, than we do now. I feel most insistent about this last "solution." Whatever else we do, we ought to begin to analyze tax from the perspective of gender justice and other political concerns. I hope that this book is a first step on what could, and indeed should, be a long road.

A QUICK SKETCH

The above survey captured the book's main themes. Here is a quick overview of the whole, which is integrated and interrelated in many ways. There are four parts, each with three chapters.

Part 1 considers joint filing under the income tax. Chapter 1 sets out some important vocabulary and concepts. Chapters 2 and 3 explore the history of joint filing.

Part 2 adds to the detailed understanding of the facts of tax. Chapter 4 considers the increasingly important, and deeply gendered, social security system. Chapter 5 adds four further factors: the tax treatment of child-care costs and other work-related expenses; the nontaxation of "imputed income"; the structure of the tax-favored fringe benefit system; and state and local taxes. Chapter 6 pulls together the five previous chapters, discussing tax facts in the context of both some general behavioral incentives and three hypothetical families of different income levels. Parts 1 and 2 together form what I call the accountant's tale—seeing the facts of tax and their effects on women as an accountant might.

Parts 3 and 4 expand the story. Part 3 deals with social and economic theory about tax, and looks at contemporary rhetoric and politics. Chapters 7 and 8 explore the theory of optimal tax, which has long recommended that we tax married women far less than married men, exactly the opposite of what the tax laws now do. Chapter 9 engages in a lengthy criticism of the contemporary tax proposals found in conservative documents such as the *Contract with America*, along with a look at "flat tax" plans.

Part 4 extends the story into labor markets. I discuss in a general way how labor markets might be expected to work in the face of a deeply gendered tax system, and I expand on the particular point that the narrowing of the gender wage gap is neither surprising nor necessarily cause for joy. Chapter 12 offers final observations on the case for and against reform, along with some more or less practical ideas for change.

CHOICES AND AUDIENCE

I have tried to write a book that many people can read. This has not been as easy as I hope that it looks, because the issues I am addressing are in many ways complex. My primary intended audience is those persons interested in issues of gender theory and justice in contemporary society.

I do not assume any specific knowledge of tax or economics; I have taken pains to be clear in these matters. I use simple examples throughout, which capture the basic essence of tax without its often dizzying details.

I hope that this audience, which might broadly be called feminist, is ready and willing to listen. Tax is important both in itself and as an example. Considering tax in depth yields an enriched look into the nature of gender bias. Yet few people, even among those with a feminist bent, are well aware of the issues at stake. This book is an instance of applied social theory. It is about how a detailed consideration of a big structure like the tax system can deepen, confirm, and shape the insights of feminist thought. A fairly straightforward, analytic consideration of tax—as most of this book will be—shows those who would look that there is much work yet to be done on the road toward gender justice in America. It is meant, in some considerable part, as a sort of wake-up call for feminists to pay more attention to large socioeconomic systems like tax.

People can of course be concerned with gender justice and other matters at the same time, and so I aim to reach other audiences. Much of this book points the way to specific reforms in the tax laws and our understanding of those laws. I consider the political history of tax and the intellectual history of the tax policy academy with regard to issues of gender and tax. I also have concerns with social theory more generally. One theme that will emerge, for example, is that we are not adequately living up to the promise of liberal democratic theory: We are not working hard enough to allow people to make diverse choices in their life plans. The labor market, for one major example, features a narrowly constricted range of job types, keeping a more dynamic work/family balance from emerging.

Finally, I do hope, however naively, that all Americans, in their roles as taxpayers and citizens, will learn something from this book. Coming to see how the tax system works and the choices that have gone into its working all along is an important end in itself. I hope that even those who disagree with my feminist and liberal social theory orientation can learn some of the facts of tax from this book.

My choice of audience dictated many other choices. I have tried to avoid technical discussions and vocabulary. For readers who want more detail, I have included a substantial bibliography at the end of the book, and I also make reference to important sources in the text. In these stylistic choices, I have tried not to sacrifice content or accuracy. The story I aim to tell has dramatic effects on just about every American life and on our understanding of the gendered structure of contemporary society. My mission is to make this story accessible to the people affected by it—that is, I believe, all of us.

PART ONE

Getting Married, Tax Style

1 Women on the Margin

Elizabeth had worked for ten years as a magazine editor, taken maternity leave, and returned to the workplace a year later. One day, as she writes in *Redbook*, "I found myself invited to a good-bye party I hadn't expected to attend—my own." Why had it come to this? A few months before, Elizabeth and her husband had met with the family accountant, who presented numbers telling a simple, irrefutable fact. After taxes and additional expenses, especially child-care costs, Elizabeth's work was *losing* money for the family. "I had to quit because I couldn't afford my job," Elizabeth reluctantly concluded.

Susan worked part time, three days a week, in the community relations department of a Connecticut public utility. As described in the *New York Times*, Susan was married with two young children, and made a comfortable salary "in the $35,000–$40,000 range." But one day Susan sat down with her husband, himself the accountant in her story. He showed her figures indicating that her job was not netting the family much money, again after taking into account taxes and work-related expenses. Susan decided to quit her job, stay home, and raise the children full time. Several years later, with her youngest child entering kindergarten, Susan returned to the part-time workforce in a different, lower-paying job. "If I had wanted to get back in where I left, I might have had to step back in salary a year or two," Susan told the *Times* reporter.

These true stories illustrate the effects of the tax system on women, especially married women with children. In each case, an accountant presented a fact to a working wife: her work outside the home was not worth much, from a strictly monetary perspective, after taking into account taxes and other expenses. Working outside the home is important for many reasons besides money. It maintains workplace skills, provides access to a circle of other workers, gives relief from the often stressful chores of housekeeping and childrearing, breeds a certain economic and social independence that can be essential in the increasingly common case of divorce, and more. But relatively few married women can afford to lose money by working away from home. Elizabeth's poignant conclusion, "I had to quit," captures her sense of enforced frustration. Many other married women, like Susan, clearly enjoy working outside the home, as well as spending time inside it with their children, but they remain conflicted about their complex and multifaceted roles. Such women are hard pressed to continue juggling two domains of work in the face of the accounting fact that their work outside the home nets little. The average working wife in a middle- or upper-income household sees two-thirds of her salary lost to taxes and work-related expenses; many wives are even harder hit by accounting realities.

Young mothers in the lower economic classes face a different dilemma. For these women, staying home is often not an option. The need for cash is too strong. What gives way for these women is marriage itself. In 1992, 24 percent of children in the United States lived in female-headed, single-parent households. A stunning 46 percent of these households subsisted below the official poverty line, and most of the rest were not far above it. Working wives are *least* likely to be found in low-income two-parent households; only about 5 percent of the poorest fifth of two-parent households feature two workers. Although in part this absence of a second worker is itself a cause of poverty, it is also an effect of the fact that second earners among the poor can face tax rates well in excess of 50 percent, sometimes even exceeding 100 percent. A bias against two-earner families is a bias against families themselves when all adults are pressed to try to work for money.

The stories of Susan and Elizabeth, and the recognition of lower-income single mothers, will be with us throughout this book. The impact of tax on women is not always as dramatic as in these cases, and women are not always as conscious of the effects. But tax exerts major pressures on all women, both in and of itself, as I consider first, and in connection with other features of the social and economic landscape, as I consider later. The basic push of tax is toward traditional single-earner families. This plays out differently across different economic classes. It pushes against stable family structures among the poor and toward traditional ones among the rich, and it makes for stress on the many women who, like Elizabeth, are caught somewhere in between. That these effects are often obscure doesn't deny their existence. What we don't know can definitely hurt us.

SOME EXAMPLES

The first tax-related factor to consider is joint filing under the income tax. Because this idea forms a core part of the tale of taxing women, I'll spend all of part 1 on it. Some hypothetical examples will carry us along the way.

Tom and Tina Traditional have been married for many years. Tom works in the paid workforce; Tina does not. Tom earns $60,000 a year as an engineer. Tina stays home with the two young children. This type of single-earner family was in fact the historical and statistical norm when major aspects of the tax system were created in the 1930s and 1940s. Laws and social practices throughout the first half of the twentieth century continued to entrench the man's dominance over the family's economic resources. Alice Kessler-Harris and other feminist historians eloquently remind us that women have always worked, and I shall take care to differentiate work in the paid workforce from work—no less important or taxing, in a nonfinancial sense—in the unpaid or domestic sectors. But we must learn to talk in terms that capture the gendered structure of society or we'll miss the biases being perpetuated and entrenched in earlier eras.

Emma and Earl Equal have been married for several years. Each works as a high-school teacher, and each earns $30,000. The Equals have young twins, and the family struggles with a variety of child-care arrangements while each parent works outside the home. There were almost no real Equals until fairly recently. When the curtain opens on the story of taxing women, around 1913, few married women worked, and only a small fraction of them, if any, would have been equal earners with their husbands. As the economic historian Claudia Goldin writes in *Understanding the Gender Gap:* "A white, married woman employed outside her home around 1900 was likely to be a manufacturing worker, and her husband was apt to be low paid, unemployed, sick, or idle for some other reason." Even today, more than 40 percent of married mothers stay home full time with their young children. In households where both parents work full time, year round, the average wife earned 63 percent of what her husband did in 1987. There are thus few real Equals, even today, but we want to have the Equals in view as an example of what could be.

I have chosen these fictional families earning the comfortable salary of $60,000 a year simply to have round numbers to work with while I explain basic concepts. The tax system has dramatic effects on women in all income classes, and we'll have plenty of occasions to look at both poorer and wealthier cases. In particular, chapter 6 will consider exemplary poor, middle-income, and rich families. By that time, we'll have a good understanding of the basic facts of tax, and we can look at contemporary reality more systematically.

To throw in a third point of comparison, consider also Sally Single, a young unmarried woman making $60,000 as an associate in a law firm. Single women have often worked. Goldin points out that "holding urbanization and nativity constant, the participation rate of young single women appears relatively stable over the period from 1890 to 1960." It has only been in very recent times, however, that such women have had access to good, high-paying jobs. In fact, at one critical juncture in chapter 3, I'm going to have to make Sally a man, to capture a fact of gender bias. But Sally is also a helpful example to have around as we unfold the central tale.

HOW MARGINAL RATES WORK

The present income tax works through a system of *progressive marginal rates*. This means that successive amounts of income are taxed at higher rates. The rate structure works like a ladder: as income moves up through the rate "brackets," it is subjected to higher rates *at the margin*. This means that it is only the most recent dollars—the ones in the higher bracket—that are subjected to the higher rates. Entering a new, higher bracket does not change the rates applied to the previous lower brackets.

Throughout the book, I'll set forth simple rate structures in a handful of tables. My examples are roughly reflective of rates in the mid-1990s, and my examples of salaries and so forth are put in 1995 dollars, unless I specifically mention otherwise. The exact schedules I'll use are rounded off and made clearer, with few brackets. Actual tax laws change all the time and are complex even at the level of specifying the relevant rates. But nothing important turns on a failure to match more precisely the current law. It is essential to our general task to step back a bit, to look for some forest atop the trees, shrubs, and weeds of modern tax laws.

Table 1 presents a simple hypothetical rate schedule for all taxpayers. What, exactly, does table 1 mean? Consider Ann, a single woman. If Ann earns $10,000, she does not have to pay any income tax; all of her income falls in the so-called zero bracket. In my simplified examples, this zero bracket automatically accounts for the standard and personal dependency deductions that, in the real world, take into account the number of children in a family. Imagine that Ann earns $30,000. How much tax must she pay? The answer is $3,000. Her first $10,000 remains in the zero bracket and generates no tax. The next $20,000 is taxed in the 15 percent bracket; 15 percent of $20,000 is $3,000, so this is her total tax. Note that being in the 15 percent bracket did not change the tax treatment of the first $10,000 of income. Note also that Ann's *average,* or what is sometimes called *effective,* tax rate is only 10 percent: she made $30,000, and paid $3,000, 10 percent of her total income, in taxes. For many purposes, this average rate is important. I'll generally be focusing on the marginal rate instead.

To drive this point home, imagine that Ann is offered a promotion, involving more responsibilities, longer hours, and an additional $5,000

TABLE 1. Basic Rate Schedule

INCOME	MARGINAL TAX RATE
$0–$10,000	0%
$10,001–$30,000	15%
$30,001–$60,000	30%
$60,001 and up	40%

in salary. What is this raise really worth to her? The correct answer is $3,500. Since Ann now makes $30,000, and the raise would increase it to $35,000, this *particular* $5,000 will fall in the 30 percent bracket, so that she would pay $1,500 in taxes on account of it. This is the relevant figure for Ann to consider. If she accepts the promotion and works harder, she will take home an additional $3,500, not the full $5,000. Her average tax rate is of no concern to her right now, for whether to accept the promotion, insofar as take-home pay matters, turns on her marginal rate alone.

The point of this example is that we live, and make our decisions, on the margin. It is marginal rates that should and do concern us; it is marginal rates that cash out into take-home dollars. The tax laws make very literal the "marginalization" of women. By adding together husband and wife under the rate schedule, tax laws both encourage families to identify a primary and a secondary worker, and then place an extra burden on the secondary worker because her wages come on top of the primary earner's. The secondary earner is on the margin. For now, we can take the secondary earner to mean the lesser-earning spouse, as it typically does. Susan and Elizabeth acted exactly as women on the margin should act. A big part of what the accountants were explaining to these women was that *their* income tax rate bracket depended on their *husbands'* wages.

Economists and accountants are used to marginal analysis, but many others are not, at least not formally, so it is worth driving home its meaning. The margin is a state of mind. We think "on the margin" when we hold factors that are not then before us, that we are not then thinking of changing, as fixed or constant. In the example of Ann contemplating her raise, it was a given that she already made $30,000, so that the additional $5,000 fell in the 30 percent bracket. Susan and Elizabeth engage in marginal analysis when they hold constant their husbands' work, as well as the fact that they have young children. The tax laws push married women like Susan and Elizabeth to think this way, and, once they do, they will come to see that their marginal tax rate is dictated by their husbands' wages. All of this contributes to the social marginalization of women as members of the paid workforce. There is a triple sense of "marginal" at work: The tax laws encourage wives to engage in marginal analysis, using a marginal rate structure, with the result that wives themselves end up on the margin of the workforce. We'll soon see just how precarious a place the margin can be.

JOINT FILING

Joint filing came about in 1948, well after the modern income tax began in 1913, and has been with us in the United States ever since. Joint filing means that husbands and wives are viewed as one taxpaying unit, filing one tax return, and paying tax under a consolidated rate schedule. This is

TABLE 2. 1948-Style Rate Schedules

INDIVIDUAL RATE SCHEDULE		MARRIED RATE SCHEDULE	
INCOME	MARGINAL TAX RATE	INCOME	MARGINAL TAX RATE
$0–$10,000	0%	$0–$20,000	0%
$10,001–$30,000	15%	$20,001–$60,000	15%
$30,001–$60,000	30%	$60,001–$120,000	30%
$60,001 and up	40%	$120,001 and up	40%

distinct from the system of "separate filing" that prevailed in America before 1948 and is today the most common method of taxing married persons in advanced democracies. Separate filing treats husbands and wives as individuals, each filling out his or her own return and paying tax under an individual rate schedule. "Married, filing separately," an option under current law, is *not* the same thing as "separate filing"; this is simply a clerical matter, and rarely used, because almost every couple would pay more tax if the spouses filed this way. "Married, filing separately" is not at all important in our main story. The distinction to bear in mind is between separate and joint filing.

Table 2, which we'll see again in its historical context in chapter 2, reflects this joint filing structure. Under joint filing, the Traditionals and the Equals both pay tax using the married persons' rate schedule set out on the right. Note that this is simply double the individual rate schedule set out on the left. The zero bracket extends to $20,000 rather than $10,000; the 15 percent bracket runs from $20,000 to $60,000 rather than $10,000 to $30,000, and so on.

Since each of our two couples makes $60,000, they each pay $6,000 in tax: nothing on their first $20,000; plus $6,000, or 15 percent, on the next $40,000. The equal tax paid by the Equals and the Traditionals reflects the norm of taxing "equal-earning couples equally." I'll get back to that in a minute, after we have gotten some more vocabulary out on the table.

THE "MARRIAGE PENALTY"

Under table 2, Sally Single, an unmarried person who makes $60,000, pays $12,000 in tax: nothing on her first $10,000; $3,000, or 15 percent, on her next $20,000; plus $9,000, or 30 percent, on her next $30,000. The fact that singles paid a much higher tax than equal-earning couples— Sally Single, the Traditionals, and the Equals each earn $60,000—gave rise to what came to be known as the singles' penalty. Congress partially addressed this situation in 1969 by creating the type of rate schedule we still have today, reflected in table 3. Table 3 is produced by holding the left-hand, singles' rate schedule constant, while reducing the level at

TABLE 3. Modern-Style Rate Schedules

INDIVIDUAL RATE SCHEDULE		MARRIED RATE SCHEDULE	
INCOME	MARGINAL TAX RATE	INCOME	MARGINAL TAX RATE
$0–$10,000	0%	$0–$16,000	0%
$10,001–$30,000	15%	$16,001–$48,000	15%
$30,001–$60,000	30%	$48,001–$96,000	30%
$60,001 and up	40%	$96,001 and up	40%

which new rate brackets take effect on the right-hand, married persons' schedule by 20 percent. Instead of extending to $20,000, the zero bracket now stops at $16,000; instead of going up to $60,000, the 15 percent bracket now goes to $48,000, and so on.

For now, I want to use table 3 to illustrate the concept of the marriage penalty. Sally Single still pays $12,000 in taxes, as she had under tables 1 and 2; the individual rate schedule has not changed in any of the examples. But the Equals and the Traditionals now pay more than they did under table 2, specifically $8,400: nothing on their first $16,000; $4,800, or 15 percent, on their next $32,000; plus $3,600, or 30 percent, on their next $12,000. That the married couples pay more under table 3 than they had under table 2, while single taxpayers pay the same, reflects the fact that the singles' penalty has been partially addressed. The relative share of taxes paid by single persons has gone down. That the Equals and Traditionals remain in lockstep illustrates the unshaken commitment to the goal of taxing equal-earning couples equally. But something else has happened in the move from table 2 to table 3: A so-called marriage penalty has been introduced.

This penalty refers to the fact that some couples pay higher taxes on getting married than they did as singles. It is in this sense—I'll explore other senses later—the Equals who pay the marriage penalty. As individuals, each making $30,000, they each pay $3,000, just as Ann did, using the left-hand schedule. On marrying, their combined tax increases from $6,000 to $8,400, under the right-hand schedule. Hence the marriage penalty; getting married increases the income tax paid. In my sample tables, the marriage penalty faced by couples like the Equals, $2,400, is in fact far higher than would result today; this follows from my attempt to use simple, round numbers. In chapter 3, we'll have occasion to look at actual figures that put the marriage penalty facing the Equals around $700. Daniel Feenberg and Harvey Rosen calculated that the marriage penalty for a family of four, where the husband and wife each earned $25,000, was $727 in 1994.

The Traditionals get a "marriage bonus" under both tables 2 and 3, because their tax goes down on marrying. Table 4 helps to summarize all

TABLE 4. Taxes and Couples

	TAX PAID ON $60,000			
RATE SCHEDULE (TIME PERIOD)	UNMARRIED EQUALS	MARRIED EQUALS	MARRIED TRADITIONALS	UNMARRIED TRADITIONALS (OR SALLY SINGLE)
I (1913–1948)	$6,000	$6,000	$12,000	$12,000
II (1948–1969)	$6,000	$6,000	$6,000	$12,000
III (1969–present)	$6,000	$8,400	$8,400	$12,000

of this. Table 4 shows us that the Traditionals, were they unmarried, would pay $12,000 in tax under all three rate schedules, just as Sally Single would. This is because Tom Traditional looks like Sally to the IRS: an unmarried person making $60,000. If the Equals were unmarried, they would pay $6,000 under all three schedules, because they would look like two Anns: two taxpayers, each earning $30,000.

Initially, getting married made no difference to either the Equals or the Traditionals, because the law, under table 1, had separate filing. Marriage was an irrelevance; the system had what came to be known as marriage neutrality. Under table 2, the 1948-style schedule, the Traditionals saw their taxes drop on marriage to $6,000. This schedule had no marriage penalties, only marriage bonuses. Under table 3, the modern-style rate schedule, the Traditionals still see their taxes drop on marrying, from $12,000 to $8,400, but the bonus is less than it had been under the 1948 schedule. Feenberg and Rosen calculate that 38 percent of all married couples got a marriage bonus in 1994.

The Equals got no particular benefit under table 2. They do not need a marriage bonus, because their tax, as unmarried persons, is as low as it can be. They take full benefit of the zero and 15 percent brackets as individuals. Put another way, the married rate schedule in table 2 is formed by doubling the figure in the individual rate schedule—that is, by assuming two spouses who earn equal amounts. But this is what the Equals are, anyway. Under table 3, in contrast, the Equals see things get *worse* when they marry. Their taxes go up to $8,400. That increase in their taxes on getting married is the marriage penalty. In 1994, 52 percent of all married couples, many of them lower income, paid some marriage penalty. (To complete the picture, 10 percent of all couples in 1994 saw no effect from marriage on their combined taxes.)

Table 1, reflecting the separate filing in place from 1913 until 1948, is marriage neutral. It has no marriage penalties or bonuses. Table 2, reflecting the initial joint filing schedule in place from 1948 to 1969, has only marriage bonuses, no penalties. Table 3, reflecting the modern-style compromise schedule in place from 1969 until the present, has both marriage penalties and bonuses in it. Tables 2 and 3, but not table 1, maintain that policy of equal-earning married couples' paying the same amount of tax.

THE SECONDARY-EARNER BIAS: OR, IT'S NOT THE MARRIAGE PENALTY

"The marriage penalty" has entered the national consciousness, or at least its vocabulary. Numerous articles now track it. From 1980 through 1995, the phrase appeared in more than 350 articles in the *New York Times* and *Washington Post*, combined. Awareness of the penalty has been heightened by its perhaps ironic increase under a Clinton administration tax bill. The *Contract with America* and its Christian Coalition cousin, the *Contract with the American Family*, which together I will call the *Contracts* and discuss in chapter 9, pick up on the concept. Some commentators bemoan the marriage penalty, while others question its practical significance: Do decisions to get married or not really turn on tax consequences?

Now I want to drive home a crucial point. The marriage penalty will become important when we look at lower-income families, because it is especially severe there, in both absolute and relative size. The penalty thus contributes to the high incidence of single-parent households—to the instability of family structures among the poor. But the marriage penalty is *not* a major part of the story of taxing women generally. The accountants were not telling Susan and Elizabeth to divorce so as to escape the marriage penalty. The major effect I want to emphasize—and it is important at all income levels—is the *secondary-earner bias*. The accountants *were* telling Susan and Elizabeth to stay home so as to escape the effect of this bias.

The marriage penalty turns out to be widely misunderstood, and I will try to clarify it later. In general, the very focus on marriage penalties is itself a gendered phenomenon: men are married in equal numbers with women, by definition, so marriage penalties become a man's concern. The modern focus on marriage penalties has been a way for upper-income families, whether or not they reflect any liberalized division of labor, to argue for and get tax relief. It has been, largely, a trick.

My main focus will instead be on the marginal burden on women as at least potentially secondary earners. In a rate structure with joint filing, the wife's wages come "on top of" the husband's: Her first dollar of salary is taxed at the bracket where the husband's salary has left her. This secondary-earner bias drove Susan and Elizabeth to call it quits, and it has *no* necessary connection to marriage penalties. We see this point most clearly in the second historical phase, from 1948 to 1969, under table 2. During this period, there was joint filing, no marriage penalties, yet a heavy bias against working wives.

This bias has two components. First, the rate structure encourages families to think in terms of a primary and a secondary worker, because there is one rate schedule applied to couples. To see this, let's focus on Emma Equal. Under separate filing, she ought to think and plan the way Ann did; actions that she is considering, like accepting a promotion or making a tax-deductible charitable contribution, take place at her marginal rate. Under joint filing, however, Emma faces a new and different question: Where does her salary come into play? That is, whose salary comes *first?* If Earl's work is taken as a fixed point, then, under table 2, *his* work triggers $1,500 in tax: nothing on the first $20,000; plus $1,500, or 15 percent, on the next $10,000. But now Emma's *first* dollar of earned income gets taxed in the 15 percent bracket, under table 2, and so her $30,000 salary triggers $4,500 in income tax. As table 4 showed, the Equals keep paying $6,000 as a couple before and after the 1948 rate change. But after that change, the internal dynamics of the marriage are altered. Emma's work is now taxed more heavily, and Earl's more lightly.

This question of where to place a spouse's income was *created* by the fact of joint filing; it did not make sense to think this way under separate filing. This same effect persists under the current flat tax plans that I'll look at more extensively in chapter 9: Earl and Emma in our example faced a large zero bracket level and then a single, flat-rate tax, just as they would under the current flat tax proposals. But as a married couple, Earl, being primary, pays $1,500 of tax on account of *his* $30,000, because he gets to use the zero bracket, while Emma, being secondary, must pay $4,500 on account of *her* $30,000. Each earns the same amount of income, but the secondary-earner wife pays *three times* the income tax on account of her earnings. The current flat-rate plans, which all retain joint filing, continue the large secondary-earner bias.

Once we've seen the first effect of joint filing—the creation of a question about the priority of the spouse's income—the second effect quickly follows. There are strong disincentives against second earners working in the paid workforce at all, because they enter it at high marginal tax rates. Since wives are overwhelmingly likely to be the secondary earner in potential two-earner families—a fact I'll discuss next—this burden falls on women. Moving from the "gender neutral" language that gives cover to the tax laws and into historical and statistical realities, this means that wives are taxed in a rate bracket dictated by their husbands' earnings. This is a big part of the accountant's tale, of the effect driving Susan and Elizabeth to call it quits, and of the economic forces breaking up lower-income families across America.

COMING IN SECOND

Once we've come to see the secondary-earner bias as the main problem, it becomes important to see why secondary earners are almost always wives. I know from extensive firsthand experience that this is a stumbling block for some: we don't want to say that the wife is "secondary" or "marginal." This is certainly understandable and commendable as a matter of our everyday speech. But insisting on inoffensive language gets in the way of understanding the actual offensive facts of the matter. Other people want to insist that a secondary-earner bias is not gendered, as a way to avoid calls for reform. But we shouldn't make it too easy for such people to avoid facing the facts of how we tax women.

There is no necessary reason to assume that the wife should be secondary. It is possible that the husband would be. It is also possible that both spouses resist marginal thinking altogether, taking as a fixed fact of their lives together that both will work outside the home. But once the question has been posed, there is apt to be a secondary earner in most families, and it is overwhelmingly likely to be the wife. However distasteful and gendered this fact might be, however we might wish for reality to be different, not seeing that women are far more likely to be the secondary earners will blind us to a very large set of problems. The nameless accountants advising Susan and Elizabeth were not so blind. They did not tell the husbands that *their* work outside the home was not worth very much; they did not propose clever solutions involving each spouse's moving to reduced or flexible-time schedules. They suggested instead that Susan and Elizabeth stay home, and these women listened. We need to see life through the eyes of these accountants to get at the current, and gendered, facts of tax.

For the most part, women are second earners simply because they earn less than their husbands. Married women make about 60 percent of what married men do. On average, two-earner families, at middle- and upper-income levels, sacrifice about 68 percent of the wife's lower salary to taxes and other expenses occasioned by her work. Because of this, there is strong pressure to look at the impact of the wife's earnings on both the family's bottom line and its general happiness. The wife's working outside the home becomes marginal or discretionary.

History is important in this discussion. Wives have long since been marginal earners, discretionary participants in the paid workforce. In the next chapter, we'll step back into the 1930s and 1940s, where there could be no doubt, in terms of economic facts or prevalent social attitudes, that the paid work of wives, when it existed at all, came second to that of their husbands. In 1936, 82 percent of all Gallup poll respondents thought that married women should not work outside the home at all, and 75 percent of the women polled agreed. In 1940, less than 10 percent of married mothers were working outside the home. Goldin writes that "as late as 1940, most young working women exited the labor force on marriage, and only a small minority would return." Marriage bars keeping married women from working in certain professions continued into the 1950s; 70 percent of school districts in 1942 did not retain single women who got married, and 87 percent refused to hire married women in the first instance. A host of law cases, which Carolyn Jones and Reva Siegel and other legal historians have brought to attention, show that the paid work of wives was often assumed to be the husbands'; working wives were simply extending their "natural" subservient role into the commercial world.

Even today, when we comfort or delude ourselves that those times are behind us, men are three to four times more likely to be the single earner in single-earner households. Where the wife happens to be the single earner, the family earns about half as much as when the husband is— suggesting lower-income families with unemployable husbands. More than 40 percent of married wives with young children stay home full time with their children, whereas fewer than 5 percent of married men do. Nor have attitudes changed much. A 1977 poll, conducted in the context of the movement then pending to ratify the Equal Rights Amendment, revealed that 62 percent of respondents thought "married women should not hold jobs when jobs were scarce and their husbands could support them," and 55 percent thought it "more important for a woman to advance her husband's career than to have one of her own." The contemporary *Contracts* show that these attitudes persist into the 1990s.

Many couples decide outright that the wife's work outside the home comes second. Mary Frances Berry, in *The Politics of Parenthood,* tells a typical late twentieth-century tale. Connie and David are married and live in Washington, D.C. Each is a graduate of Harvard Law School, and each landed a job in a prestigious law firm. But while David made partner, Connie took to a slower-paced track to give her more flexibility to deal with their children. This was a thoroughly conscious decision, by an intelligent, well-educated, and loving couple, to make one spouse the primary worker and the other the primary parent—and hence the secondary worker. Connie was put on the margin.

Regardless of the historical and statistical patterns, either culturally or for a particular married couple, the realities of childbirth tend to put the married mother on the margin. She has left her work, at least temporarily, to give birth, and the question facing the family is whether she should go back into the workforce. This question carries a large amount of gendered construction. Why is it that we face the young-mother-going-back-to-work question so often and so uneasily, while we hardly ever seem to confront the young-father-staying-at-work question? But that's part of the main story, not an objection to it. Gendered tax laws have arisen out of gendered times, and the two contribute to each other. The questions we ask have to do with the structure we have created; they spring from that structure, and they help to perpetuate it. Looking at a young mother's decision to work outside the home or not, we see that she faces a marginal income tax rate dictated by her husband's earnings.

There is one large class of families where there would seem, at first glance, to be no secondary earner: single-parent, female-headed households. In 1992, as I've already noted, 24 percent of all children in the United States lived in households with only a mother present, and a stunning percentage of them were poor. It may appear that there is no secondary earner in such cases; in fact the very strong bias against a second worker in lower-income households contributes to the prevalence of such single-parent households. Among the poor, where the need for two earners is greatest, the tax on the second earner is also the greatest. These families have nowhere to hide from the tax, except to split up. The poor may not understand the details of tax any more than the rich do, but they see the reality of two-earner families under tremendous pressure. It may at first seem surprising that among the poorest one-fifth of two-parent households, having two earners is especially uncommon; only about 5 percent of this large group has two workers. But this makes perfect sense when we consider the severe economic pressures on this particular family model.

In sum, women are and have long been at the margins of the workforce, in terms of wages, power, costs, and competing claims on their time. The tax laws both build on and contribute to this marginalization, by putting the wife's income at the margins of the family's. History, current economic statistics and reality, and culturally conditioned psychology all contribute to these facts. Every scholar who writes about the secondary-earner bias in tax, from a feminist or any other perspective, acknowledges that such earners are almost always women. I'll mainly assume that fact for the rest of the book.

A BIT OF THEORY: TAXING "EQUAL-EARNING COUPLES EQUALLY"

The equal tax burden on the Equals and the Traditionals reflects a conscious policy of taxing equal-earning couples equally. This ideal was set out and defended at great length in one of the classic law review articles on taxation and the family, written by Michael McIntyre and Oliver Oldman and published in the *Harvard Law Review* in 1977. The norm had been present in the literature long before then, including being featured in a 1948 *Harvard Law Review* article by the influential tax academic and bureaucrat Stanley Surrey, who was largely credited with the joint filing plan that became law in that same year. These are two of several articles that I will be commenting on in order to develop an intellectual history, for influential academics, bureaucrats, legislators, and judges have legitimated the gendered structure of tax, typically without evincing any awareness of this fact.

McIntyre, Oldman, and others in this tradition assumed that the purpose of an "income" tax was, after all, to measure "income," and that, as far as any essential meaning of income is concerned, a dollar is a dollar. McIntyre made this point even more explicit in an article he wrote on his own in 1980, in which he discussed a hypothetical example of a male farmer who put his first $50,000 worth of wheat into blue bags and his next $50,000 into pink ones. McIntyre then belittled as "nonsensical" the view that the blue bags were somehow more profitable after-tax than were the pink bags. In fact, this view is nothing more than the thoroughly commonsensical marginal analysis at the core of the accountant's tale. For now, though, I am just readying to examine the argument that, since the Equals and the Traditionals have the same income, they ought to pay the same amount of tax. Looked at another way, the tax laws treat each couple as a unit. As units, the Equals and the Traditionals are equal, because they each earn $60,000.

This logic has an undeniable appeal. Far from denying its force, I want to suggest that the power of this perspective turns out to be a large part of the problem: it provides an attractive cover for what turns out to be a bad set of rules. Even some critics of the current regime have taken to resting their criticism on challenging the factual assertion that families form a single unit, that husbands and wives in fact "pool" their income. It does seem as if many families do *not* act as equal pools. Many surveys and studies indicate that who earns the money matters a great deal to the internal dynamics of families. But the traditional equal-earning couples ideal is ultimately wrongheaded for quite different reasons. As a minor matter, the ideal ignores the legitimate refinements of income that ought to accompany a two-earner family. Two-earner families have much higher costs, especially for child care. If a high school teacher and a shoemaker each receives $30,000, but the shoemaker has to pay out $10,000 for materials and equipment, the two are not really "equal" earners. Two-earner families, particularly those with young children, have demonstrably higher work-related costs, like the shoemaker, and this should be taken into account in any fair tax system.

But a deeper theoretical critique is much more damaging to the traditional approach. The equal-earning ideal looks at income as a static, distributive matter. By "static," I mean at a single point in time; by "distributive," I mean a focus on objective indices of wealth, such as money alone. The traditional equality norm begins and ends with the presumption that families or married couples are a unit, and can be ranked in order of their nominal income. Equality dictates that those couples having the same level of income in any given year be taxed equally. But whoever said that these concerns should be primary? Who told us to look only to the actual dollars being paid over to spouses in a marriage, on an annual basis, no matter what else might be going on?

Suppose we begin, instead, at a higher level of abstraction, that is, with the principle that tax laws should be fair and just. Of course we do not always know exactly what the most "fair and just" rules are. This is a political matter, open to reasonable discussion and debate. But it certainly makes sense to think of tax laws in these terms—as having, that is, to satisfy our concerns over justice and fairness—and I'll often write in these consciously open-ended terms. Indeed, the goal of taxing equal-earning couples equally is appealing precisely because it strikes us, at first glance, as being fair and just. We do not think that it is some god-given necessity or that we have no other choice, but rather we think that it *is* a sensible ideal to choose. "It sounds fair," we might say. But if this is our reasoning, we should be open to criticisms of the ideal that point exactly at its alleged fairness. If it turns out that taxing equal-earning couples equally is *not* fair, then we ought to abandon that goal. Our deeper commitments are to fairness, not to handy maxims.

This is exactly what we'll find: Taxing equal-earning couples equally is terribly unfair, because in fact it leads to massive discrimination against women. This is because of its behavioral and dynamic effects, that is, the way it shapes women's choices over time. Under a system of progressive marginal rates, taxing equal-earning couples equally necessarily means that Tom Traditional's "second" $30,000 must get taxed the same as Emma Equal's "first" $30,000—in a high rate bracket, thus pushing against Emma's decision to work. This is, in any event, a decision that has historically been, and remains today, a close and difficult one for many mothers. Thus many women stay home. Indeed, the law was to some degree intended to have this effect, as we shall see. Ours are not only, or even primarily, questions of who pays what amount. We should care about how tax affects people and their life plans. That ought to matter more than any static sense of equality, more than being able to stick to a tidy, easily remembered maxim.

The common talk of "neutrality" gets to be a big part of the problem. On one level, it is not clear that neutrality, in itself, is a virtue of any importance at all. Fairness and justice are virtues, and neutrality often serves them, but whenever we have hard questions about what is or is not neutral, we should refer to the ideals of fairness and justice, not to some arbitrarily chosen neutral principle. The move to joint filing was not neutral vis-à-vis the internal dynamics of marriages: it pushed toward a primary-secondary earner delineation, and then discriminated against the secondary earner. The move to joint filing did not have a neutral effect on Emma Equal, for example. Nor are the effects neutral as to class: a bias against two-earner families pushes against families for the poor and against two earners for the rich. Since class and race remain strongly correlated in America, these effects are not neutral along racial or ethnic lines, either. White families are more likely to be traditional; minority families are more likely to be single-parent. Perhaps we should simply abandon all use of the term "neutrality." Taxing equal-earning couples sounds neutral. But we realize it is not when we look at the real-world effects on women and families.

A BIT MORE THEORY: "INCOME" IS NOT AN IDEAL

Some tax scholars see their project as working out the logic of an "income" tax. But why should we even care about this? Actually, America doesn't try very hard to have an income tax. There are plenty of deviations from any "true" income principle, even if this term could be precisely and uncontroversially defined, as it clearly cannot be. When we deviate from the income ideal, we often talk explicitly about behavioral incentives and effects, as in the case of deductions for charitable contributions, pension plans, or investments in projects like solar energy or low-income housing. Why even bother to make an argument that taxing equal-earning couples equally follows from the nature of an income tax? It seems ironic that the law insists on a slavish devotion to a formal concept of income in exactly that area where such an insistence burdens women, while it freely deviates from it in areas favoring savings, investment, and the like.

In fact, there is a very important category of income that our tax system has never attempted to tax. So-called imputed income refers to the value of work done for oneself. If Susan or Elizabeth stay home and care for their children, each "earns" $10,000 or so by not having to pay child-care costs out of her own pockets. Traditional single-earner families have demonstrably higher imputed income than two-earner families do. Why don't we take this fact into account in constructing the tax system?

The typical reactions to concerns over imputed income are either that taxing it would be neither practicable nor feasible, or that it is *good* that we do not tax it, because it encourages parents to stay home with their children. But we are saying in this and in many other cases that income is not a sacred principle after all. It has always been held subservient to other goals, such as administrative convenience or behavioral effects. Why don't we see this when sticking to a concept of income that actually hurts women? Why do we invoke logic only in the service of certain ends, typically ones favoring men? Why shouldn't income be subservient to our deepest and most cherished goals, like equal concern and respect for all individuals?

Taxing equal-earning couples equally is, of course, a certain form of equal treatment. Yet it is a form that has turned out, and was in important regards designed, to place a large burden on women—to have, that is, very unequal effects when we look at individuals, families, and the gendered structure of life in America. Once again, handy maxims ought to yield to the dictates of justice.

A QUICK LOOK ABROAD

I have often been urged to look at how other countries tax women. I have, by and large, resisted this idea. The story of taxing women is very much an American story. It requires a fair amount of historical and cultural perspective, implicates a wide range of tax laws, and ultimately depends on the particular labor markets and politics in this country. Comparatism— the cross-cultural comparison of legal institutions—is a tricky and complex business. The comparatist should be sensitive to a wide range of legal, economic, social, and cultural variables. This section gives just a quick look abroad to show that neither the American tax system in general nor joint filing in particular is somehow inevitable.

Writing in 1960 in the *Stanford Law Review*, Oliver Oldman (of the later McIntyre-Oldman collaboration) and Ralph Temple, following up on a report they had done for the United Nations, noted a wide range of practices for taxing families. At the time they clearly believed that the American model, with its joint filing, was intellectually soundest: "While there may not be agreement on just which principles of economics and equity are being pursued by progressive taxation, there is a widespread belief that, for the purposes of any reasonable policy of progressive taxation, the economic lives of a husband and wife are inseparable." Later, Oldman and Temple, despite declaring that two-earner couples should get some relief, claim that "separate taxation based on the legal precept of the equality of the married woman is . . . ill-founded." This seemed to be the dominant attitude throughout the 1960s, echoed by economists such as Harold Groves and Douglas Thorson. In 1972, Grace Ganz Blumberg began the feminist turn in tax policy scholarship and was able to find some solace in the system of separate filing then in place in Sweden.

In 1990 the noted tax policy reformers Joseph Pechman and Gary Englehardt painted a different, more complex, more nuanced picture. Looking at eleven developed countries, Pechman and Englehardt find that only three—the United States, Germany, and France—still have a system of joint filing. France actually has a more complicated per capita allocation, which includes children within the taxable unit. "The remaining eight countries consider the individual as the tax unit, reflecting the world-wide trend in developed countries away from joint taxation of married couples." Indeed, there has been a notable shift toward separate filing, away from joint. Italy converted to a system of individual filing in 1977; the United Kingdom did so in 1990.

But before we jump to the conclusion that America lags behind the rest of the world in its gendered consciousness, we face some puzzles. Pechman and Englehardt point out that because two-earner couples incur higher costs, they should get some kind of tax relief. But they do not.

"Curiously, instead of providing relief to two-earner couples, many of the countries provide relief to one-earner couples. Australia, Canada, Italy, Japan, the Netherlands, Sweden, and the United Kingdom provide such relief." Thus, in 1989, the Netherlands, the only country to recognize unmarried persons living together as possibly equivalent to married couples, paid some stay-at-home spouses as much as $4,100. Sweden, the favorable point of comparison for Blumberg in 1972, paid some such spouses nearly $6,500. Pechman and Englehardt conclude by noting that there "is very little uniformity in the tax treatment of the family" among the eleven countries they studied.

What does this tell us? Mainly it cautions against any but a long and careful look abroad. My personal sense is that the story of this book, the story of taxing women, does recur across many cultures, because its basic features—the repression of women for centuries; the gendered division of labor; male domination of political systems; a tax system that is a creature of politics and often barely conscious prejudices, all shielded by a veil of technical and ostensibly neutral language—have been depressingly global in scope. We'll have our hands full merely coming to grips with the tax system of the United States and its effects on women: its historical development, its current structure, some proposed changes, and its interface with labor markets generally. As I indicated in the introduction, I don't want to focus the project on isolated, ad hoc changes, like moving to a system of separate filing, however wise such moves might be. The prior task is to gain a deeper understanding of where we are.

A quick look abroad is sufficient to show us what we should already in some sense know. When it comes to gender and justice, there is no promised land. There has never been a promised land—here or elsewhere, now or ever. We have to try to construct one. That will involve a lot of hard work, beginning, in our case, with the task of coming to an understanding of the story of taxing women. It is time to move on, by looking back.

2   *A Bit of History, 1913 to 1948*

BACKING UP

Joint filing has a rich history. It was much discussed as it evolved in the 1930s and 1940s, and became law in 1948. Since then it has stayed in place continuously, although rejected by feminist-oriented scholars, mainstream public finance economists, and most developed nations. This chapter takes a step back to look at its evolution.

WAR AND TAXES

The Sixteenth Amendment to the *Constitution of the United States*, ratified in 1913, made income tax possible. This amendment was a single sentence, providing that "Congress shall have power to lay and collect taxes on incomes, from whatever source derived. . . ." It was made necessary when an earlier income tax was ruled unconstitutional in the 1890s. A personal income tax was enacted in 1913. This law took up just a few pages; it was, in fact, not even the major bill under consideration, just a brief add-on to a tariff bill. This initial income tax featured low rates that reached a peak of 7 percent and a limited domain; it was a surcharge on the wealthy. From 1913 to 1915, fewer than 2 percent of wage earners filled out income tax returns and paid any taxes at all.

The story of the income tax took a decisive turn with the onset of World War I. The government needed money, and it looked to its new vehicle to raise it. In 1916 a much broader income tax was enacted. This law featured progressive marginal rates that increased throughout America's involvement in the war, reaching a top bracket of 77 percent in 1918. In 1916, just over 400,000 personal income tax returns were filed, with 37.5 percent coming from persons with incomes under $5,000—a figure roughly equivalent to $50,000 in 1995. By 1918, nearly 4.5 million returns were filed, and nearly 90 percent of these came from persons reporting an income of under $5,000. The breadth of the tax increased more than tenfold during this two-year wartime period, as the tax extended downward into the upper-middle classes, or, perhaps better, the lower-upper ones.

The general history of the income tax shows the dramatic importance of the two World Wars. World War I moved the tax from a token nod in the direction of social equality toward a more comprehensive tax on the upper class. Still, the tax had a very limited reach. Throughout the 1920s and 1930s, individual income taxes typically accounted for just 1 percent of gross domestic product (GDP). As late as 1939, fewer than 8 million personal income tax returns were filed, and the nascent social security tax accounted for more than twice as much federal revenue.

World War II brought, by 1943, the legal and accounting innovation of wage withholding, together with staggering revenue needs. These propelled the income tax to become truly a mass tax. By 1945, individual income taxes accounted for 8.7 percent of GDP, and nearly 50 million returns were filed, an increase of sixfold in breadth of coverage and nearly tenfold in total burden during the war years. In the thirty-year stretch from 1916 to 1945, the number of returns filed increased by well over a hundred times, although the overall population grew less than one-and-a-half times during this span. By the end of World War II, individual income taxes were more than five times greater than social security ones. These facts are central to the tale of taxing women, because they help us to see that the manipulations of the 1920s and 1930s were, by and large, rich men's games. But the games were to affect deeply the law that came to regulate the vast middle classes of America emerging from World War II.

THOSE WERE THE DAYS (?)

The original modern income tax made no provision for joint filing. Under the initial version of the current income tax, husbands and wives with earnings simply completed their own tax returns, using something like table 1 from chapter 1. Actually, things were more complicated than that. The 1913 tax rules and subsequent ones gave a break to married taxpayers, who, given the limited reach of the tax and the gendered facts of the age, were overwhelmingly male. It gave a married man a larger exemption level or zero bracket, provided that his wife did not file her own separate return. This feature meant that most married Americans actually faced an "income splitting" regime, of the sort that emerged for everyone in 1948. A numerical example of the schedule facing married couples is shown in table 5. Table 5 is not the same as table 2 in chapter 1, which reflected the income splitting in effect from 1948 to 1969. Table 2 was formed by doubling *all* of the individual rate brackets. Table 5, in contrast, is formed by doubling only the zero bracket; the 15 percent bracket still covers $20,000 for both singles and married filing jointly, and the 30 percent bracket covers $30,000 for each, and so on.

Under a system as shown in table 5, unless a secondary-earner wife is paid more than $10,000, there is no reason not to file jointly. (Remember

TABLE 5. Effect of Double Exemption in Phase I, 1913–1948

INDIVIDUAL RATE SCHEDULE		MARRIED, FILING JOINTLY	
INCOME	MARGINAL TAX RATE	INCOME	MARGINAL TAX RATE
$0–$10,000	0%	$0–$20,000	0%
$10,001–$30,000	15%	$20,001–$40,000	15%
$30,001–$60,000	30%	$40,001–$70,000	30%
$60,001 and up	40%	$70,001 and up	40%

that I am stating these values in something like 1995 dollars—in 1913, the figure was actually $500.) If the wife earned less than $10,000, the family was helped by filing jointly and getting a full $20,000 zero bracket. If she earned exactly $10,000, it didn't matter, because separate filing would shield all of her income from tax, and the couple would still get $20,000 tax free. But if she earned more than $10,000, the couple would want to file separately, because two separate filers could get a larger 15 percent bracket. The Equals, for example, would pay $6,000 filing separately, because they would have $20,000 in the zero brackets and $40,000 in the 15 percent brackets, combined. If they filed jointly, however, they would pay $9,000: zero on the first $20,000; plus $3,000, or 15 percent, on the next $20,000; plus $6,000, or 30 percent, on their final $20,000. The system in place from 1913 to 1948 favored joint filing for most American couples in the lower- and middle-income classes, and separate filing for the wealthiest.

The initial tax was overwhelmingly a man's matter. In 1918, statistics of income reported by the government revealed that 97.2 percent of all returns involving married persons were joint returns; only 1.4 percent were "wives making separate returns." These joint returns were completed by men claiming the larger zero bracket for married men, as we've just discussed. As late as 1939, when both tax rates and the breadth of the tax had sharply increased, less than 7 percent of all returns from married persons were separate returns filed by wives. The high percentage of joint returns indicates that wives in families with substantial income were still not earning much, or the couples would not have filed jointly. This fits with evidence compiled by Claudia Goldin and others that it was considered degrading for a man to have a working wife. Two-earner families, when they existed at all, were a lower-class phenomenon. Traditionals ruled. In 1939, somewhere between 80 percent and 90 percent of all income taxes were paid by men or male-dominated households. The range exists because it is not clear how to count categories such as community income, "separate" returns of wives, and female-headed households to the extent that they involve widows—each of these categories could reflect men's wage earnings, as we shall see. Under any count, though, the world of income taxation in this era was a man's world, and we do well to keep this in mind.

PROGRESSIVITY COMES TO THE JONESES

The simple story in 1913 probably would have remained such, but for progressive marginal rates. These had increased steeply during World War I, again during Franklin Roosevelt's early reign, and again during World War II. Because progressive rates rise with income, it is better to have two persons each earning $30,000 than one person earning $60,000. I have reprinted table 1 for convenience as we explore this point; we no longer need the complexity of table 5. Note, though, that we will be considering mainly upper-income couples for the balance of this chapter.

Under the rate structure of table 1, Sally Single, making $60,000, pays $12,000 in tax. The Traditionals also pay $12,000, because to the IRS Tom Traditional looks just like Sally—a single individual who earns $60,000—and Tina would not even have to bother filing. But the Equals pay less; they pay only $6,000 in tax. Emma and Earl each file a separate return, like a single individual earning $30,000. Thus they look the way Ann, in chapter 1, did before her raise, each paying $3,000 in tax.

The reason for the lower tax on the Equals' income is simple. Because each has a separate income, the Equals get what tax professionals call "two rides up the rate brackets." While Sally Single and Tom Traditional see their last $30,000—the salary that takes them from $30,000 to $60,000—taxed in the 30 percent bracket, Earl and Emma each benefit from a $10,000 zero bracket and each is able to put $20,000 in the 15 percent bracket. Combined, the Equals have $20,000 in the zero bracket and $40,000 in the 15 percent bracket. In contrast, while Tom Traditional's "first" $30,000 is treated like each of the Equals', generating $3,000 in tax, his "second" $30,000 falls into the 30 percent bracket, generating $9,000 in tax. So the difference between the total tax burden of the Equals and the Traditionals, $6,000, can be seen as resulting from the different treatment of the families' "second" $30,000. For the Equals, this amount generates $3,000 in tax, but for the Traditionals, climbing the ladder of progressive rates, it generates $9,000. Another way to put this is that this

TABLE 1. Basic Rate Schedule

INCOME	MARGINAL TAX RATE
$0–$10,000	0%
$10,001–$30,000	15%
$30,001–$60,000	30%
$60,001 and up	40%

example features the absence of a secondary-earner bias: Emma's earnings do not come "after" Earl's.

All this created an advantage for the Equals, or for any couple whose earnings were somehow split between the spouses. Viewing couples as a unit, the Traditionals and the Equals look to be the same—each couple has $60,000—but the Traditionals pay twice as much tax as the Equals. For couples wanting to get the lower tax payments available to the Equals, there was, of course, just one minor fly in the ointment: few couples in this era looked much like the Equals.

Indeed, as Goldin's historical work helps to remind us, there were "marriage bars" in existence at this time, whereby firms could and would simply fire women who got married. Such marriage bars, particularly common in teaching positions, persisted until the 1950s, when a period of low unemployment, brought on by productivity growth, made them unprofitable. Regardless of such bars, few wives were in the paid work-force before World War II. As late as 1940, only 12–15 percent of wives appeared to be working outside the home at all, and less than 10 percent of married mothers were. Most working wives came from the lower eco-nomic classes, where, as we saw in table 5, there was no incentive to split income. The bias against working wives was reinforced by social attitudes. A 1936 Gallup poll revealed that 82 percent of all respondents and even 75 percent of the females polled, thought that a woman with an employed husband should not work outside the home.

The situation with regard to paid work was mirrored in the ownership of assets. In the nineteenth century, "coverture" laws, which gave a hus-band nearly complete control over all familial economic matters, gave way to various "married women's property acts," which allowed married women at least nominally to own property. Men nonetheless continued to have powerful legal control over money and assets deep into the twentieth century. Legal cases from the 1920s through the 1940s, for example, re-veal that courts were reluctant to take seriously the idea that wives con-tributed meaningfully to assets obtained during marriage. Reva Siegel's fascinating work in this regard is nicely supplemented by Carolyn Jones's work on income splitting for tax reasons, a topic I'll get to shortly. We'll also look at community property laws, a system prevalent in the western states, which, although in some regards more accommodating of women, also gave force to male domination in economic matters.

Lest the title of this section mislead, the contemporary flat tax propos-als do *not* significantly change the story. The flat tax plans that periodically surface—they were in the air in the 1980s, and they have come back by the mid-1990s—are not really flat-rate tax schedules at all. Rather, they are two-rate bracket schedules, featuring a generous zero bracket. Under this structure, with joint filing, secondary-earner wives are still more burdened than their primary-earner husbands, who get to use up that zero bracket. We'll see more on that later.

TRYING TO LOOK EQUAL

Much of the history of tax and marriage deals with attempts by families like the Traditionals to get taxed like the Equals without *really* becoming equal. Traditional households tried to get the maximum tax savings at the minimum social cost—costs that could include either giving wives power over wealth and assets or having them enter the paid workforce. This history breaks down into three broad phases. In phase 1, from 1913 until 1948, the law had separate filing, so the Equals paid less tax than the Traditionals. During this phase, the Traditionals tried to get the tax benefits any way at all—any way, that is, except by really becoming equal. They tried shifting property, making private contractual arrangements, inventing clever tax dodges, and, ultimately, getting state legislatures to cooperate in a sweeping tax avoidance scheme. In 1948, the Traditionals were able to persuade Congress to "come to the rescue," as a leading tax law casebook puts it, and the law created the neutrality between the Equals and the Traditionals that persists to this day, by means of joint filing. That took the pressure off the need to look equal, and the various deals of phase 1 were quickly undone.

In phase 2, from 1948 until 1969, the action subsided; little was heard, written, or spoken about taxation and the family. During this period, there were no marriage penalties, only bonuses. But there was a large secondary-earner bias, set in motion by the move to joint filing itself.

By 1969, it was a new class of taxpayers—singles and unmarried couples—who began to complain, and their voice was heard at least faintly by Congress. Ushering in this third phase, from 1969 to the present, was a change in the rate schedules to help single taxpayers, which had the consequence of generating a marriage penalty. This penalty, particularly as it falls on wealthy couples, has led to increasing attention. But as I noted in chapter 1, the focus on marriage penalties is itself a gendered, class-based phenomenon, and is not our main concern. Phase 3 has thus been characterized by a striking insistence on looking at the wrong thing.

We can understand the entire story as being driven by the attempt of traditional families to have their cake and eat it too. To be quite clear, the cake here is money, and being able to eat it means sharing it with neither the government nor women. The bottom line is that men won, and women were pretty much ignored. Let's now take a closer look at this history, in its three major phases.

PHASE 1, 1913 TO 1948: THE TAX-DRIVEN QUEST FOR APPARENT EQUALITY

Under table 1 and separate filing, the Equals are paying much less tax than the Traditionals. We are still in the 1920s and 1930s, at a time when the Traditionals are the overwhelming majority of all taxpayers. The tax is still limited to the upper classes, where the Traditionals are especially prominent, and it remains a man's concern. The Traditionals would have liked to be taxed like the Equals, but they did not want to be like the Equals, which would mean having Tina earn as much money in the workforce as Tom did, and maybe having Tom help out around the house with the children.

The potential tax savings did not escape the traditional wealthy American family. Large potential tax savings rarely do. Traditional families tried various strategies to get the tax benefits without the perceived social burdens of becoming too much like the Equals. To understand this period and the tactics employed during it, we have to distinguish between income from property or capital—that is, rents, royalties, interest, dividends, and the like—and income from wages or salary. Let's start by looking at the former.

PROPERTY OWNERS AND THE STRANGE CASE OF "BEDCHAMBER TRANSACTIONS"

If couples were wealthy enough to have large property holdings, so as to generate income from property like rents or interest, they could shift the property to make it appear at least as if the wife were earning some income of her own. Suppose that Tom Traditional owned an apartment that provided one-half of his $60,000 annual income. By deeding this to Tina, the Traditionals would look like the Equals: two spouses, each earning $30,000. The only difference would be that Tina would have income from property, whereas Emma Equal would be a wage earner. But this difference would not matter to the IRS. Separate filing encouraged this kind of transfer.

Interestingly, a later argument for joint filing was that separate filing led to what Boris Bittker, professor of law at Yale Law School since 1946 and almost certainly the most influential American tax law academic ever, referred to repeatedly as suspicious "bedchamber transactions." This charge rests on some gendered notions. In the first place, the criticism turns on administrative concerns. The structure of the argument, a familiar one in tax policy, is that the law should be changed because it would otherwise be too easy to evade and too difficult to police the evasions. Such an argument often plays out over matters like the taxation of gifts, fringe benefits, and tips. The implicit gendered dimension of the argument here is that bedchamber transactions would be a sham, that they would have no real consequences. Of course the husband would really own and manage and control the wealth, and no wife would think of making the tax avoidance transfer meaningful by asserting real ownership. As Bittker described the matter in a classic article, "Federal Income Taxation and the Family," published in the *Stanford Law Review* in 1975: "For at least 50 years, a major theme in the taxation of income from property transferred within the family has been that bedchamber transactions are suspect because the allocation of legal rights within the family is a trivial matter." The phrase "bedchamber transaction" itself suggests triviality.

There is nothing wildly inaccurate about Bittker's characterization: marital property laws of the time in fact made interspousal transfers more or less trivial. Reva Siegel's historical and legal research shows first that the married women's property acts emerging from the nineteenth century were actually a rather conservative attempt to forestall a claim by women for equal ownership of all marital assets; the property acts simply allowed women to have control and ownership over their separate earnings, which were limited in that era. But Siegel's work continues to demonstrate a second point. Even though those modern laws abandoned the law of coverture, which gave nearly complete control to husbands over economic matters, courts continued to interpret the new statutes so as to give a good deal of control to men.

Siegel's work leaves off about 1930, and she does not specifically consider tax-induced property shifts. But Carolyn Jones's work does, and it shows that judicial attitudes in the 1940s continued to be skeptical of claims that a wife could be a genuine financial partner in a marriage. As long as the formal mechanisms—deeds of property, pro forma partnerships, and so forth—were in place, property-owning Traditionals could get taxed like the Equals without any real change in the power over resources. Actually, Jones suggests that there was the potential for the tax-induced transfers to have real effects, and it was partly the fear of these real consequences that led to the more structural reform of the 1948 joint filing system. Jones even points to cases in which men argued that they should be released from documents purporting to give their wives ownership interests if these instruments were denied favorable tax consequences. We'll see this game of giving wives just enough—preferably, the appearance alone of just enough—to get favorable tax consequences play out in a grand scale, when it comes to a national shift toward a community property regime.

The bedchamber transaction objection to single filing was gendered in a second way. The charge that couples owning property would benefit more than wage-earning ones was, in essence, a charge that the law was discriminatory among *men*. The real force of the objection was that certain male-dominated households, the ones that owned property, would benefit over other male-dominated households, the ones where the men worked. Little heed was paid to the effects on women, either in terms of their incentives to work outside the home or their rights in marital property, except to the extent that this focus was negative. Bedchamber transactions had a *bad* effect of potentially creating real rights in women, and the separate filing system had the *bad* effect of inducing women to work outside the home.

THE PROBLEM WITH WAGE EARNERS

Property-owning Traditionals at least had a vehicle, the bedchamber transaction, for appearing equal before the eyes of the IRS. What of wage-earning Traditionals? They tried to get the tax benefits available to the Equals and to property owners by private contract. Tom would sign an agreement ceding one-half of all of his earnings to Tina. Tom and Tina would then file separate returns, each claiming to have earned $30,000, and each therefore paying $3,000 in taxes under table 1. Having an awkwardly egalitarian written document seemed like a small price to pay for the sizable tax savings at stake: the little deal would save $6,000 in taxes per year in our running example. Let's see how this kind of deal fared in the law courts.

THREE CASES

This section looks at three United States Supreme Court cases—two widely cited and influential ones, and a third equally illustrative of the spirit of the times—and considers their facts and their logic. Here we continue the tale of wage-earning Traditionals trying to get taxed like the Equals. I assume that most readers are not lawyers, so I will stay away from legalese. The cases are interesting as social, political, and historical texts, at least as much as legal ones.

1. Lucas v. Earl

The Traditionals were thwarted in 1930 by the United States Supreme Court in the celebrated case of *Lucas v. Earl.* Mr. Earl, a lawyer, had done exactly what Tom Traditional was doing above; he gave his wife one-half of his income by private contract, in a document dated 1901—twelve years before the income tax took effect. I had once thought that the Earls might have engaged in the practice of "backdating"; that is, using the 1901 date fraudulently to give authority to a document written later. This might still be true, for all I can prove; certainly the facts of the case raise some suspicions.

But a search of the legal record before the Supreme Court pointedly indicates two facts. One, at the time the couple supposedly signed the agreement, Mrs. Earl had substantial separate property—$30,000, equivalent to more than $500,000 in 1995. Two, Mr. Earl was ill in 1901, and the contract was intended to expedite probate matters should he die. The situation invites a couple of questions. First, isn't it a bit odd that Mrs. Earl should, in effect, be giving Mr. Earl a large amount of wealth on *his* deathbed? Since there was no gift or estate tax at the time, the only purpose of this transfer would have been to give Mr. Earl the power to disinherit Mrs. Earl of what had been, a short while before, her own property. More to the immediate point, it is interesting that the Earls and their attorney felt compelled to get these facts out, repeatedly, in their materials before various courts. After all, who would believe that any man really wanted to share things equally with his wife? The Earls needed some cover to ward off an accusation that their agreement might be a tax scam, and Mrs. Earl's wealth provided it. In any event, Mr. Earl recuperated from his alleged illness, and, in 1920, the Earls filed separate returns, each reporting one-half of Mr. Earl's salary.

The Supreme Court, in an opinion written by perhaps the most famous American jurist, Oliver Wendell Holmes, was only briefly amused by the Earls' claim. The opinion first quoted their contract and then quickly stated that "the validity of the contract is not questioned, and we assume it to be unquestionable under the law of the State of California." It then took Holmes just a single paragraph, writing for a unanimous Court, to both note and reject the argument advanced by the Earls.

I'll set out the critical portion of that paragraph so that we can go over it more slowly, for it captures a kind of "logical" thinking characteristic of this phase. I have numbered the sentences in brackets, to aid in the ensuing discussion:

> [1] A very forcible argument is presented to the effect that the statute seeks to tax only income beneficially received, and that taking the question more technically the salary and fees became the joint property of Earl and his wife on the very first instant on which they were received. [2] We well might hesitate upon the latter proposition, because however the matter might stand between husband and wife he was the only party to the contracts by which the salary and fees were earned. . . . [3] But this case is not to be decided by attenuated subtleties. [4] It turns on the import and reasonable construction of the taxing act. [5] There is no doubt that the statute could tax salaries to those who earned them and provide that the tax could not be escaped by anticipatory arrangements and contracts however skillfully devised to prevent the salary when paid from vesting even for a second in the man who earned it. [6] That seems to us the import of the statute before us.

Holmes begins [1] by noting that Mr. Earl did, indeed, have something of a case: "A very forcible argument is presented." This forcible argument is that, by virtue of the unquestionably legal contract, Mr. Earl's earnings were the joint property of his wife "on the very first instant on which they were received." This was, in fact, a forcible enough argument to have persuaded the federal appellate court to agree with it. Holmes and the unanimous Supreme Court were reversing this decision.

Even here, however, Holmes notes [2] that one "might well hesitate," because the *private* domain ("however the matter might stand between husband and wife") did not affect the *public* domain of work ("he was the only party to the contracts by which the salary and fees were earned"). But Holmes does not have to pause long on this dilemma, because there is another, stronger, public domain that overpowers the asserted consequences of the private document. [3] "This case is not to be decided by attenuated subtleties"; instead [4] "it turns on the import and reasonable construction of the taxing act."

Holmes then dismisses in the wage-earning context what Bittker had seen in the property context as "bedchamber transactions." Holmes sees Earl's contract as an instance of [5] "anticipatory arrangements and contracts . . . skillfully devised." Surely Congress could ignore such lawyerly niceties and insist on taxing salary "to the man who earned it." Holmes could barely conceive of any substantive reality to these manipulative forms. All that was left for him was to find that Congress in fact *had* done what there was "no doubt" they *could* do; that is, to find that Congress agreed with his distrust of "attenuated subtleties." And this ultimate step Holmes takes by waving his hand at it: [6] "That seems to us the import of the statute before us."

This final move is a bit odd, for the statutes before the Supreme Court said almost nothing to the point. According to the government's brief and Holmes's opinion, four statutory sections were relevant, all referring generally to tax "upon the net income of every individual." There was nothing at all about husbands and wives, men and women; nothing at all about whether a wife's legally enforceable claim to one-half of her husband's wages made that half her income. The government, in its very short brief before the Court—it was less than thirteen pages—seemed to believe that the intent of Congress was clear. But the lower federal court did not see things in that light. It agreed with the Earls. More significantly, we see none of the legal moves we expect to find in interpreting a statute: no nod to legislative history, no reference to analogous passages in other statutes, no debate about what the words in question might mean. Holmes so firmly believed that there was "no doubt" that Congress could tax "the man who earned" the wages and that it had done so, that he could deal with the latter point—the central question of the legal case—almost by silent inference. With his forceful language, Holmes sought to shut down a nascent industry of clever wage-shifting between spouses.

A Brief Aside: It's Hard to Keep a Good Tax Lawyer Down

Alas, even in regard to wage earners supposedly governed by *Earl*, clever lawyers and attenuated subtleties were hard to keep down. This was especially so as progressive marginal rates escalated as high as 94 percent during World War II. The status quo after *Earl* was that property-owning Traditionals could split their income and look like the Equals via bedchamber transactions, but wage-earning Traditionals could not. How would clever lawyers respond to this bind? The answer, to a tax lawyer, is easy: convert "ordinary" salary into "capital" property income to make wages look like property. How to perfom this particular sleight of hand? Once again, the answer is easy to a tax lawyer motivated by high rates. The Traditionals would form family partnerships or corporations, and Tom would make Tina his partner or fellow shareholder. The business would then "earn" the salaries and fees, and these would be split through the company. Each spouse, as a "co-owner" of the business, would take one-half of the business's alleged income. This kind of device was being played out, in the business world and in the courts, throughout the 1940s, with mixed results, as Carolyn Jones's work wonderfully demonstrates.

2. Poe v. Seaborn

In a curious twist of fate, the sweeping language of *Earl* was undercut by a later Supreme Court ruling in the same year, 1930. *Poe v. Seaborn* took place under the community property laws of the state of Washington, which I'll discuss more extensively below. For now, just note that such laws give each spouse an equal share of all property and income obtained during marriage; that is, the law does what the Earls' contract tried to do. California, where the Earls lived, was in fact a community property state, too, but its particular community property regime was less generous to wives than Washington's law was. California modified its law in 1927, even before *Earl* and *Seaborn* were decided by the Supreme Court, to stand on the same legal footing as Washington.

Mr. and Mrs. Seaborn, who appear from the record to look very much like the Traditionals, each reported one-half of their total income, largely from Mr. Seaborn's salary, just like the Equals. But rather than relying on a private contract, as the Earls did, the Seaborns relied on state law. Justice Owen Josephus Roberts—most famous as the justice whose "switch in time saved nine," that is, whose newfound support for New Deal legislation forestalled Franklin Roosevelt's plan to "pack the Court"—wrote the opinion for a unanimous Court. Roberts's ruling upheld the Seaborns' claim that each was responsible for one-half of the whole family income. *Seaborn* thus allowed all spouses in community property states to get the income-splitting benefit of looking like the Equals for tax purposes.

It is worth looking closely at the opinion in *Seaborn*. Let's begin with the government's position. As reported by the Court, "the Commissioner [of the Internal Revenue Service] concedes that the answer to the question involved in the cause must be found in the provisions of the law of the state, as to a wife's ownership of or interest in community property." In other words, the government agreed that state law determined who owned property. In hindsight, this looks to have been a disastrous mistake, because the IRS suffered a large setback in the case. Not only did it lose in the immediate situation, but a clear income-splitting principle for all community property states was established, allowing many traditional families to save a large amount on their taxes. The government did not have to make this concession, because there is little doubt that federal law could govern when it came to questions of federal tax. After all, in *Earl*, Holmes had simply noted in passing that the private contract was "unquestionably valid" under California law.

Why, then, did the government agree to look to state law? Ineptitude and inattention seem unlikely explanations. *Seaborn* was a carefully monitored "test case," with a large record before the Court, including a 60-page brief from the federal government, supplemented by memoranda on community property practices and legislative history, a volume outmatched by the 156-page basic brief and the 122-page supplemental brief filed on behalf of the taxpayers. No one was asleep at the switch. Two other reasons, both gendered, immediately appear for the concession. First, the government thought it would win, anyway; the government's reading of community property law—not at all a foolish one, as we shall see—was that it was every bit as patriarchal as the rest of American society in 1930. Although the property was "communal" in name, in fact and, typically, by law, all management and control lay in the husband.

But this does not fully explain the government's concessions. Even if state law was on its side, why didn't the IRS also rely on federal law and the sweeping language of *Earl*? The government could have argued that federal law required taxing "the man who earned" the wages. This gets to a second motivation: The government wanted to make a clean argument that would deny all property-owning Traditionals their shifts. If the government could tax whoever controlled wealth, then the trivial fact of nominal legal ownership could be ignored. Only men, in 1930, would be taxed.

Unfortunately for the government, its gambit did not work. The implicitly gendered argument did not persuade the Court because the Court had its own gendered assumptions at work, which cut just the other way. Roberts and his colleagues simply saw that there were perfectly clear reasons for putting all managerial powers in the husband's hands: "The reasons for conferring such sweeping powers of management on the husband are not far to seek." Roberts reasoned that lawsuits between spouses should be discouraged, and "third parties who deal with the husband respecting community property shall be assured that the wife shall not be permitted to nullify his transactions." Common sense dictated that the husband should make the deals and that the wife should not be allowed to "nullify . . . his transactions." But to Justice Roberts this did not deny that the wife had rights: "Power is not synonymous with right." To Roberts, it seemed a matter of course that the man had to manage the property, but this was not to deny the wife's ownership interest in it. It seemed perfectly natural that a man should care for his wife's property, like a parent for a child's. The government lost its argument, and community property laws were able to do what private contracts in *Earl* could not—split the husband's income, and make Traditionals look like Equals.

Another Brief Aside: Teaching Taxing Women

Earl and *Seaborn* are major cases, included in a good many tax textbooks, although neither is among the more than four hundred cases written up in the encyclopedic *Oxford Companion to the Supreme Court*. Tax issues have not particularly struck the fancy of Court scholars. But it may be worthwhile to pause at this point to consider how standard tax texts treat the subject matter of this book.

Principles of taxation and the family are typically discussed under the dry headings of "attribution of income" or "taxable unit," saved until well into the text, and then presented as a more or less inevitable problem of a practical income tax system. *Earl* is almost always included, but it gets discussed as a specific example of a more general phenomenon of income shifting that goes beyond the husband-wife context. Parents want to shift income to their children, and individuals use corporations to shift income—both tactics designed to escape high progressive marginal rates. *Seaborn*, if it is included, often gets a separate treatment from *Earl* and is usually followed by a quick synopsis of the movement toward joint filing. No tax text has an extended discussion of taxing women, grouped and labeled as such. There is no social history, no discussion of gender biases in the promulgation of the laws, no mention of the interactions between tax and wider patterns of gender discrimination. The typical tax student, like politicians, scholars, and most Americans, simply never sees the issues.

3. Hoeper v. Tax Commission of Wisconsin

Let's take a look at a third Supreme Court case from the *Earl* and *Seaborn* era, *Hoeper v. Tax Commission of Wisconsin*, decided in 1931, the year after *Earl* and *Seaborn*. *Hoeper* is not a major case included in any tax textbook; indeed, it deals with a state tax issue. But it does concern the same attitudes toward taxation, families, and gender seen in *Earl* and *Seaborn*. What makes *Hoeper* even more interesting is that it featured a divided

Court, which pitted Roberts, writing for the majority of six justices, against Holmes, writing for himself and two other justices, including the celebrated liberal, Louis Brandeis. We are able to see the contrasting attitudes of Roberts and Holmes, each gendered in its own way, in the same case.

The facts of *Hoeper* are simple. Wisconsin had a state income tax. Its law, in explicitly gendered language, provided that the husband should pay income tax on his and his wife's income. We'll see in a moment that this was the essence of legislative proposals for "mandatory joint filing" in 1941 and 1942 that were widely rejected; it also appears to have been the system in place for the income tax briefly operating during the Civil War. Mr. Hoeper had married a widow—Holmes takes care to point out this fact, which presumably explains why she had her own income—and he complained about this statute. The majority agreed with him and struck down the law.

Without ever citing *Seaborn*, Roberts followed pretty much the same logic. His opinion first notes, however, that a wife need not have any economic rights. "At common law the wife's property, owned at the date of marriage or in any manner acquired thereafter, is the property of her husband. . . . Were the status of a married woman in Wisconsin that which she had at common law, the statutory attribution of her income to her husband for income tax would, no doubt, be justifiable." No doubt! There is no doubt that Justice Roberts, as much as Justice Holmes, is a product of his times, and those times are not far removed from the deeply gendered era of coverture laws, where wives had nothing but a new last name to show for being married.

Nonetheless, Wisconsin, like most states by 1931, had moved away from coverture, replacing it with a "Property Rights of Married Women" law that gave a wife separate ownership and control of her separate earnings, except for those "accruing from labor performed for her husband, or in his employ or payable by him." Given this new regime, Roberts saw the case just as he had seen *Seaborn*. Since the state chose to give the wife separate ownership—a choice clearly not compelled, in his mind—it could not tax a wife's earnings as if they were not separate.

One final point from Roberts's opinion is worth noting. Wisconsin had argued that its statute dealt with the regulation of marriage, a traditional domain for state power, not for the federal government. But Roberts saw the law at issue as a *tax* matter, and saw tax as something different from regulation: "It is clear that the law is a revenue measure, and not one imposing regulatory taxes. . . . It is obvious that the act does not purport to regulate the status or relationships of any person, natural or artificial." This split between viewing tax as a "revenue measure," affecting little, and "regulatory taxes" or other measures affecting the "status or relationship of any person," mirrors the static-distributive versus dynamic-behavioral distinction that characterizes our thinking about taxation in general, even today. But there is in reality no distinction at all. All taxes affect behavior, whatever they were intended to do.

However interesting Roberts's majority opinion is, for its echoes of *Seaborn*, its recognition of a state's ability to be as gendered as it chooses to be in setting up its property rules, and its demarcation of a clear line between tax and social regulation, it is Holmes's dissent in *Hoeper* that makes the case most worth reading. This opinion underscores our reading of *Earl:* Holmes is relentless in seeing taxation as a matter of state power and is unwilling to consider any objection on gender grounds. Holmes's four-paragraph opinion is magisterial in its scorn for Roberts's reasoning. Holmes would have little difficulty in upholding the statutes: "The statutes are the outcome of a thousand years of history. They must be viewed against the background of the earlier rules that husband and wife are one, and that one the husband."

This is a stunning statement, by any account, but especially as coming from a jurist well known for his hostility to bare precedent. Holmes was a notorious pragmatist who believed that the past could be abandoned altogether if it no longer served the present. "It is revolting to have no better reason for a rule of law than that so it was laid down in the time of Henry IV. It is still more revolting if the grounds upon which it was laid down have vanished long since, and the rule simply persists from blind imitation of the past," Holmes had famously written in 1897. Apparently, what is "revolting" in the law of property or contracts—to rely blindly on the past—is unquestionable when it comes to matters of gender.

There is no doubt that Holmes believes in looking backward here, for he returns to the idea:

> In some States, if not in all, the husband became the owner of the wife's chattels, on marriage, without any trouble from the Constitution; and it would require ingenious argument to show that there might not be a return to the law as it was in 1800. It is all a matter of statute. But for statute, the income taxed would belong to the husband, and there would be no question about it.

No question about it! This language—full of forceful, logical self-confidence—should send a shudder through those who might believe that the ERA, for example, is simply not necessary because women already have all the legal rights anyone could want. It would be "ingenious" to Oliver Wendell Holmes, writing in 1931, to argue that under the Constitution—a Constitution that since 1920 had given women the vote—there "might not be a return" to the coverture laws of 1800.

In *Earl*, as we have seen, the statute itself could hardly be thought to be clear or to speak explicitly to questions of husband and wife. Yet Holmes found that there was "no doubt" that a Congress, to untutored eyes silent about the issue, had meant to tax the man who earned salary.

In *Hoeper*, Holmes looked at a statute that explicitly presumed that a wife's income was her husband's. This statute was at odds with other principles articulated in other statutes of the same state and with at least faintly emergent norms of women's equal rights. Yet Holmes once again had no trouble siding with the gendered taxing forces, to tax the man who must really manage the property. Again there was no doubt about it. Men can control their wives as utterly as statutes allow and, where the statutes do not seem to say so in so many words, it is simply assumed that they do.

COMMUNITY PROPERTY AND OTHER ODDITIES

That concludes the brief tour through Supreme Court cases. When we started down that path, we had been considering ways that couples might look like the Equals without having to become equal. Property owners used bedchamber transactions. Wage earners tried to write simple contracts, but the Supreme Court shut them down in *Earl;* for the time being, such salaried taxpayers are left trying more clever, attenuated subtleties, like family partnerships and corporations. *Seaborn* breathed new life into the game, bringing us to the final technique available under this first historical phase, a move to community property laws.

Community property descends directly from Spanish and, to a lesser extent, French law. In the 1930s, California, Louisiana, Texas, Idaho, Washington, Arizona, New Mexico, and Nevada were community property states. In the 1980s, Wisconsin, in an obviously liberal move, in effect converted to community property, thus undercutting the claim of major treatises written early in the century that no jurisdiction would ever willingly buy into this system. That claim is worth keeping in mind during what follows, because we shall soon see that tax incentives—but, clearly, only tax incentives—indeed motivated change in the 1930s and 1940s.

Community property laws are a complex mixture of different gendered assumptions. On the one hand, they reflect a certain unitary or "partnership" view of the family in that they automatically pool all income into a single community. Until fairly recently, however, community property laws generally made clear their gendered basis by giving the husband dominant managerial control over this consolidated family pool. All wealth was combined under the husband's control, as in *Seaborn*. California's law initially went so far in giving the husband powers that it did not get the favorable *Seaborn* interpretation until it was modified in 1927.

On the other hand, community property laws do give the wife a substantial economic stake in family wealth and thus are more favorable to women, at least in the case of death or divorce. Although states vary considerably in the specifics, wives can often, as in California, leave a marriage with an equal share of all property and income earned during it.

Wives can also pass this wealth on in their own wills, and their husbands cannot disinherit them.

Women's groups were divided in the 1930s and 1940s as to whether to support community property regimes. This paralleled the divide noted by Siegel in the nineteenth century between women who chose separate earnings as the best route to equality and those who preferred an equal share of a communal pool to achieve the same goal. This debate still plays out today. Some persons, including many feminists, believe laws that ostensibly benefit divorced women by giving them more assets on divorce in fact encourage dependence on men to the detriment of women. One of the most damaging features of our times may be simply the fact that women tend to face many more hard choices than men do. Should women have supported autonomy or communality in the debates over property rights? Men manipulated whatever answers emerged, while women were divided among themselves.

The history of community property helps to explain why such laws could coexist in an obviously male-dominated United States. Community property laws have deep roots in medieval and Renaissance Spain, as Roman Catholic power emerged to the exclusion of Moorish influences. Under the leadership of Catholic Spanish and French settlers, where divorce was officially frowned on, community property could take hold, as in Louisiana, Texas, California, and nearby states. Without having to consider divorce—even wanting, perhaps, to discourage it—such laws are at least as patriarchal, and maybe more so, than the common law, "equitable interest" rules obtaining in the heavily Protestant eastern states. Under community property, all familial wealth arising during a marriage came under the managerial power of the husband. There was nothing especially feminist about community property in its historical roots in America.

THINGS GET STRANGER

A remarkable bit of social history followed *Seaborn*. Because community property rules now generated the *tax* benefit unsuccessfully sought in cases like *Earl*, a flurry of states attempted to reform their *property* laws, generally by giving to the wife the minimal rights necessary to satisfy the Supreme Court's standards. Because the Court was not prepared to accept all community property regimes as granting the wife as much of an interest as the state of Washington did, some such states, like California, modified their laws. Oklahoma, Oregon, Pennsylvania, Nebraska, Michigan, and the territory of Hawaii actually adopted community property regimes; other states were in the process of considering a change.

In every case, there are further interesting stories to tell. Both Oklahoma and Oregon, for example, first passed community property laws that the Supreme Court held to be too close to California's initial law to get the *Seaborn* benefit; the states then had to go and try again. It was clear that the game was to give the minimum concession to women needed to get the tax benefit. Pennsylvania's community property law was declared invalid by that state's supreme court, on somewhat shaky legal reasoning, apparently in part because the court could see the 1948 federal tax change coming, which rendered the issue moot.

The disparity between these two kinds of state property systems created a political problem for a Congress that was acutely aware of the situation. There were legislative proposals to change the national tax laws through-out the 1930s and 1940s. In 1947, for example, there were extensive hearings before the House Ways and Means Committee, with many de-tailed accounts of the nature and genesis of community property laws. The level of concern is itself interesting. Recall that virtually all married families at the time looked like the Traditionals. Only about 12–16 percent of married women were employed in the paid workforce at the onset of World War II, most of them earning far less than their husbands or having husbands who did not or could not work at all. Furthermore, since in-come splitting was a concern of only wealthier families, it was even more exclusively an affair of the Traditionals. Most families who paid income taxes saw that their taxable income fell in the single lowest nonzero bracket. Under the example of table 5 (with its modern values), most families were earning less than $40,000, so income splitting did not mat-ter to them. In 1939, only some 50,000 community property returns were filed, out of a total of some 7,500,000 returns nationwide; even in California, the state with the most community property filings, there were only roughly 25,000 such returns, compared with more than 235,000 joint returns. The government estimated that any ultimate move to allow income splitting for federal tax purposes would benefit only the wealthi-est 10 percent of married taxpayers, and even that figure may have been too high.

The fact of the matter was that some states had found ways to help out a handful of rich traditional families, allowing them to pay lower taxes than they would in non–community property states. States were doing what Mr. Earl could not but property owners could; states were in effect making bedchamber transactions for their richer citizens. There was the possibility that all states would simply move over into the community property camp. Oklahoma, for example, feared that all of its wealthy men would emigrate to Texas to get the tax break available there, and so it adopted community property laws itself. Would a domino effect sweep the nation? This might not be so bad, because it would at least remove the disparity among states, and Congress could just raise tax rates if it needed more revenue. But any large-scale movement would have the un-pleasant *social* effect of working a shift in actual property rights toward women.

NOT QUITE A "STAMPEDE"

Carolyn Jones has done fine historical work in questioning the view of mainstream tax scholars that there was a "stampede" toward community property in the wake of *Seaborn*. In fact, the situation in the 1940s was even more deeply gendered than at first appears. Virtually all states did indeed consider shifting over to community property regimes, and many in fact did so. But a fear of the real social consequences of the move chilled the process. This might have been aggravated by higher divorce rates, since community property laws actually had egalitarian effects in the case of divorce, along with suspicions of a newfangled European, not to mention Catholic, legal import.

Jones has unearthed interesting reports of the fears prevalent in the non–community property states of what a new regime might mean: women marrying for money, estranged wives clamoring for economic power and interests, opportunistic women getting divorces, and so on. Newspaper accounts in Nebraska related the concerns of men that their wives would insist on "banking" one-half of the communal income; the fear here was of the financial incompetence of women. Other accounts relayed concerns that marriages would fall apart and divorce rates increase because of the new law; the fear here was of women's greed.

A good many of these stories, ironically, focused on immoral male activities. An article published in *Nation's Business* in June 1947, for example, relates two tales. In the first, a gold miner from Alaska comes down to Seattle, gets drunk, marries a woman he has just met, and buys a hotel. A divorce court orders the hotel split in two, and the author concludes by noting "how an evening in a community-property state can be profitable for a lonesome girl." This story is not even legally accurate. Community property laws would only divide up gains accrued *during* marriage, not investments made out of funds saved *before* the wedding. The story thus captures the irrationality of the fear of community property. A second story concerns the presumably more usual occurrence of a wealthy husband lavishing gifts on his mistress. A court subsequently determined that community funds could not be put to such use, so that "the girl friend was ordered to kick back half her plumage." These stories convey the message: "Imagine that: A man cannot even have an affair without being accountable financially to his wife! What will happen to the hallowed tradition of one-night marriages? Do we really want to do this to ourselves, men?"

Income splitting was still largely a rich family's issue in the 1940s, even after the expansion of the income tax during World War II. As late as 1947, a *U.S. News* story read into the Congressional Record reported that only about one in ten families would benefit from joint filing; statements before the Ways and Means Committee put the figure at 5 percent. Not many families were rich enough to care about income splitting, and a good many of those who were had already done something by 1947. We'll see in the next chapter an attempt by young Senator Hubert Humphrey to depart from the 1948 solution, not because of its effects on marriage and women, but because of its class dimensions—because it was tax relief for the rich.

The movement to community property was fueled by rich married men; it generated no tax benefit to most families. It would seem, from the evidence that Jones and others have compiled, including the ultimate repeal of all the newly adopted community property laws, to be highly unpopular for its non-tax consequences. Even so, the movement nearly carried the day. In the end, though, it was the failure or unwillingness of all states to convert to community property laws—to give up the usual way of doing business—that kept the controversy alive.

CONGRESS TO THE RESCUE, TAKE 1: 1941

Congress made various attempts to level the playing field between community property states and other states throughout the 1930s. Congress was not limited by *Seaborn*. Notwithstanding the IRS concession in that case, federal law could override state law, if Congress expressed an interest in doing so. Thus there were two ways to go to make all states equal, both of which were considered by Congress. On the one hand, the government could move toward its victorious position in *Earl*, insisting on separate filing and taxing the men who really earned or controlled the wealth, as Wisconsin had tried to do in *Hoeper*. This would mean a federal law ignoring community property for income tax purposes. On the other hand, the government could move toward *Seaborn*, allowing income splitting among all spouses. This might mean a federal law respecting private contractual arrangements, as the taxpayers had tried in *Earl*, or an elective community property regime for the whole country.

The government's revenue needs during World War II suggested the first route. The Roosevelt administration floated a proposal to tax all married couples as if they were a single unmarried person. The Traditionals and Equals would both be taxed alike—but both would be taxed as Sally Single was. This solution was identical to the Wisconsin law at issue in *Hoeper*. In the all-important bottom-line terms, this meant that all married couples earning $60,000 would have to pay $12,000 in taxes, under table 1. This would make it a tax burden for upper-income people to be married anywhere, as long as both spouses had some personal income, because one spouse's income would always simply be added on top of the other's, with no offsetting benefit in the rate structure.

Randolph Paul was a leading tax policy analyst of the era. An ardent supporter of the New Deal, he played a major role in the Treasury Department during World War II and so was intimately familiar with wartime tax policy. Paul reports in his roughly contemporaneous 1954 treatise *Taxation in the United States*, which reads like a transcript of his diaries from the period, that the 1941 proposal was met by a storm of protest:

> The joint return provision, designed to yield about $300 million, aroused violent protest. Wendell Wilkie called it a "proposal out of the dark ages," which would set the cause of emancipation of women back five hundred years. Arthur Krock of the *New York Times* said that it would put a premium on divorce, celibacy, a lower birth rate, and make for a mercenary attitude toward the estate of marriage. Arthur Graham Glasgow, a noted gas technologist of somewhat advanced years, was moved to send his opinion to the *New York Times* that the provision was immoral as well as unmoral, and allotted a premium to living in sin. The *New Republic* was afraid that it would retard marriages and discourage women from working. . . .
>
> The supporters of [an amendment against the plan] became champions of emancipated womanhood. The provision was an encroachment on the independent status and social, economic, and political individuality of women which has been won only after a long, hard struggle. It revived the old common law fiction which made the wife a chattel. Thus it was a step backward and contrary to the trend of American policy, which more and more treated women on an absolute equality with men.

Note that the proposal for mandatory joint filing, like Wisconsin's law in *Hoeper*, came from relatively liberal political factions—the Roosevelt administration and the Democrats. These liberals were concerned with increasing the effective burden of progressive rates; the proposal was a way to get at rich families. This fact created strange bedfellows: conservatives and Republicans arguing for "emancipated womanhood."

This is yet another example of the power of tax and of the linkage of the rhetoric of tax and family, which we'll see time and again, most recently in the *Contracts*. The 1941 episode drives home that what is constant in these rhetorical moves is not so much any set view of the family or the role of women as it is a fundamental opposition to tax. Conservatives were willing to wave the banner of women's emancipation and "absolute equality with men" when it could be used against a tax increase on them. Any port in a storm.

The careful reader might, however, be puzzled. Mandatory joint filing, as the 1941 proposal was dubbed, would really hurt only those in high tax brackets. Most married taxpayers were filing joint returns anyway, because they were in the single lowest bracket. But weren't the upper classes most likely to be the Traditional-like families, least likely to have significantly secondary-earner wives in 1941? The hypothetical Traditionals have been paying $12,000 in our examples, and we have noted how few real Equals there were, especially among the upper classes. Why should they care about how *Tina* is taxed?

But we should be learning by now just how strange the tale of taxing women is. By 1941 many Traditional-like families had found ways around separate filing through bedchamber transactions and, most important, community property laws. Sure enough, Paul notes that the complaints "came principally but not altogether from congressmen of the community property states." The opposition to joint filing really had nothing at all to do with women's emancipation, and that is why conservatives could advance it. The complaints were coming from couples able to *look* like the Equals, not the real Equals, and thus could be rejected as "political pap" by Democrats. We'll see this same dynamic play out in modern times, when the *Contracts* use the rhetoric of the marriage penalty to advance a tax relief program designed to encourage wives to stay home.

The proposal for mandatory joint filing died in 1941. The same proposal, put forth again in 1942, met the same fate. Congress found other ways to raise taxes, many involving the move from a class to a mass tax, as another of Carolyn Jones's articles puts it, such as the implementation of wage withholding in 1943. Everyone's taxes were increasing, women were entering the workforce in record numbers, some rich families were designing bizarre legal entities in a desperate attempt to look like the Equals, and states were dancing with the devil of community property laws. Mere anarchy seemed to have been loosed upon the world, and only peace could promise better answers.

CONGRESS TO THE RESCUE, TAKE TWO: 1948

Seven years after the proposal for mandatory joint filing went nowhere, joint filing of a different sort became law. Times had of course changed dramatically. The war was over and, as typically happened in a postwar America, tax cuts were possible. There was also much hope, or rather, much assuming, that the end of the war would mean a return to normalcy in another sense: married women, especially mothers, would leave the workforce they had entered during the war as part of the wartime production effort, and go back home. The participation rate for women in the labor force rose from 27.9 percent in 1940 to 35.8 percent in 1945, but then dipped back down to 31.5 percent by 1947; the numbers for married women alone were far lower, and for married mothers lower still. Meanwhile, in the wake of the war, birth rates shot up, as the celebrated baby boom took hold. Federal funding for child care, put in place during the war, was eliminated soon after it.

In Washington, tax and family were linked. A large peace dividend was spent in the form of tax cuts, which benefited rich traditional families. Politicians used the rhetoric of neutrality and family values to justify the change. We'll see later that this exact scenario is almost eerily repeating itself in the contemporary *Contract with America*. In 1947, there was a fierce battle between President Truman, who believed that a tax cut would be irresponsible in the face of pressing economic needs, including paying down wartime debts, and a Republican Congress bent on distributing a peace dividend again—a situation with interesting resonances to the 1990s. Truman won the battle with a veto in 1947. In 1948, however, joint filing emerged once more, like a phoenix from the ashes.

Congress considered several different ways to deal with the problem of the differing treatments of families—that is, rich families—in community and non–community property states. It considered again what had come to be called "mandatory joint filing": the rejected 1941 option. This kind of joint filing had to be mandatory because no family in which the lesser-earning spouse had any income would willingly file jointly under rate schedules that put this income on top of the primary earner's. A second option involved ignoring community property laws and focusing on the actual control of wealth—an acceptance of the government's argument in *Seaborn*. A third option was to allow family partnerships and other tax-saving dodges—an acceptance of the "attenuated subtleties" tried by tax lawyers after *Earl*. A fourth option was elective community property, letting spouses in non–community property states sign documents creating this relationship on their own—just as the Earls had tried to do. But the proposal that won out was for a system of optional joint filing referred to as income splitting. This plan was perfect for the Traditionals: It allowed tax savings with no real effects on women's property rights. The proposal, which came to be called the Surrey Plan, after Stanley Surrey, who was then working for the Treasury Department, easily carried the day.

Much of the testimony before Congress on the various proposals came from politicians and citizens of community property states, and, on first glance, a good deal of their rhetoric looks quite concerned with women's property rights. Representative Bertrand Gearhart, a high-ranking Democrat from California, for example, repeatedly argued that community property law had real effects on women's property ownership, and he chided other states for not adopting this regime for themselves. Addressing a spokesman from Florida, which had considered but failed to enact a community property law, Gearhart asked:

> The fact that they did not become community property states, their legislatures having failed to pass any laws changing their property system, would that not indicate that they did not want the change, and that, therefore, they preferred to stay under the common-law system?

Community property advocates mimicked the language of Justice Roberts in *Seaborn* and *Hoeper*, and often invoked neutrality norms. The federal government was simply and consistently taxing the "real" owner of income, which meant in community property states taxing the wife as one-half owner. Gearhart lectured another speaker about the difference in California law:

> We tax the individual's income. If, in your state, you want to insist that that income belongs to the husband and that the wife has no interest in it at all, logically he should pay the tax on it. In our state, the State of California, the husband never was regarded and is not treated as the owner of all of that income. From the instant that it is earned, according to the law of the state, it became and was the property of the community partnership. The wife owns half, and the husband owns half.

This all sounds rather enlightened, but on closer inspection the arguments begin to look disingenuous. Community property states praised their own systems and stressed their real consequences because they were worried about the 1941-style plans for mandatory joint filing, which would strip their wealthy citizens of the tax benefits of community property laws. Community property advocates repeatedly stressed their sympathies with their common law brethren, and even pointed out that the Surrey Plan would indeed help their wealthy citizens, because many men in community property states had separate property that would benefit from income splitting.

J. Paul Jackson, an attorney from Texas (a community property state) had lectured the House Ways and Means Committee, as Representative Gearhart had, on the real egalitarian effects of community property, and had stressed his opposition to a 1941-style mandatory joint-filing plan. But Jackson made clear what he thought was the best answer: "Undoubtedly a much fairer and more equitable effort to equalize is represented by the present proposal sponsored by Congressman Reed ... popularly known as the Surrey proposal." Jackson went on to explain:

> We in the community-property States cannot complain too greatly if others in the common-law States pay the same taxes we do, so long as our property laws are not jeopardized, and we are not made the exclusive mark for discriminatory legislation.
>
> Moreover, the bill frankly will serve to reduce taxes in the community-property States, in that certain incomes, namely, royalty income in Texas and income from separate property in California and Washington, now taxed to the separate owner, will be taxed equally to the two spouses.

In other words, the community property states had no objection to treating all states alike, as long as this was done on the *lower* tax plateau of income splitting.

Part of the proof of the pudding was that the plan for elective community property went nowhere. This was a regime wherein, *if* husbands ceded real property rights to their wives, then (and only then) could they get the income-splitting benefit. Once the Surrey Plan for automatic splitting without real ownership effects emerged as an answer, it easily carried the day. Although the Truman administration continued to oppose income splitting on the grounds of its cost and the fact that it only benefited the wealthy, it was not supported in this regard by Congressional Democrats, who readily backed the Surrey Plan. More proof of the pudding was to come in the lightning-quick repeal of community property laws by those states that had converted to them just prior to 1948.

Congress again voted for tax reduction in 1948. The income-splitting provision was a prominent aspect of this bill, accounting for between $800 million and $1 billion of the $6.5 billion total. This meant that about 15 percent of the total "peace dividend" would be distributed to no more than 10 percent of all married taxpayers, namely, wealthy Traditional-like families in non–community property states. Truman again vetoed the bill, but Congress handily overrode the veto. Joint filing has been with us ever since.

Paul had generally sympathized with Truman and favored more progressive taxation, and had recorded the 1941 outrage with care. Yet he readily signed off on the 1948 change, recording nary a dissenting vote: "Whatever may have been its shortcomings, the 1948 act accomplished one result which will have permanent values in income, and perhaps also estate and gift, taxation. It eliminated the longstanding discrimination giving the residents of community property states a marked income tax advantage over the residents of the common law states." Paul readily bought into the mainstream story, neglecting the fact that this was largely a "longstanding discrimination" limited to the rich, and that it could have been solved by moving to community property, ceding more power and control to wives, or, for that matter, overturning *Seaborn*. Paul was soon joined by other leading lights of the postwar tax policy academy in viewing joint filing, with its deemed income splitting, as a foundation of good tax policy.

A NEW DAY DAWNS

The 1948 Act set rates on married couples equal to twice what a single person earning one-half the total family income would pay. The community property regime was in essence adopted for federal tax purposes. All income was now *deemed* to be split between spouses, for tax purposes, without the unpleasant pressure to *actually* split it, for non-tax purposes. Couples were viewed as Equals, without any attention whatsoever to the generally contrary facts of the matter. In terms of our running example,

TABLE 2. 1948-Style Rate Schedules

INDIVIDUAL RATE SCHEDULE		MARRIED RATE SCHEDULE	
INCOME	MARGINAL TAX RATE	INCOME	MARGINAL TAX RATE
$0–$10,000	0%	$0–$20,000	0%
$10,001–$30,000	15%	$20,001–$60,000	15%
$30,001–$60,000	30%	$60,001–$120,000	30%
$60,001 and up	40%	$120,001 and up	40%

the Traditionals were now taxed like the Equals—but at the *lower* rate of the Equals. Both couples would now pay $6,000, leaving Sally Single, alone, to pay $12,000.

Above I repeat table 2 from chapter 1, which now appears in its historical context. Notice what is going on in the table. The rate schedule for married couples, set out on the right, consists of brackets that are simply double those for single persons, set out on the left. Thus, both the Traditionals and the Equals would now pay $6,000, as the Equals had all along, while Sally Single would still be stuck paying $12,000, because the left-hand side, the rate schedule for individuals, has not changed. The Equals themselves get no particular benefit from table 2, since they already had had two rides up the rate brackets; they really were equal earners, so they did not have to be deemed so. We shall see shortly, however, that the 1948 law *did* change matters for the Equals, in a way that put Emma Equal on the margin.

One way to understand the 1948 style of joint filing schedules is that all couples, including the Traditionals, are assumed to pool their earnings, so that equal-earning couples really are equal from an economic point of view. Stanley Surrey, writing in 1948, seemed to believe this, and it was a key assumption driving the classic McIntyre and Oldman article some thirty years later. Marjorie Kornhauser and others have questioned the fact of this matter. Not all married couples in fact pool their incomes, and many unmarried couples do, including gay and lesbian couples who, not surprisingly, have been left out of account in all of the legislative action on taxation and the family.

But we can question not just the *fact* of pooling, which looks to income once again as a static, distributive matter, but also its *relevance*. Even if couples do pool their income, there are gendered effects to a system of joint filing. The combination of spouses puts the lesser-earning spouse on the margin, and therefore at a higher rate, whether or not the family pools its income. The two issues—pooling and the secondary-earner bias—are distinct, just as the marriage penalty and the secondary-earner bias are distinct. Another way of getting at this point is to look at the law's effects on individual spouses *within* couples, as distinct from its effects on couples as units. In taking for granted the notion that couples are best understood as units, public discussion over joint filing simply did not consider its impact on individual spouses.

LOOKING AT EMMA

It looks at first glance as if 1948 brought no change to the Equals because they paid $6,000 both before and after the new rate schedule. This shows that there is no marriage penalty. Even if a couple consisted of two equal earners, they paid the same tax filing separately, under table 1, as they did jointly, under table 2. In contrast, if the couple were *unequal*—if, say, Earl made $50,000 and Emma $10,000—they would pay less tax under joint filing, or on getting married. In viewing this couple as consisting of two $30,000 earners, by fiat, the law would shift $20,000 from Earl's higher bracket into Emma's lower one. From 1948 to 1969, there were no marriage penalties, only bonuses.

But let's go back to the $6,000 tax paid by the Equals and look at how it is allocated between the spouses. Before 1948, with Earl and Emma filing separately under table 1, *each* had a $10,000 zero bracket, and *each* paid $3,000 in taxes. After 1948, the *couple* has a $20,000 zero bracket, and the *couple* pays $6,000 in tax. But now there is an inducement to think of the couple as consisting of a "primary" and a "secondary" earner; now there is one rate schedule for married persons, so there is an accounting question of who comes first. This is a question that did not exist before; it is the question that puts Emma on the margin.

Imagine that Emma gives birth to a child and that she is now considering whether to exit the workforce, like Susan or Elizabeth in our opening stories. Before 1948, Emma would think that she would be sacrificing $27,000 in take-home pay: her $30,000 salary minus the $3,000 tax. Now what? It turns out that Emma would be sacrificing $25,500 in salary. The $6,000 in taxes is no longer split equally between the Equals, if we consider that Earl comes first. If he alone continues to work, the couple pays $1,500 in tax: the first $20,000 generates no tax; the next $10,000 is taxed at 15 percent. By virtue of the consolidation of husband and wife, in one meaningful sense, Emma's tax has gone up, and Earl's has gone down; $4,500 gets pegged to Emma's work, and only $1,500 to Earl's.

Bringing spouses together under the rate structure encourages them to think this way. We are back to the accountant's tale. This has a very important *behavioral* effect that can be dramatic over time. The effect can swamp whatever justice is served by the sterile norm of taxing "equal-earning couples equally." The secondary-earner bias led Susan and Elizabeth to change their lives and run the risk that they may never get back to their former jobs or level of career satisfaction.

The fact that Emma's implicit tax burden went up, and Earl's went down, under a rate structure that has no marriage penalty within it—and that continues, to this day, to be advocated as an ideal of fairness and neutrality in tax—perfectly illustrates a central point from chapter 1: the marriage penalty is *not* the same thing as the secondary-earner bias, and there are good reasons to care far more about the latter, at least at the middle- and upper-income levels.

WRAPPING UP (?)

After 1948, all couples looked like the Equals to the IRS. But America got there not to help the Equals, and not even thinking of them at all, but rather to help their opposite number, the Traditionals, who relentlessly pursued the tax goodies at stake from 1913 on. No one mentioned the creation of the secondary-earner bias, and no one paused to see that society was marginalizing women and keeping them at home, except to comment, as Stanley Surrey explicitly did in 1948, that this very inducement to return home was a *good* thing.

Celebrating the 1948 law, Surrey wrote that now, "Wives need not continue to master the details of the retail drug business, electrical equipment business, or construction business, but may turn from their partnership 'duties' to the pursuit of homemaking." Note how Surrey repeats, mantra-like, the word "business" after each of his bizarre examples (retail drug, electrical equipment, construction!); how he encloses in quotation marks the obviously facetious word "duties"; and how he closes by invoking, almost absurdly, the Declaration of Independence, in his reference to the noble "pursuit of homemaking." Surrey was quite clear about what he thought married women should be doing. The absurdity of a tax system that could have induced women even to pretend to learn the world of business could not have been lost on his audience. That audience, not incidentally, happened to include the Congress of the United States. And that Congress, again not incidentally, happened to be about 99 percent men.

3 Still His Story, 1948 to the Present

PHASE 2, 1948–1969: PEACE AT HOME

Soon after 1948, all of the recently made community property states reverted to their former non–community property laws. This gave the lie to the arguments, propounded before Congress and elsewhere, that the moves to community property represented a sincerely motivated advance for women. Peace brought a return to normalcy, or so it appeared. A large peace dividend was spent to foster and reward wealthy, traditional households. Now women could go back to the noble "pursuit of homemaking," and men could stop pretending to give their wives assets. This happy reception should not surprise us at this point.

But it should puzzle us. The widely praised 1948 change had much the same structure and effect on women as the roundly criticized 1941–1942 proposals for mandatory joint filing, but just at lower rates. Both imposed a consolidated rate schedule on married couples. Both taxed equal-earning couples equally. Both placed the secondary-earner wife's wages on top of her husband's, at the margins of the tax structure. Yet while Randolph Paul and others reported that the 1941 act was viewed as "anti-woman" and "anti-family," the 1948 act was readily accepted and widely praised by Paul himself, Stanley Surrey, and others. What could this possibly mean?

Partly the reaction was due to the absence of working women among the upper classes; no one saw the secondary-earner bias because there were so few secondary earners. More important, the 1941 proposal had only marriage penalties in it; the 1948 one had only marriage bonuses. The class dimensions of this political drama ensured that only a small percentage of married couples and few, if any, real Equals were affected. Still, no one paid any significant attention to working wives.

The status quo that emerged was a tax system that combined the incomes of husbands and wives, and, in most of the country, a nontax property-rights system that kept them separate. Perhaps this sounds inconsistent. It is not. In both cases, men won. The overall regime was, not coincidentally, optimal from a strictly male point of view. Men had worked diligently for this result all along. Now they could go back to their usual ways of doing business, without fear of losing wealth to taxes or to their wives.

NOTHING TO TALK ABOUT?

For two decades after 1948, the story of taxation and the family drifted off into sleep. Paul reports an interesting anecdote from the United States Senate in 1951. Hubert Humphrey, during his first term in the Senate, led a campaign for a more progressive tax system. At one point he turned to the split income provision. Humphrey noted that this was "an area of the tax bill where angels fear to tread." He made clear that he did not support any return to the pre-1948 state of affairs, and no one at all seemed to be thinking of the biases against working wives: "The Senator from Minnesota explained that 'no one with a sense of equity in his heart' would wish to restore the inequity which had worked discrimination prior to 1948 against married couples in the common-law states," Paul wrote. What was Humphrey's objection? Split income brought no benefit at all "to a married man with two children receiving an income of $4,000." Humphrey's Republican opponent, Eugene Millikin of Colorado, admitted that the benefits of the provision started at $10,000 of income—more than $60,000 in 1995.

It was the unfairness of the 1948 reform along distributive lines that bothered Humphrey, and he proposed a change in the rate schedules to eliminate the advantages of splitting income for richer taxpayers. This meant moving toward the rejected 1941 joint filing option. Humphrey's proposal was projected to raise more than $300 million a year—about $2 billion in 1995—and it would have come packaged with tax relief for middle-income taxpayers. The Senate, with Democrats in the majority, soundly rejected Humphrey's proposed amendment, 62 to 15.

There was some congressional tinkering around the margins of the story. In 1951, a "head of household" rate schedule was passed, exactly splitting the difference between the single and married filing-jointly schedules, for unmarried individuals supporting an unmarried dependent child or grandchild. In 1954, a rather limited child-care deduction of $600 was granted to the middle- and lower-income classes, and it was occasionally modified during this phase. But there were no big issues on the table, like the joint filing debates leading up to 1948. There was no widespread move to revisit that joint filing solution, no provision for secondary-earner relief, no rethinking of the social security system's skew against working wives, which grew much worse during the period. Things were quiet on the legislative front.

Things were also sleepy in the academy. Major articles on the subject more or less stopped appearing in law reviews. There was no marriage penalty, which left nothing much to talk about. Emma Equal had lost badly in 1948, by the creation of the secondary-earner bias, but still there seemed to be little to talk about. Oldman and Temple published an international comparative study in 1960, following up on a United Nations report the prior year. The clear message of this endeavor was that Americans, with their system of joint filing and their norm of taxing equal-earning couples equally, had gotten it right. Oldman and Temple did note, in distinction to McIntyre and Oldman's 1977 article, that some relief for two-earner families would be appropriate, to compensate for the greater out-of-pocket costs of having two workers.

Harold Groves, an economist at the University of Wisconsin, published a volume prepared as background for a Brookings Institution conference in 1963, *Federal Tax Treatment of the Family*. He devoted less than three pages to the problems of "working wives," noting that "a strong consensus supports the view that the proper taxing unit is the family unity; that is, that two couples with equal taxable income should pay the same tax regardless of the technical legal division of the income." Groves did see that "a strong case can be made in terms largely of extra expense incurred by working wives and the non-taxability of the imputed value of services of nonworking wives, for granting some concessions to the two-job family," but he would have any benefit here "restricted to low and modest incomes."

Most interesting in this volume is its report of the conference discussion attendant on Groves's paper. Brookings had gotten twenty-seven of the leading tax policy experts together, among them Stanley Surrey, Joseph Pechman, Walter Blum of the University of Chicago Law School, eventual Nobel Laureate James Buchanan, Alice Rivlin, who was to go on and have a distinguished career at the Federal Reserve Bank and become President Clinton's budget chief. An early note about the topic addresses the discomfort some felt: "I don't think that 27 economists should have been assembled to address themselves to problems which are really partly anthropological, partly sociological, partly anything except what we have competence in." Somehow putting these doubts aside, a consensus seemed to emerge that the gravest problem area lay in the taxation of single taxpayers, anticipating the 1969 reform that we'll soon see:

> A final note was sounded, namely that if there were to be politically acceptable changes in the existing law, they would probably take the form of modest mitigation of the "unconscionable" tax burdens now cast upon single taxpayers. Not much sympathy was to be expected for bachelors and spinsters; according to code they shirk the responsibilities which families shoulder. The point was made that many single people are elderly widows and widowers, of whom no such criticisms can be made.

This representative quotation confirms the wisdom of the economists' skepticism. Perhaps this particular set of tax experts should have left the matter to the anthropologists.

In 1965, another economist, Douglas Thorson, published "An Analysis of the Sources of Continued Controversy over the Tax Treatment of Family Income." Thorson noted that "horizontal equity requires the taxation of the imputed income of the nonworking wife or deduction of extra expenses for the working wife," and later pointed out the "adverse incentive effects on the working wife." This shows that the ideas were clearly present for all to see, as they had been in 1963, and indeed at all times since 1948. But Thorson did not make much of these points; he concentrated his discussion on other issues, mainly on how the law should adjust for family size.

In his 1966 book *Federal Tax Policy*, Joseph Pechman, a major force at Brookings and in tax policy for most of the postwar period, devoted just three of 300 pages to the topic of taxation and the family. Pechman, who in 1959 had testified before the Congress that income splitting should be seen as a solution "for all time," now noted a few "theoretical objections" to it—mainly that some single persons with families were penalized—but concluded his brief discussion by commenting that the 1948 solution was "fairly popular" and thus "Congress has not considered alternative methods of allowing for marital status and family size." It seemed as if the compromise of 1948—in truth, an unequivocal victory for the Traditionals—had laid the matter to rest.

This is more or less the central theme of Boris Bittker's 1975 article. It moves us beyond the period immediately under discussion, but in many ways Bittker delivered the crowning touch to this period of relative complacency and silence. He saw with characteristic clarity the objections to a system of joint filing, including those relating to secondary earners. But with equal clarity he saw that these problems were the inevitable consequence of a basically sensible legislative compromise. Commenting on a current proposal to return to the pre-1948 system of single filing, Bittker wrote:

> The achievement of equality in taxes between married couples with the same income has been so commonly regarded as a permanent part of our tax structure—adopted in 1948 "for all time"— that its abandonment by a current legislative proposal, sponsored by a politically diverse spectrum of more than 150 Congressmen and Senators, is *nothing less than astonishing*. (Emphasis supplied.)

Bittker cited Pechman's testimony in the middle of this sentence, making a connection with this tax policy stalwart who, by the mid-1970s, was wavering in his support for joint filing.

I'll take an extended look at Bittker's canonical article later. The point for now is to see that the 1948 solution was so widely accepted that its potential abolition, some twenty-five years after the fact, was considered "astonishing." Surrey, Pechman, Paul, Bittker, McIntyre, and Oldman—leading academics and tax intellectuals who battled, sometimes fiercely, on a range of issues—all agreed on this central point. And yet it was exactly the 1948 change that put women like Susan and Elizabeth on the margin.

SOMETHING TO TALK ABOUT

The social history, however, did not end in 1948. The marginalizing of married women did not draw much attention, but another by-product of the 1948 law ultimately did. The joint filing regime created what came to be called the singles' penalty. We saw some concern for this—although limited to "widows and widowers," not "bachelors and spinsters"—in the 1963 conference reported in Groves's book. Pechman, in a 1959 paper submitted to Congress, was also much concerned with the plight of single taxpayers.

Before 1948, under table 1, the Equals paid $6,000 in taxes, while both the Traditionals and Sally Single paid $12,000. After 1948, Sally alone paid the higher amount. Even if a couple looked like the Traditionals—with one spouse earning all of the income—this couple got the benefit of two rides up the rate brackets. But Sally got only one ride. This was precisely the intended effect of rejecting the 1941 joint filing option and implementing the 1948 one, which had simply doubled the individual rate schedule in constructing the one for married persons. Pechman and others noted a specific objection to this scheme. Widows and other single taxpayers with dependents paid a price for not being married, even if they qualified for the somewhat restricted head-of-household category, which split the difference between the two schedules. This intellectual point languished until 1969, by which time single taxpayers had grown in numbers and political importance.

At this point, let's add another couple to our story: the Untraditionals. Ulma Untraditional makes $60,000 as a singer in a rock-and-roll band. Her boyfriend, Ronnie Rebel, makes nothing at all, having rejected the bourgeois notion of earning his own keep. To show his liberation from traditional patriarchy, and to make my naming convention a bit easier, Ronnie adopts Ulma's last name, but the two refuse to get married. Ronnie and Ulma are an unmarried couple living together—and paying a hefty tax penalty on account of their refusal to get married. The Untraditionals pay tax of $12,000, like Sally Single, because they refuse to join the ranks of the Traditionals and the Equals.

Same-sex couples who had unequal earnings among themselves paid a higher tax than married couples did, too, although they had no choice—and still don't. The tax law refuses to consider that some couples who are not married may pool their incomes, possibly even more fairly than many married couples do. Perhaps this is because "according to code they shirk the responsibilities which families shoulder," as the conference participants in Groves's 1963 book put it. The failure even to consider the claim of same-sex couples, however, gives the lie to the idea that actual income pooling was the driving force behind joint filing. The failure of Congress to insist that couples agree to share property as a condition of getting the favorable income-splitting tax treatment had also rendered this theory suspect. A wife cannot sue her husband to get one-half of the family's economic pool on the grounds that the tax laws say she owns it. Conversely, gay and lesbian couples who do pool their income cannot be taxed as if they do. In any event, the syndrome of unmarried individuals bearing a high tax burden came to be known as the singles' penalty.

SAL (NÉE SALLY) GOES TO CONGRESS

Notwithstanding my choice of a woman, Sally Single, to pose this example, it should not escape us that the complaints about single filers were mainly men's issues. We have come to the point where Sally Single must become a man—let's call him Sal. Most high-earning singles who did not want to be compelled to marry—with all that marriage meant in terms of economic rights for lesser-earning spouses (not coincidentally, such rights had been growing since 1948)—were, of course, men. The gender gap between men and women was so stuck during this period that "59 Cents" became a slogan of the ultimately unsuccessful campaign for the ERA. Why should rich men be induced to marry just to save taxes? This is like the question asked in the 1940s, regarding community property: Why should rich men have to pretend to give their wives property rights just to save taxes? American men have wanted to do two things throughout: pay as little tax as possible, and cede as little to women as possible. Why should they have to choose? The record has been stuck on this tune for quite some time.

Sal, Ronnie, and Ulma took their complaints to Congress. To rectify the perceived injustice, or at least to garner votes, Congress adjusted the rate schedule in 1969. Married couples now pay more than two single persons each with one-half of the combined income, but still less than one unmarried person earning the whole amount. Interestingly, the benefits of this single-person rate schedule extend to all singles, including bachelors and spinsters.

Modern rate schedules look like table 3, which we now see in its historical context. Note what has happened, compared with table 2. To mollify singles, Congress raised the rates on married couples by shrinking

TABLE 3. Modern-Style Rate Schedules

INDIVIDUAL RATE SCHEDULE		MARRIED RATE SCHEDULE	
INCOME	MARGINAL TAX RATE	INCOME	MARGINAL TAX RATE
$0–$10,000	0%	$0–$16,000	0%
$10,001–$30,000	15%	$16,001–$48,000	15%
$30,001–$60,000	30%	$48,001–$96,000	30%
$60,001 and up	40%	$96,001 and up	40%

their brackets. The married persons' schedule is no longer double the singles' schedule. Table 3 is formed by multiplying the married-rate schedule of table 2 by 0.8: The zero bracket now extends to $16,000 rather than $20,000, the 15% bracket to $48,000 rather than $60,000, and so on.

The Equals and Traditionals still pay the same amount of tax; the policy of taxing equal-earning couples equally is intact. But this married persons' tax has gone up: it is now $8,400 on $60,000 of earnings (zero on the first $16,000, plus 15 percent of the next $32,000 ($4,800), plus 30 percent of the remaining $12,000 ($3,600). This is less than the $12,000 tax still paid by Sally Single and the Untraditionals, but is higher than it had been. In reality, the increased tax on married couples could and did fund a tax reduction for singles. I don't mean to suggest a pure act of spite on the part of single taxpayers; I just want to keep the examples as simple as possible, and that's why I have kept the singles' schedule fixed.

HERE COMES THE MARRIAGE PENALTY

As a result of this latest rate change, the marriage penalty enters the picture. It is in one sense the Equals who pay this, for were they not married, each would pay $3,000, using the unchanged rate schedule for individuals. By marrying, the tax paid by the Equals goes up because the right-hand rate schedule is less favorable.

But let's note some facts about this state of affairs. One, the 1969 rate change hits especially hard on *Emma* Equal, the secondary earner in that family. If the 1948 act led families to think in terms of a primary/secondary earner split, then the 1969 change made it worse to be the secondary earner. Table 6 sets out the total tax burden paid by the Equals, and its allocation between Earl, as primary earner, and Emma, as secondary earner, under each of the three basic rate structures we've considered. What has happened to the Traditionals in the three major phases is that their tax first went down, from $12,000 to $6,000, and then went up, to $8,400. Table 6 illustrates what has happened to the Equals. Their total tax at first stayed at $6,000, then went up to $8,400: they paid a price for being hitched to the Traditionals.

TABLE 6. Primary-Secondary Tax Allocations

Rate Schedule	Total Tax	Primary-Secondary Allocation
I: Pre-1948	$6,000	$3,000/3,000
II: 1948–1969	$6,000	$1,500/4,500
III: Post-1969	$8,400	$2,100/6,300

More important, though, consider what has happened, in an accounting sense, to Emma as the secondary earner. As a result of the 1948 change, her share of the tax burden went up, while Earl's went down: 1948 led the family to consider her a secondary earner and then penalized her for being one. The 1969 change then adds to her burden. Emma continues to bear the brunt of the tax—specifically, she pays three-quarters of the change—because she is on the margin, in the higher tax brackets. Think again of what happens if Emma stops working outside the home. Her $30,000, which had been $27,000 after taxes in phase 1 and which went down to $25,500 in 1948, has now been further reduced to $23,700. If Earl alone works, and earns $30,000, the family will owe $2,100 in taxes, so $6,300 is saved when Emma stays home. Here is a striking fact in the story: of the six major players in this drama—Earl, Emma, the Equals as a unit, Tom, Tina, and the Traditionals as a unit—only Emma Equal's tax was increased in both 1948 and 1969. We might think of 1969 as a high point for liberalism in general; it was just another in a series of low points for working wives.

It is also important to remember the baseline. Since the Equals and Traditionals were linked together in their tax burdens in 1948, the Traditionals, too, paid a penalty in 1969. Their taxes went up just as much as the taxes of the Equals did in 1969. This is a very significant point, because we'll continue to see, right down through the *Contracts*, a focus on the Traditionals when the marriage penalty is brought up. If society were really concerned with the plight of the Equals, Emma in particular, it should consider separate filing or some secondary-earner relief, but the law has almost never done this.

Let me be clear on this point, and put it a slightly different way. The Equals pay a marriage penalty because their tax as a couple goes up when they marry. In general, this marriage penalty is less important to our story than is the secondary-earner bias, which sees the wife's tax in effect go up, and the husband's go down, on marriage, with or without a marriage penalty in the rate schedule. We saw that in 1948. The Traditionals do not pay a marriage penalty in this sense; their tax goes down when they marry, so they still get a marriage bonus.

But the Traditionals do pay a marriage penalty, in the sense that the rate schedules are not as favorable to married couples as they were from 1948 to 1969. This is a relative marriage penalty, which looks to the way things could be and in fact have been. In phase 3, we'll see that the system— mainstream politicians and academics—have shown little interest in alleviating the marriage penalty in its first sense, insofar as it falls on the Equals. The system has, however, taken a strong interest in alleviating the penalty in this second sense, insofar as it falls on the Traditionals.

PHASE 3, 1969 TO THE PRESENT: TALKING ABOUT THE WRONG THING

There are two different effects at work in table 3. Married couples still get the *benefit* of income splitting, as they have since 1948, but they also get the *burden* of a higher rate schedule, as they have since 1969. Every married couple is treated as if it had two equal earners, whether or not this is in fact true. This was the point of the 1948 change—a windfall for couples with unequal earnings. But then those two equal earners must pay tax under a higher rate schedule than unmarried persons use. To see this, divide the right-hand schedule in table 3 in half: You will see a zero bracket extending to $8,000, a 15 percent bracket extending to $24,000, and so on. That this is a higher rate schedule is the point of the 1969 change to accommodate single persons. This change hurts all married couples. The Traditionals are still net winners, for the 1948 income-splitting victory was greater than the 1969 tax-rate defeat. The Equals are net losers, because they got no benefit as a couple in 1948, so only the 1969 loss stands. Emma Equal lost both times.

Whether there is an actual marriage penalty under the general rate structure depends in one sense on the relative allocation of earnings between spouses. Those that already have a 50/50 division, like the Equals, receive no benefit from income splitting, and simply pay the price of the higher rates. Those who have a 100/0 split, like the Traditionals, see the benefits of split income predominate over the burden of higher rates. The precise figures vary from year to year, but in 1994 Feenberg and Rosen found that 52 percent of all married couples paid a penalty, 38 percent got a bonus, and the remaining 10 percent were unaffected. This study took into account, as others had not, the earned-income tax credit that I'll discuss later in this chapter. This credit generates a very steep marriage penalty for lower-income families; when the credit is not accounted for, the percentage of couples paying the marriage penalty appears much smaller.

Congress wanted to prevent couples from having a beneficial "heads I win, tails you lose" choice between filing jointly under the married-rate schedule or filing separately, which would have in effect reintroduced a singles' penalty by giving married people an option that unmarried people didn't have. So Congress set the "married, filing separately" schedule at one-half the "married, filing jointly" one. This married, filing separately schedule is thus less favorable than the singles' schedule. Specifically, it has a zero bracket extending to $8,000, a 15 percent bracket extending to $24,000, and so on. It almost never makes sense to be married and file separately, since this sacrifices the benefits of income splitting *without* getting a more favorable rate schedule.

The Equals, for example, would still pay $8,400 under the married, filing separately schedule. Earl and Emma would each pay no tax on their first $8,000; but would pay $2,400, or 15 percent, on their next $16,000; plus $1,800, or 30 percent, on their final $6,000. This adds up to $4,200 each, or $8,400 in total, as before. In contrast, the Traditionals, or any married couple with unequal earnings, would see their taxes go up; the Traditionals would pay $14,400 if Tom were foolish enough to file separately. (I'll skip the math this time.) It is neither surprising nor irrational that only a small percentage of married couples file separately. Most of these separate filers are estranged or otherwise living apart, and simply unwilling to sign the same form, even to save taxes. "Married, filing separately" is an irrelevance in this book, as it pretty much is in real life.

UNDERSTANDING THE MARRIAGE PENALTY

We're about to see the somnambulance of phase 2 give way to the fervor against the marriage penalty—never our main concern—in phase 3. Recall that when we started the story in 1913, with only table 1 before us, the Equals paid $6,000 in tax while the Traditionals and Sally Single paid $12,000. The point of the 1948 change, captured in table 2, was to bring the Traditionals down to the tax level of the Equals, $6,000. This left Sally alone at $12,000, and it was this fact that led to the singles' penalty complaints and the 1969 changes set out in table 3. After these changes, both the Equals and the Traditionals move up, in lockstep, to $8,400. Table 7 summarizes this contemporary picture. Much of this came to pass because of the fixity of the norm of taxing equal-earning couples equally. Because of this linking together of the Traditionals and the Equals, the fortunes of the Traditionals, too, are tied to the marriage penalty.

If what we mean by the marriage penalty is the additional tax certain

TABLE 7. Taxes and Status, Post-1969

Family Type	Tax Owed
Unmarried Equals (each earning $30,000)	$6,000
All married couples earning $60,000 (Equals and Traditionals)	$8,400
Single persons and Untraditionals earning $60,000	$12,000

couples pay on getting married—if we are looking at the incentive to marry or not—it makes sense to consider the unmarried Equals as paying a penalty and the unmarried Traditionals as getting a bonus. Looking at table 7, we see that the unmarried Equals increase their taxes on marrying; the unmarried Untraditionals decrease their taxes when they marry. But there is no reason why we have to think of the marriage penalty that way. Talk of marriage penalties can come from—and, I am arguing, does come *primarily* from—traditional families.

Proof of this claim is easy to come by. There are three general responses to the marriage penalty. One, we could go back to the system of separate filing that the United States had from 1913 to 1948 and which most advanced democracies now have. This system has marriage neutrality, because marriage is an irrelevance as far as the tax laws go. The Equals would stay at $6,000 in taxes, and the Traditionals at $12,000, whether either couple were married or not. The fact that the Traditionals would be hit hard under this plan indicates why it must be made mandatory.

Two, we could view the marriage penalty as a particular problem of the Equals, and offer relief targeted to secondary earners; we could deal with just those couples whose tax goes up when they marry. There are two general ways to do this. First, we could have a system of optional separate filing that would allow married couples to file separately under the more favorable rate schedules for unmarried individuals. A couple would choose the joint filing option if the income-splitting benefits prevailed over the burden of the higher rate structure, but not otherwise. The Equals would choose to file separately and pay $6,000, while the Traditionals would keep filing jointly and pay $8,400. This would help the Equals without directly hurting the Traditionals, as mandatory separate filing would. A second way to help the Equals is to allow some kind of secondary-earner relief, like a deduction or credit for the work-related expenses of two-earner families. This also would flow only to the Equals; the Traditionals would not be affected directly.

Three, we could lower rates on married couples generally, keeping all equal-earning couples together. That is, we could go back toward the 1948–1969 rate schedule of table 2, which had no marriage penalties. Under this approach, both the Equals and the Traditionals would see their taxes fall to $6,000. In sum, the first option hurts the Traditionals directly, the second has no direct effect on them, and this third one benefits them directly.

It should now not surprise us which solution to the marriage penalty has been most commonly advocated and implemented in American politics. It is the third one, the one that favors traditional families. The first, of mandatory separate filing, is what Bittker dismissed in 1975 as "nothing less than astonishing." The second, of looking directly to the secondary-earner bias, is exactly what the laws choose *not* to do, as we shall see. This refusal to move seriously toward either of the first two approaches, separate filing or secondary-earner relief, confirms the political fact that talk of the marriage penalty is fueled by a desire to take the final approach. Consider now the history of dealing with secondary earners, or, more accurately, not dealing with them.

ON (NOT) HELPING SECONDARY EARNERS

The story of this part is the inexorable move toward a system of joint filing that has the effect both of leading married persons to think in terms of a primary and an at least potentially secondary earner, and of then heavily taxing that secondary earner's work outside the home. Emma Equal is the big repeat loser in this story. The problem was set in motion in 1948, with the adoption of joint filing, but it got little attention until after the 1969 rate change designed to mitigate the singles' penalty. This change introduced a marriage penalty, neither identical to nor necessarily connected with the secondary-earner bias. Now we face another set of puzzles: how society goes about addressing the marriage penalty. If the concern over the marriage penalty is particular to the Equals, we should be looking at one of the first two answers, separate filing or secondary-earner relief. But this we have rarely done.

A Bit of a Twist

A curious episode happened at the height of World War II. In 1944, the tax law was amended to provide for an exemption or zero bracket of $500 per individual against the normal tax, which had a rate of 3 percent. The new provision stated that "in the case of a joint return by husband and wife . . . the normal tax exemption shall be $1,000, except that if the adjusted gross income of one spouse is less than $500, the normal tax exemption shall be $500 plus the adjusted gross income of such spouse." Immediately prior to this time, individuals had a $500 zero bracket, but married couples filing jointly had a $1,200 one. This was the kind of structure discussed in connection with table 5, only with a more generous married zero bracket. It was this feature which meant that some 90–95 percent of American taxpayer couples would derive no benefit from income splitting, even though they looked like the Traditionals. The new law decreased the zero-bracket benefits for married couples from $1,200 to between $500 and $1,000, depending on the wife's earnings.

The new provision actually did more than that. It carried, for the first time, an insistence on true separate filing for all married taxpayers. The wife had her own $500 zero bracket, which she could use to offset her wages. The couple could file jointly, but the law only accommodated this as a clerical matter; the married zero bracket was no longer *automatically* at least double the single person's one. If the couple filed jointly, the wife simply transferred her own zero bracket—which would effectively be the lesser of $500 or her own earnings—to her husband.

This meant that the provision was a tax increase on traditional families. Prior to 1944, it didn't matter to the vast majority of American men, for tax purposes, whether their wives earned anything at all. The Traditionals and the Equals alike had a zero bracket of $1,000 (actually, $1,200 in 1943). But for two years, 1944 and 1945, at a time when many American married women were indeed in the workforce in connection with the war effort, families would sacrifice up to $15 in taxes if the wife did not have her own earnings. Now the Equals would have $1,000 in their zero bracket; the Traditionals would have only $500. For the first time, the law featured a true separate filing system; husbands could not simply take a double-exemption level, whether their wives worked or not. This was also—not coincidentally—the same limited period during which the federal government, under the Lanham Act, provided money for child care for working mothers.

Joseph Pechman, in his 1966 book, identified the joint filing provision, minor as it was, as the only "working wife credit or deduction" we have ever had in the United States. This is, in a sense, true, because it was the first time that working wives were acknowledged as a significant enough phenomenon to affect tax policy. Before that time, the law more or less assumed that wives earned nothing. The system of separate filing was set up so that the typical married man could and would be *the* separate filer in a family. What Congress did in 1944 was nothing other than make separate filing a reality, insisting on each spouse's having his or her own exemption level. Ironically, Congress was also *increasing* the tax on middle-income traditional families by this insistence on true separate filing. The law was a revenue raiser.

That Pechman thought Congress would see fit to give wives working during wartime a $15 break—a sum equivalent to just about $150 in 1995—is itself interesting. That this really wasn't so—that Congress was only acknowledging, for the first time, that lots of wives did have their own earnings, and was insisting, again for the first time, that couples truly be separate filers—is also interesting. Interesting as well, especially considering the failed 1941 and 1942 attempts at mandatory joint filing that would have raised the taxes paid by *rich* Traditionals, was the fact that the 1944 provision was in effect a tax increase on *lower*-income Traditionals. But most interesting of all is the fact that Congress repealed the law as soon as the war ended, and went back to the old system in 1946, a system that allowed middle-class families to be Traditionals without adverse tax consequences. Only for two years, at the height of World War II, and as part of a tax increase, did Congress bring itself to admit that some wives worked outside the home. Its quick repeal of the provision suggested a "return to normalcy" effect for the vast middle classes, exactly parallel to the quick withdrawal of federal funds for child care.

The Standard View, and a Lone Dissent

Putting this wartime episode aside, the idea of secondary-earner relief would surface occasionally, as in Oldman and Temple's 1960 article, Groves's 1963 conference paper, or Thorson's 1965 article. But the mainstream tax policy community hardly placed the issue at the top of its agenda, and often belittled it. Let's return to Bittker's classic and canonical 1975 article.

A principal theme of Bittker's highly influential work is that, in the collision between the goals of (1) progressive marginal rates, (2) marriage neutrality, and (3) taxing equal-earning couples equally, something had to give. Bittker clearly supported at least moderate progressivity throughout his illustrious career. Note that if we had truly flat marginal rates, it doesn't much matter whether we have joint or separate filing. All of the tax rate tables become redundant, because all income gets taxed at the same rate. (This is, however, not true of the contemporary flat tax plans, with their large zero brackets, which I'll consider more fully in chapter 9.) Bittker also clearly and strongly endorsed the goal of taxing equal-earning couples equally, along with Surrey, Paul, McIntyre, Oldman, Pechman, Groves, and the rest of the chorus. That's why Bittker found the reconsideration of joint filing nothing less than astonishing.

That then left marriage neutrality as the weak point in the system. Under a system of progressive marginal rates with equal-earning couples being taxed equally, there would be singles' or marriage penalties, or some combination of each. Taxing the Traditionals and the Equals alike under progressive marginal rates necessarily means that Tom Traditional's "second" $30,000 gets taxed like Emma Equal's first and only $30,000. Some couples would see their tax burdens go up on marriage, some would see them go down, or there would be some of each. The rejected 1941 mandatory joint-filing plan, like the *Hoeper* plan, had only marriage penalties in it, as all married couples were taxed alike at the Traditionals' high rate. The widely accepted 1948 income-splitting plan had only marriage bonuses in it, as all married couples were taxed alike at the lower rate of the Equals. The 1969 revision still in effect today has some bonuses and some penalties, as all married couples are taxed alike under rates that fall in between the higher Traditionals' and the lower Equals' ones. Ever since 1948, the law has kept equal-earning couples together, at the price of marriage neutrality.

Bittker saw the dual-earner problem, all right. Two-thirds of the way into his lengthy article, he turns to the problem of the "two-job married couple." By 1975, Bittker began wryly, this problem had "moved to the center of the stage in the ever changing but never ending drama entitled 'Victims of Tax Injustice.' " Indeed, by this point in the story, there was a growing consciousness of just this problem. In 1972, Grace Ganz Blumberg published a law review article, "Sexism in the Code: A Comparative Study of Income Taxation of Working Wives and Mothers," which carefully laid out the burdens facing working wives and mothers. As Bittker was aware, Blumberg, while a teaching fellow at Harvard Law School, had testified in 1973 at the hearings on the Economic Problems of Women before the Joint Economic Committee of Congress, along with Pechman and Babette Barton of the University of California at Berkeley School of Law. (This session was chaired by a woman, Representative Martha Griffiths, and apparently was attended by only one other Congressperson—Senator Charles Percy, who showed up late.) Blumberg had also participated in a conference at New York University on the problems of taxation for women, organized by now Supreme Court Justice Ruth Bader Ginsburg, whose husband is a prominent tax lawyer. Bittker, who had attended this conference, includes in his text a "plausible example offered by a critic"—he then cites Blumberg's testimony in a footnote—"involving a married woman whose $10,000 salary yields a net of only $1,600."

This is just like the stories of Elizabeth and Susan. In the mid-1990s, with income tax rates dramatically lower than when Bittker was writing (the top bracket was then 70 percent), the story of taxing women is still every bit as dramatic as it was in 1970 or so. Bittker saw the accounting facts and did not question their accuracy; he found the example "plausible." It might appear that we were on the brink of having a major tax policy academic, Boris Bittker, join the cause.

Nothing of the kind happened. The wry introduction should have tipped us off: Bittker saw this "problem" as just another in an endless series of gripes against taxation of any and all sorts. Having repeated Blumberg's example and having noted that the burden against secondary earners is overwhelmingly likely to fall on wives, Bittker retreated. In the next ten pages of his text, he argues against doing anything much at all for wives. During one stretch, he frets that any earned income allowance extended to working wives would have to extend more broadly:

> *Everyone* who works away from home—not just the working wife—must get to the job site, dress as the job requires, and pay for lunch if it is inconvenient to bring it in a brown bag. Similarly, *everyone* who works has less time and energy to keep house, prepare meals, and look for bargains.

This language, which is inaccurate in some ways, gendered in others, is frequently cited in tax textbooks as an authoritative argument against secondary-earner relief. Yet it contradicts the greater common sense evidenced in Groves and Thorson, each of whom had seen a strong argument for secondary-earner relief because of both the greater expenses of two-worker couples and the nontaxation of the imputed income of stay-at-home spouses.

Bittker goes on to note how even the kind of "modest allowance" then being discussed by Pechman and others would not "constitute a major economic breakthrough for the housewife" but would generate large revenue losses for the government. Bittker failed to see it as a virtue that the lower tax rates for secondary earners would be financed out of higher taxes on primary earners. Perhaps because Bittker's logic has led him to see men and women in the same boat ("everyone who works has less time and energy to keep house") or because he cannot consider a more radical inversion of the status quo, he is only able to see possibilities for limited, ad hoc changes—which he then rejects on that very account. The argument runs as follows: (1) All we can do, consistent with logic, equity, and commonsensical understandings of our revenue needs, is to offer modest relief; (2) modest relief would do little to solve a big problem; (3) therefore we should do nothing.

After the discussion of possible earned-income allowance for secondary earners, Bittker spends five pages discussing the possibility of moving to separate returns for married couples—a proposal, as we've already seen, that he finds "nothing less than astonishing." As noted above, Bittker cites Pechman, who, although he had earlier written that the 1948 move to joint filing was "for all time," was by 1973 arguing along with Blumberg for some accommodation to two-earner couples. It is as if Bittker had to remind his now wandering ally, Pechman, about the facts of the matter.

After all of this, Bittker does concede a possible, limited role for some earned-income allowance for secondary workers that would address the particular marriage penalty faced by the Equals. But Bittker was skeptical of this solution, and he concluded that there might at most be some *small* accommodation of dual-earning couples, as "a symbol, however minor its financial value, of Congressional 'approval' of employment outside the home." He went on to add that even this limited symbol should be "phased out as obstacles to the employment of wives are eliminated."

This whole view is disturbing. The burden on women like Susan and Elizabeth was hardly minor by 1975, as Blumberg's article and testimony made clear. Why would Congress even have to show its "approval" of women working outside the home, in 1975? Who asked *them*? Who needs their "approval"? And why should this approval, if it is to be given at all, be nothing more than symbolic? The tax system is marginalizing women and helping to keep them at home. Isn't it a bit ironic that Congress, a large culprit in this story, should give a nod and a wink—should say that it is all right for married women to work outside the home—even while keeping in place all but a minor fraction of the very large disincentives to their doing so? After all that, why should the relief be phased out as "the obstacles to the employment of wives are eliminated"? The tax system *itself* is a *large* obstacle to the employment of wives.

Alas, the kind of heightened awareness of gender suggested by my rhetorical questions did not yet play a role in 1975. Instead, Bittker proved characteristically prescient; indeed, he seemed to influence the course of history. This was not at all surprising, given his exalted status as a tax scholar. The separate filing system that Bittker found "astonishing" was not adopted. In 1981 a very limited secondary-earner deduction was passed—and repealed five years later.

In a final subsection of his discussion of the problem with two-job married couples, in which he seems not even to be recommending the moderate, symbolic nod he had above, Bittker begins: "The search for a remedy for the two-job couple's complaint has taken us far afield." But how could the problem of working wives be "far afield" in an article magisterially entitled "Federal Income Taxation and the Family," one that appears to have been intended to, and in fact did, become the canonical statement of tax policy wisdom on the subject for decades? What field was Bittker on? Our project is to craft a new field, from the ground up—a field that women and men can build equally, and on which all individuals can stand and be treated with equal concern and respect.

The Curious Case of Section 221, Part I: Implementation

The most decisive evidence that the political understanding of marriage penalties is not about a heightened concern for equal-earning couples comes from the legislative history of Internal Revenue Code Section 221. This provision was put in place in 1981 to help secondary earners. It was specifically linked in congressional discussions to the marriage penalty, which was the subject of extensive hearings before the House Ways and Means Committee in 1980. Once again, note the contrast between the silence that greeted the secondary-earner bias in phase 2 and the intense noise over the marriage penalty in phase 3. At these hearings, Pamela Gann, economist June O'Neill, and many others testified, as Congress considered three plans to address the marriage penalty. These hearings give us a window into the political understandings of tax and gender issues.

One plan, sponsored by Representative Millicent Fenwick and co-signed by more than two hundred Congresspersons, would have given married couples a choice to file jointly or separately, under the favorable singles' schedule. As we saw above, this "optional" separate filing would have helped the Equals without directly hurting the Traditionals: there would be marriage bonuses for the Traditionals and neutrality for the Equals. Still, the Traditionals can be expected to resist optional separate filing, because it lowers the taxes of the Equals and thus costs money, none of which they get. The relative share of the tax burden borne by the Traditionals increases. Despite apparent initial widespread congressional support, this plan went nowhere.

A second option was a return to the pre-1948 system of separate filing, or, equivalently, "mandatory" separate filing. This would have been less costly to the government than the Fenwick plan was, precisely because it would have deprived the Traditionals of their income-splitting benefit. Indeed, it was the worst possible outcome for the Traditionals. The Equals would see their taxes fall to $6,000, as under the first option, but the Traditionals would now see theirs go up to $12,000, just as they had been under phase 1. Like the reconsideration of separate filing in the 1970s, this plan went nowhere.

The third option was to allow a limited deduction for the secondary earner. The ultimate law allowed a deduction of 10 percent of the earnings of the lesser-earning spouse up to $30,000 of wages (that is, a deduction up to $3,000). The ceiling was designed so that the benefit would not extend too much into the upper classes, and hence marks a theme that we'll see more of—a greater willingness to help lower- and middle-class secondary earners than rich ones. This provision would allow the Equals, in our example, to deduct $3,000, saving them $900 in tax and dropping them out of parity with the Traditionals; the Equals would now pay $7,500 in tax. Further, all $900 in savings would come out of the second earner's taxes. For the first time in our history, Emma got some help. Of course, the vast majority of families would save significantly less than $900 because the secondary earner in 1980 was unlikely to be making $30,000 (a figure even now well above the average income of a working wife) and the family's marginal tax bracket was apt to be lower than the 30 percent one the Equals face. A family with a second earner making $10,000 and in the 15 percent rate bracket, for example, would save $150: 15 percent of 10 percent of $10,000.

Section 221 was exactly the type of limited relief suggested by Bittker. It fell short of any systematic rethinking but was at least a step in the right direction for working wives. One may thus think that it marks a deviation from the basic story of policymakers having little concern for secondary earners or of marriage-penalty talk being fueled by the Traditionals. But we should pause. In the first place, this option was the least expensive and therefore—to the Traditionals—the most favorable of the three under consideration. The first plan gave the Traditionals no benefit, but cost a lot of money; the second plan would have raised the Traditionals' taxes. So it is no surprise where the Traditionals came out. But they obviously would have preferred yet a fourth option: a return to the 1948 rate schedules, which simply had lower taxes on all married couples. They are about to get just that, as the story progresses.

Politics, as Usual

There is much that is interesting in the 1980 hearings. Robert S. McIntyre, the director of the public interest-oriented Citizen's Tax Reform Research Group, who was to play a large lobbying role in the major Tax Reform Act of 1986, openly argued for a return to the 1948 joint filing schedule. He blamed all of the current problems on the 1969 accommodation of single taxpayers. Michael McIntyre, of McIntyre and Oldman, submitted a written statement with a strong endorsement of joint filing, and a specific rejection of the secondary-earner argument. McIntyre and Oldman, in their 1977 article, had previously weighed in in favor of the precise 1948–1969 rate structure: "For married couples, we propose attributing one-half the total income to each spouse as was required by the pre-1969 income-splitting rule. Such a fifty-fifty division is based on the realistic assumption that married couples do pool their income, each obtaining more or less equal benefit." This "realistic assumption," however, was based on little more than McIntyre and Oldman's intuitions, and has since come under fierce attack by the likes of Marjorie Kornhauser, who actually troubled to survey couples on how they in fact pooled their income.

Perhaps the best flavor of what the powers that be were thinking can be garnered from Representative Fortney H. (Pete) Stark, a high-ranking Democrat from California. Stark had been elected to the House in 1973 from Oakland; he had been educated at the Massachusetts Institute of Technology, had received a Master's degree in Business Administration from the University of California at Berkeley, and had worked as a banker in private life. Here's some of what Stark had to say:

> I am curious here. As I understand the problem—and I don't know if Mr. Sunley [Emil Sunley, Treasury official] and the gentleman from Virginia would agree—it is a teeter-totter and we can't have both ends in the air at the same time. So we have to rank groups of people. And I have tried to do so just as I sit here this morning.
>
> Let me just try it on the gentleman from Virginia. If we are going to give tax breaks or penalties, then we ought to have some social purpose. I am not sure I actually think these are mine but I think they might get the most votes in a referendum; that the people who ought to have the highest tax break are the one-earner couples with children, and then the second highest tax break ought to go to one-earner couples on the theory that jobs are scarce and that if only one of two people is using up a job we ought to give them a break. Third, it would be married couples and, fourth, unmarried couples.

In his tax logic Stark is picking up—in the reference to a "teeter-totter" that "can't have both ends in the air at the same time"—a theme from Bittker and Edwin Cohen, a Treasury official who had testified before Congress to this effect in 1972. The idea is that it is impossible to have marriage neutrality and the equal taxation of equal-earning couples at the same time in a system of progressive marginal rates.

But Stark goes beyond this accounting logic; he takes the paradox as an occasion for making political judgments about *which* marriages to favor. Stark's judgments rank Traditionals with children first, and then, perhaps most shockingly, Traditionals *without* children next, "on the theory that jobs are scarce and that if only one of two people is using up a job we ought to give them a break." Only then does Stark get to two-earner families, followed by those true dregs of the social spectrum, unmarried couples. Surprisingly enough—or, then again, not—Stark was in tune with his times. As I've noted above, a nationwide survey conducted in 1977 found that most Americans thought married women's paid work was discretionary and should not come at the expense of men's paid work.

Stark repeatedly returned to this theme throughout the hearings. In a curiously refreshing bit of honesty, he put his finger on what may be the biggest problem in the tale of taxing women:

> But the problem . . . is that we do have some preference now in the law and if we change that preference we are apt to hear screams from those people who enjoy an advantage, and obviously plaudits from those whose disadvantage is alleviated.
>
> I am quite sure that we will do whatever really is politically most popular. Congress is never courageous in the even years and it is not usually courageous in the out years, but we do actually respond. In other words, if there is an overwhelming majority of the people in this country who feel that to live together and be unmarried is not an American way, we probably are not going to do anything in the tax code that would make it economic for unmarried couples to live together and get some kind of tax advantage.
>
> You just accept that. If a great majority of families feel that being a homemaker is the most important part of one partner to a marriage's life—and it would be that group by the way that would have their tax advantage lowered if we made any changes, relatively lowered—I am not [*sic*] sure what the politics of that are.

Stark's words were prescient. They point to a problem that feminists concerned with gender justice in tax still face today: positions concerned with justice for women may not be popular. My belief in writing this book is that Americans generally are not seeing the biases and the inequities of tax. The illusion of neutrality is clouding our vision. I hope that, once we do see, the dictates of justice and fairness will motivate change. But the periodic forays we've made into the political world indicate just how far feminists will have to go to win the battles, even after they have come to see the importance of fighting them.

Faced with three options to address the marriage penalty and the particular problem of secondary earners, Congress in 1981 rejected both variants of separate filing and adopted instead a moderate secondary-earner deduction, the least expensive solution. That was just the beginning of a story that would prove Stark a good forecaster. His political insights, that single-earner families should be most favored, were confirmed in 1986, are appearing again in the contemporary *Contracts* tax proposals, and seem to have played a role in those European tax systems that give credits to stay-at-home spouses.

Pamela Gann, later to become dean at Duke Law School, testified before Stark and others at the hearings in 1980. In her 1983 article "The Earned Income Deduction: Congress's 1981 Response to the 'Marriage Penalty' Tax," Gann saw Section 221 as a step in the right direction, but only a limited one, and she continued to advocate separate filing, as she had in an earlier article. She concluded with a call for more action:

> By retaining the joint return and adding [Section 221] in 1981, Congress again illustrated its tendency to temporize. Only by adopting a system of individual tax returns and eliminating marital status as a factor in the determination of tax rates will Congress provide an acceptable long-term resolution of the appropriate filing-unit issue.

The Curious Case of Section 221, Part II: Repeal

Alas, whatever hope there was proved short lived. Section 221 became law in 1981. Gann saw it as a decent first step. Instead, Congress took it back. In repealing the statute just five years later, Congress moved toward the third solution to the marriage penalty problem. This meant neither separate filing nor secondary-earner relief, but instead a step in the direction of the flattened 1948–1969 rate schedules.

The repeal was linked to the sections of the act lowering general tax rates. An influential congressional staff published a report explaining the new law that included a chart showing the relative marriage penalties before and after the 1986 act. This was part of a discussion of the repeal of Section 221. The chart is reproduced in table 8, which shows the marriage penalties before the 1986 changes on top, and the marriage penalties afterward on the bottom. Negative numbers indicate a marriage bonus.

Table 8 gives a good sense of contemporary values. We know by now that the marriage penalty is worse for couples like the Equals; by following along the main diagonal, where husband and wife each earn the same amount, we see this clearly. The Equals themselves, for example, who each make $30,000, paid a marriage penalty of $733 before 1986, and $774 afterward. Conversely, the Traditionals get a marriage bonus. Where the husband makes $100,000 and the wife makes $10,000, this bonus was $2,337 before the 1986 act and $1,548 afterward.

TABLE 8. Marriage Penalties, Pre- and Post-1986

INCOME OF HUSBAND	INCOME OF WIFE				
	$10,000	$20,000	$30,000	$50,000	$100,000
$10,000	$88	$63	− $15	− $404	− $2,337
	$150	$150	− $443	− $443	− $1,548
$20,000	$63	$131	$403	$613	− $885
	$150	$158	$466	$466	− $210
$30,000	− $15	$403	$733	$1,310	$325
	− $443	$466	$774	$774	$529
$50,000	− $404	$613	$1,310	$2,609	$2,243
	− $443	$466	$774	$1,284	$1,389
$100,000	− $2,337	− $885	$325	$2,243	$3,974
	− $1,548	− $210	$529	$1,389	$1,494

Table 8 is misleading because it does not take into account the phasing out of the earned-income tax credit; this would dramatically increase the marriage penalty on lower-income couples, as I'll explain shortly. But it is interesting to note that even without this important effect, the 1986 act actually *raised* the marriage penalty for most couples, lowering it only for the fairly wealthy. The Equals at $10,000, $20,000, and $30,000 each saw their marriage penalties go up. Only couples making $70,000 or more saw any real benefit: the couples splitting $50,000/$20,000 made $150. The big winners were the very wealthy Equals: a couple where each spouse made $100,000 saved $2,500 under the change. Once again, class, family, and tax make for strange bedfellows.

The reason for all of this is that the 1986 act followed the strategy, advocated by Robert McIntyre, Michael McIntyre and Oliver Oldman, and others, of lowering rates generally, and thus helping *all* married couples, especially the wealthier ones. The repeal of Section 221, a limited provision that had *particularly* helped the Equals, was used in part to finance a general rate reduction that helped *all* married couples, the Traditionals included. This is a good example of the Traditionals' using marriage-penalty rhetoric to serve their own ends without evincing any particular concern for working wives.

The 1986 act did not, as many lobbyists had advocated and as the Traditionals would have preferred, return the law precisely to the 1948 status quo and hence eliminate all marriage penalties. But it got close: it lowered rates dramatically enough—the top rate fell from 50 percent to 28 percent—so that it all mattered less. That's what table 8 is really showing, and that's all it's showing. For, while the 1986 act may have lowered the magnitude of the marriage penalty, the relative incentives for secondary-worker participation are still skewed, as Susan and Elizabeth found well after the 1986 act had taken full effect.

Missing the Point

The marriage penalty and the secondary-earner bias are different issues. Congress continues to pay attention to the marriage penalty—an issue that affects men as well as women and can even be shaped to concern wealthy traditional households—rather than the secondary-earner bias, which is far more narrowly a women's issue. It turns out, as Pete Stark sensed, that none of the three options considered in 1980 was the preferred way to deal with the marriage penalty, because none of these benefited the Traditionals. It was another approach, of lowering taxes generally, that they sought. They were more than willing to pay for this *general* benefit with a repeal of the *particular* benefit given to the Equals.

Another bit of irony drives the point home. Various women's groups appeared before Congress to testify against keeping Section 221. These traditional housewives found the "benefit" to working women offensive and degrading. Helen M. Coyne, president of a group called "Mothers at Home, Inc.," testified that "America's families want a Tax Code which is career neutral; that is, a code which does not create an unfair economic advantage for either two-career families or families choosing to have one spouse stay home." Note the selective invocation of "neutrality" concepts. It was Section 221 that was seen as non-neutral, not the underlying tax system with its secondary-earner biases or other skews against working wives.

But Coyne did not predicate her recommendations for increased standard and personal deductions and for individual retirement accounts (IRAs) for homemakers on any "neutral" data. She relied instead on letters written to her group: "Our mail indicates that mothers whose families are struggling financially feel rewarded for taking a job outside the home and penalized for making the decision to remain home full-time with their children." One might well question how generally representative letters addressed to a group called Mothers at Home, Inc. might be, but Coyne and other Traditionals were making a powerful rhetorical argument to a receptive Congress. It is exactly what Stark had sensed in 1980.

This is typical of a set of arguments that we'll confront throughout. Any attempt to change the law to "favor" working wives is viewed as "social engineering" or as subverting "family values." At the same time, the status quo is defined in the language of "neutrality." Changes to help working wives are then by definition not "neutral." But this baseline, and the particular concepts of neutrality at work, are themselves highly gendered. The 1948 change was justified in part on the grounds that it would get women back to the homes they had left during the war. What does it take to see the point? Women are being taxed, and taxed very heavily, but this tax has become so entrenched and hidden that its *alleviation* has come to be viewed as an unwarranted "bonus" to working women and as subversive of the status quo. But this status quo has long been predicated on imposing the tax in the first place.

Curiouser and Curiouser: The Contracts with America

The final installment in this mini-saga of the secondary-earner bias and the marriage penalty concerns the tax provisions in the *Contracts*. These documents skillfully invoke talk of the marriage penalty, which had been increased under a Clinton administration tax bill, in order to advocate tax relief for traditional families. The *Contracts* feature child, not child-care, credits, and they attack the idea of any particular help for working parents. We will examine the relevant documents in chapter 9.

All of this history comes down to the same old story. Although there has been talk of marriage penalties ever since they were introduced in 1969, a far larger problem, in terms of gender justice, remains the secondary-earner bias. As we have seen, there is some relation between the concepts, in that one view of the marriage penalty problem focuses on two-earner couples like the Equals. But if that were the main social understanding of the problem, we should address it by way of a return to separate filing or provisions for the relief of secondary earners. We don't. Instead, the preferred means of dealing with the marriage penalty benefits the Traditionals as much as the Equals—and it does nothing at all for working wives and mothers.

A FINAL TWIST: THE EARNED-INCOME TAX CREDIT, AND A LOOK AT THE POOR

An important part of the tax system's rate structure—and one generally left out of discussions of the marriage penalty until fairly recently—comes from the earned-income tax credit. The credit is so enormously complicated that many who are entitled to it do not claim it. This is especially distressing because this credit, unlike the child-care credit or the child (not child-care) credit featured in the contemporary *Contracts*, is a refundable one. This means that the government will mail a check to anyone whose credit is higher than the amount of tax owed. The earned-income tax credit is a benefit program for the working poor.

The credit is thus a good example of the "workfare" trend in welfare reform; it was central to several of President Clinton's policy proposals and began to elicit extensive academic attention in the 1990s. The credit was first put in place in 1976 and was significantly expanded in the 1980s. I'll present a simplified version, noting just the essentials.

The credit potentially applies to any individual or married couple who has at least one dependent child. Higher benefits are available to families

TABLE 9. Simple Earned-Income Credit Table

INCOME	CREDIT
$0–$10,000	+20%
$10,001–$15,000	0%
$15,001–$25,000	−20%

with two children; above two there is no further increase. There are three relevant dollar limits. There is a maximum amount above which taxpayers get no credit; this is about $25,000. There is also a maximum amount for which a credit is given; I'll use $10,000. Finally, there is an intermediate figure, where the "phase-out" of the credit begins; I'll set this at $15,000. Assume that the credit itself is 20 percent. These figures are shown in table 9. The federal government will give taxpayers who earn up to $10,000 an additional 20 percent of their earnings, as a pure benefit. When a family earns $10,000, for example, it will get a check for $2,000 from the government, offset by any other taxes owed. This amount holds constant from an income level of $10,000 to $15,000.

Once the family makes $15,000, however, it becomes "payback time." Over the range of income from $15,000 to $25,000, the family will *lose* the credit at a 20 percent rate. The reason for this phaseout is to avoid two problems. One is having a "cliff" effect, whereby taxpayers lose the entire credit all at once: If this happened, families would cluster together earning just under the $15,000 level. The second problem is cost. Not having a phaseout makes the whole credit program much more expensive. By the time a family has earned $25,000, it has paid back all of its credit, and the whole thing becomes mainly academic.

To give an example, consider the Lowers, a family of the lower-income class. Larry and Laura Lower are married, with two young children. If Larry works and earns $15,000, the family's net income taxes are a *negative* $2,000. The Lowers would pay no regular income taxes under table 3, and would qualify for an earned-income credit of 20 percent of the first $10,000 that Larry made under table 9. So the government would mail the Lowers a check for $2,000. There is now even a program in place for Larry to get this benefit throughout the year, through his paychecks.

What happens if Laura goes to work at a job paying her $10,000? The tax of the Lowers now goes from a *negative* $2,000 to a *positive* $1,350. Because Laura's wages put the family's income at $25,000, they lose all of the earned-income credit. Laura's wages come in the phaseout range, so her $10,000 results in a loss of $2,000 of earned-income tax credit. Meanwhile, Laura's work also pushed the family into the 15 percent rate bracket under the regular income-tax rate schedule from table 3. (Specifically, the $9,000 over $16,000 gets taxed at the 15 percent bracket, for a total positive tax of $1,350.) Once the family is in the 15 percent bracket, Laura—a poor woman from a poor family—is in a 35 percent marginal federal income tax bracket, when we add in the earned-income tax credit phaseout. This is a higher bracket than almost any other American faces.

While the phaseout of the earned-income tax credit makes some sense, an effect of it is exactly the same as a general tax. Losing a benefit is the same thing as paying a tax. Both involve giving money to the government that one would otherwise spend or save. This 20 percent phaseout creates a higher marginal rate bracket for lower middle-income taxpayers. There are similar phaseouts under other welfare-type programs. The secondary earner in lower-income households—as it turns out, this is precisely that income which could raise the family out of the lowest income levels—is often taxed at effective marginal rates over 50 percent. Sometimes the rates even exceed 100 percent. This means that second earners can lose money by working, strictly because of taxes—that is, even without any other work-related expenses to consider.

In terms of the marriage penalty, the earned-income tax credit and similar programs make no provision for two earners. The credit works like the rejected 1941 option, where all families are combined under the same high rate structure. Thus, families are taxed worse than single taxpayers are. The resulting marriage penalty falls only on the relative poor. Feenberg and Rosen calculated that a family of four like the Equals, where Earl and Emma each earned $10,000, would have paid a marriage penalty of $3,717 in 1994. In contrast, a family where each spouse earned $25,000—a family two-and-a-half times wealthier, before taxes—would have paid a penalty of just $727. In and of itself, this shows once again how the focus on marriage penalties has come from upper-income Traditionals and how there is a very important class dimension to our tale.

Recall the outrage expressed against the proposed 1941 changes, which would have treated married couples as a single taxpayer, under a schedule with only marriage penalties, no bonuses. This is *exactly* what the earned-income tax credit does. Just as the plight of secondary earners has by and large been ignored, but for the brief and ill-fated Section 221, so has any marriage penalty affecting lower-income families. When marriage penalties affect the rich, there is outrage, and the system responds by lowering the tax on all families; when marriage penalties affect the poor, there is silence.

There is a strong argument on grounds of social policy and fairness that this focus on marriage penalties only among the rich is exactly backward. We should care about the secondary-earner bias, not the marriage penalty, at middle to upper levels of income, because decisions to marry or not are unlikely to be affected by tax factors, but decisions for women to work or not are affected. It is exactly the opposite among the poor. Decisions to work or not are matters of economic necessity; what can give way is the decision to marry or stay married. Addressing the marriage penalty among the poor will alleviate the secondary-earner bias as well, but perhaps the most pressing concern is the pressure on two-earner families themselves.

Finally, by the middle 1990s, with increasing academic attention to the issue, Congress took some notice of the marriage penalty facing lower-income families. But, as of this writing, there has been no real change. Indeed, the most talked about and most likely reform of the earned-income tax credit is to get rid of it altogether or cut it back drastically, throwing the baby out with the bathwater. Ironically, and cruelly, lower-income persons are blamed for the fragility of their family structures. Society seems to assume that poor persons freely "choose" to live in single-parent households, not seeing the tremendous barriers to doing anything else. Poor families, just like women, and sometimes Uncle Sam, join the ranks of victims of male-oriented tax policymakers—and only Uncle Sam has been able, on occasion, to fight back successfully.

SUMMARY

Let's revisit Susan and Elizabeth for a moment, each sitting around the kitchen table with the family accountant. The first thing that accountant is explaining is that *their* income tax rates are set by their *husbands'* income. Using table 3, assume that each husband was earning $48,000. Holding that income as fixed—the proper accounting reasoning—Susan and Elizabeth are seeing their incomes reduced by 30 percent at the start. If Elizabeth had thought she was making $16,000, and Susan $40,000, the accountant has to disillusion them: Elizabeth is really making only $11,200, and Susan $28,000. This is what life on the margin means. Life for Laura Lower is even worse; her $10,000 salary adds only $6,650 to her family's net income, because of both income taxes and the earned-income tax credit phaseout.

For those curious about how the men are faring in Susan's and Elizabeth's households, the answer is, quite well, or at least not nearly as poorly as Susan and Elizabeth themselves are. Each of these husbands will pay $4,800 on his $48,000 salary. To put this in other terms, Elizabeth's husband is making *three* times as much as she is, but paying the *same* amount of federal income taxes on account of his salary. Susan's husband is making $8,000 *more* than his wife, but paying $7,200 *less* in federal income taxes on account of this. Looked at yet one more way, although I have generally been looking at life on the margin, the effective or average tax rates are not irrelevant: They often factor into decisions to work at all. Here, the husbands are effectively taxed at a 10 percent rate, the wives at 30 percent. Among the Lowers, Larry's work bears a negative 20 percent average rate while Laura's carries a positive 33.5 percent one.

For now, we must hold on. We have explored only the first of six tax factors burdening working wives and mothers. By the end of chapter 5, we'll be ready to see for ourselves the sobering fact that Elizabeth is losing money by working, Susan is barely showing a profit, and Laura Lower is affected worst of all. The gap between these women and their husbands, after taxes and expenses, will become even greater than it is now. Yet throughout all this we will continue to hear some recurrent chants. We will keep hearing the siren call of "neutrality" as a justification of the status quo. We will hear the plaintive cry of men who get taxed, and, sometimes, of traditional families asserting "family values." We will hear the rich complain, whenever and however they can. We will hear everything but the voice of the true sufferers—women. That we'll have to provide.

PART TWO

Beyond Joint Filing: Getting Worse

4

Social Security Isn't What It Looks to Be

Part 1 discussed the way that the income tax places women like Susan and Elizabeth on the margin. By bringing together husbands and wives under a single rate structure, the tax system first leads families to think in terms of a primary and a secondary earner and then taxes the secondary earner at rates dictated by the primary earner's salary. Since women are overwhelmingly likely to be the secondary earner, so conceived, in two-worker families, we are off and running with a gendered dynamic.

This would not happen under separate filing. Yet the history of the income tax in America presented an inexorable move to joint filing, and then a fixation on that structure as a linchpin of tax neutrality. Throughout this evolution, little attention was paid to women, except to the extent that any tax system that might encourage women to work outside the home, or to own property, or that failed to pay due respect to women who did *not* work outside the home, was seen as silly, astonishing, or something worse. Only occasional, limited, and ultimately repealed relief—the secondary-earner deduction in place from 1981 to 1986—broke the monotony of the basic tale.

Whereas part 1 established the idea that women are on the margin, part 2 will show just how bad that margin can be—just how heavily society weights the burden against secondary-earner participation. This burden will fall especially heavily on married women with children, but its force will be felt on single mothers, too, because the high burdens against lower-income working wives make family structures themselves fragile among the poor.

Part 1 ended with Susan and Elizabeth each seeing their first dollar of paid wages taxed at a 30 percent marginal rate, and Laura Lower at a 35 percent rate. This part adds five more features to the story: social security taxes, the tax treatment of child-care and other work-related expenses, the nontaxation of imputed income, the structure of tax-favored fringe benefits, and state and local taxes. By the end of part 2 we'll see why Elizabeth is in fact losing money by working and why Susan is barely breaking even. We'll also see that life is hardest of all on Laura Lower; she may end up separated from Larry.

To set this in the context of the whole book, there are four broad themes, corresponding to the four parts. One, the tax system puts women on the margin. Two, the margin is a very rocky place to be. Three, economic theory and a commitment to ideals such as equal concern and respect for all citizens—buttressed by a measure of educated or enlightened common sense—suggest that women on the margin should be taxed *less* by the fiscal system. Four, the large distortions of the tax system interact with labor markets to create severe gender discrimination, and, relatedly, constraints on the emergence of satisfactory new models of work and family. It turns out that we not only do exactly the wrong thing, from the perspective of fairness and economics, but we do it with a vengeance. We pile a burden on the margin.

LOOKING AT SOCIAL SECURITY

Tax policy discussions often ignore the social security system. This is a mistake. Social security and Medicare taxes, which I will combine and call "social security," now account for about 85 percent as much revenue as the personal income tax does. Making a usual assumption on the "incidence" of the employer's share of the tax—this is a concept that I'll explain presently—social security taxes represent a greater burden than the federal income tax does on all but the highest-earning Americans. For lower-income taxpayers, the skew is especially dramatic. A family earning $20,000 can pay no income taxes but more than $3,000 in social security taxes.

I will drop the misleading euphemism "contributions" and simply refer to social security taxes. Social security payments are not set aside for the payor's individual benefit, like some type of personal retirement plan, but are instead used much more like a general tax. There is no necessary reason to connect the benefits side with the tax side. Society makes one set of decisions, to pay out benefits, and another set, to raise the money to finance them. In fact, it was precisely a certain decision to split the benefits from the burdens of social security that set in motion the gendered dynamics we'll consider in this chapter.

Looking at benefits strictly in relation to burdens is difficult. But, as throughout the book, my concern is not just or primarily with the static, distributive questions of who pays what amount. The main question is not who wins or who loses in the sense of net transfers of social security money. We should care about behavior, about how tax affects individual life plans. The social security system turns out to have a distinctly and highly gendered structure and history that contributes to behaviors over time, and so perpetuates gender bias in society. This will continue to be our main concern.

We begin this stage of the story with a touch of irony. Part 1 showed how the law brings together husbands and wives for purposes of the income tax, under joint filing. It turns out that the law tears spouses asunder for purposes of social security. Actually, this statement is only half true. Spouses are separated for purposes of paying social security taxes, but only partially so for purposes of receiving benefits. Each spouse must pay into social security as though he or she were not married, but the ultimate benefits a spouse receives turn on marital status. The deeply gendered structure of this tax emerged in the 1930s and then remained in place, all but unexamined, notwithstanding the system's dramatic evolution since then. Let's first get a better look at the mechanics of social security, then explore its history.

SOCIAL SECURITY IS A BIG DEAL

The social security system is a complex institution, with all sorts of actuarial and other nuances built into it. In and of itself, this bears noting, for while the complexity of the income tax is the subject of incessant academic, popular, and political attention, few commentators seem to take notice of social security. It is difficult, even for a specialist in tax law, to get answers to basic social security questions.

As a tax system, social security operates like a flat-rate wage tax levied from the first dollar of earnings, up to an upper limit. It is thus a regressive tax: lower-income persons pay a higher average rate than upper-income ones do. This is both because those individuals with unearned income from property are not taxed, and because high-income persons exceed the maximum amount subject to the tax and so pay a lower average rate.

Specifically, each person, whether married or not, pays a flat rate on her wage earnings up to a maximum. For our purposes, I'll use a rate of 8 percent, slightly higher than the 7.65 percent in effect as I write this; it includes social security proper as well as a similar contribution for Medicare. The maximum taxable amount of salary, rounded off, is $60,000. There is no ceiling on the Medicare component, which I'll take to be 1.5 percent.

Employers also pay an equivalent amount of tax, but the standard economic assumption is that the actual incidence of this portion falls on the employee. That is, the employer's share actually comes out of the pocket of the employee. How can this be? The employer offers the employee a single wage, "tax included." But the employer knows full well about the social security payroll tax, and he calculates it into the offered wage. In a rational economic market, employers can and will pay employees what they are worth—what their "marginal physical product of labor" is, in technical economic jargon. If employers did not pay employees this amount, some other employer could, at least in theory, bid the employees away. On the other hand, if an employer paid her employees more than they were worth, that employer would be losing money, and headed toward bankruptcy. So employers, in standard economic theory, pay employees just what they are worth: no more and no less.

Here is the immediate rub: it does not matter to employers whether this employee-specific payment is in cash, fringe benefits, or taxes. One way or another, employers have to pay the money on account of the employee. So if an employer hires Fran for a nominal $10,000 salary, say, Fran gets $10,000 minus the income tax due on account of the $10,000, and minus 8 percent for her own share of the social security tax. But the employer must *pay* $10,800 under current law: the $10,000 to Fran, plus $800, or 8 percent, to the social security system for the employer's share of the tax. It is this figure, the $10,800, that is relevant to the employer: Fran must be worth at least this much. But if this is true, then Fran is really paying the employer's share, too.

Looked at another way, if the law were changed so that the employer no longer had to pay a social security contribution on behalf of each worker, Fran, and not the employer, should get the additional $800. Otherwise, as noted above, Fran should go to work for a higher bidder. If the reader is thinking something like, "Come now, that all sounds good in theory, but is Fran really going to be able to get the amount formerly paid for social security?" she should ask herself why it was in the first place that Fran was getting $10,000 while the employer had to pay $10,800. If employers had unlimited power to set pay scales, all workers would get minimal wages. In this example, the employer has decided that Fran is worth $10,800; changing the social security system, all by itself, would not change this calculation at all. Fran should be able to ask for an $800 raise the day she learns of the repeal of the employer's share of the tax. If the employer balked, some other employer could step in and offer Fran a better deal. (This fact of incidence is why discussions over who pays, such as transpired over President Clinton's proposed health-care "mandate" in the early 1990s, are typically misleading. The public debate over whether employers or employees should pay for health-care coverage had little real economic content.)

In any event, the relevant figure for the burden of the social security tax, for some purposes at least, is 16 percent: for every dollar in wages an employee earns, 16 cents goes to the government. Using the 16 percent figure, this means that social security taxes pose a higher burden for all but the wealthiest Americans. A married couple using table 3 from chapter 3, which is fairly representative of a mid-1990s rate schedule, does not pay an effective rate of income tax in excess of the 16 percent social security tax until the family's income exceeds $68,000—a solidly upper-income figure. The reason is simple: since taxpayers first have a zero bracket, and then a 15 percent bracket under the *income* tax, they must go well into the next higher bracket before their *average* income tax rate exceeds 16 percent. But social security just starts at a full 16 percent rate on the first dollar of wages. The average rate of social security taxes is 16 percent on the entire first $60,000 of earnings per individual.

Looked at another way, payroll taxes generate 85 percent as much revenue as the income tax does. But the income tax gets a large percentage of its total from the wealthy, who have income from property and who are subject to progressive rates with no ceiling. For payroll taxes to be so large a source of revenue, a good many lower- and middle-income people will pay more under them. For many married couples, the comparison reveals an especially high skew toward social security taxes because of the many possible deductions from the income tax, none of which apply to social security. For example, having children increases the personal exemptions and therefore expands the zero bracket for federal income tax purposes, but it does not affect social security taxes at all.

A HISTORICAL PERSPECTIVE

So far, the point has been that social security is a big tax, one that has grown steadily over the decades since it was put in place in 1935. Indeed, whereas the federal income tax as a percentage of the national economy has been more or less fixed over the entire post–World War II era, the social security tax has steadily risen.

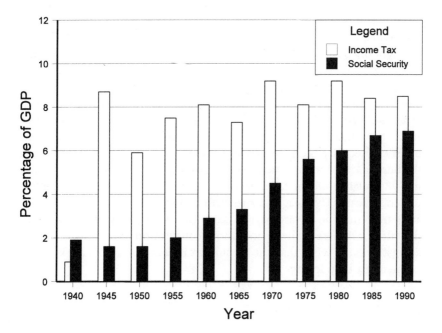

Figure 1. Income and Social Security Taxes as Percentage of GDP, 1940–1990

Figure 1 shows income and social security taxes from 1940 to 1990, as a percentage of GDP. It tells us a good deal. First, note how relatively minor both income and social security taxes were in 1940, at the start of World War II. We saw in chapter 2 how the income tax escalated dramatically during the war; figure 1 shows that with some fluctuation, it has stayed fairly high since the war. Social security, however, has followed a different time path.

When the social security system was first enacted in 1935, the contribution rate was 1 percent each for employer and employee, or a total of 2 percent; the rate was scheduled to rise in 0.5 percent intervals, reaching 6 percent, combined, by 1949. In fact, however, Congress continually deferred increasing the rate during the 1940s; it was not until 1950 that it rose, to a 3 percent combined employer-employee level. Thereafter, payroll taxes began a steady rise of roughly 3 percent in total rate per decade: the rate was 6 percent in 1960, 9.6 percent in 1970, 12.26 percent in 1980, and 15.3 percent in 1990. At the same time, the base—or the types of wages subject to the tax—also increased, so payroll taxes have been on a steady and dramatic upward move.

In 1940 social security contributions represented a flat 2 percent payroll tax on some portion of the United States economy—a limited portion, because the initial system extended only to most workers in industry and commerce. It did not cover railroad workers, farm workers, domestic employees, or government personnel. Even so, this small and limited tax in 1940 was twice as large in its total burden as the income tax—highlighting how limited the size of the income tax was. World War II wrought big changes. The income tax quickly moved to a mass tax, greatly eclipsing social security as a percentage of the total economy. The next interval, 1950, shows the slight "return to normalcy" effect, as a good chunk of the postwar peace dividend was spent to reduce the income tax. From the early 1950s down to the present, however, the story becomes a steady tale: the income tax more or less hit a ceiling as a source of revenue, but social security taxes have risen inexorably and now they almost equal the burden of the income tax. Note, for example, that from a certain peak in 1980 relative *income* taxes decreased, but social security taxes continued to increase. The Reagan tax reduction "revolution" was largely a shift away from income toward payroll taxes. This is definitely part of our central tale, for if there is any socioeconomic institution more heavily skewed against working wives than the income tax is, it is the payroll tax. Working women just keep losing.

IT AIN'T NECESSARILY SO

The social security system might be considered fair if it were simply a form of publicly required retirement system. The taxes paid by each individual, including the working wife, might be set aside for her particular benefit. If this were so, we ought to weigh the future benefits to be given to her against her current contributions. But social security does not work this way. Putting aside questions of whether the system will be able to fund its obligations at all in the future, the rules of social security have distinct, and strong, gender biases.

The gender bias begins with the fact that spouses of wage earners get benefits regardless of whether they have worked outside the home, in paid labor markets. While the husband is alive, the wife receives credit for the greater of her own or 50 percent of her husband's "potential insurance amount," in social security lingo. This means that the wife is treated as if she earned one-half as much as her husband. Since the husband is receiving 100 percent credit for his own work, the couple gets to pool at least 150 percent of his benefits. On the husband's death, the widow receives credit for the greater of her own earnings or 100 percent of her husband's. That is, on the *benefits* side, the social security system rewards single-earner families like the Traditionals. Wives like Tina Traditional get benefits without ever paying taxes.

This may sound fair, like the norm of taxing equal-earning couples equally. After all, stay-at-home spouses, especially when they become widows, may be thought to need social security, too. The problem is that there is *no* marginal return to the taxes paid on the first dollars earned by a secondary-earning spouse. Since such a spouse would get benefits anyway, as a presumed dependent on her husband, she does not receive her own benefits until she has established herself as a persistent and large earner, relative to her husband: until the "greater of her own or 50 percent of her husband's earnings profile" comes to mean "her own." The reason she needs to be a persistent as well as a high earner is that the social security system looks to earnings weighted over time, so that in-and-out workers, or "gappers" as they are sometimes called—workers who have stretches of being absent from the paid workforce—are penalized. Of course, it just so happens that women are far more likely to be gappers than men. Just ask Susan and Elizabeth.

To give an example, a wife like Emma Equal, whose husband earns $30,000, would have to earn more than $10,000 before she received *any* benefit from the 16 percent effective social security tax on her earnings, and the number would have to be higher if she, as is often the case, were an intermittent participant in the labor force. While the whole system has some obvious appeal, as protection for economically dependent widows, it further undermines the incentive of the potentially second-earning spouse to enter the workforce. It means that couples like the Equals are actually subsidizing ones like the Traditionals. Emma Equal, receiving no benefit for herself on her first $10,000 of earnings, is just flat out giving away $1,600 to the fund, for people like Tina Traditional and others to use. Note, by the way, that even if we wanted to benefit stay-at-home spouses like Tina, we do not have to get second earners like Emma to foot the bill. Contributions and benefits are separate. We could give Emma a break, and get funds for Tina from somewhere else.

The puzzles of taxing women grow. We have seen the relentless movement toward joint filing under the income tax. This was fueled by the ostensible desire to tax "equal-earning couples equally" at a time when the Equals were taxed less than the Traditionals. Since 1948, these two couples have been taxed the same; the Equals are largely responsible for pulling down the tax of the Traditionals. Under social security, equal-earning couples, at least when both spouses earn less than $60,000, are and always have been *taxed* the same. But they do not get the same *benefits*. The Traditionals typically get more than two-earner families do. Yet there has never been a general push for a norm that would have "equal-earning couples benefiting equally"; there is no sense of outrage at *this* disparity. One suspects that the fact that such a norm would operate to the relative benefit of the Equals may have something to do with its absence.

In 1994 C. Eugene Steuerle and Jon M. Bakija of the Urban Institute published a helpful book, *Retooling Social Security for the 21st Century: Right and Wrong Approaches to Reform*. Steuerle and Bakija do not dwell on the gender injustice of the system, but they note and puzzle over the treatment of two-worker couples. Focusing on the pattern of spousal benefits, the authors are unable to find any compelling rationale at all for the status quo. The system is not responsive to arguments based on need ("the size of spousal benefit is related inversely to need," write Steuerle and Bakija), treating like cases alike, or an insurance rationale. About the best the authors can do is to guess that the system responded to some "'natural' order in the design of pension plans"—as if a band of technocratic actuaries had taken over the Social Security Administration. There is something to this interpretation; a large part of the obscurity of gender injustice in tax is due to the technical veneer of the laws. Still, the explicitly gendered dimensions in the history and political development of the social security system that we're about to consider may be more deeply explanatory of the current law.

It is hard to present data on patterns of social security benefits, because the system works in a complex actuarial fashion, and families have very different patterns of earnings. Steuerle and Bakija's book is helpful in setting out some of social security's basic features. The authors worked out the patterns of increased taxes and benefits for families as the wife enters the labor market. Table 10, adapted from Steuerle and Bakija's work, shows how dramatic the secondary-earner bias under social security is. Families can easily see their contributions go up by one-half or even double, all for a negligible increase in their benefits. Steuerle and Bakija perform their calculations using national average income figures; in 1994

TABLE 10. Costs and Benefits of Wife's Work under Social Security System

Family Wage Pattern	Increase in S.S. Taxes Due to Wife's Working	Increase in S.S. Benefits Due to Wife's Working
Husband High/ Wife Average	43.3%	1.0%
Husband Average/ Wife Low	46.6%	1.2%
Husband Low/ Wife Low	103.6%	15.2%

a "high wage" individual made $60,000 a year, an "average wage" one $24,444, and a "low wage" one $11,000. The details of the analysis are less important than the general theme, which emerges across a wide range of cases: Working wives are working in part to support stay-at-home ones.

THE WEBS WE WOVE

Social security benefit rules seem to illustrate a basic paradox: given that there are many traditional, single-earner families, society often tries to protect widows and divorcées, who face problems due to their economic dependence on men. But in protecting such spouses, we often create a bias against secondary earners, or two-earner families like the Equals. This paradox is by no means insoluble, but we have never tried very hard to solve it. There is good evidence that rather than viewing as problematic any possible competition between the Traditionals and the Equals, social security reformers saw an opportunity to reward and encourage the Traditionals at the expense of the Equals.

In fact, the social security laws rather dramatically favor only single-earner families that stay together, until death do them part. That is, the law has decided biases against divorcées. Although the law works reasonably well for widows, a category initially favored with a pure bonus in 1939 set at 75 percent of their husband's entitlement, which was increased to 82.5 percent in 1961 and a full 100 percent in 1972, it has numerous pitfalls for divorced or remarried spouses. These include in particular the rule that a divorced spouse has to have been married for at least ten *years* to be able to claim under her ex-spouse's earnings. Even then she can claim only up to a 50 percent level. The average number of years married before a divorce has long been about seven; far less than half of all marriages that end in divorce make it out to ten years.

The result is that the social security system puts women in a bind. If they do specialize in unpaid housework and child care, as numerous social incentives—including the large and intrusive tax system—push them to do, women run the risk of having little security in their old age if they divorce. The law makes this problem worse: it does not allow courts to compensate divorced people for the spouse's greater social security entitlement by giving them a larger share of some other assets. On the other hand, unless a woman is to earn a significant proportion of her husband's salary and persistently stay in the paid workforce, her social security contributions are a pure tax. These contributions benefit her only as a hedge against divorce; other than that, they discourage paid work effort. This is a serious matter. Divorce is increasingly common in America: more than one-half of all marriages now end in divorce. Many middle- and even upper-income stay-at-home wives will one day find themselves lower-income divorcées with limited job market experience. To add injury to injury, most of these women will have *no* social security benefits saved up from their years of marriage. This is one of the many hidden costs of the way we tax women.

The law partially protects stay-at-home spouses in traditional marriages, on the condition that they *stay* stay-at-home spouses in traditional marriages. The feminist psychologist Nancy Chodorow wrote a splendid book, *The Reproduction of Mothering*, describing the psychoanalytic mechanisms whereby women are led to become mothers from one generation to the next. What we see here are the ways that a large socioeconomic system like tax is set up, sometimes consciously, other times not, with particular family models in mind, and how it perpetuates them. The social security system makes a perfect illustration. If women stay home, the system, working in tandem with men's work, will provide for them, at least as long as they don't leave the home or their men. If, on the other hand, women try to get out and work outside the home, the system purely and unequivocally taxes them. All of this was quite deliberate, it turns out, in the formulation of the social security system.

GETTING THERE: MORE OF HIS STORY

Social security was created in the 1930s, a decade, we have seen, of intense activity in the story of taxation and the family. Alice Kessler-Harris, a feminist-oriented labor market historian, has written an illuminating essay on the gendered assumptions at work behind the pivotal 1939 reform amendments of the system. This is the same time period that saw the Traditionals jockeying for the illusion of equality for tax purposes in chapter 2, so the gist of the tale here will come as no surprise. But Kessler-Harris's work is particularly striking for its use of direct testimony from members of a panel appointed to consider social security reform. Kessler-Harris was able to unearth evidence confirming, in almost exactly parallel ways, the tale told in chapter 2.

The social security system began during Franklin Roosevelt's first term, becoming law in 1935. The law has always had two components: various provisions meant to serve a welfare, or need-based, function, such as disability and old-age assistance, and then the major portion, designed to serve an insurance function, labeled old-age insurance. We are concerned predominantly with this latter portion.

The initial law functioned only to collect revenues: 2 percent of covered wages, as mentioned above. The plan was not to pay out any benefits until 1942, when a suitable reserve would be established. By 1937, however, a large reserve was beginning to accumulate, and, under the influence of Keynesian thinking—John Maynard Keynes's celebrated *The General Theory of Employment, Interest, and Money* had been published in 1936, and triggered the notion that social spending might be good for the macroeconomy—the government decided that it would be better to stimulate the economy by spending the reserves rather than allowing them to amass. The federal government set up a Social Security Advisory Council, composed of academics, politicians, and representatives of labor and industry, with the explicit mandate to figure out how to spend the large social security reserve.

In this sense, the advisory council faced a task exactly parallel to what Congress faced after World War II, and again in 1981, 1986, and in the mid-1990s: how to spend money. It fashioned an answer strikingly similar to what Congress did on these other occasions; it decided to use the money to foster and reward traditional families. The advisory council did this by extending the benefits of a husband's contributions to his wife; the wife was able to get credit for 50 percent of her husband's wages while he was alive, meaning that the couple could draw on a pool based on 150 percent of the husband's wages. Once he died, the man's widow would get credit for 75 percent of his earnings, that is, one-half of the larger pool. This is the structure described above. The widow's portion was increased to 82.5 percent in the 1960s and to 100 percent in the 1970s. The initial law was even explicitly gendered, in that it spoke of husbands and wives; over a period of time and in the face of certain Supreme Court cases, this literal gender bias was eliminated. But that is not my main concern here: the deeper, darker, and in many ways more important gender bias remains, and has grown.

Kessler-Harris, through reading the transcripts of the advisory council's hearings, was able to establish that the council made a conscious decision to transfer resources to wealthy men. The council saw what it was doing as simply increasing a married man's take to 150 percent of what it would otherwise be. Families like the Traditionals were the clear exemplar before the panel. Indeed, the council explicitly noted that the 50 percent payout to wives, whether they worked or not, had the effect of giving no benefit to just about all of the wives then working—the effect we've noted above—but considered that a *good* thing. A leading member of the council, the academic economist J. Douglas Brown, opined that the benefit structure might even have the salutary effect of discouraging working wives, for it would "take away the urge to go back and compete with the single women."

There is a strong social norm in the United States that women's work outside the home is marginal or secondary within the entire economy; whenever paying jobs are scarce, women are supposed to cede theirs. In 1937 the advisory council saw married women competing with single ones; in 1977 a nationwide poll found that most of Americans felt that "married women should not hold jobs when jobs were scarce and their husbands could support them"; in 1980 Pete Stark thought that single-earner families should be explicitly favored "on the theory that jobs are scarce and that if only one of them is using up a job we ought to give them a break." Need we more proof that women are thought of as secondary workers? There is also a growing body of psychological evidence suggesting that men identify strongly with the breadwinning role and resent women's working anywhere outside the home. The social security reforms in 1939, which have been further strengthened since then, fit perfectly with this basic picture: Men rewarded their own breadwinning behavior while penalizing married women for working outside the home.

Kessler-Harris establishes that the advisory council was aware of an "earnings sharing" concept that would not have all these gendered effects. But it dismissed this idea with barely a whimper; even its three women members did not pay it much heed. The council clearly and deliberately preferred giving the 150 percent benefit to working husbands to alternative ways of spending money, especially those that would have had the effect of transferring the reserve's resources to lesser privileged groups, particularly southern blacks. The council was concerned to keep its southern Democratic members "on board," and benefiting traditional families seemed like the perfect touch. Recall the overwhelming support, even among congressional Democrats, for the income-splitting move in 1948 that benefited only the richest families in America.

Like the work of Carolyn Jones and of Reva Siegel, that of Kessler-Harris is well worth reading. It shows just how important history is to understanding the gendered structure of the present, and, conversely, just how much is missed when history is left out of account. Michael Boskin, a fairly conservative economist who had a prominent position in George Bush's administration, and Douglas Puffert, a fellow economist, wrote a fine study in the middle 1980s, showing how the social security system results in large distributive transfers from two-earner to one-earner families; this tale is picked up and expanded upon in Steuerle and Bakija's book. What neither Boskin and Puffert nor Steuerle and Bakija note, though, was that this was the *intention* of the crafters of the regime. A historical perspective greatly enriches the abstractions of economics and accountancy.

SAME OLD STORY

The insight into the decisions of the government in the late 1930s confirms the tale told in chapter 2, at a time when social security was in fact a far bigger tax than the income tax was. We see an explicit decision to reward the Traditionals, a conscious desire to get working wives back in the home, and a deliberate use of familial rhetoric to facilitate transfers of resources to relatively wealthy men, to the conscious exclusion of less privileged groups. The script played out again in 1986, when tax reduction was directed toward all families and away from two-earner ones. It is happening again in the 1990s.

The structure that emerged for social security confirmed the image of the Traditional family in all its glory. The wife would stay home and would even be discouraged from working. Meanwhile, the man's work was validated and enhanced into a breadwinning model: The husband not only provided for his family during his working days, but beyond them, as well, even from beyond his own grave. Society simply made real that the man's work stood as a proxy for the family's work, and attached to his paid work an added bonus—one that would keep the wife at home from worrying about what would happen to her if her man retired early or died. She would not have to worry about anything at all except raising the kids: her husband and Uncle Sam had seen to that.

One further striking feature of the social security story is how little it has been subjected to rethinking, although the burden of the system has grown almost 800 percent since 1940. There have been a few minor reforms in the benefit structure, but these only tended to confirm and solidify the gendered structure, as by increasing the widow's share. Much more attention has been paid to the fiscal solvency of the system, its budgeting procedures, the contribution and payout levels, and so on. In the 1970s and 1980s, a series of United States Supreme Court cases invalidated the most obviously gendered provisions—those that denied a widower benefits while granting them to widows. Ironically, men won in these cases. Women just keep getting taxed.

The dramatic shift from income to social security taxes effected during the Reagan presidency may be seen as one of the more ingenious ways of taxing women, since the social security system is even more heavily skewed against working wives than the income tax is. That this could have occurred in the 1980s, with barely a whimper—notwithstanding the dramatic increase in working women and in particular working mothers since 1940—is testimony to the obscurity of tax, as well as to the dangers of that darkness. A central theme of this book is that it is time for those concerned with issues of gender justice to wake up to the facts of tax.

SOME SURPRISINGLY EASY ANSWERS

As I said in the introduction, I don't want to get bogged down in particular discussions of particular answers. But part of the story I've been telling is that the entire engine of tax has been driven by gendered assumptions. This is a comment about intellectual history, about how logic and formal rhetoric are used, selectively, to produce gendered law. As was the case with the system of joint filing, where an easy answer is to move toward separate filing, and an answer almost as easy is to provide some relief for secondary earners, specific policy recommendations regarding social security are rather easy to conceive—yet have never been attempted.

One idea is to continue the current benefit policy but change the contribution rules so that a secondary worker need not pay tax until she is at a level where she gains at least some marginal benefit. Thus, a secondary earner would not start to pay into social security until her earnings profiles exceeded one-half of the primary earner's. This would be a type of secondary-earner exemption that would eliminate the unfortunate situation whereby secondary earners, who pay a pure tax, are subsidizing stay-at-home spouses, among others. Note once again that we could do this independently of setting benefits for traditional stay-at-home spouses. Widows like Tina Traditional could keep getting paid, but just by someone besides working wives and mothers like Emma Equal.

One large advantage of this solution is that it would help to alleviate the secondary-earner bias of the *income* tax. Since wives are generally entering the workforce at high income tax rates, as we saw in part 1, and giving up imputed income, as we'll see in the next chapter, they could at least benefit from a break on social security taxes. Indeed, the rebate of social security taxes could be provided on an income tax return. Interestingly, part of the theory of the earned-income tax credit is that the very lowest income workers should not pay any net positive tax; the credit, administered through the income tax system, can be seen as giving back to the working poor their social security payments. But recall that a secondary-earning wife in a lower-income household is apt to see her earnings fall within the phaseout range of the earned-income tax credit. Whereas Larry Lower, the primary-earning man, is in a zero bracket because his social security taxes are offset by the earned-income tax credit, Laura Lower, the secondary-earning wife, is in a 50 percent or higher bracket because she faces income taxes, social security taxes, and the phaseout of benefits.

A second possible change, aimed especially at the dynamic problem of the divorced stay-at-home spouse, has been called "earnings sharing." This plan works like community property. The law would simply allocate half the earnings of both spouses during marriage to each spouse, and would allow the earnings credit to be fully "portable." That is, Tom's $60,000 would be split between him and Tina. Tom and Tina would each be viewed as having earned $30,000, whether they divorce or stay married. This would make real, and literal, the deemed income splitting present in the income tax since 1948. The fact that the law does not actually split earnings in a situation where it has the complete power to do so—and where it would have possible real consequences—underscores one of the primary lessons learned thus far. Men only wanted to appear equal with their wives for purposes of saving taxes. They had no intention whatsoever of becoming equal.

Such proposals for reform were squarely before the Social Security Advisory Council in 1937. They were explicitly discussed then, and have since been brought up repeatedly, at least by a handful of academics and astute political reformers sensitive to issues of gender justice. Reform proposals have been discussed by prominent law professors such as Grace Ganz Blumberg and Mary Becker, and by prominent economists such as Marianne Ferber. Standard textbooks and treatises on social security now note the gendered biases of the system, and typically mention these obvious possibilities for reform.

It is also a fact that no action has been taken on any proposal to cure the gender biases. Indeed, these were made worse by the expansion of the widow's benefit percentage and, more important, by the nearly eightfold increase in the rate of the tax since its inception, all despite the further fact that social security has been the object of several highly prominent general reforms. Gendered structures do not attract the kind of attention that moves real change. They seem to stay in place and shape our lives, generally unconsciously, forever.

BACK TO THE ACCOUNTANT'S TALE

Gendered as the tale of the benefits side of the social security story is, our central story has a different focus. The structure of social security benefits is a problem that women like Susan and Elizabeth will face years down the road. Right now, the problem is that social security has become a big part of the tax base. Recall that we left these women, at the end of part 1, in a 30 percent tax bracket, strictly on account of their husbands' wages. Now we should just add 8 percent to that. This figure, by the way, is correct in an accounting sense, because the other 8 percent—the employer's share—will not come out of the wage offered. The full 16 percent is a drag on Susan's and Elizabeth's salaries, but they will see only half of it coming out of their paychecks.

Some would defend the law as gender neutral. It is true that social security taxes no longer speak explicitly of men and women, widows and wives. On the face of it, the law looks the same for men and women. But, as I hope we are learning, we have to look beneath "the face of it" when it comes to tax. When we do so for social security, the gender bias has at least four components.

One, if men are the primary earners, the 8 percent or 16 percent is initially added on to their zero, and possibly even negative, marginal tax rate, depending on the earned-income tax credit. Men as primary earners enter the workforce at a virtually zero rate; women as secondary earn-ers will typically enter close to 50 percent, all things considered. We are still building up this story, but it is true across all income ranges that secondary-earner wives face high marginal tax rates; indeed, the story is most severe at the upper and *lower* income levels.

Two, the primary earner's benefits are at least part of a personal retire-ment plan, in a way that the secondary earner's are not. The primary earner is getting up to 150 percent credit for *his* contributions; the sec-ondary earner is getting nothing for hers, until she is a nearly equal earner; recall table 10. The 1939 amendments confirmed the man's role as breadwinner. Husbands provide for their families, during life, on re-tirement, and in death, the latter two courtesy of the government's sys-tem. This future is a long way off, and many individuals may not be think-ing much about their ultimate retirement years, but the social security system has some real present effects. The largesse shown to primary earn-ers at least partially frees the man from what would otherwise be the pos-sible expense of financial instruments like annuities and insurance. The government has given husbands a large fringe benefit, at least partly paid for by a pure tax on working wives.

Three, once a primary-earning man has gone through the $60,000 ceiling, his marginal tax rate is *lower* than his wife's, not just by the 6.5 percent drop in his share of social security, but by a full 13 percent. Once an employee hits $60,000, his employer no longer has to pay social secu-rity on his account and can afford to give him a more generous raise. We'll see this effect later, when we look at upper-income families.

Finally, as with the income tax, social security taxes have a bias toward imputed income, or the invisible income generated by self-supplied labor. Two-earner families face dramatically higher costs than single-earner ones do, especially for child care. If a married mother leaves the home to go into the workforce, she must earn at least *double* the costs of child care and other work-related expenses because for every dollar she earns, the government will take one-half. We'll see this in the next chapter; my point here is that social security has an imputed income bias in it, felt at the full 16 percent rate. Money that replaces self-provided services bears social security tax. Put yet another way, working wives are taxed without being benefited; stay-at-home spouses are benefited without being taxed.

We need to put the whole tax structure together, for it is as a whole that the system can best be seen as taxing women. The gendered history begins with the fact that little attention was paid to the possible biases against working wives in the 1930s, except, again, to see that these were good. Social security was then allowed to increase dramatically from 1950 onward, with barely a whimper being heard about its effects on women. But this should not surprise: it echoes the story of chapters 2 and 3. It was the Traditionals we heard in chapter 2, asking for joint filing. It was again the Traditionals we heard in chapter 3, complaining about the marriage penalty. It was the Traditionals who benefited from the social security reforms in 1939. And now, we might assume, it is again the Traditionals we hear, complaining about the fiscal soundness of social security, or various moves to tax its benefits under the income tax. No one is rushing to change the system to improve its gender justice by alleviating its biases against working wives, though the relevant changes would be simple to implement. Some things we never seem to see; one wonders if we want to.

5

Piling It on the Margin

BACK ON THE CHAIN GANG

Part 1 ended with Susan and Elizabeth in the 30 percent marginal income tax bracket for their first dollar of wages, on account of joint filing. Things were even worse for lower-income wives. Chapter 4 added social security, and the tax rates facing Susan and Elizabeth went up to 38 percent, while Laura Lower was in a 43 percent bracket. Yet working wives got virtually no benefit from their social security payments, which really are contributions in their case, while men in traditional families reaped a windfall. This chapter completes the accountant's tale by bringing in four final factors: the tax treatment of work-related expenses, especially child care; the nontaxation of imputed income; the structure of tax-favored fringe benefits; and state and local taxes.

CHILD CARE AND OTHER WORK-RELATED EXPENSES

Child care constitutes a large set of problems facing mothers today. At the Fourth World Conference on Women, held in Beijing, China, in 1995, child care emerged as one of the biggest and most troubling issues facing women in all cultures, the problem being limited, unsatisfying, and costly options. An article in the *Wall Street Journal* described the problem:

> As women in nearly all regions of the world play a growing role in politics and business, child care, once viewed as a family affair, has emerged as an economic issue. Concerns about inadequate child care "will pervade the meeting" as women at the parley seek ways to close the gender gap in areas ranging from pay to education. . . .
> In most cultures, even when both parents are present, finding care usually remains the responsibility of the mother. Though the poorest women typically rely on relatives and friends, the majority of others in most countries can't afford to hire someone to come into their homes and must find group child care instead.
> For millions of women, that means a nerve-racking search in loosely regulated environments. With exceptions in France and

Scandinavia, most women face a trio of day-care obstacles: poor availability, high costs and low quality.

A host of evidence confirms that child care is largely the wife's concern—psychologically, logistically, economically—even in two-parent households. The tax system aggravates this problem, for reasons we'll consider more fully when I discuss the next factor, imputed income, and does pitiably little to alleviate it, for reasons we'll look at now.

A Little Tax Theory

Child care and other work-related or "mixed business-personal" expenses, as they are often called, have long been a troubling area of the income tax laws. The economists Harold Groves and Douglas Thorson made reference to the problem in the 1960s, and Grace Ganz Blumberg and Joseph Pechman presented strong testimony to Congress in 1973 on the issue; child-care expenses also featured prominently in Blumberg's 1972 article. The way that the traditional tax policy literature has approached this set of issues is, by now, familiar: as a matter of cold logic, divorced from any sense of the real world, let alone a heightened concern for gender injustice. Tax scholars have seen the problem as one of "drawing lines." Tax logic allows a deduction from "gross" or total income for legitimate business expenses in order to arrive at "net" or taxable income. A knotty question for tax legislators has been how to separate out personal items, which should not be deductible.

The celebrated Haig-Simons definition of income, named after the economists Robert Haig and Henry Simons and from which a good deal of traditional tax policy—including the traditional equal-earning couples ideal—derives, holds simply that income equals consumption plus savings ($I = C + S$, in short form). This basic accounting identity points to an interesting fact: We can define "income" by looking either to the *sources* or the *uses* side of the identity. That is, we can look to how taxpayers use their income ($C + S$), just as much as how they earn it (I). Either they spend it (C) or they don't (S). This insight has fueled much contemporary discussion of consumption taxes: if income equals consumption plus savings, then consumption equals income minus savings ($C = I - S$). This means that we can, and often do, have a consumption tax: whenever we subtract savings, such as pension plans or IRAs, from taxable income.

The Haig-Simons definition of income also points to the fact that taxpayers should pay income taxes on what they spend for personal consumption. The question for child-care costs is whether they are personal consumption, and hence appropriately taxed, or business expenses, and hence appropriately left untaxed. This question sets the stage for how almost all tax policy scholars have viewed the matter.

False Neutrality, Again

Neutrality rears its head at this juncture. Since all workers incur work-related costs, many scholars and politicians seem to believe that the tax laws cannot give special treatment to certain workers, such as secondary earners. Boris Bittker expressed this sentiment most forcefully, in 1975:

> *Everyone* who works away from home—not just the working wife—must get to the job site, dress as the job requires, and pay for lunch if it is inconvenient to bring it in a brown bag. Similarly, *everyone* who works has less time and energy to keep house, prepare meals, and look for bargains.

These words are frequently quoted in tax textbooks, and Bittker's logic gets picked up in lobbying efforts against relief for secondary earners. Yet, as a first cut, we can question who it is in America who keeps house, prepares meals, and looks for bargains. The fact of the matter is that men rarely perform any of these activities, even if they are married to a woman who works full time outside the home. Bittker also curiously avoids any direct mention of children, the source of the most tiring and important of all unpaid domestic work. Women do most of the caring for the children in America, once again even when both spouses work.

As a second cut, the standard deduction and exemption levels—the zero bracket amount—are designed for just such reasons. The first earner is able to make a large sum before he starts paying any income taxes. The primary-earning husband can use this range of income in which his earnings are not subject to income tax to pay for his and his family's clothing, meals, and transportation. Looked at another way, this is a point where the average tax rate may be relevant, as well as the marginal rate: a primary-earning married man who earns $48,000 under table 3 pays $4,800, or 10 percent of his salary, in income tax, leaving plenty of money left over for necessities. The secondary-earner wife, by contrast, *enters* the paid workforce at an income tax rate bracket of 30 percent, and a total tax bracket, all things considered, of close to 50 percent. Her very first dollar gets split with the government, and her one-half share must then first pay for the necessities occasioned by her act of leaving home to go to work.

Further, not every worker has child-care costs, in many ways the most important category of expenses. Only working parents do, and, more specifically, only working single parents or two-earner households. It was only when and if Susan and Elizabeth went to work outside the home that the need for paid child care arose. Just as important, not everyone enters the workforce at a zero rate of income tax; only primary workers do. These are serious criticisms, and it is puzzling that the normally careful Bittker did not anticipate them, but they are not my main point. I am yet again less concerned with static and distributive matters than with behavioral and dynamic ones. Here the problem gets worse. Bittker's logic is one more feature of the seemingly neutral tax laws that has a disparate and devastating impact on women. We begin to see this impact clearly when we consider the real-world costs of child care.

The Costs of Child Care

It is difficult to get good figures for child-care expenses, in part because many women use low-cost options, and in part because there is surprisingly little attention paid to this important set of issues. Jonathan Veum and Philip Gleason reported that average weekly expenditures on child care were about $60 for younger women and about $45 for older women, translating to per hour charges of $1.80 and $1.56, respectively. These numbers are low because they include cases where relatives care for the child at nominal fees. Sandra Hanson and Theodora Ooms found that the average middle- and upper-income, two-earner family sacrifices two-thirds of its higher income over a single-earner family to the costs of having a second earner. Hanson and Ooms report average annual expenditures on child care for two-earner couples to be $376, 485, and 417 for lower-, middle-, and upper-income families, respectively. These numbers are so low in part because they include completely unpaid options.

Both sets of figures (Veum and Gleason, Hanson and Ooms) are based on 1980–83 consumer expenditure surveys, and so need to be adjusted upward—roughly doubled by 1995—due to inflation. A 1990 national child care survey reported average weekly expenditures on child care for families with at least one child under five and a working mother to be $63; surprisingly, the figures for full-time working mothers, $68, were not much higher than for part-time ones, $51. This same survey found in-home care to be the most expensive option, at $94 a week. A Commerce Department study reported in *USA Today* in 1995 revealed that for families making less than $14,400 a year, 25 percent of the family income was spent on child care for preschoolers.

There are compelling reasons not to use the low figures that appear in such studies for our immediate purposes. Because many women for whom inexpensive child care is available are apt to be working, our focus on the *marginal* secondary earner leads us to look at a woman who has no such option. By far the largest category of child-care arrangements in the *USA Today* study, for families with young children not cared for by a parent, was care by relatives: 41 percent. Families that have a grandparent, an aunt or an uncle, or an older sibling around to help are apt to be using such a person. But we care about women who are on the margin of working or not, like Susan and Elizabeth; we care about women who are not working, just because it is not economically viable. We should also care that there is so much pressure to save on child-care costs: this pressure may prevent better, more diverse child-care options from arising. For women on the margin, we would have to adjust upward dramatically the figures found in the studies. A *New York Times* article from 1991 notes that $300 a week is a typical expenditure for a full-time, in-house sitter. My own experience with friends and colleagues in Los Angeles indicates that typical upper-income families spend $200 to $400 or more per week on in-home care when both spouses work. It is not uncommon to hire two child-care helpers, working a combined 60 hours a week, at $6 to $8 an hour, often plus taxes.

For most Americans, paid in-home care is not an option. The *USA Today* study revealed that only 5 percent of families with preschoolers and some form of child care had paid in-home caregivers. It was more common for the child to go to work with his or her mother (6 percent of total). Interestingly, there was no category for going to work with Dad. Many families pay to have their child cared for in someone else's home, in some kind of family day-care arrangement: 17 percent in the *USA Today* survey. Other Americans use more institutional child-care centers: 30 percent.

In chapter 6, I'll use a range of expenses for child care: $50 a week for the lower-income family; $100 a week for the middle; and $200 for the upper. These figures seem reasonable. Among other things, it is important to have the expenditures increase with class, because there is good evidence that families will spend a large portion of their available resources on child care. This is one reason why child care seems to be as much a source of stress in the first-world United States as it does in third-world countries like China. Even families making more than $54,000 spend 6 percent of their income on child care for preschoolers, as a national average; this is far less than the 25 percent figure for the poorest group, but still large, as an absolute matter. The Equals, for example, with their $60,000, would be expected to spend $3,600 a year, or $300 a month, for child care. Many wealthy families with two full-time workers would be expected to pay far more; the 1990 National Child Care Study found average weekly expenses for in-home care of $94 a week. It is important to consider their situation as well as that of less well-paid families.

An Aside on Cost Allocation

I have lived with the project of this book for a long time, and shared it with a wide range of readers, commentators, and critics. In the process, I've learned a good deal from the range of reactions. One of the more puzzling criticisms I have received—from labor market economists, among others—is that allocating child-care costs to the secondary worker, or the wife, is essentially arbitrary. Why should these costs be tied to her salary, if both spouses are working? If Elizabeth and her husband each make $20,000 a year and the family spends $5,000 in child care, who is to say that this amount comes out of *Elizabeth's* salary?

Like much else that we have seen, there is a superficial appeal to this objection. If it were somehow a given, a fact of life, that both spouses worked, then it would be arbitrary to assign primary or secondary status as between them, or to allocate child-care costs to one salary. But the problems we are considering stem from exactly the fact that there is no such given in life. The reluctance to allocate child-care expenses to the wife parallels the reluctance to see the wife as secondary earner. Congresswoman Martha Griffiths, leading hearings before the Joint Economic Committee of Congress in 1973, admonished Grace Ganz Blumberg and Joseph Pechman not to use the phrase "secondary earner": "I hope you won't say the secondary earner. . . . In my judgment the one who supplies the children's music lessons, and their clothing, and pays for the schooling is the primary earner. And the one who buys the booze and the outboard motor and the fishing tackle is the secondary earner."

Representative Griffiths' observations underscore the offense to women's work in attaching the secondary label to it. But as we've learned by now, the failure to see the world as an accountant does—to insist on *language* that is not offensively gendered—blinds us to a deep and troubling gendered *reality*. Allocating child-care costs to the secondary earner is simply another instance of marginal thinking, of the kind that the tax system induces us to do. It was not arbitrary to assign $4,500 of the $6,000 total tax burden shared by the Equals to Emma, and it is not arbitrary to assign child-care costs to women.

The accountants had no difficulty in allocating child-care costs to Susan and Elizabeth. These accountants were not necessarily gender biased themselves: the central purpose of this book is not enlightened consciousness-raising for accountants. The tax technicians simply said something like "Look, if you stay home, and care for the kids yourselves, you'll be saving money." My guess is that the accountants did not even think of saying that to the husbands. In Susan's case, remember, the accountant and the husband were the same person. Susan and Elizabeth looked at the numbers, considered the situation, and decided to stay home. Plenty of other married women with children do so as well: 40 percent of mothers of young children do not work outside the home. But almost no married men with children stay home. These are facts, and we ought to be facing them.

Another Embarrassing Legal Case

How did the law respond to the problem of child-care expenses? The first and still most fundamental answer came from a court case, decided in 1939 by the low-level Board of Tax Appeals. This case ruled that child-care expenses were nondeductible since they are caused by the personal decision to have children. The discussion of the Haig-Simons definition of income showed how damaging it is to have an expenditure classified as "personal" consumption; this means it gets taxed. Let's take a closer look at this legal case.

Mr. and Mrs. Smith both worked in the paid workforce in 1937. They took a deduction from their joint return for "sums spent by the wife in employing nursemaids to care for [their] young child." The Smiths justified this deduction as a general business expense. Just as the shoemaker would deduct the costs she paid for leather and other materials necessary to do her job, the Smiths viewed the costs of child care as necessitated by business. How could Mrs. Smith work otherwise? The court did not agree; in half-mocking tones it attempted to ridicule their argument. As with *Lucas v. Earl,* I have numbered the sentences in the following excerpt for ease of analysis:

> [1] [The Smiths] would have us apply the "but for" test. [2] They propose that but for the nurses, the wife could not leave her child; but for the freedom so secured, she could not pursue her gainful labors, and but for them, there would be no income and no tax. [3] This thought evokes an array of interesting possibilities. [4] The fee to the doctor, but for whose healing service, the earner of the family income could not leave his sickbed; the cost of the laborer's raiment, for how can the world proceed about its business unclothed; the very home which gives us shelter and rest and the food which provides energy, might all by an extension of the same proposition be construed as necessary to the operation of business and to the creation of income. [5] Yet these are the very essence of those "personal" expenses the deductibility of which is expressly denied.

Let's put aside the various sexisms employed in the court's language: that the court has no problem allocating child-care expenses to "her" child [?] or that it refers to the man as "the earner of the family income" [4]. Let's zero in on the court's logic.

The court's reasoning is at first plausible, even persuasive. How are we to distinguish child-care expenses from an array of other mixed business-personal ones? In all cases, these expenses seem to have multiple causes and effects—in personal and in business life—and so will not satisfy the "but for" test in regard to business alone. On closer inspection, though, the court is simply wrong, because it has incorrectly specified the logical test. The court asks a question with the logical structure, "but for X, would there be Y?" [1], [2]. It then uses the expense as the X and the earning of income as the Y—but for the expense of the nurse, would there be income? [2]—and reduces the argument to an absurdity in the long sentence [4]. It is true, the court concedes, that but for the child-care expense, there would be no income, but this is also true of expenses for medicine, food, and clothing [4]. This would make almost every-thing deductible.

The court's mistake is in getting the X and the Y backward. The correct accounting reasoning would make the job the prior, X, and the expense the posterior, Y. That is, we ought to ask, "But for the business or income, would this expense be incurred?" And then we would see that the answer, as to food, clothing, and medicine [4], is yes. These are expenses that are independent of work. Everyone eats, wears clothes, and takes medicine, at least if they can afford to: these expenses do not depend on working, and should not be deductible under this logic. But it is precisely *not* true of child-care expenses: But for her paid work, Mrs. Smith would not have generated child-care expenses [2]. The court not only missed this point; it also added insult to injury by mocking the argument, which was, in fact, a serious and compelling one.

The court continued:

[6] We are told that the working wife is a new phenomenon. [7] This is relied on to account for the apparent inconsistency that the expenses in issue are now a commonplace, yet have not been the subject of legislation, ruling, or adjudicated controversy. [8] But if that is true, it becomes all the more necessary to apply accepted principles to the novel facts. [9] We are not prepared to say that the care of children, like similar aspects of family and household life, is other than a personal concern. [10] The wife's services as custodian of the home and protector of its children are ordinarily rendered without monetary compensation. [11] There results no taxable in-come from the performance of this service and the correlative ex-penditure is personal and not susceptible of deduction.

Once again, I'll refrain from extended comment on the gendered lan-guage—here, the wife's emerging as "custodian of the home and protec-tor of its children" [10], in distinction to the husband's role, expressed earlier, as "the earner of the family income." Let's concentrate instead on the substance of the court's reasoning.

Two points need emphasis. First, the court responds to the unquestion-ably "novel" issue—finding no other legal authority "on point," as law-yers say—by turning to "accepted principles" [7], [8]. This is puzzling because the very absence of "legislation, ruling, or adjudicated contro-versy" [7] may be taken to mean that there is no accepted principle to decide the case: it's the court's job to come up with one. Here, there was a statute in place allowing taxpayers to deduct all reasonably necessary business expenses; the Smiths argued that, in the facts of their case—with two spouses working—child-care expenses were in fact business-related. As in *Earl*, the court had to apply an abstract and vague statute to the facts of marriage and family. As in *Earl*, it relied on "accepted principles" to give a gendered answer, although to an untutored eye there was no answer yet given. Sexism operates as a master default rule: we assume that silence is gendered.

But there is an even greater puzzle in this second quoted passage. The court is clearly noting the imputed income effect, which I'll discuss next, in referring to the fact that the "wife's services . . . are ordinarily rendered without monetary compensation" [10]. This somehow leads the court to conclude that there should be no deduction when such services, on account of the wife's leaving the home to go into the paid workforce, become the source of out-of-pocket costs [11]. A plausible case for fairness, however, would hold just the *opposite*. Since the self-provided services of child care are not taxed, the working wife should not have to pay tax on the dollars she earns simply to replace those services. Put another way, the costs of child care—whether performed by a natural parent or a paid third party—should not be taxable. That's a "neutral" rule. As with the irony of reducing to an absurdity a logical argument—the "but for" test—that it gets wrong and that is in fact far from absurd, the court's self-serving logic undercuts itself, again. The court is unmistakably wrong, for the reasons it itself gives.

The troubles with the *Smith* opinion, even as a matter of straight tax logic, have not escaped commentators. The law professors Grace Ganz Blumberg and William Klein, among others, have each criticized the case at length, with no effect on the gendered forces of tax. Not only has *Smith* remained good law for well over fifty years, but its clear dismissal of child-care expenses as a personal, nondeductible expense has shaped the broader discussion over the legislative treatment of such expenses, to which I now turn. These legislative developments get seen as a matter of the government's largesse, not as a basic matter of tax logic, fairness, or justice. The "neutral" baseline emerges as one of *not* allowing any deduction for the costs of child care, and any such provision is then seen as "special." Had the case gone the other way, as it easily could and indeed should have, then the neutral baseline would have been to allow child-care deductions for secondary earners, and any limitations on the deductions would have been seen as the "special" rules.

Congress to the Rescue, Sort Of

The *Smith* case remains good law, as a matter of the general business expense deduction. A taxpayer is not able to argue that child-care expenses are automatically deductible. As the court noted, however, child-care expenses soon became a "commonplace," and Congress ultimately acted. There are presently two means of getting some tax benefit for child-care expenses. Both are limited, and each has an interesting history.

The older and still far more common method is by way of what is now the child-care credit of Section 21. This provision was first put in place in 1954, as a deduction. Throughout its history, the provision has been consciously oriented to lower- and middle-income working wives. From 1954 to 1971, the deduction was limited to $600. Initially, in 1954, the deduction was phased out as taxpayers earned between $4,500 and $5,100 (about $30,000 1995 dollars). Not having yet thought of the technique of a credit, this phasing out of the benefit was the best way to limit it to the lower- and middle-income classes; Congress has consistently viewed child care as a class matter.

The child-care deduction was a minor concession to a major problem. Groves, describing the $600 deduction in place in 1963—a provision worth $90 a year to taxpayers in the 15 percent bracket—called it "niggardly." In fact, Congress changed the law in 1964, but only to make "husbands with incapacitated wives" eligible for it, and to raise slightly the threshold for the phaseout range. It was not until 1971 that the deduction was increased, at that time all the way up to $4,800. Other changes followed; in 1976, Congress replaced the deduction with a credit. Credits, unlike deductions, do not depend on a taxpayer's marginal rates. A credit gives the same benefit to everyone, whereas a deduction is worth more the higher one's rate bracket is and therefore favors upper-income taxpayers. The clear congressional policy throughout has been to give a begrudging bit of assistance, aimed at middle- and lower-income working wives.

Today, the child-care credit is set as a percentage of actual expenses, specifically, 30 percent of expenses up to $2,400 for one child under the age of thirteen, and up to $4,800 for two or more children. In this regard, it resembles the earned-income tax credit, by benefiting up to two children, but not differentiating for larger family sizes. The applicable rate declines by one percentage point for each $2,000 of adjusted gross income above $10,000, until it reaches 20 percent at $30,000. This provision restricts the benefit flowing to the rich. A couple having two or more children and earning at least $30,000 can have their taxes reduced by $960 as a result of child-care expenses (20 percent of $4,800); another couple earning $10,000 could receive a credit of $1,440 (30 percent of $4,800). The amount of child-care expenses given tax relief cannot exceed the salary of the lesser-earning spouse. The credit is also available for single parents, or heads of households as the tax code calls them.

On first glance, the modern child-care credit looks reasonably generous, especially for the poor. In fact, however, whether the taxpayer is from lower or upper levels of income, the credit is woefully inadequate. Unlike the earned-income tax credit, the child-care credit is not refundable. This means that lower-income families, who generally pay no net income tax, receive little or no benefit from it. Figures 2 and 3 capture this story circa 1993.

For both figures, the horizontal axis shows income class, in $1,000s.

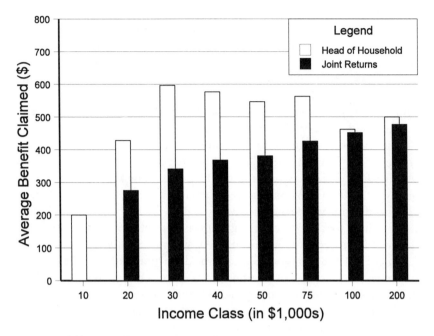

Figure 2. Child-Care Credit, 1993, Amounts Claimed by Income Class

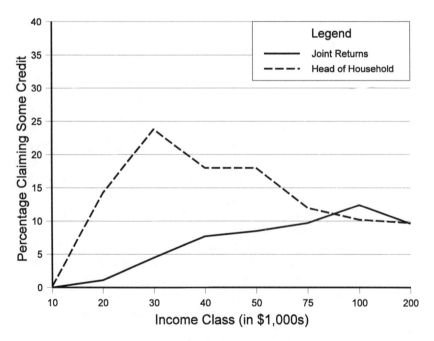

Figure 3. Child-Care Credit, 1993, Percentage of Filers by Income Class

The figures place at 10 those filers in the zero to $10,000 range; at 20 those in the $10,000 to $20,000, and so on. The vertical axis in figure 2 is the dollar amount claimed; in figure 3 it is the percentage of filers claiming any credit at all. Both figures depict joint-return and head-of-household filers separately. What the figures demonstrate is that the child-care credit is not particularly generous and that most of it is going to head-of-household filers.

Among married couples filing joint returns, *none* who made $10,000 or less claimed the credit. Only 1.1 percent of joint filers making $10,000–$20,000 claimed a credit; and they received an average annual benefit of just $275, or a little more than $5 a week. Both the percentage figures and the average dollar amounts for heads of household are consistently higher than those for joint filers until the high income ranges are reached. At the $20,000 to $30,000 level, for example, 23.8 percent of single-parent households claimed the child-care credit, with an average benefit of nearly $600, but only 4.5 percent of joint returns did, with an average benefit of about $325. Even the relatively higher (but still low) percentage for heads of households is a little puzzling, given that most taxpayers in this category have dependent children. Among all married couples in America in 1994, 47 percent had children under 18 present at home; 31 percent of all married couples had a child under 17 living with them and a working mother; 14 percent had children under 6 and a working mother. Yet, among joint filers, the proportion claiming a child-care credit rises above 10 percent only at the $75,000–$100,000 range, and then it tapers off. Interestingly, only those couples making more than $200,000 who claim the credit actually average as much as a $500 benefit, or $10 a week from it. Notwithstanding the planning that went into limiting the credit to the lower and middle classes, the average amount claimed among joint filers in fact steadily increases with the family's income.

Rosanne Althuser and Amy Ellen Schwartz confirm the above analysis. In examining tax returns from 1983, they found that less than 18 percent of taxpayers with dependents received any child-care credit at all. No taxpayers in the poorest 10 percent of families with dependents claimed a credit; less than 3 percent in the poorest 20 percent did. The poor families who claimed a credit received an average of $177, or a little more than $3 a week.

In all income ranges, the child-care credit is rare in its occurrence and limited in its generosity. Among the poorest couples, in particular, it is virtually nonexistent. A major reason for this is the fact that the credit is not refundable. A family has to be paying positive income taxes before it can benefit from a nonrefundable credit, and most lower-income households are not. This does not mean, however, that lower-income households, especially the secondary earners among them, are not paying significant taxes. They are, but these taxes are serving to phase out the earned-income credit, or being paid into the social security system. A lower-income wife like Laura Lower can easily be in a 43 percent marginal rate bracket without qualifying for a single penny of the child-care credit.

Still Mucking It Up

In part because of criticisms that the child-care credit is inadequate and too complex, lawmakers developed a second way to help with the costs of child care. In 1981, as part of the early Reagan administration law that also added the secondary-earner deduction discussed in chapter 3, Congress added Section 129, sanctioning "dependent care assistance programs." These allow employees to take up to $5,000 of their pay, free of taxes, including social security ones, in the form of child-care services. This has the same practical effect of a deduction and thus undermines whatever rationale there was in having Section 21 be a credit: the Section 129 provision is indeed worth more to higher-bracket families. Wealthy families can receive a tax benefit of $2,000 or more, even if they have only one child, as opposed to a credit of $480 (20 percent of $2,400) under the same facts.

The dependent-care program requires an employer to establish a plan. This is typically an accounting mechanism, whereby the employee puts aside money that would otherwise be salary in a separate account maintained by the employer. The employee then submits receipts for child-care expenses as she incurs them. Somewhat surprisingly, given the potential tax savings, but not surprisingly, given the administrative inconvenience, only a small number of employees even have access to such plans. In 1992 the child-care credit cost the government, by its own estimate, $4.6 billion in forgone revenue; the Section 129 dependent-care provision cost about $100 million. The credit, that is, was 46 times as costly as the dependent-care deduction.

One may thus wonder why Congress even bothered with Section 129. Why not just make the child-care credit more rewarding? While there may be some social benefit in encouraging employers to establish child-care programs, there are obvious objections to making tax benefits turn on the vagaries of one's employment. Even odder are some strange twists in Section 129's application: for one big example, employees have to estimate in advance how much to set aside in their dependent-care account, and they simply lose money that they do not spend. The whole thing is once again an odd and minor concession to a pervasive and large problem.

What's going on? There appears to be an interesting subtext in the Section 129 story. Flexibility for working mothers has become an issue of some concern to large corporations. Big businesses would like to solve their own problems in attracting, retaining, and increasing the productivity of their women employees, and they are willing to look to the government for help—help limited to them. This no doubt explains part of the reason for the provision's being a deduction: it's an executive class issue. This all shows how important it is to have an agent lobbying for tax reform—as Pete Stark so keenly intuited. It also demonstrates, yet again, the absence of a general constituency arguing for broader gender justice in tax.

An Odd Aside: Child, Not Child-Care, Credits

The two contemporary *Contracts* both advocate child (not child-care) credits, and both make the credits nonrefundable. This is a perfect way, it turns out, to reward traditional middle- and upper-income families, while doing nothing for the lower-income classes or two-earner families. The focus is not on work-related expenses, which would benefit only two-earner couples, but rather on children, which benefits all families with children. The nonrefundable feature means that more than one-third of all American children, living in families too poor to have positive income tax due, will get no benefit at all, and another 10 percent will get less than the full amount on account of their poverty. Expanded personal exemptions, as reflected in many flat tax plans, have a similar effect.

This serves to drive home the stakes in the 1939 *Smith* case. By seeing child-care expenses as a personal item when the issue first arose, the stage was set for the limited, begrudging, and rather openly manipulative legislation that has followed ever since. Helen Coyne, President of Mothers at Home, Inc., testified before the House Ways and Means Committee in 1985 in favor of a "career neutral" tax system. Heidi Brennan, co–executive director of the same group, appeared before a Select Committee of the House on Children, Youth, and Families in 1991 to ask that, among other things, Congress "transform the current dependent care tax credit into a universal young child credit that does not discriminate between the choices made by families to care for their children." What we should have seen from the above discussion is that a neutral logic can easily justify complete deductions for child-care costs for two-earner couples, but we've never been there. The neutrality we follow serves other ends.

Not Just Child Care

The child-care provisions of Sections 21 and 129 are limited in their intended and actual effects. Nor are child-care expenses the only additional costs for two-earner families. A 1991 study by Hanson and Ooms suggests that up to 68 percent of the second income of middle- and upper-income two-earner couples are sacrificed to work-related costs. These costs include payments for housekeeping, dry cleaning, more meals at restaurants, commuting, work clothes, and so on. Except for the limited secondary-earner deduction, in place between 1981 and 1986, the tax code has done nothing to help working wives with regard to these costs. Admittedly, all of these expenses fall within traditional tax policy's great gray area of "mixed business-personal" ones, and there is some superficial appeal to the customary argument, à la Bittker, that all employees, not just working wives, must incur such costs. But at least four responses to the traditional argument are in order.

One, it isn't all that accurate. Married women, especially those with young children, incur particularly high costs of entry into the labor force. Two, the typical employee receives a standard deduction, possibly an earned-income tax credit, and the benefit of initially lower rate brackets to shelter some of his inevitable job-related expenses. These benefits are long gone when the married mother faces her own marginal labor decision. Three, the failure to make provision for the wife's costs of earning income works alongside the imputed income effect that we'll consider next. Homemakers are not taxed for the services they themselves provide, but working wives are taxed on the value they pay to third-party providers who merely replace this lost imputed income. We've encountered each of these points already.

Four, and most important, we can question the very premises of the traditional thinking. There is nothing overwhelmingly compelling about the analysis that simply equates married working mothers with "all other employees," or even that denies "personal" deductions in all cases. Being neutral, as between primary and secondary workers and as between one- and two-job couples, and taxing all personal consumption equally, ignores the effects of social practices, rules, and realities—including tax itself—that deter secondary-earner participation in the labor force under a wide range of circumstances. In important respects, we are not being neutral as regards different models of the family. We are exalting traditional single-earner households over all competing visions.

IMPUTED INCOME

The tax treatment of work-related expenses such as child care relates directly to an issue I've been skirting for a while: the tax treatment of "imputed" income. Imputed income refers to the value of services that taxpayers provide for themselves. As we saw in the *Smith* case, if a wife stays home and plays her role as "custodian of the home and protector of its children," her services, although very valuable, generate no taxable income. In fact, they generate no monetary income at all. The "income" is invisible, or imputed.

The problem of imputed income ripples through the tax system. Both the social security tax and the official income tax fail to tax imputed income. Indeed, we can understand the history of social security reform as a decision to give stay-at-home spouses credit for that imputed income on which they were never taxed. This observation drives home the two-pronged nature of gender bias in tax. Society burdens women working in the paid workforce directly, by taxing them, and it also benefits women who work at home, by granting them social security benefits, by not taxing their imputed income, and by other mechanisms. But then the benefits that a woman gives up when she enters the paid workforce become additional sacrifices she must make. The system is saying to women: stay home, and we'll take care of you; go to work, and we'll punish you.

Virtually all of the services that the spouse who stays at home performs constitute untaxed imputed income, and it is clear that the need for such services increases, first with marriage, and later, dramatically, with children. Consider Susan and Elizabeth again, leaving the home to go to work outside the home. The family would then have to pay for a variety of services—child care and housekeeping primary among them—with after-tax dollars. By performing these services herself, Susan or Elizabeth obtains a tax benefit for the family: it is precisely as though she were receiving a discount of her marginal tax rate. At a 50 percent tax rate, a wife would have to earn $20,000 merely to replace the $10,000 in services that she had been supplying to the home.

Economists have now begun to study the responsiveness or "elasticity" of unpaid housework, as well as paid work, to tax rates, and are finding distinct gender-based patterns. When tax rates go up, married women move back into the home, and the converse also holds—lower taxes bring married women back into the paid workforce. This distinction between paid and unpaid work reveals the bias in the more traditional "labor-leisure" distinction, whereby some scholars divide time into paid work and all else, which they call "leisure." Women are working all the time, but they seem to be making reasonable decisions as to where they can most effectively use their energy. Women are choosing between domains of work. This jockeying back and forth among domains will be a central part of the economic stories I'll tell later.

The imputed income effect has been noted by many scholars and has long played a role in feminist criticisms of the tax status quo: Rolande Cuvillier, a European, focused on the imputed income effect in a 1979 article, "The Housewife: An Unjustified Financial Burden on the Community." The kind of hostility toward housewives evidenced in Cuvillier's title is not needed to make out the case for reform, nor is it especially attractive, but Cuvillier's polemic at least captures the sense of bias, even if she puts the blame in the wrong place. Nancy Staudt, a young American tax-law professor, is working on an argument that the tax system should tax imputed income as a way of valuing it, and making sure that it gets credit in our various programs, like social security, which are tied to market income. Though Staudt's perspectives on imputed income and housewives are in many ways the exact opposite of Cuvillier's, she comes out in the same place in terms of a policy recommendation. Yet the problem with imputed income has not moved the system to make any fundamental change or to rethink itself. To the contrary, many parties seem to like things just the way they are.

Revisiting the Income Ideal

A good deal of the intellectual case for joint filing rested on a certain logic of what an "income" tax was or should be. In their imperious 1977 article, "Taxation of the Family in a Comprehensive and Simplified Income Tax," McIntyre and Oldman set out to do exactly that: they intended to construct a "normative model for the tax treatment of the family" based on attributing income "to the person who uses or benefits from the income." McIntyre and Oldman relied heavily on the logic and definitions laid down by Henry Simons, who wrote two influential treatises on what an income tax should be, published in 1938 and 1950. Simons himself did not propose taxing imputed income for household services, in part because of his settled conviction that "income must be conceived as something quantitative and objective. It must be measurable," but he did recommend taxing homeowners on the imputed income they got from not having to pay rent.

More puzzles arise. An "income" tax ought to be concerned with all "income," including imputed income, as Simons saw, however dimly. In fact, the failure to tax imputed income is a far bigger conceptual problem for an income tax than separate filing had been. There is no question that under separate or joint filing, all income could be taxed. Income shifting keeps "income" constant, it just moves it around the rate brackets. But imputed income is a matter of what gets included in the income tax base. A failure to tax imputed income is a failure to tax income. It is a failure to have an income tax. Rather than taking imputed income as the occasion to look elsewhere altogether—to admit that we don't really share a commitment to an income tax ideal after all—society seems to accept it as a minor inconvenience in a predominantly income tax structure. Alas, it is a minor inconvenience that severely affects women.

Doing Nothing

If not taxing imputed income is a problem, what should be done about it? The typical answer is nothing. One response is that imputed income is too difficult to measure. A somewhat related objection to doing anything is the idea that the distribution of imputed income is arbitrary or random. As McIntyre and Oldman put it, the "correlation" of imputed income to one- and two-job couples "is too tenuous to justify differential tax treatment." Neither McIntyre and Oldman nor others who take this position base it on any data. McIntyre and Oldman, for example, admit: "Since we have no organized data, we must rely on intuition, experience and observation." In fact, there are plenty of reasons to doubt these intuitions. Actual data show very clearly that two-job couples have higher expenses for child care, housekeeping, dry cleaning, and restaurant meals than single-earner families do. It is precisely the freedom from these costs that represents the Traditionals' imputed income.

Other responses have been made to the imputed income problem. Concerns about liberty are raised. How can a tax system deal with private and nonmarket activities? Liberals often talk or write of taxing imputed income as if it were "commodifying" people's lives and time, or as if it were somehow akin to indentured servitude. But none of these objections—that imputed income is hard to measure, randomly distributed, or offensive to liberty—is compelling, because each begs a central question: the solution to the problem. Seeing that there is a problem with imputed income—seeing that the tax system is not in fact neutral among different types of income and that this bias has a distinct behavioral effect—can lead to several different answers. These do not necessarily involve a direct tax on imputed income at all. To take a ready example, expanded child-care deductions are a perfectly sensible response to imputed income. Since we do not tax the value of domestic work provided by a taxpayer herself, we should not tax the labor market earnings that simply replace that lost imputed income. That is, *Smith* was exactly and precisely wrong in its reasoning on this score.

Once again we need to set the imputed income phenomenon in a behavioral context. Measuring levels of imputed income for purposes of making static-distributive comparisons about what couples are really "spending"—McIntyre and Oldman's view of the project—is difficult and in some ways offensive. But that need not be the point. What is important to see are the behavioral effects that flow from the fact that the marginal-earning spouse must compare taxed labor market income with imputed earnings, which are not taxed. Rather than using the imputed income problem as an occasion to rethink first premises, tax scholars have squeezed the problem itself into a frame shaped by those first premises. But we don't have to be slaves to words or definitions. We should be servants of justice and fairness instead.

Except for a small handful of dedicated semanticists, people making the imputed income objection are not seeking a comprehensive definition of "income" and its practical incarnation. Rather, these objections are contextual. The point is that the failure to tax *this one particular category* of imputed income, homemaking and child care, results in a distinct *behavioral* bias that is offensive along independently dictated lines of gender justice and fairness. Scholars who are opposed to taking imputed income into account, like Bittker and McIntyre and Oldman, often leave child care off their list of examples. Bittker referred to "keeping house, preparing meals, and looking for bargains"; McIntyre and Oldman wrote that "the variety of self-performed services which in some sense constitute income range from the sublime to the ridiculous, from the priceless poetry of an Emily Dickinson to the thumbsucking of a small child." When scholars miss child care, they miss the very point of the objection. In a long litany of examples that follows the above passage, the closest to the important and onerous chore of child-raising mentioned by McIntyre and Oldman is "reading bedtime stories to one's children." Presumably, this was something men did, even in 1977.

Just the Way Men Like It

Some people argue, and many others seem silently to assume, that the imputed income effect benefits families by encouraging personal care of children and other dependents. We saw this kind of argument directly in the Social Security Advisory Council's deliberations in the 1930s; it was also part of Stanley Surrey's clarion call for the "pursuit of homemaking" in the 1940s. Lest anyone think that it is behind us, it was at least a subtext in Pete Stark's comments in 1980, in the lobbying efforts to repeal Section 221 in 1986, and it is in the contemporary *Contracts*. I have also had the objection pressed on me, forcefully, in discussions with academic colleagues around the country at workshops and conferences.

I want to be perfectly clear here, because this is a point that is often misunderstood. I have no objection to parents spending time with their children. Indeed, I am inclined to agree with the trend in social scientific evidence, as well as common sense, that direct, personal parenting is a good thing. Maybe we want to reward and encourage it as a society, and the tax system is not an inappropriate place to look. One of my themes is that tax is necessarily political. So we can certainly look at tax vis-à-vis its effects on parenting. Indeed, there is a sense in which we have to, for to ignore the issue is to address it by default.

When we look at the effects of not taxing imputed income within the current tax and social structure, however, what is disturbing is the push toward a gendered division of labor. The tax laws were set up with a traditional, single-earner family in mind. The rhetoric of parental care almost always picks up this structure, looking to a stay-at-home spouse, always at least implicitly the wife. Confirming this, the fact of the matter is that, in the traditional single-earner household, the effect of the *wife's* imputed income will be measured relative to her *husband's* income. The dynamic can be perverse. Given that the wife is apt to have less labor market power and perhaps be socialized into the role of caregiver, it becomes more likely that it will be she who takes advantage of the imputed income bonus. Note the irony: the more the husband earns, the more he is taxed, the more we "pay" the wife to stay home, and, perhaps, the more the man works to compensate for the loss of income due to taxes.

Cycles

Feminist and other observers of the contemporary structure of work and family have often noted the cyclical nature of gendered patterns. Nancy Chodorow's psychoanalytic work turns on the concept of the social production and reproduction of mothering roles. Mary Frances Berry and her example of Connie and David show a certain self-perpetuating cycle at work. Education and decisions about how much education to pursue also perpetuate gendered cycles. Susan Hanson and Geraldine Pratt point out that geography often works this way, too: families choose homes based on the husband's work needs, and the wife's work must follow suit. And so on.

It is worth reflecting on this general theme, for the imputed income effect contributes dramatically to what we may well think of as vicious gendered cycles. Consider the following passage from Arlie Hochschild's book, *The Second Shift:*

> It sets up a cycle that works like this: because men put in more of their "male" identity in work, their work time is worth more than female work time—to the man and the family. The greater worth of male work time makes his leisure more valuable, because it is his leisure that enables him to refuel his energy, strengthen his ambition, and move ahead at work. By doing less at home, he can work longer hours, prove his loyalty to the company, and get promoted faster. His aspirations expand. So does his pay. So does his exemption from the second shift.

Hochschild goes on to describe the parallel cycle for women—leading them to stay home and develop domestic skills—and to note the general fact that the higher up the corporate ladder a man is, the more likely he is to have a wife who stays at home.

This is the cycle that Connie and David have started on, more or less deliberately. We'll see in the next chapter that the tax-induced push for wives to stay home is especially strong among the upper-income classes. Labor market economists have found the same effect. Joni Hersch and Leslie Stratton write that "wives do more housework than their husbands, in part because they earn less on average than their husbands. Further, their greater time spent on housework exacerbates this earnings differential, both indirectly and directly." Hersch and Stratton go on to note that "allocation decisions that result in women doing more housework than men set up a vicious cycle which is hard to break." We are now seeing directly that tax just adds to this effect. The more the man works, the more the woman is taxed if she tries to work outside the home, and the more tax benefit she gets from staying at home. The tax system is wired to magnify Hochschild's effect. Tax works along the same dynamic lines, just compounding and accelerating the effect.

Let's get back to the argument that the imputed income bias is a good thing, because it encourages parents to stay home with their children. Note that there will be an imputed income bias under any income, or other wage-based tax system like social security, that fails to tax imputed income. But there is no reason for this bias to be gendered. Under a system of separate filing, for example, much of the imputed income incentive would be shifted over to primary earners. Primary earners would be taxed at a high rate and thus would be highly rewarded for staying home; secondary earners would face an initial zero bracket, just as primary earners do now, and so would not be deterred, by tax alone, from entering the paid workforce. That is, the imputed income incentive effect, so lauded by men, would be shifted to fall in large part on *them:* men would get the bonus if they stayed home a little more. More creative two-parent/two-worker arrangements might follow. That's the kind of dynamic, behavioral effect I'm after in this book.

One more thing is disturbing about the argument that the imputed income bias under existing law is good: its form is social engineering of the crudest sort. Advocates of a positive imputed income bias are openly admitting that there are behavioral effects in our tax system and that, in the case of the imputed income bias, these are desirable. But they are often the very same people who cry loudest and longest against some relief for secondary earners or for child-care credits, often invoking the language of neutrality. It is time to admit that tax has behavioral effects; that these effects are by and large at least as important as narrowly distributive ones; and that we should all have an open and political dialogue about what these effects should be. It is time to cast aside the wolf's engineering functioning so effectively under the sheep's clothes.

NOT REALLY "FRINGE" BENEFITS

By approaching the tax treatment of a given set of issues systematically we are able to see connections within the maze of tax laws that a more traditional analysis would miss. Consider the taxation of fringe benefits. Both the law and the economic effects of fringe benefits are extremely complex, and I'll just touch on some of them here. My focus will be on two basic facts.

First, the tax laws encourage employers to provide compensation to their employees in the form of tax-favored benefits. The tax advantage comes from the fact that employers can deduct the expenses, but employees need not count the benefits as income. Consider Tom Traditional in a 40 percent marginal tax bracket. If his employer offers him a $10,000

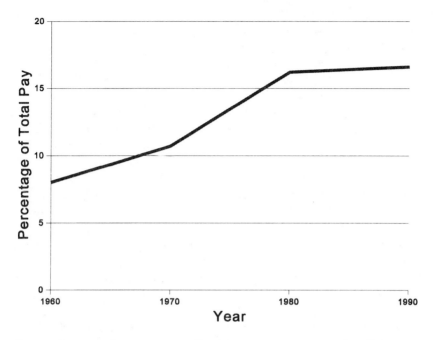

Figure 4. Fringe Benefits as a Percentage of Total Wages, 1960–1990. Originally published in *UCLA Law Review* 41:1861. Copyright 1994, The Regents of the University of California. All rights reserved.

raise, and if Tom takes it in cash, the Traditionals will only see $6,000 of the money after they pay their $4,000 in taxes. But if the employer pays $10,000 for a life insurance policy that is not taxable, Tom gets the entire policy. Even if he himself would pay only $8,000 for similar insurance, Tom will prefer it to the $6,000 after-tax in cash. This is just a simple example of a basic phenomenon: people prefer to get paid in a way that avoids taxes. Getting something tax-free is like getting it at a 40 percent discount. It is therefore not surprising that government statistics show that nearly 30 percent of all compensation by 1993 was through fringe benefits, almost all of which are tax-favored.

The second fact is that tax laws allow these benefits to extend beyond the individual employee to cover his or her family. This is not really surprising, given the history behind the first factor. Fringe benefits took off in the postwar era, a time of rising tax rates. Figure 4 charts this growth from 1960 to 1990, showing that the relative weighting toward noncash benefits nearly doubled over the period 1960 to 1980 and slowed down thereafter. The actual percentages are lower than the 30 percent figure mentioned above, because of different means of computing the figure in different sources, but it is the trend that I mean to emphasize. The rise of benefits was due in part to the increased cost of benefits such as medical insurance, but it also represented a predictable bias in favor of tax-free compensation.

Throughout most of this period, the government was not very systematic about treating fringe benefits as taxable income; this was a "loophole" of sorts that exploded. Congress tended to consider noncash benefits on an ad hoc basis, allowing employer-provided medical insurance, group term life insurance, pension coverage, and other benefits to be tax-free, by law. Most of the cat was already out of the bag by the time Congress got around to articulating a general approach to the situation. Not until 1984 did the law make clear that all noncash benefits not specifically excluded by another law would be taxed as income. At the same time, Congress attempted to apply some antidiscrimination rules to fringe benefits generally. Rather than risk a taxpayer revolt and live with a series of provisions that were difficult to administer, Congress accepted much of the benefit structure that had emerged, health insurance and pension plans as the two biggest examples. During the time when these benefits were expanding, the Traditionals reigned, so it is not surprising that the benefits should have extended beyond Tom to cover his family. After all, Tom surely wanted these things for his wife and children; Tom's employer could buy them more cheaply than Tom himself could, in large part because of the tax structure; therefore it was a natural move to extend benefits to the whole family.

In a case decided in 1950, *United States v. Drescher,* a high-ranking executive of Bausch and Lomb argued that a private annuity or retirement plan, purchased for him by the company, was not presently taxable as income to him. Mr. Drescher lost, in part because the judges could easily see that such a policy was a natural object of desire for a wealthy married man. As one judge wrote: "In the light of modern conditions of life, the satisfying of the highly natural and indeed burning desire of most men of middle age to obtain security for their old age and for their widows at death seems so clearly an economic benefit that I wonder it has been questioned as much as it has." This is the same image of the husband as breadwinner for the family throughout his life and from beyond the grave that was entrenched in the Social Security Act Amendments of 1939. The Supreme Court concluded that the policy was a benefit to Drescher just as cash would be, because he obviously wanted and needed it.

Mr. Drescher's loss was just a temporary setback. Employees are now allowed to receive presently tax-free retirement funds under "qualified plans," regulated by the highly complex but not ungenerous provisions of the Employee Retirement Income Security Act of 1974, known as ERISA. These provisions enable a primary-earning man to save enough for both himself and his spouse on his retirement and to provide for his spouse in the actuarially likely event of his earlier death.

Today, in a wide range of cases, either regulations or practices, including the vital ERISA regulations, even compel every full-time employee to accept certain benefits. This is all harmless enough, and even beneficial, for there is good reason to believe that employees might save too little for their retirements or buy too little medical insurance without some kind of tax incentive. Employers can also be efficient purchasers or providers of insurance. But the picture changes somewhat when gender justice is put on the table. A familiar problem repeats itself. The seemingly neutral tax laws foster traditional single-earner families by rewarding specialization of labor. The primary earner is able to provide full benefits to the family. The secondary earner, by contrast, will undervalue a portion of her compensation. Once the family has medical insurance and adequate retirement security, it will not value these benefits when they are also part of the secondary-earning wife's pay package. She would prefer cash, even cash reduced by taxes, to unnecessary benefits.

There has been some movement to address this problem through such devices as "cafeteria plans," which allow workers to choose from among a menu of different benefits. This solves at least part of the problem, because the secondary-earning wife can choose benefits not covered under her husband's plan, as by adding in dental care or disability insurance. But this remedy is partial, and only major employers offer it at all, as with the case of Section 129 dependent care assistance programs.

More common techniques are various "coordination of benefit" provisions, which seek to limit double coverage between two employed spouses. These provisions stipulate that, in cases of two-job couples, one of the medical insurance packages will be primary, the other secondary. A common way to make these operational is to legislate as primary whichever spouse's birthday comes earlier in the year. While this is perfectly sensible, the whole structure still has much the same effect as the social security system—two-earner couples subsidize single-earner ones. The subsidy occurs because the two-earner couples, governed by coordination of benefit rules, cost less under the group plans than single-earner ones. One might think that married women could command a higher wage, because their health care costs less under benefit plans. But the coordination of benefit plans makes it unclear which spouse's health care in a two-earner family will be the greater expense. In any event, general labor market antidiscrimination laws, perhaps ironically here, would not allow women to be paid more on account of their marital status. This should, by now, ring a familiar note. Primary earners get to provide a benefit for the whole family, and secondary earners just see a portion of their salary go to a program that does not benefit them much at all.

We've Seen This Before

The rules for pension plans, the second largest category of employee benefits, are highly complicated. To a striking extent, however, these rules parallel the social security story. On the payment side, the limits on contributions are set without regard to marital status, and the complex antidiscrimination rules essentially compel all full-time employees to participate. These provisions have mixed effects. On the one hand, they might reward two-earner families by giving them more tax-favored retirement savings. On the other hand, mandatory pension plans decrease flexibility by locking each worker into a private pension system, even where a second household worker might prefer immediate cash. The ERISA rules also play a large part in discouraging employers from making accommodations for part-time, reduced-time, or flexible-time work.

On the benefits side, there is once again solicitude for the single-earner family. When spouses divorce, the federal pension law allows state laws to govern the ownership of pension rights. In community property states, this will give the spouse a one-half interest in the pension accrued during marriage. Even in non–community property states, a nonworking spouse typically benefits from the working spouse's pension savings. On the death of one spouse, the survivor is specifically given a federal right in the deceased's pension. The leading casebook on pension law, by John Langbein and Bruce Wolk, explains the rationale for this provision as follows: "Although expressed in gender-neutral terms, the guiding purpose of the legislation was to enhance the retirement income security of the widow in traditional support marriages, in which only the husband has had significant earnings opportunities outside the home." The pension system is even set up to make it simple and advantageous for a retiree to withdraw funds under a "joint and survivor" annuity program, which automatically continues after the death of the first spouse to die, in favor of the surviving spouse.

As with the social security system, we see the paradox of accommodating existing "traditional support marriages" while generating incentives that make such families more likely in the first place. From the perspective of gender justice, the problem is not so severe in this case. It is not true that a second earner fails to benefit from her own contributions, which will always increase her retirement savings, as well as her husband's. Pension plans work like the "earnings sharing" recommendation for social security. But this just helps to show why earnings sharing alone may not be ideal from the point of view of unraveling gender bias. An adverse incentive effect is brought about by the knowledge, made secure by law, that a nonworking spouse will benefit from the working spouse's pension. The whole scheme, like social security, gives the family an incentive to have a single well-paid member able to maximize the tax-favored pension savings available to the whole unit. Tom and Tina approve.

One More Problem

A very important, though seemingly unintended, effect of fringe benefit rules is that they slant the employment market toward a stark separation between high-quality, long-workweek, full-time options, and low-quality, short-workweek, part-time ones. This is an effect I'll consider at greater length in the next chapter, but its causes are manifest already. As employers pay out a large share of fringe benefits that tend not to vary with an employee's hours, they will look for long hours of employment, as the cost to them of an additional hour of the employee's time falls. On the other hand, employers will try to keep some workers away from legally requiring the costly benefits, by keeping them temporary or part-time workers or as "independent contractors"—a tax and labor market term of art that denotes nonemployee status. All of this explains part of the reason why a more vibrant part-time labor market has not developed.

Just about all fringe benefits contribute to this effect. Consider again the two major items: medical insurance and pension plan coverage. The cost of medical insurance does not depend on hours worked. An employer faces a large, one-time cost in providing this benefit for its employees, at whatever point that practice or the law sets as the threshold for being covered—say, thirty-five hours a week. A predictable result is that this point becomes a bit of a Maginot Line. The employer tries to keep many workers beneath it, but will want those who go over it to go quite far, say to work forty or fifty hours a week, because the cost of medical insurance is now sunk, or behind the employer. There is an incentive to have a workforce consisting of some part-time and temporary workers who are getting no benefits, and some working long hours who are getting the same benefits as those working the minimum number of hours to be covered.

Pension benefits do depend on total salary, and so vary with hours worked. At first glance, therefore, these benefits do not give an employer a reason to prefer full-time employment. But the antidiscrimination rules of ERISA dictate which employees must be covered in a pension plan and then make all covered employees part of a common pool for purposes of calculating overall pension limits. These rules create the same incentives as medical insurance. Once again, an employer will want to get much of its work done by low-hour part-time help, temporary workers, and noncovered independent contractors. These workers need not be part of the pension plan. High quality part-time workers are not favored, because they both come under the pension plan and lower the benefits that others can get. Meanwhile, secondary-earning wives cannot opt out of this structure all by themselves, either by creating good part-time work or by getting paid more for full-time work by forswearing the pension benefits that their husband has already provided. Working wives must struggle to do the best they can, in a world not set up to help them at all, but rather to tax them at every turn.

STATE AND LOCAL TAXES

I have thus far concentrated on the federal tax system, but state and local taxes are becoming an increasingly important part of fiscal life in America. These simply add to the problems of working wives and mothers. By 1992, net federal government revenues had dropped below one-half of all government revenues in America, capping a steady trend that accelerated noticeably during President Reagan's years in office. A complete picture of what is facing Susan, Elizabeth, Laura Lower, and other working women should take these considerable taxes into account.

State and local taxes include income, property, and sales and use taxes. State and local income taxes, which largely mimic the federal structure and thus have all of the biases we have discussed, accounted for just under 14 percent of total state and local receipts in 1992, ranking below both sales taxes and property ones, respectively, as a source of revenue. Still, state and local income taxes accounted for almost 25 percent as much as federal income taxes did in 1992, and the story is complicated by the fact that nine states, including Texas, do not have a statewide income tax. Thus, in those states with such a tax, it is typically more than 25 percent of the federal income tax bite. Further, other state and local taxes, such as "contributions for social insurance"—a category that, by 1992, accounted for 56 percent of what state and local income taxes did—are directly tied to labor market earnings. Even sales taxes correlate positively with having a second spouse working. Two-earner spouses spend more on transportation, clothing, dry cleaning, and restaurant meals, typically subject to a variety of state and local taxes. Paid child-care expenses often generate employment and other state and local taxes, and so on.

It would get increasingly difficult to build in more specifics here, because of variation among the states and the need to make projections about spending patterns. To keep things fairly simple, I'll just add on a flat 10 percent rate for state and local income and other taxes occasioned by the secondary earner's working outside the home. Wealthy taxpayers in some states may pay higher income tax rates but then get some of it back in the form of a federal tax deduction; lower-income workers in low-tax states may pay less; most two-earner families will pay more in sales and use taxes, and so forth. A 10 percent rate captures the relative burden of state and local taxes in comparison to federal ones and may even be, on balance, on the low side. But I am trying to keep things as simple as I can, and 10 percent is at least a nice round number.

SOME (ONCE AGAIN, SURPRISINGLY EASY) ANSWERS

This chapter has completed the tale of six factors in taxing women by dealing with items three through six. We saw, in part 1, that the first factor, joint filing, emerged in the 1930s and 1940s and has at least one easy answer—the system of separate filing that obtained in America before 1948 and that most advanced countries have since adopted. In part 2 we discovered that the second factor, the social security system, is strongly and deliberately skewed against working wives. Here, too, there were easy answers, widely known and available—a secondary-earner exemption, or earnings sharing. So, finally, in this chapter, there are surprisingly easy answers to the remaining three factors. The surprise comes when we consider how little serious attention these answers have received.

The easiest answer to child-care expenses is to reverse the *Smith* case and allow deductions for such costs, up to the secondary earner's salary. Some further limit on these expenses may be appropriate as a way of avoiding excessive or lavish child care, but this is a standard problem in the tax laws. There are plenty of situations, such as those involving business travel and entertainment, where the law has to monitor unquestionably legitimate business expenses that could become excessive. More important, a deduction seems to be the right approach. Child care should be thought of, contrary to the *Smith* case, as a reasonably necessary cost of earning income for two-earner families. Stepping outside of income tax logic altogether, we should simply face the social fact and the problem of child care in a more open and helpful fashion, as working women around the world have been asking us to do for years. Any accommodation of child-care expenses should extend to upper-income levels, as well. Child-care costs are a concern for wealthy mothers, too, and we ought to care about them, as I'll discuss later. There is something gendered about only looking at the problems facing lower- and middle-class working wives—the law continues to assume that only such wives who have to work should do so.

It may seem as if the imputed income problem is genuinely unsolvable. How are we going to value and tax the invisible income that stay-at-home spouses provide for themselves and their families? But this is not so. Once we have come to see the behavioral problems of not taxing imputed income, we can look for solutions to these behavioral problems, whether or not they fit within tidy academic definitions of "income." We could, for example, give a subsidy to secondary earners, like the earned-income tax credit, paid for out of higher rates on primary earners. This change would not entirely solve the imputed income problem—no traditional income tax will—but it would shift its effect. Let's consider what would happen to the Traditionals under this plan. If Tina still stayed home full time, she would in essence be taxed by giving up the subsidy available to her if she worked. On the other hand, if Tom cut back on his hours of paid work to help with the children and around the house, he would save the large taxes he is paying at his marginal rate. Details aside, this is precisely the type of solution we may want in order to begin unraveling centuries of gendered patterns.

Another perfectly sensible approach to the imputed income problem is to treat it together with the problem of child-care costs. Allowing a more generous child-care deduction is a way of dealing with imputed income, too, because it corrects the nonneutrality that leaves self-provided child care untaxed, but requires care provided by third parties to be paid for in after-tax dollars. A working mother would have to earn only $10,000 to replace $10,000 of her own child-care services if she didn't also have to pay tax on these earnings. Seeing tax as a matter of justice and fairness leads to sensible answers not revealed when we look at tax merely as a matter of accounting definitions.

The problem with fringe benefits could be cured easily enough by allowing secondary earners to opt out of certain coverages and get cash instead. More systematically, we should examine the whole structure of fringe benefit and other laws that put a crimp in the development of a more flexible and vibrant part-time labor market. State and local taxes could be made less gendered along the lines discussed above for federal tax.

Of course, there are plenty of details to work out, plenty of transitional regimes to fret over, which is why the main point of this book is not to get bogged down in overly specific practical proposals. Rather, one of my purposes is to show just how easy, and how available, some answers are, to make us reflect more deeply over our failure to adopt them in the first place. The initial step on what will be a long road is to admit just how much, and how unfairly, we are taxing women.

PUTTING IT ALL TOGETHER: THE ACCOUNTANT'S TALE TURNS TRAGIC

Getting back to the kitchen table with Susan and Elizabeth, we can now play the role of their accountants. We begin by telling each of them that they are in a roughly 50 percent bracket, considering federal income taxes (30 percent), social security (8 percent), and state and local taxes (10 percent). So Elizabeth's after-tax pay drops from $16,000 to $8,000, Susan's from $40,000 to $20,000.

Let's say that Elizabeth can get child care for her two children for $100 a week, or $5,000 a year. Under the child-care credit, the government will credit her with $960, which I'll round up to $1,000. So the net child-care expense is $4,000. Subtracting this from $8,000, Elizabeth is down to $4,000. If her work occasions $100 a week in other expenses—house-cleaning, transportation, work clothes, dry cleaning, her own meals out, and more restaurant meals for all—she drops solidly into the red, all by virtue of the decision to work for money. Under these simple, plausible assumptions, Elizabeth is losing $1,000 a year by working at a job that pays her $16,000.

Let's turn to Susan, whose comfortable $40,000 job was quickly cut to $20,000 by taxes. Indeed, Susan may well fare worse under tax rates alone, because some of her salary, again when added to her husband's, may have climbed up into the 40 percent income tax bracket, bringing her effective marginal tax rate to 60 percent. But I'll keep things simple and keep her rate at 50 percent. Susan and her husband may spend more for child care; wealthy parents tend to. Let's assume $200 a week, or $10,000 a year. If we generously assume that Susan can somehow have access to a Section 129 plan, she'll get $2,500 by virtue of the $5,000 deduction in the 50 percent bracket; otherwise, she gets the same $960 that Elizabeth does. Using the more likely lower figure, Susan's net child-care expense is $9,000, reducing her take-home pay to $11,000. If the increased and nondeductible work-related costs to Susan and her family are $150 a week, or $7,500 a year, Susan is left with $3,500 from her $40,000. Whereas Susan had thought that she was making a decent contribution to the household's income, she now learns that she is actually taking home something less than $300 a month to be away from her children. She, too, will stay home. And life, on the margin, will go on.

LOOKING AT THE GUYS

We've been focusing on taxing women. The accountant's tale has shown us that, in a wide range of circumstances, married women's work outside the home does not net the family much income, and it can even lose money. Susan and Elizabeth knew this before we did, but we have now come to understand their situations. In the next chapter, we'll pull together what we have seen thus far, by considering three illustrative families. This exercise will also enable us to see the income class dimension more clearly.

But first, let's pause for a moment to ask about the men, the unnamed husbands in the stories. Don't all the burdens I've been talking about apply to them? It is true that they face the same marginal income tax rate as their wives do and the same state and local taxes. Until they earn a higher income, about $60,000 a year, they also face the same social security tax rate. But there are important differences. The husband's additional work occasions few, if any, additional child-care expenses; there is no loss of imputed income, precisely because he has not been around the house much contributing imputed income in the first place. The husband's employer has already provided medical insurance and other fringe benefits in most instances; a raise can be passed through to him in cash. Either he is above the $60,000 social security ceiling, and hence in fact in a lower tax rate than his wife—lower by the full 13 percent drag of social security—or his additional work translates into higher benefits down the road for him and his wife.

As we'll see in the next chapter, in almost all cases it makes more short-term economic sense for the husband to work harder to get a raise, put in more hours, or take a higher-paying job than it does for the wife to work outside the home. Married men do indeed work, full time and with full commitment, with astounding rigidity and predictability. Men's wages go up on marriage, and women's go down. Recall Arlie Hochschild's description of the cyclical dynamics of families and Nancy Chodorow's psychoanalytic tale of the social reproduction of the mothering role across generations. It all turns out to be a perfectly predictable response to the way we are taxing women, on several levels. There's good reason to believe that some of us planned it, and many of us like it, just that way.

6 Taxing Families

IN A FAMILY WAY

This chapter concludes the accountant's tale. It has two major themes. First, it focuses on some of the general behavioral effects of the laws we have considered. Second, it makes the accountant's tale more vivid by considering the cases of three sample families: the Lowers, the Middles, and the Uppers. By holding the husband's annual salary fixed—Larry Lower at $15,000, Mel Middle at $25,000, and Umberto Upper at $60,000— we can focus in on the wife's marginal decisions. We can also see, clearly and systematically, how economic class matters.

I mean the examples to be broadly realistic. When it comes time to fill in a precise number, such as the costs of child care, I'll look to the real world of experience. My central goal is to set out the basic essence of a story, or set of individual stories, that is complex and variable in its details, yet pervasive in its practical effects. Examples should help.

THE SIMPLE TRUTH

It is time to confront head-on an ambiguity in the central theme of a "bias against two-worker families." Among the lower classes, such a bias is against families themselves, against two-parent households. Lower-income families don't have the luxury of stay-at-home spouses. Among upper-income families, the same bias turns into one against the second worker, that is, against wives working. Rich families have the funds to have a stay-at-home spouse, and they are heavily pressured to do just that. In the middle, women are squeezed between these two extremes and given second-best choices between working full time outside or inside the home. The tax system was not set up with dynamism in mind. In fact, society has systematically failed to develop attractive alternative work-family arrangements, such as a model of two part-time-worker couples.

These biases are reflected in the three most common family arrangements for American households with children. In 1992, 24 percent of the 65 million children in the United States lived in female-headed, single-parent households. A stunning 46 percent of these households subsisted below the official poverty line, a figure that has been constant at least since 1970, when it was 45 percent; most of the other female-headed households were not far above official poverty. Another 40 percent of the children lived in two-parent, two-earner households; statistics suggest that the vast majority of this percentage involved two full-time workers in middle-income households. Finally, 23 percent of the children were raised in two-parent, single-earner households; most of these families saw the father as the earner, and a good many of them were upper-income. A recent survey of high-ranking executives in American corporations, for example, revealed that fully 80 percent were men with stay-at-home wives. These are the pressures—against two-parent households among the poor, toward stress in the middle, and back to the Traditionals at the top—that I'll explore in this chapter.

Before we get to walking through the accounting facts facing the Lowers, Middles, and Uppers, let's first consider three decisions affected by tax: to marry or not; to be a household of one or two earners; and for the secondary earner to work full or part time. These are the types of behavioral, dynamic effects that tax policy must take into account—they shape our lives, the kind of people we are. As things turn out, one effect is especially dramatic for each family. The marriage penalty among the Lowers puts pressure on stable family structures. The bias against part-time work among the Middles contributes to a stressful sense of limited options. The push toward single-earner families among the Uppers makes Traditional families prominent among the rich and powerful and deprives women of important positions at the top of the social hierarchy.

TO MARRY OR NOT

I've already noted some ironic facts about the so-called marriage penalty. On the one hand, complaints about such penalties turned out to be largely driven by wealthier, Traditional families. Had the concern been over the situation of the Equals, where both spouses earned roughly the same amount of money income, society should have looked to separate filing or some tax relief for second earners. But the law almost never did this. It looked, instead, to the 1948–1969 income-splitting rate schedule, which most favored the Traditionals.

Discussions of the marriage penalty also meet with skepticism over its consequences. Do tax factors really play a role in the decision to marry? How many couples even understand the magnitude of the issue? Especially given that not all couples suffer a marriage penalty, and that there are many other things going on in the decision to marry, it seems unlikely that a marriage penalty under the tax laws actually matters much at all.

Now, I believe that this skepticism about the marriage penalty is warranted, but only on two conditions. One, the penalty is unlikely to have effects on the decision to marry if we are considering relatively wealthy, or at least middle-class, families. Among poor families, in contrast, economic burdens on marriage, even if they are not consciously understood, can easily turn into conditions of unhappiness and stress. The existence of effects does not depend on knowledge of the causes of those effects. Few people ever understand, in anything approaching completeness, why their marriages fail, or why two people do not get married in the first place. These are complex matters, both for the individual and across society. A deep-seated social pattern of failing to support marriage is unlikely to be noticed, especially as so much contemporary rhetoric is pro-family. But this hardly means that burdens on marriage don't exist or don't matter.

Further, the tax system's bias against lower-income, two-earner families is picked up in important aspects of the welfare system. At exactly the point where two-earner families are most strongly needed, and where marriages are most fragile, the tax system most burdens them. Thus, it should not surprise us, although it often does surprise social commentators, that two workers are especially rare among the poorest two-parent families. Only about 5 percent of the poorest one-fifth of two-parent households feature two workers. Of course, one reason for this is that a second income moves the family up in the income rankings. But it is also the case that secondary earners are *most* heavily taxed in the lower- and lower-middle classes. That's a problem.

There is now a debate among economists about how much marriage penalties affect family structure among the poor. Almost everyone thinks that there is some effect, but there are those who argue that it is slight. Revealing my own biases, I have strong doubts about these studies. They generally proceed in standard statistical fashion, by holding "all else constant." If we hold all else constant, do family structures respond to changes in the tax rates? But the problem is that there are so many overlapping causes it is hard to see just which ones are doing the work. There is no doubt that family structures among the poor are fragile, and there is also no doubt that lower-income, two-parent families face steep marriage penalties. That's almost enough, to my taste, to make out the case for doing something to ameliorate the situation. Lower-income marriage penalties are a social disgrace.

Consider now a second qualification to the skepticism about the marriage penalty. Whether we care about such penalties depends on whether we care about consequences. Consequentialism is a philosophic view that considers the merits of a rule strictly in terms of the results or consequences that follow from it. In the case of the marriage penalty, the skeptical objection presumes that we are considering whether people marry or not because of tax laws. But there is more going on in discussions of the marriage penalty. For example, although the almost universal academic understanding of the marriage penalty is that it falls on couples like the Equals, we came to see how couples like the Traditionals—in many ways the opposite of the Equals—have been able to exploit discussion of the marriage penalty. The role of consequences in considering the marriage penalty is likewise complex and value-laden.

Truth and Consequences

Throughout this book I have been criticizing the traditional approach to questions of tax, one that looks at the subject solely as a static, distributive matter. This approach considers how many dollars individuals or families earn, and then dictates that fairness means taxing families on the basis of these observed dollars, and in the same rank order: the more dollars, the more tax. I've attempted to move the discussion into a richer dimension, one that gives more weight to behaviors and other factors. A central theme is that these behavioral effects should count in our basic normative theories of tax, especially as there is no logical mandate for doing otherwise.

It may seem as if my focus on behaviors would lead me to conclude that what is important about the marriage penalty is whether it affects decisions to marry—whether, that is, it has consequences. But I do not believe that matters are so simple. There is a difference between being concerned with behavior and adopting a measure of social policy that looks *only* to behavioral effects. My basic orientation to questions of tax and other social matters is to search for a just and fair answer, openly admitting that what is "fair" or "just" can be complicated and controversial. Questions of tax are deeply important, affect a range of vital interests, are not dictated by any logic of law or economics, and have evolved, both consciously and unconsciously, in a gendered fashion.

But however unclear questions of fairness or justice may be, they are not necessarily the same as questions of consequences. Questions of fairness or justice are like questions of rights or privileges. We believe in the right to free speech, for example, even though in some and perhaps a good many cases, this has bad consequences—as when the Nazis march through a town full of Holocaust survivors or when magazines that are offensive to most citizens are sold in public places. Consequences are relevant to the setting of rights, to be sure, but they are not the sole metric of evaluating or establishing rights.

And so it is with tax in general, marriage penalty talk in particular. We may think it a wrong thing to burden married couples disproportionately, even if this burden results in no noticeable behavioral effects, that is, even if it does not affect the marriage rate. Certainly we would be deeply offended if we placed a tax on religious observation, as on going to church (such a tax would in fact be unconstitutional in America), although few of us would give up our religion in the face of a moderate tax. The marriage penalty strikes a similar chord. A "marriage penalty" sounds wrong, perverse. It sounds like the opposite of "sin taxes" on cigarettes and alcohol; it sounds like a "virtue tax." That's why it makes for such a powerful political appeal quite independently of its consequences.

Back to Getting Married

Now observe an ironic feature of the dialogue over the marriage penalty. Recall where we are. I've already noted, first, that complaints over such penalties have come from families like the Traditionals and, second, that there is a plausible skeptical objection to such talk, because it seems unlikely that the marriage penalty actually affects decisions to marry. I proceeded to qualify this plausible skepticism on two counts: one, that we were not talking about the lower-income classes, and, two, that we were, in fact, concerned with consequences. Among the poor and for nonconsequential reasons, the skeptical objection was not fatal: in the former case, the grounds for skepticism are not present; in the latter, they are not relevant. This second provision invited an aside, in which I made explicit a view that I have had at least implicitly throughout: We need not approach questions of tax in narrowly consequentialist terms, even if we sometimes care about consequences and are attempting to get beyond a traditionally narrow, distributive view.

Here then, finally, is the irony: the Traditionals making the marriage penalty complaints have taken up the second of these two qualifications, and have used this move to avoid taking the first. Complaints about the marriage penalty persist in moralistic terms that do not invite specific consequential investigation and that avoid the need to take on a particular solicitude for the poor. This set of argumentative moves allows the Traditionals to continue to focus on consequences when dealing with the poor. Conservatives often talk openly about whether welfare breeds dependency or laziness, whether workfare "works," and so on. This talk treats the Lowers as an appropriate source of consequential manipulation, in a way that would offend us when talking about those who are not poor. A delicate balance allows us to object both to being taxed and to spending government resources, and it leads us to an outcome that favors those with money. We don't tax marriage, because marriage is sacred, and we don't ask any further questions about that. But we don't give breaks to the poor, because breaks to the poor don't work. We are having our cake and eating it, again.

Thus the first effect looks at the tax-induced burden of being married, especially among two-earner couples. The language of "marriage penalties" may not be helpful in this regard and may even mislead, because it is not necessarily a question of the relative tax rates of singles, married couples, and unmarried couples. Rather, it is a question of how the tax system burdens particular marriages, making certain work-family arrangements especially difficult. A bottom line of sorts is that the tax system is set up against two-earner marriages, and a bias against two earners is a bias against marriage itself whenever economic conditions compel everyone to try to work.

TO WORK PART TIME OR FULL

The second incentive effect is to work full time, to make a certain "all or nothing" decision in regard to the labor force. The tax part of this story operates on several levels. First, on an aggregate level, a system set up for single-earner families is going to be biased against two-worker families. This fosters unstable family structures among the poor and stay-at-home wives among the rich. Meanwhile, men in all income ranges are pressed into working full time, even sometimes extra hours to make up for their wives staying at home. Also working full time are the large number of single mothers among the poor, themselves partly the result of a social system tilting against two-earner families. The pool of potential part-time workers on the supply side is thus limited. All of this begins to point to a "collective action problem." Individuals who want to work at good part-time jobs, or who want to fashion modern and creative work-family balances, are forever swimming upstream.

Second, the fringe-benefit laws, heavily shaped by tax, create incentives for employers to divide the workforce into two groups. One is fully compensated and receiving full benefits, a group from whom the employer will expect particularly long days and solid work. The second is a transient group of part-time workers, temporary help, and independent contractors, all kept off the fringe-benefit rolls. Firms have little incentive to offer jobs between these extremes, although these are just the kinds of jobs that a more flexible and dynamic workforce might feature.

Third, on an individual level, wives as potential second workers enter the workforce at high marginal rates, dictated by their husbands' salaries and aggravated by social security. Yet working wives get very little tax assistance for their sizable work-related expenses. Economies of scale make the costs of full-time work less than double those of part-time work. It will very often be the case that part-time work is simply not worth it, in a bottom-line, accounting sense. Susan and Elizabeth heard these facts straight from the accountant's mouth.

All of this leads to another example of complex cycles of cause and effect. Because of tax and other obstacles, few women or men look for good part-time options, and most employers look for solid full-time workers and low-grade part-time ones. Men contribute to the problem by clinging to a more or less unquestioned full-time model of work, which continues to set a certain social default. Women either accept this mode of work or stay home. The system leads to a cycle against new, creative, dynamic work-family arrangements, especially ones that might include high-quality part-time work.

I have often been surprised at reactions to this part of my analysis. People both with and without some detailed knowledge of labor market conditions in America today often scoff that there is, in fact, a vibrant market for part-time work, that many women are indeed working part time. Others seem to think that more part-time work is my solution to the problems of gender discrimination today, and thus that the best answers should come on the firm or demand side; we should somehow legislate to make part-time work more available and more attractive. These misunderstandings are part of what has led me to be wary of centering my description of deep problems over anything that might be construed as a narrow political solution. Whenever an answer is even hinted at, it seems to become the salient point for discussion. Deep problems have no "answers" in that narrow sense; it is important to understand the problems first.

The Facts of the Matter

The basic fact of the matter is that we most decidedly do *not* have a rich and vibrant part-time labor market. It is true that something like 25 percent of women who work do so part time: not a trivial number, by any means, but also not an overwhelming one. But we have to look far behind this number to get at the real story.

First, the percentage of married *mothers* who seem to be working part time—anything less than thirty-five hours per week, as the government defines it—is actually rather low, less than 20 percent, and has been falling over the past several decades. Second, a good deal of part-time labor is *involuntary*—situations where the part-time workers actually want to work more, but the employers do not want them to. This is, in other words, a result of demand-side pressures, looking to what firms or employers want. But a liberal political morality should be concerned with the individual worker's side of the labor story. We should care about people. Here, the puzzle is that the massive influx of women of all demographic sorts into the workplace since World War II has not been matched with a correspondingly large rethinking or reshaping of models of work and family. We have many more choices in breakfast cereals or cars than we do in work arrangements, and this ought to puzzle us. Working wives and mothers seem to be disproportionately stressed by this lack of flexibility. Third, almost no fathers work part time. Statistics are hard to come by, but it seems to be the case that less than 5 percent of married fathers work part time. Finally, almost no families consist of two part-time workers.

The rosy view that we have a rich and vibrant part-time job market is a product of looking selectively at a few statistics. A different picture emerges from talking to women, surveying the various studies on women's attitudes toward work, careers, and families, or simply checking out the articles in popular magazines portraying the plights and perils of the modern working woman. In the so-called real world, there persists an overwhelming sense of the time stress and other pressures facing women, especially married women with children who try to work outside the home, too. Many women working full time wish they could be working part time. This is an ironic counterpart to the involuntary part-time market. Women with "good" jobs feel locked into a full-time pattern. Women with "bad" part-time jobs would rather have good full-time jobs, willing to consider the sacrifices in time for the money and job satisfaction of better work. In both cases women lose out because of a lack of flexibility. What many women seem to want is good part-time work.

Men do not seem to mind the status quo so much. Discouraging women from working pushes men to work more. Some men moonlight or work extra hours; many other men continue to work as men have worked ever since the turn of the century—full time, with full commitment. Psychological and workplace studies continue to show that the average man identifies strongly with a full-time working model and indeed often resents women who work full time and get paid as much or more than he does. Men are by and large not clamoring for reduced time at work or for more flexible work-family options. But perhaps they ought to be. Perhaps we ought to be taxing men more.

Looking Forward

This interim discussion of the part-time labor market hints at what I feel is a crucial direction for change. We need more flexibility, more options for integrating work, family, and career in a complex economy where men and women can be true equals. It is not all a matter of simply making part-time work more available for married women with children. It is, rather, a matter of making more options available to all persons and of involving men more directly in the process.

We cannot know what a future of true equality of concern and respect for all citizens, women and men, would hold. We have never been there. But we can see that something is wrong in the present, that women continue to bear a disproportionate weight of what is wrong, and that what is wrong has a strong connection to a lack of flexibility and change in the options for work and family facing us all. We are learning that this is all part of the script laid down in the 1930s, 1940s, and 1950s. As its constraints have grown in force, they have become less visible. Our first and most essential task is to come to see them.

TO BE SINGLE- OR DUAL-EARNER FAMILIES

The third incentive effect involves the pressure toward being single-earning, traditional families. I've already identified the burdens facing Susan and Elizabeth and other married women with children, which push them toward staying at home. There should therefore be nothing new or surprising here, except perhaps to see that it is among the upper classes where the incentive for wives to stay home is most pronounced. Even that shouldn't be too surprising. It was the wealthy Traditionals who took the lead in the 1930s and 1940s, and an image of working wives as being a lower- and middle-class phenomenon has been around at least since the 1950s. The push for single-earner families and against two-earner ones puts a stress on marriage itself among the poor, but it plays out differently for the rich, who care less about extra dollars. For the upper classes, the incentive is simply for the wife to stay home.

We need to be mindful of our political leanings here. Liberals and progressives might think that under a fair tax system upper-income families should be taxed more. Upper-class wives often fail to generate much sympathy. With a focus on gender justice rather than just the traditional distributive concerns of tax policy before us, however, there are important reasons to care about the fate of upper-class families, upper-class wives in particular. Our consideration of the Lowers, Middles, and Uppers will allow us to see striking discontinuities in the taxes on women as we move through the income scales. This discontinuity across income ranges is itself a problem for women. Of course, there are also some constant themes: women everywhere are taxed, and men everywhere go on working as usual.

Let's turn now to the Lowers. Tables 3 and 9 are reprinted here, since we'll need them again as we go through these family examples.

THE LOWERS

Among the lowest income earners, all three behavioral effects are rather severe. There is a pronounced marriage penalty, which punishes the very

TABLE 3. Modern-Style Rate Schedules

Individual Rate Schedule		Married Rate Schedule	
Income	Marginal Tax Rate	Income	Marginal Tax Rate
$0–$10,000	0%	$0–$16,000	0%
$10,001–$30,000	15%	$16,001–$48,000	15%
$30,001–$60,000	30%	$48,001–$96,000	30%
$60,001 and up	40%	$96,001 and up	40%

TABLE 9. Simple Earned-Income Credit Table

INCOME	CREDIT
$0–$10,000	+20%
$10,001–$15,000	0%
$15,001–$25,000	−20%

formation of the family. Among the two-parent households that remain, the high marginal tax rates facing a potential second earner and the inadequacy of the child-care credit strongly encourage one spouse to stay home. This putative secondary worker faces an all-or-nothing choice, because it will generally be difficult to cover the high after-tax costs of working on a salary sharply reduced by taxes.

There are other incentives, such as to have one child, but at most two; for single parents to work; and for all poor families with children to earn at least the earned-income tax credit ceiling, $10,000 under table 9. These incentives are similar to ones generated by the welfare system. Indeed, the earned-income tax credit may best be understood as simply a part of the welfare system. Especially relative to lower-income classes, it is important to consider the entire tax and transfer system together. Unlike social security benefits, which pay off down the road, welfare benefits and the loss thereof have immediate effects on home economics: they translate into dollars and cents in the present tense.

Hitting the Poor Hard

Most striking for the Lowers is the marriage penalty. First, let's meet them more formally. Larry Lower earns $15,000 working in a nearby factory. The Lowers have two children, so they qualify for the maximum earned-income credit of $2,000 under table 9. Let's assume that Laura Lower is considering a job paying $10,000, before taxes, to help make ends meet. At 50 weeks a year, 40 hours a week, this comes to $5 an hour, just above minimum wage, so it ought to be clear that we are, indeed, dealing with lower-income opportunities. What impact would Laura's job have on the family's bottom line?

First, the Lowers would lose all $2,000 of their earned-income credit. Nine thousand dollars of Laura's wages would fall into the 15 percent income tax bracket under table 3, costing the family another $1,350. Social security taxes take away another $800, and, at a flat 10 percent for state and local taxes, another $1,000 goes. Laura faces a marginal tax rate in excess of 50 percent in this example, with the earned-income credit phaseout (20 percent), income (15 percent), social security (8 percent), and state and local (10 percent) taxes. I have not factored in the effect of the employer's share of social security, or the loss of other government benefits from need or income-based welfare programs. Gene Steuerle has shown that welfare recipients often face marginal tax rates of 70 percent, sometimes higher than 100 percent, meaning that they simply lose money by working, even without taking any work-related costs into account. Looking at taxes alone, Laura's $10,000 has added less than $5,000 to the family's take-home pay.

To get a clear look at the marriage penalty in this setting, consider what would happen if the couple were to divorce. In the above example, with Laura working, the family has a net federal income tax of $1,350—the Lowers get no earned-income tax credit, and have to pay taxes under table 3. We can put aside social security taxes, which are unaffected by divorce. That is, in all cases, both Lowers pay a steady 8 percent, and there is an additional drag on their pay due to the employer's share: social security benefits are affected by divorce, but social security taxes are not. If the couple divorces and Laura takes the children, Laura would pay no federal income taxes under the individual rate schedule in table 3. In fact, she would be able to use the somewhat more generous head-of-household schedule, but this is an unnecessary complication for our purposes. Laura and her husbandless family would get the full $2,000 earned-income tax credit. Larry would pay $750 under table 3's individual rate schedule. He would have $5,000 taxed in the 15 percent bracket. Combined, the couple would, if divorced, pay a *negative* $1,250 in taxes: Larry's $750 minus the $2,000 Laura and the children get.

Given these simple facts, the Lowers's marriage penalty is $2,600, well over one-half of Laura's take-home pay, before it is reduced even further by nontax expenses. This is a staggering number, in absolute and relative terms, for a lower-income couple. Yet under various actual situations the marriage penalty on a couple like the Lowers can be even more severe. Daniel Feenberg and Harvey Rosen calculated a 1994 marriage penalty of $3,717 for a couple with two children where each parent earned $10,000. The earned-income tax credit is responsible for a good deal of this lower-income marriage penalty. The current structure of the credit creates a large penalty, and this comes at exactly the point where legally sanctioned marriages might be most sensitive to economic conditions.

Two financial aspects of this lower-income marriage penalty are especially striking. First, it hits on the very first dollar of income that a potential secondary worker might earn. This is unlike the usual case under the rate structure, where there is actually a marriage bonus until one spouse earns at least 20 percent of what the other does. Second, the lower-income marriage penalty is extremely high in both absolute and relative terms. Feenberg and Rosen calculated that a couple where each spouse earned $25,000—two-and-a-half times the $10,000 per spouse family—paid a marriage penalty of $727 in 1994, less than *one-fifth* what the poorer couple paid. A family with a primary earner making $50,000 and a secondary earner making $30,000 paid a marriage penalty of $2,418, still far less than the couple who earn one-fourth of what they do. Not until a family earned $90,000 did its marriage penalty possibly exceed that of the $20,000 family.

Not Helping Laura

Consider next the push toward single-earner households. The Lowers see this because of the high marginal tax rates facing Laura and the woefully inadequate child-care credit. Laura faces marginal tax rates easily approaching or even exceeding 50 percent. This creates an obvious disincentive to work and a corresponding incentive to spend her time generating tax-free imputed income. Cutting against this pressure is that we would expect the "marginal utility of money income"—in plainer English, the desire for cash—to be high, driving lower-income families to work for money. But if both parents do try to work outside the home, they run into the penalties against two-earner marriages that we've just sketched. The Lowers are hit hard, wherever they turn.

Studies by economists like Jane Leuthold and others show that lower-income families generally react to higher tax rates by increasing their labor market participation *and* having both spouses put in additional non-market labor, thus leaving little time for leisure. Low-income couples also look for low-cost options to replace lost imputed income—as by having relatives care for the children. Jonathan Veum and Philip Gleason found in 1991 that 40 percent of mothers aged 23 to 39 relied on relatives to care for their children while they worked; wealthier women were significantly less likely to invoke this option. The study reported in *USA Today* in 1995 similarly showed that more than 40 percent of families with child-care needs used relatives to meet those needs. These figures are exactly in line with the 1990 National Child Care Survey.

The tax laws simply fail to help with any of Laura's job-related expenses. The two-earner deduction has been repealed, but it never would have been much help to Laura anyway: in our example, the deduction would have saved her $150 (10 percent of her $10,000 salary, in the 15 percent bracket). The earned-income tax credit is also typically unavailable for secondary-earner spouses, since primary earners use it up. Finally, the child-care credit, although written with the appearance of concern for the poor working wives, is in fact not very helpful to them.

Let's assume Laura earns $5,000, all of which goes to pay for child care. That is less than $100 a week, and as the Lowers would be making $20,000 combined, it is consistent with the *USA Today* study showing that lower-income families spend 25 percent of their income on child care. The Lowers will ostensibly get a child-care credit of $1,200: the 30 percent child-care credit is reduced to 25 percent at $20,000 of family income. Twenty-five percent of $4,800 is $1,200, the maximum amount the law takes into account for child-care expenses. In fact, though, the

Lowers would get *no* child-care credit at all, because the credit is not refundable. The Lowers, who are still paying back their earned-income tax credit, don't owe any positive income taxes yet. Nonrefundable credits, like the child—not child-care—credit proposed in the *Contracts*, don't help the poor at all.

For Laura's $5,000, the Lowers will lose $1,000 in the earned-income tax credit, and Laura will have to pay $600 in income taxes, $400 in social security, and another $500 for state and local taxes. Over this range in which every penny Laura earns simply goes to pay for child care, Laura is still in a 50 percent marginal tax bracket. The Lowers are losing $2,500, not counting any other expenses and notwithstanding a child-care credit seemingly designed to help them.

By the time Laura earns a full $10,000, the child-care credit has fallen to a potential $1,050 if the Lowers spend $5,000 on care. At least this $1,050 does offset some of the $1,350 positive income taxes now due, reducing them to $300. But, once again, we still have to consider social security, the loss of the earned-income tax credit, and state and local taxes. Considering taxes and child care, but no other expenses, Laura's $10,000 job will bring home $1,050 to the family: she faces $5,000 in taxes and $5,000 in child-care costs, reduced only by the $1,050 credit. Additional expenses of just $50 a week would bring Laura's net yield down to a *negative* $1,450.

About the only options for lower-income individuals like Laura and Larry will be saving on child-care costs—something that surveys indicate they do—and splitting up to avoid the high marriage penalty. If Laura can cut in half both her child care and other work-related expenses, her $10,000 job would at least bring in a positive sum, about $1,800, to the family: she still pays $5,000 in taxes, but only $2,500 in child care and $1,250 in other expenses, and the Lowers get a $550 child-care credit. This is not great: It's like being taxed at an 82 percent rate. But at least it beats the absurdity of losing money by working. Whether or not it's better than divorce is a question we'll leave for the Lowers.

Life Is Hard

Consider the final incentive effect, that wives will make all-or-nothing labor decisions. This follows naturally from the above discussion. Unless Laura enters the workforce at a sufficient level, her salary will not cover the high after-tax costs of working. For the Lowers, it is probably enough to see that working just to pay for child-care costs is a losing proposition. Unless Laura can earn much more than the costs of paying for child care, she might as well stay home. Part-time work is unlikely to do the trick.

When we factor these elements together, a deeply unpleasant picture emerges. There is certainly pressure on our lowest-income families. The earned-income and child-care credits seem designed to alleviate some of this stress, but in fact neither one does much to help two-earner, lower-income families. The law ironically discourages marriage in the first instance. The child-care credit seems to have two-earner couples in mind, but in practice it does little to help the poor. Because of the strong economic incentive to work, the discouragement of secondary workers at this level pushes marriages to the breaking point.

Contrary to the conservative cultural wisdom on work and family, rules that generally discourage two-earner families will also discourage marriage, especially among our poorest citizens. By fostering and rewarding traditional, single-earner families, the law is not sensitive to the economic realities of lower-income life. In fact, single-parent households are most common among the poor, and, among the two-parent households that do exist at this income level, two-earner families are especially rare. For our lowest-income citizens, we see the worst of two worlds—labor markets featuring low pay, few benefits, and little flexibility, and family structures in disarray. Tax rules play a role in generating these effects. More to the point, tax policy could be more sensitive and helpful, especially if it freed itself from the seductive allure of naively neutral rules.

THE MIDDLES

Among the middle-income ranges, the incentive effects we've been discussing are not as severe as they had been for the Lowers. First, the marriage penalty is comparatively small. Under table 3 a couple earning $40,000, with each spouse earning $20,000, pays a maximum marriage penalty of $600. We saw similar figures in chapter 3, when we looked at the marriage penalties before and after the Tax Reform Act of 1986 in table 8. Feenberg and Rosen calculated a marriage penalty of $727 for a family of four with each parent earning $25,000 in 1994. Although the Middles make $15,000 more than the Lowers do with both spouses working, the Middles' marriage penalty is $2,000 *less*.

Second, the relative push toward single-earner families is also much smaller. The marginal rates facing Molly Middle are lower than they are for either Laura Lower or Ursula Upper. The child-care credit is also helpful for Molly in offsetting at least the tax costs of her working to pay for child care. But the third incentive, that toward all-or-nothing labor decisions, is clearly present, as Susan and Elizabeth helped us see. The reason is that these workers still face high marginal tax rates when and if they enter the workforce, and they generate sizable work-related expenses while receiving only limited tax relief. The need to cover both the high costs of child care and the miscellaneous other costs of work with reduced pre-tax dollars makes part-time work infeasible. In a complex cycle of cause and effect, these incentives play out against a backdrop in which part-time work is not very attractive in any event.

Now let's consider the Middle family. Mel Middle earns $30,000 as a policeman, putting the family squarely in the 15 percent federal tax bracket. If Molly Middle leaves the two children at home and enters the workforce, she will face a combined social security, federal, and state and local tax rate of 33 percent. This is no small rate, although it is significantly lower than the 50 percent or higher rate facing Laura Lower, who had to deal with the phaseout of the earned-income tax credit and other welfare benefits. Notwithstanding this one-third tax bite, the tax laws do not help Molly much with her work-related expenses, except for very partial relief with respect to child care.

Molly Makes a Choice

Let's look at two options facing Molly. One is a full-time position, 40 hours per week, paying $20,000 a year, which is approximately the median income for a married American woman and captures the relative situation of many wives to their husbands' earnings. Two is a part-time position, 20 hours per week, paying $10,000 a year, each figure being one-half the full-time option. Taking taxes into account, the take-home pay for the two choices immediately falls to $13,400 and $6,700, respectively.

Assume that the Middles find some child-care arrangement for $100 per week, a reasonable midrange figure in America today. The relevant yearly costs for child care, assuming a 50-week schedule, are $5,000 and $2,500. At this income range, the child-care credit is approximately as favorable as the Section 129 deduction for dependent care, were that available. The Middles would get a credit of $960 in the full-time example and $500 in the part-time one. After taxes, child-care costs and the child-care credit, the Middles are left with $9,360 in the full-time case, and $4,700 in the part-time one.

Finally, assume that Molly incurs additional work-related expenses of $50 a week if she works full time, $25 if she works part time. These are again reasonable, if low, estimates of the additional costs of house-cleaning, commuting, clothing, dry cleaning, restaurant meals, and other expenses associated with work. Taking these nondeductible expenses into account, the full-time Molly is down to about $6,900 a year; the part-time Molly will net $3,450. This is almost exactly the two-thirds effect from the Hanson-Ooms study.

Now let's take a closer look at this example. First of all, note that, compared with Molly's staying at home, the Middles are left with less than $300 a month more from having her work part time, and less than $600 if she works full time. In either event, these amounts will have to compensate the Middles for the loss of imputed income, leisure, and time that Molly would have spent with her children. Quite often, the part-time numbers may not seem worth it, as appeared to be the case in Susan's story.

Second, the whole discussion has so far presumed a proportionality in both the cost and benefit sides for part-time labor. That is, I assumed that Molly could be paid one-half as much and incur one-half of the costs of full-time work simply by working one-half of the time. These assumptions are unrealistic. Part-time labor in America, especially for the non-professional classes, is low in pay, prestige, and satisfaction. At the same time, the costs are not likely to rise precisely in line with time spent, especially over the initial ranges of hours worked. There are apt to be some fixed costs of getting into the labor market and economies of scale in other expenses. Commuting, for example, is unlikely to cost twice as much just because the work hours are twice as long. The 1990 National Child Care Survey similarly showed that households with part-time working mothers incurred 75 percent of the average weekly child-care costs that those with full-time working mothers did.

So we should revise our example. Let's give Molly's part-time opportunity 40 percent of the salary and 60 percent of the costs of the full-time option, to reflect biases in pay and economies of scale in costs. The part-time position now generates $1,460 a year, or about $120 a month. It is easy to imagine such an option losing money, in a cash flow sense, as happened to Elizabeth. The reason for the qualifier "in a cash flow sense" is that such work may generate net lifetime gains, the long-term benefits of staying in the paid workforce outweighing the short-term costs of losing money during early child-rearing years. But many families will not be able to pay a mother of young children to continue to work outside the home, even if this may help her in the long run.

Looking at Mel, and for Something Else

How about Mel Middle? At all relevant ranges, Mel will be in the same tax bracket that Molly faces. This shows the nominal neutrality of the law. But when we consider practical reality, a strong bias persists. Mel's additional working—whether it is greater effort to generate a higher salary, taking on a second job, or working overtime—will not occasion the explicit child-care expenses that Molly's working did. Mel's work is also almost certain to come at a higher wage level, reflecting a full-time bias. Mel's employer has already paid for his fringe benefits, for example, and so can pass on additional dollars straight to Mel. When Mel works harder he is also likely to generate lower work-related costs than Molly would if she entered the workforce. If, for example, Mel gets a raise by putting in extra hours at his job, there is no added commuting cost, and the family is probably no more likely to eat out at restaurants on account of Mel's situation than it was before.

Mel thus faces pressure to work harder as Molly faces pressure to stay home. I'll sketch out the numbers when it comes to the Uppers, where we'll see that this effect is especially dramatic—that is, a primary-earner husband can bring home additional income for the family much more easily than can his secondary-earning wife. Indeed, just as labor force participation drops for mothers, it increases for fathers. Even where the tax laws are nominally neutral, we can see in the interface between tax and reality a significant impetus toward specialized—and gendered—divisions of labor.

The all-or-nothing effect has some unfortunate consequences, especially in conjunction with the other two tax-induced incentives. The effect may make women's presence in the labor force unstable because, as circumstances change—most notably, as children enter the picture—the major option facing the family is for the wife to leave her job. Simply cutting back one's hours is often not feasible. In fact, women are much more elastic—that is, more likely to move into and out of the workforce. To the extent that women remain committed to their jobs, the all-or-nothing effect makes it especially difficult and costly to have children in the first place, or forces the couple to juggle two full-time careers and child care. This latter solution puts pressure on the marriage itself, since two equal earners with children are the most burdened family, as we have seen throughout. The all-or-nothing effect forecloses options and contributes to the stressful sense that society is not fostering creative alternatives to traditional family models. It is not just hard to be a family of two full-time earners. It is hard to be a full-time/part-time family, and harder still to be a family of two part-time earners.

On an intuitive level, something seems wrong in the contemporary reality of work and the family. More and more households are becoming two-earner families. But where these families also have children—despite the numerous economic, including tax-related, disincentives for doing so—we would expect a growing part-time and flexible-time job market to accommodate the competing demands of home and work. This is not happening. Nor does the growing participation of women in the labor force appear to be fostering marketplace or domestic equality between the genders.

This example of a representative middle-income family gives one possible explanation for the apparent paradox. Molly Middle and many others like her face an all-or-nothing choice, and women on both sides of her in the economic spectrum are pushed even harder. Poorer women, likely to be single parents, must work full time, and wealthier women can just as easily stay home. And so the part-time market is hampered on the supply side. We are really not seeing women's "true" preferences here, for their choices are shaped by their options. Ask married women with young children what they want, and many will say they want good part-time work with a flexible schedule. Yet more than 40 percent of all married mothers stay home full time, and another 48 percent work full time. Far less than 12 percent are doing what would seem to be a most attractive option—

that is, working part-time at good jobs. A significant portion of the married women working part-time are unhappily doing so while they look for full-time work. At the same time, few married husbands are staying home, few of any type of workers are working part time, and the two part-time-worker household is extremely rare.

The Middles have done all right, by and large, in certain obvious, visible ways. They pay a small marriage penalty, if any, and the pressure to be a single-earner family is not especially severe—not as severe as among the Lowers or the Uppers. This ought to come as no big surprise, for the middle classes have contributed the lion's share of tax revenue ever since World War II, and we would expect some ostensible solicitude toward their values—and their earnings capacities—in setting up the tax system. But the middle class is nonetheless being squeezed in other, more subtle and insidious ways. They are paying the price of a lack of institutional flexibility. They have few choices. We generally seem unable to see the absence of something, perhaps especially a choice, as itself a social problem that we can do much about. We don't pay heed to the dog who did not bark; we often fail to think about what is not happening. But sometimes what is not happening is the worst thing of all.

THE UPPERS

Finally, let's look at the highest-earning Americans. There are good reasons to care about upper-income families, as we'll see, and there are also strong tax effects at work on them. The marriage penalty on wealthy two-earner families is significant. And there is a strong bias in favor of traditional, single-earner families.

A paradox immediately presents itself. In the real world outside of tax rules, the image of two-earner families is strongest in the upper-income levels. Such couples are apt to be younger and better educated than the more traditional single-earner families, and their incomes are generally higher. But the tax laws by and large do not support this reality. Tax continues to be the product of decisions made in the 1930s and 1940s, when the Traditionals reigned supreme. The results are tax-related incentives not to have children, not to marry if the spouses' incomes are apt to be equal, and to specialize in either unpaid housework or paid labor-market work. The fact that many, although by no means all, upper-income families have resisted these incentives is testimony to the appeal of different family models, as well as to the flexibility that money can provide. It does not disprove the tax effects. These are too well grounded in the facts.

A good many wealthy families do indeed fit the Traditional mold. As one piece of evidence, 80 percent of the chief financial officers of large American corporations surveyed in 1991 were men with stay-at-home wives. Arlie Hochschild points out that the cycles inducing a gendered division of labor are especially acute at the upper-income levels, where wives are indeed more likely to stay home and support their husbands' careers. The top 5 percent of families, who won tax victories in 1939 and again in 1948, and who warded off Hubert Humphrey in 1951, have continued to do quite well for themselves, and to change rather little in the process.

Ursula's Work Doesn't Much Count

Let's meet the Uppers. Umberto Upper earns a comfortable salary of $60,000 as a lawyer. When we ask whether Ursula Upper will work outside the home, too, very strong incentive effects emerge, especially if one option is for Umberto to put in more hours at his work, or otherwise to increase his salary. Suppose Ursula is offered a job paying $30,000 a year. She would face a marginal tax rate of at least 48 percent: an income tax rate of 30 percent, social security of 8 percent, and state and local taxes of 10 percent. Many upper-income wives actually face higher tax rates, because the primary earner has pushed the family into a higher income tax bracket: at $96,000 under table 3, for example, the Uppers enter the 40 percent bracket. These days there are numerous phaseouts and other more or less hidden, complex tax provisions that also have the effect of raising effective marginal tax rates on wealthier individuals.

Note a peculiar irony here. The joint filing compromise of 1948 created a dilemma for tax policy reformers. Any attempt to increase progressive rates on wealthy, upper-income Americans will now especially burden the potential secondary-earner wives in such households. We saw this happen in 1969, when the attempt to mitigate the singles' penalty fell especially hard on Emma Equal. The richer a family, the more a wife is taxed on her first dollar of earnings. Just as gender and class intersect among the poor, so they do among the rich. Here the search for distributive equality and justice is put in direct conflict with the search for gender equality and justice. To resolve this dilemma by ignoring the particular plight of wealthy wives is hardly satisfactory.

Getting back to Ursula, to keep matters simple I'll put her in the 50 percent bracket. Her $30,000 salary is immediately cut in half, to $15,000. Making the not unrealistic assumption that child care will cost the Uppers $200 a week, these expenses subtract another $10,000. Now some readers will have a tendency to scoff at a family considering spending $200 or more per week on child care. Who cares about *them*? If they are that rich, why should the tax laws pitch in to help? One saw such attitudes, for example, in the public uproar over Zoe Baird, President Clinton's nominee for attorney general, who turned out not to have paid all of the social security taxes on her household employees in a timely fashion. Much of the public's sense of hostility toward Baird seemed driven by resentment of her wealth, which allowed her to hire several people to assist around the house. We'll see a direct animosity to tax provisions for the child-care costs of upper-income taxpayers in chapter 9, when we look at contemporary flat tax proposals.

I believe, however, that this tendency to belittle the child-care problems of the rich, while understandable, is a mistake for at least two reasons. One, the wealthier the family, the more expensive child care is apt to be. It is simply a fact that child-care expenses get a high priority in most households. And we probably want them to; we want to encourage parents to do well by their children. Given their ability to afford it, it will most likely be a fact that the Uppers will want good stay-at-home care if Ursula goes to work.

But there is a second reason why a lack of concern with the child-care problems of the Uppers is inappropriate. The burdens of such indifference fall on *Ursula* Upper. This gives us another look at the devilish paradox generated by the compromise of 1948. In general, when we add gender and class to our matrix of social concerns, strange things happen. It is important to the gendered dynamics in society that upper-income women not be tied to the tax brackets of their husbands. Otherwise, rich women join poor women as the most heavily taxed—with unnerving results across the gender-class spectrum. The common case of divorce haunts this picture, too: Ursula, staying at home today, may find herself alone and unable to find work tomorrow.

If the Uppers are fortunate enough to have an employer with a Section 129 dependent-care assistance program in place, and if they are willing to use this option, they will gain about a $2,500 tax benefit, using their 50 percent bracket and recalling that only the first $5,000 of child-care expenses is eligible for relief. Without such a program, the maximum child-care credit of the Uppers will be $960: 20 percent of $4,800. Ursula Upper's net contribution to the family's cash income has now fallen to between $6,000 and $7,500: she has lost $15,000 to taxes and $10,000 to child-care costs, and has gotten just $1,000 to $2,500 in tax-related "benefits."

Now let's look at Ursula's additional work-related expenses. Hanson and Ooms find that among middle-income households, two-earner families spend $1,868 a year more than one-earner families do on work-related expenditures other than child care, pension contributions, and taxes: thus these expenses include additional transportation, meals out, housekeeping, and clothing. Among upper-income households, two-earner families have a disparity of $1,752. Over a 50-week working year, these figures translate into weekly disparities of $37 and $35, respectively. The figures are drawn from the 1980–83 Consumer Expenditure Survey; inflation since that time would roughly double those numbers by the mid-1990s, to $74 and $70. Further, the figures are not broken down separately into full- and part-time workers; they average both types together.

Hanson and Ooms used a cutoff for upper-income families of $33,560 a year; even after adjusting for inflation, this would be about $60,000 in 1995. Note that this is far less than the Uppers would earn if they both worked—$90,000, in our running example. Finally, we are once again concerned with the marginal family, the ones most affected by tax. Costs for this family are likely to be higher than on average. For the New York City upper-income couple portrayed by Tamar Lewin in 1991, for example, additional expenses on work clothing, commuting, and meals totaled $4,178, or $84 a week over a 50-week year; the comparable figures for the blue-collar suburban family were $2,522 and $51. Factoring all this together, I'll use $100 a week for Ursula—again, these are the costs of the paid housework, commuting, and so on occasioned by her work outside the home.

Ursula Upper's $30,000-a-year job has now brought a bottom line to the family of between $1,000 and $2,500. I'll average and round up to $2,000. These numbers are consistent with many cases I have observed firsthand. The Uppers will have to balance the $2,000, or $167 a month, at an income level where money has presumably become less important, against the loss of leisure, imputed income, and time with children brought about by Ursula's full-time job. How many wealthy parents would leave their children to work full time at a job *grossing* $30,000 but *netting* only $2,000 a year? Ursula will stay home, as a large majority of the wives of highly paid corporate executives do.

Umberto's Work Counts

Before making a few final observations about the behavioral incentives, let's consider the case of Umberto taking on a second job, or putting in additional effort to get a raise, or some such thing. Umberto's added work effort will not occasion any direct child-care costs. It would also be expected to generate less of an incremental increase in work-related costs than Ursula's working would: Umberto won't be driving any extra miles if he just stays in his office longer. Umberto also faces a marginal tax rate of 40–43 percent, at least 6.5 percent less than Ursula does, since he has already paid off all of his annual social security contribution. In fact, an entire 13 percent weight has been lifted from his shoulders, because his employer will not have to pay 6.5 percent on his account, either. His employer has also already paid off medical insurance for Umberto's entire family and has perhaps made a maximum contribution to Umberto's pension plan. It is easier, on these accounts, to give Umberto a raise.

If his costs of additional work were $50 a week, and Umberto, like his wife, faced the possibility of making $30,000 more, the family would net about $16,000 from *his* efforts—just about *eight times* the take-home effect of Ursula's earning the same level of income. Indeed, under realistic assumptions, Umberto would have to increase his income by just$4,000—

that is, by less than 7 percent—to obtain the same financial benefit to the household that Ursula would by making $30,000. Umberto's $4,000 is reduced by 40 percent or so for taxes, to $2,400. His extra work at this level may not occasion any additional costs at all. Even if we allow him another $25 a week for more meals out or whatever, his small raise beats Ursula's full-time job as a matter of bottom-line cash flow.

We can even now imagine Umberto explaining all of this to his boss, along the following lines: "Look sir, my wife is thinking about going to work, and she's been offered a position paying $30,000 a year. I've talked this over with my accountant, and it turns out that, if you can give me a raise of $4,000 a year—that's $80 a week—we'll be able to keep the wife at home, because I'll be bringing as much cash home as that job of hers would. I'm willing to take on a few extra duties around here. You know, if we can keep her at home, I'll lose much less time due to kid stuff, like child-care emergencies and other headaches. What do you say?"

Now I don't think that many conversations like that actually take place—although it does resonate with the plot of many movies and television shows, like *Parenthood*, that feature a young father hunkering down to work harder to enable his wife to stay home with the kids. But the fact of the matter is that men do solidify their full-time work status and commitment when they become fathers, and many men even start taking second jobs, or moonlighting, to maintain the family's dollar income. Meanwhile many married mothers do stay home. The incentive for a specialized division of labor is clear.

At Least Some Choice for Ursula

The final incentive effect, which tilts away from part-time work for secondary earners, is relatively modest for Ursula. This is in large part because the full-time option is so unattractive that it is hard to imagine part-time ones being less so. On the one hand, part-time labor is even less likely to survive the familial algebra presented above. A $15,000, half-time job for Ursula, were it available, might net the Uppers just slightly less than the full-time option. But Ursula is rather unlikely to be working for immediate cash flow purposes; if the family were in need of greater funds, it would make far more sense for Umberto to look for more income, as we have just seen. Part-time options may fit better with Ursula's desire to balance child-rearing tasks with a presence in the job market. Upper-income wives are in fact more flexible in the numbers of hours per week they work; being rich has its benefits.

We can readily imagine, for example, Umberto explaining to his wife that she does not *need* to work—in fact, her salary won't really matter much—but, if she insists, a part-time job might be a nice way for her to get out once in a while. The same goes for the volunteer work that wealthy women and stay-at-home spouses seem to do: there is actually an argument pressed by groups like Mothers at Home for not penalizing stay-at-home spouses, lest charitable activities suffer. All of this simply illustrates the greater flexibility that the wealthy have to structure their work and family lives.

As I've said, it would be a grave mistake, from a richer, behavioral, and gender justice perspective, to ignore the upper classes. The greater income of the wealthy is actually apt to make their workforce behavior *more* responsive to tax rules. Lower-income women, where income needs dominate, continue to work from necessity. Upper-income women have more choices and freer ones, but this flexibility just makes it more problematic when we burden one choice particularly heavily. Clearly, wealthier families may take a longer-term perspective and may be more likely to consider nonmonetary matters, including each spouse's career satisfaction. Such factors will often cut in the other direction, toward labor market participation by wives, and may explain the appearance of two-earner families among the affluent. But *these* tendencies are independent of tax. They thus suggest just how strongly married women really do want to work; they don't refute the particular incentives generated by tax laws. Whatever else is going on with the rich, tax makes it especially hard to be a rich working wife. That many still choose to do so doesn't change that fact.

ADDING IT UP, AND LOOKING ACROSS INCOMES

There are important reasons to care about the labor market decisions of the upper-income classes. Encouraging women to stay home at these income levels deprives all women of powerful, symbolically important roles. Wives of the rich and powerful perpetuate the prominent role of the Traditionals in our national culture. Meanwhile, the evidence of discrimination against women in upper management continues to be pervasive. Divorce also complicates the situation. Today's stay-at-home upper-income wife may be tomorrow's divorced woman with few assets and little job market experience. Perhaps even more important, the situation of upper-income families—indeed, the whole range of treatment by class—introduces highly unfortunate discontinuities.

We see this by putting the three income classes together. Among the lower classes, the tax laws threaten formal family structures. This makes economic improvement to the middle class difficult. At the middle-income levels, the laws encourage women to work full time or stay at home. Either such women fail to develop valuable job market skills, or they find themselves pushing against the upper-income levels. But as soon as they do, they face even greater incentives to stay home. Secondary earners in general, married women in particular, are thus pushed in different directions as they cross income levels, and the whole pattern is replicated in a social structure that finds poor women alone, middle-class women in a bind, and upper-class women disempowered. The disparate economic effects also drive wedges into the women's liberation, or feminist, movement, as women in different economic classes confront different problems and needs. Not that it was intended, but the discrepancies play out a "divide and conquer" strategy quite nicely; women are set against each other by economic class. One among many ironies is that the tax system which plays a central role in this story is defended precisely on the grounds of its supposed neutrality.

TALLYING THE ACCOUNTANT'S TALE

This brings the accountant's tale to a close. Many married mothers like Susan and Elizabeth barely make money by working outside the home, and, over a good many ranges, they lose money. This puts a stress on lower-class marriages; it places middle-class wives on the horns of an all-or-nothing dilemma set against attractive part-time work; and it encourages upper-class wives simply to stay home. Laura, Molly, and Ursula helped us to see this. The factors leading to such an unhappy state of affairs are joint filing under the income tax, the social security system, the nontaxation of imputed income, the failure of the tax laws to take child care and other work-related expenses of the secondary earner adequately into account, a fringe benefit system set up like the social security system on a single-earner family model, and state and local taxes.

Academics and politicians have generally not seen these issues in their totality and their sweep, or in their vivid and painful details, but accountants have. The accountants presenting the facts to Susan and Elizabeth have been our Greek chorus throughout, and they have been singing a tragic tale to us, if only we could bring ourselves to understand. With the accounting facts of the matter behind us, we can take, in the next two parts, a deeper look at just what is wrong, from a social and gender justice angle, with this strange but all too true accountant's tale.

PART THREE

Theory, Practice, and Rhetoric: On (Not) Getting It

7 Some Taxing Hope

THE NEED FOR HOPE

As the story opens on part 3, the accountant's tale told to Susan and Eliza-beth from the start of chapter 1 has come home to roost. By the end of chapter 5, we had come to understand how Elizabeth was losing money by getting paid $16,000 a year to work outside the home and how Susan was barely breaking even notwithstanding her $40,000-a-year job. Chap-ter 6 generalized these tales and factored in a class dimension. We came to see how heavily poor wives are taxed, in a way that hits stable two-earner marriages among the lower classes especially hard. Middle-class wives face the difficult choice of working full time outside the home or staying full time inside it. Upper-class wives at first appeared to have an easy choice, to stay home, because their work could scarcely be expected to matter much to the family's bottom line. But this strong effect on upper-class married women made for an uneasy gendered dynamic across the range of classes, as poor women were left alone, middle-class women were stressed, and upper-class women remained at home. Women are both taxed and deprived of the wealth and power that we think of as incident to the price, however unwanted, of being taxed.

Bad as these practical effects are, we could equally well despair over the political and intellectual histories that run parallel to the accountant's tale. Significant and significantly gendered features of modern tax laws were constructed in the 1930s, 1940s, and 1950s. These features were then legitimated by the tax policy academy, invoking concepts of logic, neu-trality, and common sense at every turn. As the tax system expanded dra-matically, first principles were not revisited. An emergent feminist voice struggled to be heard. A rhetoric of family was co-opted by traditionalist forces, sometimes to argue for changes to favor their chosen family model of a single-earner, breadwinning husband and a stay-at-home wife, other times simply to get tax reform for the rich. Confused and confusing con-cepts like the marriage penalty arose in lieu of a more systematic and sustained behavioral focus on women, their wants, and their needs. Com-plaints about the secondary-earner bias, when heard at all, were dismissed as mere gripes, inevitable by-products of any practical tax system or even, as in 1986, as attempts to subvert traditional family values. Meanwhile, the dominant schools of tax politics and policy had little difficulty in moving to a behavioral focus when behaviors important to the male-oriented economy, like savings or investment incentives, were at stake.

A WAY OUT?

There is bad news aplenty, and thus plenty of need for hope. The good news is that tax itself affords some such hope. Just as tax has been a large part of the problem facing modern women, so it can also be part of the solution. Tax affords an attractive mechanism for affecting individual incentives, maintaining a focus on individualism and change without "top down," centrally mandated policies. It is no coincidence that economists have long seen tax as a good way to respond to failures of the free market, as by getting polluters to bear more of the costs of their own activities. Tax is a powerful means to control individual behaviors, as society at large has found out by taxing cigarettes and gasoline.

Indeed, that tax could affect behavior was one of the insights of the traditional forces invoking tax policy toward their own ends in the 1930s and 1940s. We'll see later that the contemporary *Contracts* are also trying to use tax actively, to further their own conservative vision of society. One hope is to reverse course, to use the same means toward different—more just and fairly chosen—ends. It turns out that a standard idea in public finance and economics, the theory of "optimal tax," which I am going to explore shortly, has long recommended the strongest practical proposal of this book: tax married women less and married men more. This is an exciting idea, not just for tax policy, but for concepts of social theory more generally.

If the idea that tax can provide hope for change is good news, it is good news that has a dark underside. Optimal tax theory, with its recommendation to reverse the way society taxes women, has been widely available for decades; its development was roughly coincident with the beginning of the feminist voice in tax policy in the early 1970s. But the theory's pro-woman message and the feminist critique of tax more generally have been linked in other, more depressing ways. Each has suffered the same political fate: death by silence.

Optimal tax is concerned with "utility" and "wealth maximization," with the economic ideal of "efficiency"—all terms I'll explain in due course. Optimal tax's most general lesson, against high marginal tax rates on upper-income earners, has indeed been picked up. It became a staple of the "supply side" economists and social critics influential in spawning Ronald Reagan's revolutionary decrease in tax rates. When Reagan took office, the marginal rate on the highest incomes was 70 percent, as it had been fairly steadily ever since the Kennedy administration. Within six years, Reagan had overseen the lowering of this top rate to 28 percent, creating the general shape of the rate structure that I am using in this book.

But another principal recommendation of optimal tax theory—to change the way society taxes married women—has not enjoyed the same success. Relatively conservative economists like Michael Boskin, eventually chairperson of the Council of Economic Advisors for George Bush, advocated rethinking the way America taxes secondary earners, whom Boskin knew overwhelmingly to be married women. The theory of optimal tax in one important way completes the accountant's tale, by demonstrating the large behavioral burden on women and its social costs. The theory also allows the criticism of the status quo to avoid charges of wanton social engineering—of the replacement of traditional family values with newfangled liberal ones. Optimal tax theory gives a solid, more or less "objective" groundwork for criticizing the way we do things.

Yet while optimal tax completes that story, brings it to a certain close, it also merely continues the intellectual history of the selective and gendered logic of tax. Why is it that a growth-oriented theory is followed when it favors the economy generally, and rich men and traditional families particularly, but not when it favors women? Another day, another gendered dynamic, another rhetorical question—and still no good answers.

A WORD FROM THE SPONSOR

I am about to get on with the theory of optimal tax. But first I want to exercise my authorial privilege and note something of the intellectual history of my own project, because this personal history plays a particularly important role at just this juncture in the story.

I have lived with the ideas of this book for many years. Ever since I developed a keen interest in tax as a law student, precisely for its social and political importance, I have been struck by its gendered aspects. This impression deepened as I began to teach and, later, as I read the scholarly literature—noticing both the persuasiveness of the relative handful of feminist critics of the status quo, like Grace Ganz Blumberg and Pamela Gann, and the suppression of their voices in the mainstream analysis.

I wrote two lengthy law review articles, each nearly two years in production, before turning to this book. I cannot ultimately complain about my personal academic good fortune, but the path has not always been smooth. Colleagues and superiors, in and out of tax, puzzled over my choice of topic and questioned the gendered basis of tax. Was I merely out to curry favor with the "politically correct" crowd? Was this all just about my own experience? (My wife happens to be a wonderful and wonderfully talented medical doctor, and we have two young daughters.) My specific findings were questioned and challenged. The law was indeed neutral, I was told repeatedly; it never spoke of gender directly, for example. Political theory and tax just could not mix. There would be no way to cure the problems I was noting, if they were indeed problems. I was just trying to substitute a two-worker family for the traditional single-earner one, and there is no disputing such tastes, at least within the confines of presumably neutral academic theory alone.

Sometimes the conversation became even more deeply gendered. Many colleagues told me, typically in the safety of private discussions, that traditional families with stay-at-home wives were good for society, for children, for men, even for women. The not so subtle message was that I should not rock the boat. Everywhere the gendered logic of tax had answers. Either the law was neutral, or whatever biases there were, such as the imputed income effect, were good. The world we live in could be very differently characterized, but always as the best of all possible worlds. I was advised to give up the project.

In the face of this opposition, I came to see that my project and I were simply living themselves out. By the early 1990s, when I was coming of age as a scholar, it had become acceptable, or at least accepted, that some women scholars would write about "feminist" topics. But men who wrote about feminist concerns were viewed with suspicion. The very charge that my personal life, politics, or preferences were somehow entering into and tainting my scholarship presumed some model of a pure, neutral style of scholarship to which men were supposed to aspire. Never mind that most of the colleagues who pressed criticisms on me were married men with stay-at-home wives; they just happened to be subscribing to independently neutral principles. All of these attitudes were especially powerful and entrenched when it came to financial and economic subjects like tax.

I came also to see that there was more than just gender and false conceptions of neutrality at work in triggering resistance to my project. It is not just that I am writing about families and family structures, a subject that obviously invites deep-seated value judgments and psychoanalytic twists. I am also writing about tax. Tax hits close to the bone. I recall interviewing for jobs in legal academia in the late 1980s. At the time, I was talking of simplifying the tax laws from a liberal political perspective. I found many sympathetic ears—until I mentioned the possible repeal of the mortgage interest deduction. This quite literally struck too close to home for most of my interviewers, as many contemporary politicians have since learned.

The link between tax and family is not just strategic or rhetorical. People react strongly against being taxed, and their thought processes in opposing tax may often be subconscious. Defenses go up, and arguments follow suit. My central proposal calls for taxing married men more. Almost all of my vehement opponents have been married men. I learned a lesson that politicians like Walter Mondale, George Bush, and Jim Florio have pondered in their enforced retirements from public office: People really do hate being taxed.

Alas, I continued to believe in my story, and I remained true to it throughout. I began to feel like some wild-eyed young inventor or screenwriter in an old Hollywood movie (Jimmy Stewart would make a nice leading man). If I could just find some way to sell the idea or tell the tale, people would no doubt see the light. After each encounter with hostile scholars, I would go back, consider the facts of tax law, reconfirm my beliefs, and write more assertively and specifically. The extended accountant's tale was intended to drive home the idea that the gendered basis of tax is not a fiction of a too active and too liberal imagination; it is a fact of life that any certified public accountant can see. Extensive historical references also helped to emphasize that there really is something here. Complaints of gender bias are not just a matter of one more complaint in the "never ending drama entitled 'Victims of Tax Injustice,'" as Boris Bittker sardonically put it, but a legitimate reaction to a deep and gendered history.

By the time I had finished my first article on taxation and the family, I had embarked on a formal study of economics. My growing understanding of economic forces, combined with the work I had done on tax, led me to believe that the story could not end with tax. This resulted in a second article, and many of the ideas we'll meet up with in the rest of the book. Once again, a pattern of denial, questioning, and hostility followed my project. The same rhetorical moves I had confronted in tax now came at me from the broader field of economics. Economics was neutral or, if it was not, ours was still somehow the best of all worlds. How could I be bending, twisting, even contorting economics to advance a feminist agenda?

No part of my project met with greater confusion, fear, or hostility than my use of optimal tax theory, although I see this theory as a helpful response to many basic questions and criticisms. Friends and critics alike on the left have been suspicious of my use of any economic theory at all. Friends and critics alike on the right have leveled charges that I am engaged in "social engineering," manipulating time-honored tools to serve a personal agenda. Those in the center have been, as they often are, puzzled. What is this theory of optimal tax? Do I really believe that we should move to some kind of crazy, counterintuitive, unequal, and perhaps even sexist plan of taxing men more than women?

Part 3 is meant to answer these questions, to explain, in a nontechnical way, the theory of optimal taxation and why I think that it is an important part of the story of taxing women, even if there are plenty of perfectly good reasons why we shouldn't just give in to it altogether. Once I have sketched out the basic theory of optimal tax, including its traditional grounding in utilitarian social theory, I will show how it yields important insights into a social theory not explicitly utilitarian, but concerned instead with issues of gender and justice in a complex and open-ended way. This set of moves should address centrist and other concerns. I have no intention of advocating a complete abandonment of practical tax politics to optimal tax theory and all of its counterintuitive recommendations. But optimal tax theory should help us to see the problems of taxing women in a better, brighter light, to generate reform proposals, and to see that this is not just a matter of one set of modern "liberal" preferences being set up against earlier, more "conservative" ones. Optimal tax theory adds to the chorus begun by the accountant's tale and further amplified by the excursions into political and intellectual history, all telling us that there is something deeply wrong with the way the United States taxes women.

I most definitely do not mean by any of this that optimal tax theory is neutral; the manipulable myth of neutrality has done enough damage in taxation already. As in all matters of tax, we have to make political judgments in deciding when, where, and to what extent to accept the precepts of optimal tax. But such theory does provide an external grounding for what I've been talking about throughout this book. It points to something outside the private subjective preferences of any one author, or of any liberal, culturally elite vanguard. It thus deserves a central position in the larger story of taxing women.

USING ECONOMICS

Just as we've seen that there is plenty of room to hide in tax, behind veils of neutrality or common sense or logic, economics is also invoked, consciously or not, as a way to avoid confrontation with gender. This explains some of the resistance to my invocation of optimal tax theory in a feminist context. Economics is neutral, the story goes; it is about utility and wealth maximization and real things like that. Feminist-oriented concerns are about politics and preferences, and have no part in the technical domain of economic theory. Commentators have often told me that I should not be "using" economics to advance feminist concerns, but should rather follow whatever "truth" economics ultimately reveal. This is a charge that hints at intellectual dishonesty, at result-orientation and ideological blinders.

To the extent that economics is or can be purely descriptive, there is something to this sentiment. We should be able to look to objective data to help test and check our political instincts. Economics—for which discipline I have a profound respect—is indeed often at its best and most powerful when it is most counterintuitive, most likely to change our ways of thinking. Yet a sense of gender injustice is so deep, so well confirmed by the equally factual teachings of ancient and recent history and the superficial workings of the law revealed in such renderings as the accountant's tale, that one has a right to expect that economics will bear out a general perception of gender bias, or else itself be suspect. What would we think if economics somehow told us that there was no bias against women, that everything had somehow become wondrously and perfectly "fair" and "neutral"? Would it be economics or the sense of gender justice that is more called into question?

But that is a bridge we most decidedly need not cross, because economic theory tells us that indeed there are severe biases against women, as long as we take a broad enough view. True intellectual honesty consists in stating prior beliefs up front, while holding these open to criticism and revision, for these beliefs cannot help influencing a search for and interpretation of real world data. My principal point in this and the next chapter is that an ostensibly neutral, objective, quasi-scientific economic theory precisely agrees with the long-standing feminist critique and the general lesson we've learned thus far: society is taxing women far too much, in exactly the wrong ways. A theme to emerge later is that the gender wage gap, another more or less objective index, has indeed been narrowing, but not at all for reasons that should lead us to believe that the quest for gender justice is at an end. People who are looking at the gender gap alone, or at certain other signs of women's participation in the paid workforce, are not looking at the whole picture.

If we begin our investigations of real-world data with the ideas that everything is fine, that women have been helped enough already, that there is no longer any real bias against women in America, and that markets work better than social interventions, we'll find numbers to back up these beliefs. But if we begin our empirical search instead with the firm conviction that something is wrong, we'll be led beyond the gender wage gap to ask questions about why it might be closing notwithstanding the continuing disproportionate stresses on women. If we are diligent and creative, we might come to something like the tax system, and a sense, which I shall expand on in part 4, that the particular narrowing of the gender gap is a part of the pattern of gender bias, not the harbinger of its end.

Even if we thus merely use economics as a tool for understanding the facts of our world—for better describing it—we confront and deepen our belief in gender injustice, as long as we are looking at the right places. But there is something uncomfortably incomplete in this view of things, which would confine economics to a purely descriptive domain and afford it a logical and intellectual priority over the subjective, normative, value-laden world of politics and preferences. Economics gives us just the facts, so this story goes, and our political theories should be built on a firm foundation of facts. What will it take to see that this is a dangerously and foolishly false dichotomy? That the world of finance, economics, and tax is ineradicably political? In some deep-seated ways, the priority of economics as scientific, positive description gets it backward. Economics is best understood as being about means, or instrumental reasoning; our ends have to come from elsewhere. What better place than the goal of equal concern and respect for all of our citizens? Shouldn't that come first?

What I want to make clear is why I am persisting in the use and description of optimal tax theory in this book on taxing women, notwithstanding the confusion or hostility to the idea from a wide range of sources, including my book editor. I am going to try and make my editor happy, at least, by setting out the theory of optimal tax briefly and simply. Then we can discuss why it is, and is not, relevant to the central tale.

OPTIMAL TAX, TAKE ONE: APPLES AND ORANGES

The basic insights of optimal tax theory are simple, and I can get them out easily enough with an example and a few pictures. Imagine a small island where the only goods are apples and oranges. In a given time period (the precise length of time does not matter), 100 apples and 100 oranges are bought, each for $1, by the 100 citizens. The government decides that it needs to raise $100 by a tax on apples and/or oranges. What tax should the government set?

The most intuitive answer is that the government should impose a 50 percent tax on both apples and oranges; it will then get one-half of the $100 spent on oranges and one-half of the $100 spent on apples for its needed total of $100. This simple answer appears neutral to us. The government is not picking and choosing between apple and orange growers or consumers, just applying a flat, across-the-board tax. This answer corresponds to the ideal of taxing equal-earning couples equally that has played such a large role in our discussions. But the problem with the simple and apparently neutral tax is that it ignores behavioral responses, just as the norm of taxing equal-earning couples does. In the case of the taxation of goods, this deficiency of naively neutral theories has been noted since at least 1927, with the seminal public finance work of Frank Ramsey. He pointed out that the responses of individuals to taxes have to be taken into account in assessing the real burden of any tax.

ELASTICITY, SUPPLY AND DEMAND, AND OTHER TERMS OF ART

This leads us to the technical term and concept of "elasticities." An elasticity measures the percentage change in one variable relative to the percentage change in another. I'll be concerned primarily with the "price elasticity of demand." This means that I'll look at how much demand for a product, which I will call a good, changes when its price does. An elasticity of 1, for example, means that a 10 percent fall in price leads to a 10 percent increase in quantity demanded; an elasticity of 0.5 means that a 10 percent fall in price leads to a 5 percent rise in quantity demanded, and so on. We are directly concerned with tax, of course, but because tax affects price, I can simplify and talk of price and quantity alone. The basic question now becomes, What happens to the price and quantity of apples and oranges purchased when the government imposes its 50 percent tax?

The price of a good is set by the intersection of supply and demand curves; the two curves operate like the blades of a pair of scissors, in Alfred Marshall's famous expression. In a competitive market, the supply curve is set by the "marginal cost" of a good—what it costs a producer to make one more item. This is another example of life on the margin. If a producer can get paid what it costs to make one more good, including a reasonable profit (because if the producer cannot make a reasonable profit on her investments, she might as well put her money in the bank), she'll do so. Let's assume that our island has such competitive markets and that the supply of both apples and oranges is perfectly *elastic*. This means that it costs farmers $1 to produce an apple or an orange, and they could produce an unlimited number at this price. This assumption keeps the example simple, without adversely affecting the analysis. Figure 5 gives a picture for this state of affairs. The *s* curves or lines in figure 5 stand for the supply curves; these are straight to capture the sense of perfect or infinite elasticity—farmers can supply any number of apples or oranges at the $1 price.

ENTER TAXES

The next question is, What happens to the price of apples and oranges after the government imposes the tax? The answer is that each rises to $2.

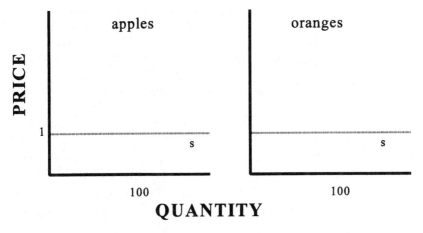

Figure 5. Supply of Apples and Oranges

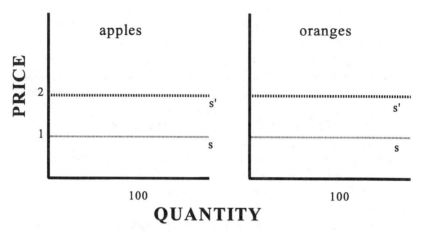

Figure 6. Supply of Apples and Oranges, after Tax

Why? At a 50 percent tax rate, the farmer has to pay one-half of what she receives for her apples or oranges. But it still costs her $1, before the tax, to produce an apple or an orange. It cannot cost her any less after the tax—the tax just adds one more cost, without affecting the other costs at all. She will have to raise her price to $2 so that she can keep the $1 she needs to cover her own costs and pass another $1 over to the government. Figure 6 adds this wrinkle, showing another supply curve, s', parallel to but above the first curve by the amount of the tax.

As an aside, note that we have already seen the point illustrated by figure 6: it is a point about incidence, just like what we saw when discussing social security. I noted then that the employer's share of the tax had to come out of employees' pockets. The same thing is happening with the island's apples and oranges. It looks as if the government is taxing the farmers, but the real burden is falling on consumers. The price just goes up to effect this shift. Most readers see this every day, when they purchase a good that is subject to a sales tax, and the seller just tallies the tax into the bottom-line price.

The final question is, What happens to the sales of apples and oranges—that is, the quantity bought and sold—when, after the government has imposed a 50 percent tax on each, the price of both rises to $2? Here comes the classic economist's answer, as Ramsey saw in 1927: it depends. On what? On the price elasticity of the demand for apples and oranges, in the technical language we learned a few paragraphs back. In other words, it depends on the shape of the demand curves for apples and oranges.

A DRAMATIC EXAMPLE

I'll exaggerate to drive home the basic point. Let's say that each of the 100 citizens of the little island simply must have an apple. Perhaps they all believe in the saying that an apple a day keeps the doctor away, and no price would make them want to see a doctor rather than eat an apple. Their demand for apples would then be completely *inelastic*. In other words, the price elasticity of demand for apples would be zero. The islanders would still want 100 apples, even at a $2 price.

You may be asking yourself, at this point, Why didn't farmers just charge more for apples even before the tax? The answer lies in the double-edged nature of supply and demand. Since apples cost only $1.00 to produce profitably, no farmer could get away with charging $2.00; some competitor would pop up next door, charge $1.75, and still make a large profit. The process would repeat until the price came down to the minimum profit level of $1.00. This is the importance of competition, and why many economic actors try to escape it—they try to get monopoly power so that they can raise the price to meet demand. Just imagine what would happen if some evil corporation bought up all of the world's water. How much would you pay for a drink on a hot afternoon? But how much do you in fact pay for a typical drink of water? Competition is good for consumers.

Back on the island, perhaps in part because they are so devoted to apples that they are willing to spend just about any sum on them, the islanders are not fully committed to oranges. It just so happened that, at a price of $1, they were each willing to purchase an orange. But for $2? Forget it, is their simple response; who needs oranges? In technical terms, this set of facts or preferences would mean that the demand for oranges is *highly elastic*—highly sensitive to price. Using an elasticity of 1 would mean that the 100 percent increase in the price of oranges, from $1 to $2, was matched by a 100 percent fall in demand for them, from 100 to zero. Figure 7 shows this final stage of our story, by bringing the demand curves into the pictures. Figure 7 reveals that, at a price of $1, consumers on the island would purchase 100 apples and 100 oranges, which is where this story started. But once the tax has increased the price of apples and oranges to $2 each, note what happens. Consumers still purchase 100 apples, as before, but now they purchase *no* oranges. The seemingly neutral and simple tax has resulted in a complete shutdown of the market for oranges!

AN AWKWARD CONVERSATION, AND A SURPRISING RULE

The tax now hardly appears neutral to the orange growers. Imagine that you are the government official in charge of tax policy, and a delegation

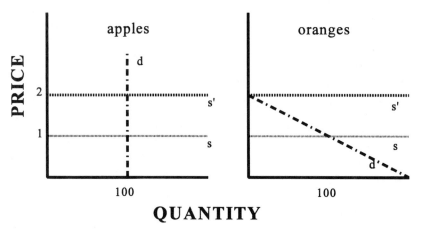

Figure 7. Supply and Demand, Apples and Oranges

of orange farmers comes to you in protest. What would you say? You could point to the apparent neutrality and appeal of the tax before it was put in place. But the orange farmers would know that the effect of the tax on them was wildly disparate and devastating. You could say that this is just plain bad luck—that neutral rules often have nonneutral effects. But the orange farmers would reply that you should have known better, that you should have done some research, conducted a few polls. Even a cursory investigation would have revealed the islanders' deep commitment to an apple a day, so that the eventual response to the tax was in fact fully predictable. There was nothing at all random, or a matter of pure luck, about the effects.

The orange growers are doing well enough in this rhetorical encounter, but they have an even stronger trump to play. As a curious fact, note that it would have been a far better government policy to impose a 50 percent tax on apples alone. This would have raised the price of apples to $2, as above, and brought the government its $100, but would then have had no effect on the market in oranges: 100 apples and 100 oranges would still be purchased. This would actually be a win-win situation, about which no one on our simple island ought to complain. Apple farmers would not care, since they would still sell 100 apples for a net, after-tax price of $1. The government would not care, since it would still get its $100. But orange growers and consumers would be downright happy. The orange growers will forgive you for your initial sin of believing in a naively simple neutrality, one that took no account of behaviors at all, as long as you will rectify the mistake now by doing the right thing and repealing the tax on oranges at no cost to anyone.

It turns out that this simple tale has captured the essence of what is known in public finance as "Ramsey taxation," "optimal commodity taxation," or, sometimes, the "inverse elasticity rule." The rule states that taxes on commodities should optimally be levied in inverse relation to their elasticities. Inelastically demanded goods, like apples, should be taxed at high rates; elastically demanded goods, like oranges, should not be. I'll discuss in the next chapter what is and is not so "optimal" about this approach. For now, the apples and oranges example shows that there is a good deal of sense—if not quite untutored "common" sense, something close to it, and in any event far short of wild-eyed liberal theory—in Ramsey taxation.

Indeed, society often follows the precepts of Ramsey taxation. We tax things like gasoline, for example, which are inelastic. On the other hand, we have had bad experiences with "luxury taxes" on yachts and other high-cost goods, precisely because we found out just how elastic the demand for such goods is. When George Bush imposed a luxury tax, he soon found out that people just stopped buying expensive new yachts: they had their old ones upgraded instead. Bush had to drop the tax soon after it was imposed, much to his embarrassment. Cigarettes and alcohol are more complicated stories: demand here is fairly inelastic, which means that these are good objects of taxation, if the government is after revenue, but hard behaviors to change, if that is the social goal. This dilemma often leaves a government dependent on harmful activities as a source of revenue; Mikhail Gorbachev found this out in the former Soviet Union, when his campaign against alcohol led to a plummet in government receipts from liquor taxes. In America, states eagerly advertise for lotteries that are, in essence, taxed at rates of 50 percent and upward; demand for this form of gambling is pretty inelastic.

It is time to point out one final curious fact: men as labor suppliers in America look like apple eaters, and women look like orange eaters. That is, men go on working in the aggregate, more or less the same way, no matter what the tax rate does to their take-home pay, but women do not. Women have two spheres of work, and they bounce back and forth between the paid workplace outside the home and the unpaid workplace within it. Even the seemingly bizarre, exaggerated numbers—a zero elasticity for apples, and an elasticity of 1 for oranges—are not so far off what has been found for married men and women. The story of taxing women is a curious one, indeed.

OPTIMAL TAX, TAKE TWO: ON INCOME, MEN, AND WOMEN

It took a while for the simple insights of Ramsey to be applied to income taxation, in part because there are some technical difficulties in making the transition, but the move has now been made. Optimal income tax theory began in earnest in the 1970s, with the pioneering work of British mathematical economist James Mirrlees and others. Ignoring most of the additional complications, a couple of which I'll mention in a moment, optimal income taxation simply involves making a few changes to the apples and oranges story set out above.

We are now concerned with individuals as labor suppliers; firms demand labor. As above, I'll simplify and put the firms largely out of the picture, here by assuming an infinitely elastic demand. Firms are willing to pay employees their "marginal product," or what value they add to the firm at the margin, again allowing for a reasonable profit to the firm. Let's assume that this marginal value, for all employees, is $10 an hour. At this wage, firms make a reasonable profit; if they paid higher wages, they would go bankrupt. Once again, with competitive markets, the wage rate should rise to this level. If any firm tried to get away with paying its workers $8 an hour, some competitor could lure the entire workforce away with an offer of $9, and still make a large profit, and so on, until the wage rate hit its competitive level of $10.

In the story of this subsection, men and women replace apple and orange eaters. Suppose men and women each work 40 hours per week at $10 an hour, but then a flat 50 percent income tax is put into effect. Of course, we should all know by now that married women are getting taxed at higher rates than men, but I'll keep it simple here.

The first question is, What happens to the wage rate paid by firms? The answer is that it stays at $10 an hour. Just as the tax on apples and oranges did not change the other costs facing the farmers, so an income tax, all other things being equal, does not change the marginal value of employees. This parallels the social security and fringe benefit story told before. Firms just keep paying wages equal to the marginal value of their workers. Employees bear the cost of taxes, and they sometimes choose to take out some of their value in the form of noncash benefits. But while the employer continues to pay $10 an hour out of its pockets, the employee now faces a $5 an hour wage rate after tax; this is his or her take-home pay.

Now what happens? Figure 8 tells the basic story. Figure 8 is much like figure 7 except that it substitutes varying supply curves for demand ones. Demand is almost always downward sloping, because if prices increase then demand decreases. Supply, on the other hand, is typically upward sloping, because if wages go up, hours worked also typically go up.

Figure 8 is drawn to show that men, like apple eaters, are inelastic in their work patterns. Men work 40 hours a week no matter what the wage. But women, like orange eaters, are very elastic. Lower the wage from $10 to $5 an hour, and the number of hours they work declines. The story is even more complicated, of course, and worse for women, because the labor market in America is not flexible: this is the "all or nothing" effect noted in chapter 6. Women are unlikely to find any options at all at the point where their supply curve intersects with their new after-tax wage

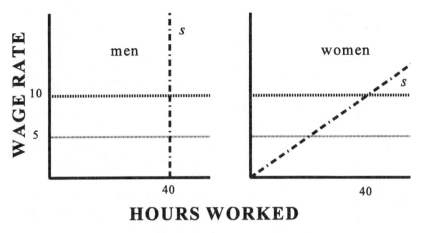

Figure 8. Men's and Women's Labor Supply, with Taxes

rate, so they will have to make second-best choices among working 40 hours per week, or not at all, or taking an inferior part-time job.

The principal idea of optimal income tax is, then, just the same as for optimal commodity tax: the inverse elasticity rule. Optimal income tax has become much more refined and complex than this simple discussion illustrates. But its major recommendations of relevance to us in this book are twofold, and are now easy to see. First, tax rates should generally be kept low, and perhaps ought to decline as income increases, because upper-income taxpayers tend to be more elastic than lower-income ones are. Second, married men should be taxed more than married women, because men are less elastic. It should not surprise any reader which one of the two recommendations has been taken up in the public political sphere—and which one utterly ignored.

A BIT MORE COMPLEXITY

I want to introduce just one further complication in the story, a complication that is easier to see with labor supply and income taxes before us. The elasticities I've been discussing can be broken down into two effects: an "income" one and a "substitution" one. When any tax is imposed, two things happen to workers. First, they have less money, because now they have to pay the tax. In our example, men who used to have $400 from their 40-hour job paying $10 an hour now take home $200. This is the *income effect* of the tax—any tax increase decreases income.

The second effect is that work looks less attractive after it has been taxed relative to other uses of time, which economists sometimes lump together and call "leisure," as in the phrase the "work-leisure trade-off." There is something gendered about this phrase, and about not having an equivalently standard reference for the "paid work/work at home/leisure" trade-off, which is a large part of what makes married women's elasticities so much higher than men's. (Many labor market economists have begun to use a more subtle, more accurate vocabulary to get at the three-part trade-offs involved.) This second effect is called a *substitution effect*. When a wage tax decreases the take-home wage rate, leisure becomes more attractive. A worker who was willing to put in another hour at the office for $10 may decide to just go home for $5. We can see this in different settings. A worker may be willing to put in longer hours if she is paid overtime, but not otherwise, and the orange eaters in the prior example were eager to choose substitute products when oranges went up to $2.

In the case of taxes on wages, income and substitution effects typically push in opposite directions: income effects lead people to work harder in the face of a tax, substitution ones push them to work less. The income effect means more hours of work are needed to make ends meet; if one of the men in our example had to have $300 a week to pay the family's bills, he would have to work harder in the face of the tax, which has reduced his take-home pay to $200. If the income effect is strong enough, elasticities of labor supply could even "bend backward," or go negative: decreasing take-home pay by increasing taxes could lead to *more* work. Such negative elasticities are in fact sometimes observed, especially in the case of married men. But the substitution effect cuts in the other direction: for a net $5 an hour, our hypothetical worker may prefer to stay home or go to the beach. When taxes go up, work pays less and therefore looks like a less attractive thing to do. Yet, for whatever reason, men do not seem to want to substitute leisure for work over a wide range of wage levels.

WOMEN'S "CHOICES"

For women, the story is once again more complicated. Married mothers have a choice that few men make: to stay home and care for the children, as Susan and Elizabeth did. Indeed, it seems that there is simply no realistic leisure option for most Americans at all. Substitution effects are weak, because there is no compelling choice but to work. In the face of this, as it now stands, men have no option at all but to work outside the home, while women, and women alone, have a choice—to work inside or outside the home. The situation is different yet again for lower-income households, and it is bleaker: Their "choice," whether consciously faced or not, is to be two-earner or single-parent households. Elasticities for lower-income women, and for members of racial minority groups like African Americans, many of whom are poor, are generally low. Poor women must work to make ends meet; what gives way for them is family structure itself.

To put this another way, the substitution of unpaid household work for paid market work, at least for the middle- and upper-income classes, is a reaction to income as well as substitution effects. Whereas income effects would strongly lead men to work more at their jobs, women typically have another potential source of income: the imputed, untaxed income they can get from staying at home, as Susan and Elizabeth did. Thus, while the effect of income on the primary worker, the "breadwinning" husband, is unambiguously in the direction of more paid work, the income effect on the secondary, marginal earner, the "homemaker" wife, may cut in the other direction, toward staying at home.

If the tax brings the value of the woman's paid work below her imputed income value, she will, rationally, stay home. Suppose that childcare and other household maintenance expenses are $6 an hour. If there is no tax, a woman who could make $10 an hour in the paid workforce could do so, keeping $4 after paying expenses. But once a 50 percent tax is put in place, this woman loses money by working, just as Elizabeth did; she will make $10, pay $6 in expenses, and give $5 to the government. In such a case, *income* is increased by *not* working outside the home. The income effects of a tax on wages, in effect, drive some women to work at home. It is not surprising that studies have consistently shown that married women react to tax increases by leaving the workforce.

There is a further wrinkle in optimal tax theory and the family that I am generally avoiding in this chapter: it is the idea of cross-elasticities—how a husband's behavior responds to his wife's, and vice versa. In most families, decisions about when and how much to work are obviously interconnected. The high elasticity of married women tends to play directly into a low elasticity for married men: As wives react to income and other effects by working less outside the home in the face of a tax increase, their husbands react to *both* the tax increase *and* their wives' withdrawal from paid work by working more outside the home. For all the complex economic theory and jargon embedded in optimal income tax theory, it is telling us what we already know. It is simply another telling of the accountant's tale that Susan and Elizabeth lived out. It is what at least some social reformers in the 1930s and 1940s wanted to happen, to drive women back home. It also points to the cycles portrayed by Arlie Hochschild and confirmed by common experience. The perversion of our tax system is exaggerating the gendered division of labor.

JUST THE FACTS

I have simply stated that women, especially married women, have higher labor supply elasticities than do men, especially married men. This is indeed true, as has been shown in many studies over a long period of time. I am not going to break with my habit at this point and extensively discuss these numbers in the text. I do, however, want to indicate a few points and puzzles about the numbers from these studies and suggest the ways that they might, and might not, be used in facilitating social debate and reform.

First of all, a great many studies have shown that "uncompensated" or "observed" elasticities for married women are higher than they are for men, and those studies that have looked at "compensated" elasticities, which is a harder thing to do, have shown that these, too, are higher for married women. Compensated elasticities are corrected for the income effect to look only at substitution effects; uncompensated elasticities, as we will see, are not. These studies cover periods from the 1970s through the effects of the Tax Reform Act of 1986.

Michael Boskin, writing with co-author Eytan Sheshinski in a 1983 article, observes that "studies invariably conclude that the labor supply of wives is much more elastic than that of husbands," and remarks that "the compensated wage elasticity of wives is five or six times as large as that for husbands." Boskin and Sheshinski go on to conclude that the optimal tax rate on husbands, under certain plausible conditions, "would be roughly twice that on wives." Robert Triest, writing in 1990 and reviewing two decades of research, concludes that "male labor supply is very price and income inelastic in all variants of the model estimated," and that the situation for women is more complex. I'll get back to Triest's observations on women's labor supply elasticities shortly. Mark Killingsworth and James Heckman, surveying the field in 1986, reported that "most of the estimates suggest that female labor supply elasticities are large both in absolute terms and relative to male elasticities."

So striking is the variance between male and female labor supply elasticities that the literature has split; economists who study such matters tend to specialize in one gender or the other. Chapters in major public economic sources are simply and exclusively devoted to male labor supply elasticities; large-scale studies focus on married women or married men. Men have generally been found to have observed or uncompensated elasticities ranging from as low as −1—meaning that they increase their work to keep exactly even with taxes as taxes increase—to zero, meaning that tax changes have no effects on them. John Pencavel, surveying the literature on men's labor supply patterns in 1986, gives his findings: "If a single number has to be attached . . . then for American prime-age men the (uncompensated) wage elasticity of hours of work is −0.10." Later, summarizing the "great deal of research" he found on male labor supply, Pencavel concludes that "the vast proportion of that work . . . indicates that the elasticities . . . are very small."

Women's observed elasticities, in contrast, tend to range from zero to well over 1. Anthony Atkinson, summarizing matters in 1995, found that nearly 50 studies of married women's labor supply published through the mid-1980s found on average a strikingly large elasticity of 2. The ranges are somewhat more constricted in the case of compensated elasticities, which may be thought to get at "true" preferences, unaffected by income. Once again, though, men's compensated elasticities are surprisingly low, typically very near zero. This indicates that men are wedded to existing patterns of work. Women's compensated elasticities, in contrast, typically range from 0.3 to 1.0 or higher; Atkinson found very little difference between compensated and uncompensated elasticities for married women in the 1970s and 1980s. These numbers indicate that women are conflicted about work outside the home and are quite sensitive to the wage level. Recall that an elasticity of zero simply means that whatever one's preferences for work are, they are unaffected by tax or wage rates. A high elasticity is thus inconsistent with a woman's preference for staying at home—it means she is quite willing to go to work, for the right wage.

A second set of observations, coming from economists who focus on women's behavior, is that wives reallocate their time from the paid workforce to unpaid work at home. As noted above, women's elasticities are not about a "work-leisure" trade-off, but a more complex one: "paid work/unpaid work/leisure." Jane Leuthold, an economist, wrote in 1983 that "while taxation has a small positive influence on total home production, it results in wives devoting more hours to home production and husbands fewer." In an article published a year later, Leuthold looked specifically at the effects of income splitting—a central feature of American law since 1948. Leuthold found that income splitting induces women to stay home: "The higher the tax rate on the first dollar the woman earns, the lower her disposable wage and the lower the probability of her participating in the labor market." Leuthold went on to find that women's participation in the paid workforce might increase by 25–35 percent or more under various plans for separate filing, with "the greatest percentage increases in labor-force participation . . . among wives in the higher income brackets." Once again, history, the accountant's tale, and economic theory are all singing the same song. Recall that the incentives to stay home were greatest on Ursula Upper, and this is exactly what the wealthy Traditionals in the 1930s and 1940s wanted.

Leuthold is not alone. In an article published in 1981, "Taxation and the Wife's Use of Time," the economists Janet Hunt, Charles DeLorme, and R. Carter Hill conclude that "the hypothesis cannot be rejected that wives *completely* reallocate hours of effort from market production to home production, with no change in leisure time, given a change in the marginal tax rate." This trio of economists goes on to note a point we'll encounter again: "The real loss may occur in the form of human capital depreciation of wives because of reduced labor-time attachment and lower hours of market work, an aspect of the tax structure that has been ignored." The "human capital depreciation" referred to by the economists is the loss of job market skills and experience that occurs when women, influenced by taxes among other factors, decide to stay home full time. The resulting fall in earnings potential can be especially harmful in the case of divorce. Today's stay-at-home wife often becomes tomorrow's divorcée struggling to make ends meet in a job market that values work experience outside the home—experience she lacks. Society is still ignoring this aspect of taxation, which would look to the widespread social effects of a tax system chosen, in part, to have just those effects. One wonders if there is a method, and a malice, in the seeming ignorance.

The class dimensions of the elasticity tale are also striking, and bear out our own more intuitive understanding gleaned from looking at the accountant's tale and the sample families in chapter 6. Nada Eissa, an economist, recently completed a detailed study of the labor supply reaction of married women to the Tax Reform Act of 1986. This law lowered marginal tax rates considerably, especially for upper-income taxpayers, although it also repealed the secondary-earner deduction. Eissa found an uncompensated elasticity of 0.8 for married women, which is quite high—recall the -0.10 number Pencavel found for men. Eissa was able to break this figure down into equal parts elasticity at the participation stage and at the stage of hours worked.

Lower-income women were less elastic. But this is what we would have guessed: upper-income women are subject to high tax rates, but at the same time have more flexibility in pursuing part-time jobs, precisely because they may care less about take-home pay. Thus, wealthier wives can be elastic when it comes to decisions about whether to work *and* how many hours per week to work. Lower-income women, in contrast, have to work, and have to work full time. The only question is the stability of their marriages. High tax rates on secondary earners at the lower-income levels translate into single-parent households. In other words, income effects are weak at upper incomes but strong at lower ones. Thus, we would expect a low observed elasticity for poorer wives at both the hours and the participation decision.

The case for changing the way we tax lower-income women rests more squarely on questions of gender justice and fairness than on optimal tax theory; the elasticity they have is in family structures. This once again brings us to the point that society should be concerned about marriage penalties among the poor, and secondary-earner biases among the middle and upper classes. In fact, though, society seems hardly to have noticed either effect. We continue to pay attention to the marriage penalty, not the secondary-earner bias, among the middle and upper classes; we pay attention to almost nothing about the poor, except for the costs of "helping" them. Time and time again, though, the data support our expectations—no surprise, given how well grounded in the facts are these expectations and how deeply gendered those facts are.

SOME TROUBLES WITH THE FACTS

All of these numbers have been shown fairly steadily. There are, however, numerous discrepancies and technicalities. Elasticities vary, based on when they were measured, who was in the study, and what time frame was used. Standard economic theory predicts that behavior will be fairly inelastic at first but will become more elastic in the long run—people change in the face of taxes, but not always quickly. There are numerous technical complexities in how models are specified; for example, how "cross elasticities," an issue I alluded to above, are employed. (These look to how the decisions of husband and wife interact.) One trend is that measures of labor supply elasticity in general seem to be getting smaller over time; current research has come in at the lower end of the spectrum. Partly this represents changes in prevalent economics methodology.

There is also a noticeable trend of working women's elasticities beginning to converge with those of working men. This is what Triest found when he looked at women's elasticities. When he sorted women into categories of workers and nonworkers, he found the elasticities of working women to be much lower, approaching men's. Triest found that "one interpretation of the results for women is that while hours of work conditional on participation are relatively inelastic . . . the participation decision is quite elastic with respect to the net wage." This is interesting, and it is consistent with the tenor of our general story. There is not a great deal of flexibility in *how* one works, so the high elasticity is concentrated at the point of working at all or not. James Heckman, one of the foremost experts in the field, surveyed twenty years of labor supply research in 1993. Heckman first noted the same effect Triest saw, namely, that married women's elasticities were getting smaller, although "generally still somewhat larger in absolute value than male labor supply elasticities." He then wrote of all workers that "elasticities are closer to 0 than 1 for hours-of-work . . . estimated *for those who are working*. A major lesson of the past 20 years is that the strongest empirical effects . . . on labor supply are to be found at the extensive margin—at the margin of entry and exit—where the elasticities are definitely not zero."

Of course, we have seen all this before: it is the "all or nothing" effect. The Uppers were not as pressed by this effect because Ursula had more latitude to work for other reasons than bottom-line dollars and cents, including maintaining her workplace skills for longer-range purposes. Hence Eissa's finding that wealthier wives are elastic relative to both hours and participation decisions is not surprising. But Susan and Elizabeth and Molly Middle know this all too well; their life stories confirm Heckman's observation. Heckman's words also bring us back to the importance of focusing on marginal decisions, as these women know.

Now, all this complexity and variation would be a problem, if we were social scientists bent on optimizing the tax system. I, at least, am not. I am interested only in gender justice, in achieving equal concern and respect for women. This leads me to look at the broad picture painted by optimal tax, one that confirms our sense that something is wrong. We have no need to be precise in implementing optimal tax precepts. Indeed, there are good reasons not to base rather permanent features of the tax system, like the rate structure, on transient and volatile data. There is, for example, a powerful and coherent story to be told about changing preferences over time—that in statistical terms women are beginning to occupy a position similar to men's because they have been given no other choice. We'll consider that later.

It is enough for now that we harden our resolve to look more closely at what is going on in tax, to rethink the gendered history and accountant's tale. After all, even if the labor supply elasticities of married women and men were identical, society shouldn't be taxing wives *more* than husbands. But that's just what we are doing, as a matter of fact. Something's definitely not optimal in the actual story of taxing women.

8 Not Just the Facts

ANY WAY YOU LOOK AT IT

In the previous chapter I gave a brief exposition of optimal tax theory and concluded with some of the data on which the theory rests its recommendation to tax married men far more than married women. In this chapter I mean to get somewhat more theoretical, to explain why we ought to pay some attention to optimal tax theory even though we would be wary of going all the way down an "optimal" path. I'll discuss what is, and is not, optimal about optimal tax theory.

The greatest payoff of the theory is that it adds an economist's tale to the accountant's, which had seen Susan and Elizabeth stay home after considering taxes and other work-related expenses. Much of what we've learned about the politics and intellectual history of taxing women should already be giving us pause. We have seen, time and time again, gendered decisions masked by superficially neutral logic and language. The accountant's tale added a certain practicality and common sense to all this. The economist's tale now shows us that it is hard to justify the current laws under any but the most gendered of lights, and that society is paying a large price—in terms of money and psychological stress heaped on women—for the status quo.

SEEING THE WORLD THROUGH ECONOMICS GLASSES

Recall the distinction between income effects, which look to the fact that taxes make people poorer, and substitution ones, which look to the tax-induced distortions in the price of goods and activities. Most economists, when working out a problem like an optimal tax one, care only about substitution effects. The reason can be variously stated, but basically it runs as follows: Since all taxes have income effects, the variable is the substitution effect, and economists care mainly about variables. Another way to put this point is that income effects reflect a desired transfer of resources, something the government wants to do, whereas the substitution effect interferes with market prices, thus distorting the allocation of resources.

To illustrate, a government official would not be worried about substitution effects if she wanted to alter prices. Let's say a reformer wanted to make dangerous, polluting, or unhealthy activities, like automobile driving or cigarette smoking, cost more in order to curb them. The substitution effect would be exactly what this reformer wanted; she *wants* consumers to make other choices. But the converse is that, if such price effects are not consciously desired, then they are unwanted distortions of people's choices—as we saw earlier with the apples-and-oranges example in chapter 7.

To see more clearly the reason economists care only about substitution effects, imagine that the government put a tax on something like apples and oranges and then returned the money to the very same people being taxed. Say that the government places the 50 percent tax on apples and oranges and prices of each go up to $2. The 100 islanders each pay $2 for their daily apple, and thus lose $1 to the tax. But then the islanders each get a check from the government for $1. One might be tempted to think that nothing but a silly give-and-take had transpired in this case, but that is not right. There has been no *income* effect due to the compensation that offsets the tax; with or without the tax, each islander has an apple and $1 more to spend. But the *pricing* or *substitution* effect of the tax remains in place. Apples and oranges still cost $2 after the tax, which will still be enough to shut down the orange market altogether. Economists are concerned about this pricing effect, and thus have developed complex means of converting observed or uncompensated elasticities, which reflect both income and substitution effects, into compensated elasticities, which look only to substitution effects. (Compensated elasticities thus have nothing to do with *real* income, on account of the fictional correction; this can seem counterintuitive at first.) That all sounds a bit odd, no doubt, but we'll see that it has a direct parallel to the actual means of taxing women and, curiously enough, to the practical tax proposals contained in the *Contracts*.

That's about as much complexity as I think we need, with one final note: Using compensated elasticities measures *utility* losses, and using observed or uncompensated elasticities measures *wealth* losses. By wealth, I just mean money; by utility, I refer to a psychological state of happiness or pleasure. Much economic and other social theory these days is utilitarian, in that it accepts as a goal the maximizing of individuals' happiness. We don't need to get into a broader discussion of all the problems and controversies with utility and how to measure it, in part because I have no intention of making a thoroughgoing utilitarian recommendation. Utility is, however, a helpful idea to entertain, precisely because it looks to some measure of well-being other than dollars alone.

When we correct for income effects, as the economists do, we are looking at some purely psychological loss. We can see this in the modified apples-and-oranges example. When the government gave the $1 back to each islander, wealth was not affected, so the only loss is the happiness that consumers got from being able to buy oranges for $1 each. But that is indeed a loss. The islanders will now do something else with that $1, but it will not bring them as much joy as the orange did: if it did, they would not have bought the orange in the first place, when it too cost $1.

In contrast, when we don't correct for income effects, we are looking at real, observable behavior, and this affects wealth. When women work less after a tax increase because their actual—observed or uncompensated—labor supply elasticity is high, there is less wealth in the society; money disappears. This is the essence of the Laffer Curve argument for lower taxes: If marginal rates get too high, people just stop working, and everyone loses. That argument looks to observed elasticities.

ADAM, EVE, AND THE GOVERNMENT

To see this latter point, let's say that all that exists on earth is Adam, Eve, and the government. (I apologize for the frightening prospect, but we really do need the government slithering around.) Adam and Eve each work 40 hours a week, making $10 an hour. The total social wealth is their $800 combined salary. Now imagine that the government puts a 50 percent tax on each. As Adam's observed elasticity is zero, he continues to work 40 hours a week, paying one-half of his earnings, or $200, to the government. But Eve's elasticity of 1 means that she cuts back 50 percent on her hours in the face of the 50 percent tax, and works only 20 hours, making $200 and giving $100 of it to the government. The total social wealth on the island is now $600: the government has $300, Adam $200, and Eve $100; Adam and Eve have $300 as a family.

Say that the government wants its $300, but decides to follow an optimal plan. What should it do? The answer is, once again, to tax only Adam, raising his tax rate to 75 percent. He still works 40 hours a week, as always, but now gives 75 percent of that, or $300, to the government. But Eve goes back to working 40 hours a week, and again earns $400. The island now has $800 of total wealth: $400 for Eve, $300 for the government, and $100 for Adam; Adam and Eve have $500 rather than $300 between them. By placing the tax on both, the society is throwing away $200.

Most economic theory has been concerned with maximizing utility, but most politicians are concerned with maximizing wealth. It is striking, though, that both wealth and utility maximizing argue for taxing married women significantly less than married men—that is, both observed and compensated elasticities for married women are significantly higher than they are for married men, as we saw at the end of chapter 7. We are not committed to being thoroughgoing wealth or utility maximizers, but there are still reasons to discuss both the psychological burden and the observed behavioral effects on women. Perhaps most puzzling of all—though the puzzle is beginning to look pretty familiar by this point—is that the United States is doing *exactly* the opposite of what utility and wealth maximizing, as well as compelling accounts of justice and fairness, dictate. We are taxing married women much more than married men. We are throwing away utility and money just to tax married women who try to work. The rest of this chapter explores these puzzles of social theory.

WHAT'S SO "OPTIMAL" ABOUT OPTIMAL TAX?

I've been a bit negligent in not getting more quickly to what must seem like an obvious question for many readers, namely, why these tax theories are called optimal. But just to answer that perfectly sensible question, we have needed the technical apparatus discussed so far. To an economist, optimal taxation is optimal because it "maximizes utility, subject to constraints." This language gives the standard form of most modern economic problems. Economists are always trying to maximize, to get the most of something. Being engaged in the science of scarcity, they are also always running up against constraints or limits—of money, time, technology, behaviors, and so on. What does this mean in the case of an optimal tax problem?

The economist begins with some "social welfare function," that is, some way of combining or aggregating individual utility levels. The easiest way is just to add up each person's utility, but many social welfare functions try to weight the utility of poorer classes more heavily. Whatever social welfare function is used—the specification of one is characteristically left outside the domain of economics itself—the goal of the economist as social planner is to maximize it. In trying to accomplish this result in an optimal income tax problem, there are two major constraints. First, there is a "budget" constraint; the government wants to raise a certain sum of money. There are ways of making this figure part of the problem itself, but, in standard and easier form, it is just a given, as I had the government wanting $100 in the apples-and-oranges example, or $300 from Adam and Eve.

The second constraint concerns the simple fact of life that people don't much *like* to work: they like money, and thus work to get it, but they also like leisure. In formal economics language, this leads to a "participation" or "incentive compatible" constraint. In a simple optimal income tax problem, a single utility function is specified for all individuals. The utility function incorporates preferences about work and leisure. In terms of our discussion so far, this comes down to incorporating the labor supply elasticities into the problem or model, as an economist would call it. The common sense of all this is, again, easy to see. If the government taxes the wrong people too much, they will just stop working, and everyone will lose.

The apples-and-oranges example illustrates an optimal tax problem. The government wants to maximize utility, subject to (1) its need to raise $100, and (2) individual preferences that lead to given compensated elasticities of zero for apples and 1 for oranges. What should it do? The answer is to tax apples only. Here again is the inverse elasticity rule. Taxing oranges simply results in a pure utility loss—no one buys oranges, and so the government gets no more money, but all the islanders lose some happiness. To a utility-maximizing economist, this is inefficient or wasteful. She would have no difficulty in granting the orange growers' petition to repeal the tax on oranges.

Now let's consider a hypothetical government official who cares only about bottom-line dollars and cents. She thinks in terms of balanced budgets and in publicly known measures of productivity and growth, such as GDP. She thinks that all talk of psychological utility is gibberish. It turns out, however, that this typical official would do much the same thing as the utility-maximizing economist, only she would try to maximize social wealth, not utility, subject to a constraint involving observed, not compensated, elasticities. This is, once again, the Laffer Curve idea behind the various "supply side," pro-growth, "pie expanding" arguments for lower taxes. Indeed, optimal tax in its general recommendation for lower marginal tax rates provided the intellectual backing for Laffer. All the government cares about is its own take and GDP. How can it raise the billions of dollars it needs with the least effect on GDP? The answer is, yet again, the inverse elasticity rule, only using observed elasticities. In the case of Adam and Eve, the government is happier with a total social wealth of $800, so it will tax Adam alone.

That's it. That's what's optimal about optimal tax. Using compensated elasticities, optimal tax shows how to maximize social utility given a government's need for revenue and individuals' aversion to working to pay taxes. Using observed or uncompensated elasticities, optimal tax shows how to maximize social wealth subject to the same two constraints.

Now it is time to get back to what we really care about in this book: equal concern and respect for women. What could all of this optimal tax stuff possibly have to do with that?

WHY SHOULD WE CARE?

Women, especially married women with children, have much higher compensated and uncompensated labor supply elasticities than do men, especially married men. Now the question is, So what? Why should we care? Surely people concerned with equality for women are not thoroughgoing wealth or utility maximizers. Most social theorists are disturbed by too much talk of utility functions and levels; almost no one but a particularly crude politician would be concerned with money, per se, to the exclusion of important norms such as equal concern and respect. And yet we, in our story of taxing women, are indeed concerned with both the utility and the wealth-maximizing parts of optimal tax theory, and a few things more. Partly I'm just continuing the intellectual/historical theme: Why has society followed the part of optimal income tax's recommendations that suggests lower rates on men and not the part that suggests still lower rates on women? Why is America 180 degrees backward in the way it taxes married women? But there is more. Let's look at the utility and wealth parts separately.

Utility, Neutrality (Again), and Psychologically Taxing Women

Using compensated elasticities that remove income effects from consideration shows us something that we've suspected all along, from the manifest signs of everyday life: women are bearing more of the psychological stresses of modern living than are men. It is not necessary to believe fully in objective, measurable utility, much less become a utilitarian, to see this. Even once we've put income effects off to the side, men are more committed to the workplace than are women. Men like to work outside the home, and women are conflicted about where to work. Psychological studies and common experience confirm that men, in the aggregate, are strongly committed to the full-time workweek model and are uneasy about women's entering into "their" domain of work, especially on terms and conditions equal to or better than what they, the men, get. The history in part 1 gave us a look at these attitudes in action. Social attitudes remain unchanged; a majority of people still seem to think that married women should give up their jobs when jobs are scarce and their husbands can support them. All of this means that women are pushed around more by changes in the tax law, and lose happiness more than men do when taxes increase. Women look like the orange eaters, who see all their pleasure from eating oranges disappear even if they are given their money back.

Several points are worth noting here. First, the compensated elasticity figures give the lie to an idea, subtly but misleadingly exploited in conservative political rhetoric, that women really want to stay home and rear their children. This is very often a myth of oppressors—that the oppressed somehow like it that way, or that nature dictates that things be so. For this reason alone we should be suspicious of arguments that take this form, and we should subject them to strict scrutiny. In this particular case, they do not survive even a mildly critical look.

Second, as strange and counterfactual as the "compensation" that goes into compensated elasticities may sound, it is, in fact, exactly what the tax laws have often done and what the conservatives aim to do again. Optimal tax, with its alien vocabulary, helps us to understand the dynamics of the *Contract with America* and other conservative tax plans. The linchpin of the *Contracts'* agenda, as we'll see in the next chapter, is child, not child-care, credits. The precise effect of such child credits is to give families money, while leaving in place the price distortions that disfavor secondary-earner work. This is what America did in 1939, when it gave away the social security pot of gold to the Traditionals, and again in 1948, with the postwar peace dividend. It is also what many other countries do when they give financial breaks to stay-at-home wives. The child-credit plan looks like the modified apples-and-oranges example, where the tax was left in place to distort prices but the money was rebated to the islanders.

Third, optimal tax theory, using the language of compensated elasticities and utility, gives us an affirmative argument, a way to ground the feminist criticism of tax's status quo. There is plenty to concern us anyway: the history of gendered provisions, the facts of the accounting tale, the manifestly conflicted state of American women today. But optimal tax theory helps to explain all of this and to show us that society really is taxing women—in both a psychological and a fiscal sense—more than it taxes men. Men do not face pressure to change their life choices. Men are not on the margin. Women are. Optimal tax theory tells us one more time that America is doing something wrong, and it is the voices of real women, through the observed data, telling us that.

Not Going All the Way

Most of us would not want to turn our political life and social theories over to a thoroughgoing utilitarianism. As one example, optimal tax would suggest taxing life-sustaining drugs—for which the demand is very inelastic, indeed—at high rates, and candy bars or other trivialities at low rates. Most of us would find that improper. Of course, most economists would find this improper, too, and would modify their social welfare function to take the problem into account. I don't mean to impugn economists or their tools, only to illustrate the need for sound moral judgments in applying those tools. But optimal income taxation of men and women shows us that society is acting against utility in a particularly troubling way. It leads us to do something that we often do in practice but rarely discuss in theory: to examine what is behind private preferences, their relative importance or "urgency," to borrow a term from the philosopher Thomas Scanlon.

We don't have to be slaves to the dictates of optimal tax, but we can use it to raise a red flag or two. When optimal tax tells us that we are doing something wrong, we can examine the charge and see if there is anything politically or socially appropriate in not following the "optimal" path. Optimal tax, like much of economics, can be thought of as a method for revealing the costs or trade-offs involved in any given policy. In the case of demand for life-sustaining drugs, for example, we feel that the inelasticity is appropriate and compelling—it reflects an obvious urgency—and we would feel wrong in burdening it. The elasticity of candy bar consumption strikes us as a more trivial matter. When it comes to candy bars and life-sustaining drugs, we can put utility-maximizing aside because of our objective, reasonable, social and political judgments: we are willing to pay the price of not being "optimal."

In the case of men and women, optimal income tax theory tells us to tax married men more, and married women less. At a minimum, this should lead us to abandon our perverse practice of doing exactly the opposite, of taxing wives more. We should definitely go at least as far as instituting separate filing for earnings and the other modifications discussed in prior chapters, and perhaps optimal tax's greatest political insight is just that. Should we go further?

We ought to be asking why it is that married women have higher compensated elasticities than married men. Then, once again, our minds will be directed toward history and the many gendered bases of our culture. Men are socialized into a role as breadwinners. Having had power over tax and other socioeconomic systems, men have set these up to protect and perpetuate their roles, often deliberately, and even at the cost of ignoring and burdening women. Indeed, men have actively tried to distort women's choices, have tried to keep them at home. The historical investigations in part 1 join with modern psychological studies in supporting this view, and the next chapter will show that some parties are still very much at it. A male-dominated society saw women's conflicted, tentative desires to get out of the home and explore the world of work, in the 1940s and thereabouts. Concluding that such a desire was not only not urgent, but was contrary to their own desires, society then *over*taxed women, in an attempt to nip the rebellious desires in the bud. Respectful equality ought not to tolerate such behavior.

Women have struggled throughout American history to emerge as free and equal participants in our social life. The high compensated elasticity of many women, especially throughout the 1970s and 1980s, and even more especially among married women not yet in the paid workforce, reflects many of the pressures and ambivalences they confront in juggling the roles of mother and worker. It reflects the pressures of having two spheres of work. Nancy Chodorow's ideas are pertinent here as well. Burdened by countless generations of the imposition of the mothering role on them and by its social reproduction, women are now struggling to define new roles outside the home as well—and society has thrown a massive fiscal tax at them, to make it all the harder. Even the low observed elasticities of women now working outside the home should raise some troubling questions. Why have women's preferences changed so much, so quickly? Why are women beginning to look more like men, from a statistical perspective? It is not clear that this pattern is all to the good, as I'll continue to discuss later.

Meanwhile, men generally have never faced particular stresses about juggling their roles as father and worker. These roles have grown up alongside each other for most men, who also do not face the heaviest burdens of taxes on their choices. Recall the social security system, as amended in 1939 and hardened thereafter. The 50 percent share given automatically to wives of working men, and their 100 percent widow's share, confirmed the man's role as breadwinner, rewarded his work, and gave him as a matter of pure largesse what a good solid provider would want to purchase, anyway—old age and disability insurance for himself and his "dependents," meaning principally his spouse. Contrast what happens to the wife's labor market earnings under social security. Over most ranges, these are subject to a pure tax. The law just takes money from wives who work outside the home and gives them nothing in return. Women are paying a tax for the privilege of working, and the tax is being passed in large part to men so that they can better play the role of breadwinners in families where the women stay home. The fringe benefit system plays out this same dynamic. Traditional forces used their power over the tax system and the economy more generally to perpetuate and entrench these gendered roles. That ought to have been, and ought still to be, unconscionable.

The income effect on men is simple and consistent: it pushes toward more paid work, because men have not developed the major imputed income skills of childrearing and housekeeping. But men should not be rewarded for their selective incompetence. Real and more dramatic changes may not come until men, too, bear some of the psychological burdens of a world that they have largely created—and this is *exactly* what optimal tax theory is telling us. It tells us to tax people like the apple eaters, who simply must have their way, just exactly to the point where their behavior becomes as sensitive to the effects of tax as everyone else's behavior is. Men have insisted on having their way at every turn, and they have changed very little during a period in which women and women's roles have been in turmoil. A strong argument can be made that we should tax men and reduce the tax on women until the two genders are equally buffeted about by tax's influence; this is where a dynamic, behavioral focus leads. The hands of society are imprinted on the elasticity figures. There is nothing random or arbitrary about the numbers for women's and men's labor supply preferences; this is not like the cases of candy bar eaters or life-sustaining drug users.

Another way to put this final point is that optimal income tax theory is in a certain sense "neutral." Optimal tax strives for equality in terms of impact—placing an equal burden on individual choice. Viewing families as equal or not on the basis of the dollars they have earned in the workplace sacrifices important questions of behavior to static facts of income. How much utility is lost? To what extent are people's choices distorted by taxes? This is the task that Frank Ramsey set for himself in 1927 and that has been followed by economists to this day. Taxing people with a high compensated elasticity means that we are depriving them of happiness and distorting their choices. What optimal income tax theory tells us is that we should distribute the psychological pain of tax evenly, and this means that we should be taxing married women far less than married men. What we are doing is exactly, completely, purposefully the opposite.

What about the Poor?

Another puzzle raised by our consideration of optimal tax theory is what to do about the poor. Lower-income women are rather inelastic. One suspects a large gap here between compensated and observed elasticities; such women may well want to stay home, but they are pushed to work by income effects. This suggests that it is indeed efficient to tax lower-income secondary earners, but we get this money at the price of stable family structures. The high labor supply elasticity of married women among the middle- and upper-income classes suggests that it is the secondary-earner bias, and not the marriage penalty, that we should be looking at there; the fragility of marriages and family structures among the poor suggests that it is the marriage penalty, not the secondary-earner bias, that we should be looking at there. Instead, society gets pretty close to doing the opposite. We endlessly focus on the marriage penalty among the middle and upper classes, and we don't think about the poor much at all.

Lower-income women and their low elasticities illustrate a central point that I have been implying for some time: Optimal tax is not everything. Economists combine the techniques of optimal tax with the tools of social welfare theory, and they are quite capable of taking into account values that favor redistribution. A standard policy recommendation, for example, is that society should help out the poor with lump-sum transfers of money, educational assistance, vouchers for food or housing, and so on. Perhaps we should take care to give an added bonus to lower-income married couples, because marriage itself is so fragile among the poor, because we generally value marriage, and because many studies have shown that stable marriages are good for children and for the economic development of the entire family unit. But at least we shouldn't be *penalizing* marriage among the poor, as we clearly are.

We really don't need a sophisticated economic theory to tell us that there is something troubling about families in the lower-income classes. Our eyes and ears should be sufficient. The facts of tax give us valuable insights into the problems of the poor, because we can see the high marriage penalties there. Optimal tax is more helpful in getting us to see the problems of the other income classes, where we've generally been focusing on the wrong thing: we should be looking at the secondary-earner bias, not the marriage penalty.

Looking at Money

A parallel line of reasoning follows the wealth-maximizing, observed elasticity effect. Once again, I suspect that most readers are not so concerned with wealth maximization—making the dollar value of goods and services as high as possible—that they would be willing to sacrifice all norms of equality and fairness to it. A simple substitution drives home this skepticism. Let's replace Adam with a dedicated child who works constantly to provide for a sick parent. I'll replace Eve with a generic loafer who prefers hanging out on the beach to working. Once again I suspect that we would recoil at the optimal income tax recommendation here: Tax the dedicated child, and leave the loafer alone.

But perhaps even more than with the necessarily abstract argument about the psychological dimension of utility, those who care about the gendered aspects of taxing women ought to care about the observed elasticities of men and women. There are at least three reasons. One, observed changes in the behaviors of married women affect social stereotypes and the rational decisions of employers. A large problem facing each individual married woman in the labor markets is that all married women, as a group, are more elastic than men. This is what businesses see. Women move back and forth between the paid and unpaid markets—working all the time—and employers rationally conclude that women are less stable employees. This sets in motion a series of vicious cycles that we've already seen and will explore further.

A second reason to care about observed elasticities and their metric, money, is that wealth *does* count, even among those who would not worship falsely at its feet. The higher elasticity of married women, combined with the perversely higher marginal tax rates facing them, keeps women at the margin and less wealthy than men. A friend once asked me whether rules governing the ownership of property as between men and women are not more important than tax. The question puzzled me, for, knowing what I do about tax, I could not see the distinction it implied. Even if one independently cares about the wealth and power of women, for their own sakes—and there are, indeed, very good reasons to care about just this, as feminists such as Catharine MacKinnon and others have been powerfully arguing for some time—tax is a large part of the problem.

Current tax laws push women to stay at home, and they push men to work more. We saw how dramatic these incentives were for the Uppers, the only segment of society likely to have significant wealth and real assets. Susan came to see that her comfortable salary as a secondary earner in an upper-income home didn't add much to the family's bottom line, but it kept her away from her children a great deal, so she, too, stayed home. Most high-ranking executives in America today seem to be married men with stay-at-home wives. When women leave the paid workforce, altogether or for long stretches, they sacrifice a very important form of property—their own earning capacities, what economists refer to as "human capital." This sacrifice will fall especially heavily on the large class of divorced women; one-half or more of all American marriages end in divorce.

Under these conditions, the only way to see that women get more wealth is to move toward a community property regime, in which women share in the family's total assets. Now this may, indeed, be a good idea, on a variety of grounds, but it has a paradoxical effect under current tax laws: it would further encourage a gendered division of labor. On purely economic grounds, giving a wife a one-half stake in the family's assets encourages her to think of ways to maximize the family's wealth, and this will often mean, as with Susan and Elizabeth, that she'll stay home, accepting the role of marginal or secondary earner. Recall here the story of the Washington lawyers, Connie and David, who openly and upfront decided to put the wife's career second. We saw how Umberto Upper's $4,000 raise could bring the same bottom line to the family as Ursula's full-time, $30,000-a-year job.

Feminists have long been on the horns of this dilemma, as Reva Siegel's work about nineteenth-century women's rights advocates helps to show. Should one encourage women's autonomy by rewarding their separate labor or instead encourage greater wealth and power by allowing women to share in all of the family's assets? This problem takes on a particular urgency in the common case of divorce. That this is a deep bind for women, likely to split their ranks, while it is little more than a possible threat to men, is another disturbing aspect of the gendered structure of our political and economic consciousness.

Third, as with the above discussion under compensated elasticities, we are drawn on pragmatic and sensible grounds to ask why the observed preferences are as they appear. In the case of the dedicated child and the loafer, we are prepared to put optimal tax recommendations off to the side because here we have no compelling moral reason to follow its counterintuitive precepts. The dedicated child's low elasticity is driven by a strong need for money that we find morally sympathetic; the loafer's high elasticity is driven by a strong desire for leisure—not to work—that we find morally unsympathetic.

But with the observed elasticity gaps between men and women, things are different. Why are men so doggedly devoted to paid work, while women move back and forth between two spheres of work? The hands of society are implicated in this status quo. It is precisely because domestic work has been gendered for so long and because we have long had—and no doubt still have—much labor market discrimination against women, that women face a choice men do not. The inflexibility of the labor market fits in at this point, too. A rigid workplace complements the male patterns of work that have remained fixed throughout the century. Since men have not had to change, their chosen model of work has not had to change, either. Yet another issue is child care and its various costs, financial as well as psychological. Since we have implicitly pegged these costs to women, in terms of both social norms and the financial reality of the accountant's tale, married mothers are highly elastic at the point of deciding whether to work at all—the child-care cross is theirs, alone, to bear.

Men ought not to stand around while women are tossed in all directions. If society really believes in equality, men ought to bear more of the burden financially and psychologically. If we think that all this talk of gender and equality is formless and unspecific, optimal tax theory tells us otherwise: we are doing *exactly* the wrong thing, if we care about utility, wealth, or women—that is, if we care about anything other than men alone.

NAVIGATING SCYLLA AND CHARYBDIS

A dilemma faces modern social theory. On the one hand, the individualistic orientation of classical liberalism has led to norms of autonomy and freedom that suggest we should respect individuals' private preferences and let markets work themselves out on their own. This is the ideal of "consumer sovereignty" that is taken to distinguish the great American democratic-capitalist spirit from the central planning of socialist states and failed communist regimes. We'll get a good look at this cluster of ideas in the words of Richard Epstein, to be examined in chapter 12. But if we simply take all revealed preferences as inviolate, what role is there for social theory? Are we doomed, as liberals, to accept whatever there is as the best of all possible worlds? Indeed, much modern normative economics theory seems obsessed with coming up with situations where a given change will make everyone happy; this is known as "Pareto superiority," the central norm of contemporary social welfare economics. But one can well ask how much there is for social theory to do if it is limited to pointing out situations where individuals, for one reason or another, have simply and uncontroversially failed to help themselves.

If the passivity and inertia of market-oriented theories hold out one danger for the social reformer, their opposite number is the unbridled subjectivity of non-individualistic norms. Reformers often try to get around actual, observed preferences by claiming that we are all "socially constructed," that preferences emerging from a flawed society need not be respected. But this line of reasoning has its own obvious limits. Once we have left the autonomous realm of the market, aren't we immediately at the other extreme? What is to prevent government officials from imposing their own values on others? This is paternalism, at best, tyranny, at worst. Indeed, a good deal of the appeal of laissez-faire, abstentionist arguments flow simply and easily from the horrors, real and imagined, of government intervention. We are left, then, doing too little or too much—both unappealing choices. The deck is stacked in favor of doing too little, as is our human wont.

Optimal tax theory provides, in one important category of cases, a way to navigate these twin perils. It tells us how to tax individuals in a way that is responsive to their revealed preferences. Nothing in optimal tax theory rests directly on feminist or other liberal attitudes or beliefs about the family, or about the ideal roles of men, women, and work. Optimal tax theory does not set out to substitute a "liberal" model of family for a "conservative" one. To return to the warning against the use and abuse of economics theory, feminists and other progressive critics would indeed be in a dilemma if the numbers came out differently—if, for example, they showed us that women really did want to stay home. Then the progressive bent on change would indeed have to argue against revealed preferences.

Optimal tax theory shows that we have to do no such thing. Not that we would not want to. History and the accountant's tale provide plenty of ammunition, resting on concerns over justice and fairness, that things ought to change. The neutral principles held up to impede the quest for gender justice in tax have been shown to be mere facades from a patriarchal past. But we don't have to fight out that battle all the way. Basic norms of justice and decency, buttressed by history and the accountant's tale, can count on arguments from utility- and wealth-maximizing to support them. This leaves us only to wrestle with the puzzle, and the embarrassment, that society has failed to follow the advice and plaintive cries of both economists and feminists. We have nowhere left to hide.

ELASTICITIES AND THE PUZZLES OF TIME

Let's get back to the facts of the matter—the statistics on labor supply elasticities. If we were really serious about optimal tax, we would have a puzzle in looking at elasticities. Women's elasticities are high now, in part because they are on the margin, and men's are low, because they are not. But it may not always have been so. Perhaps women once did more readily accept their role as homemakers, and so were inelastic: no offered wage could lure them out of the home. There is also the effect noted by Triest, Heckman, and others, namely, that women who work outside the home start having a commitment to the workforce that looks like men's always has; this is an effect that is especially important among lower-income women.

In general, there has been a swing in academic economics thinking of late, toward estimating that elasticities and other behavioral responses to tax are low. This is in itself an interesting piece of intellectual history, for the trend was at the opposite end of the spectrum—toward thinking that the behavioral responses to tax were strong—in the 1970s and early 1980s. This was a time when the main reform issues on the table happened to be high marginal tax rates in general. These, of course, happened to be tax matters that affected the traditionally male spheres of work and savings. Putting this curiosity aside, it seems clear that elasticities both are subject to widely varying estimations and, in fact, change over time.

Looking at how labor supply elasticities change over time, which few economists (Claudia Goldin is a notable exception) and fewer general social theoreticians have done, is interesting, for it paints a picture of just how preferences respond to social circumstances. This approach is different from the ad hoc dismissal of private preferences as "socially constructed," which we sometimes encounter. Looking at how preferences change over time gives insight into the very facts of changing tastes. It is not a dismissal of private preferences but a deeper, more complex look at them. There is a coherent story to tell about how married women's labor supply elasticities could go so quickly from low to high, then back to low. At first, wives more or less had to stay home, and they made a virtue of this necessity: they came to value their role as homemakers, and they were inelastic. When formal barriers to their outside work were lifted, women were curious and ambivalent—so they became highly elastic. But women soon learned that they could not be elastic in the man's world of the workforce—a world set up for and still largely peopled by full-time, fully committed, inelastic men. Women changed, again, to look statistically like men. This is not, of course, an altogether happy tale, and I'll get back to it later.

Still, the puzzle forces us to pick a specific period whose elasticities are to count if we want to implement an optimal tax solution. True fidelity to optimal tax also requires us to revisit the issue periodically—something we might want to do anyway, but not out of a quasi-scientific demand. Finally, time presents another puzzle, which we'll have to grapple with at some point: what do we do now, when many families have been set up along the traditional model that the structure of the law encourages? Can we just pull the rug out from under them by taxing their choice particularly heavily? Justice would seem, at first thought, to dictate some fidelity to existing patterns built up in reliance on the status quo, although it would be perverse, indeed, if the gendered structure set up in the 1930s and 1940s was ours "for all time," just because we hadn't come to see its pernicious effects sooner.

Optimal tax buttresses the accountant's tale and the lessons of history. Something is wrong—indeed, something is precisely backward—unless society is trying deliberately to impose an especially large burden on women, keep them at home, and maintain a gendered division of labor, all at a significant real cost in national wealth. Optimal tax, in the service of maximizing utility or wealth, would suggest taxing married men more than married women, perhaps two or more times as much. We don't have to go that far, but we should at least stop the unjust and wasteful practice of taxing married women more than married men. And we should be unapologetic in doing so, and hardened against the selective charges that we are the ones engaged in social engineering. The engineering in serving this end is less interventionist, and more just, than the gargantuan project of social construction that has gone into building up the gendered morass we live in today.

A FINAL NOTE: TAXING MEN

This book is about taxing women; that's what titles are for. But it should not escape any reader that the practical drift of my ideas is to tax married women less and married men more. Most of my efforts have been on the first prong—establishing the practical effects, the intellectual and political history, the economic theory, all pointing to something wrong in how society is taxing women. But optimal tax has also led us to see the reasons for, and importance of, taxing men more, even if this kicks up intense and often subliminal psychological resistance to the plan. It is time for things to change, as we'll see even more urgently later.

I want to emphasize that I do not present this idea as any kind of "male bashing." Occasionally one reads of proposals, mildly satiric and Swiftian in tone, that we should tax men more than women. Often these arguments point out the facts that men generate a large share of the costs of crime in this country, use up more resources such as health services, are often financially irresponsible parents, and so on. I have no particular position on these ideas—a main thrust of this book is that tax *is* political, after all, so these points are fair game—but I want to make clear that they differ from the drift of the recommendations we have just seen.

Taxing men more and women less is an efficient, wealth-maximizing move, and so should allow tax rates to come down while GDP grows. But this is really the least of it. A core problem in taxing women is that women are multiply stressed—by modern life itself, by tax and other laws set up by a patriarchal society in part to keep them at home, by conflicting roles of mother and worker, by the vestiges of discrimination, by employers acting rationally in the face of observed behaviors transpiring under markedly gendered conditions. Men are not bearing their full share of the psychological burdens of tax. Women are on the margin, and the margin is being taxed especially heavily. What we have now seen is that society should tax the margin especially *lightly*. In practical terms, this means that things ought to change. Men ought to pay their fair share.

Another way to reach this point is to consider that the low elasticities of men reflect in part the fact that the imputed income spheres of child-rearing and housekeeping are not viable for them. Whereas women move back and forth between domains of work in response to increased taxes, men only have one place to turn. Indeed, as women withdraw from paid work to generate more imputed income, men are drawn more to the paid workforce, to replace the cash lost when their wives stay home. But why should we take the fact of male incompetence at home for granted, as a fixed point for all time? Taxing men more encourages *them* to develop imputed income skills—to stay home with the kids once in a while.

One of the stronger and more common objections leveled against my project by colleagues, as I noted above, was that society should like the imputed income bias because children benefit from being cared for at home. True enough, I would reply, but why should it always and only be the *wife* who has the incentive? Any real-world income tax system has an imputed income bias that encourages self-supplied labor. Taxing men more just shifts some of this inducement to them. It indeed turns out that *paternal* involvement with children has positive effects, and much feminist social theory is concerned with an image of two-*parent* households, the domestic analogue to two-worker families. The nearly exclusive focus on the changing roles of women has ignored the near total fixity of men's roles. But this fixity is part of the problem. Once again, think of the general patterns of work. As long as men are not compelled to consider helping out at home, they can go on working full time or even longer hours; the long work week remains the norm, and Arlie Hochschild's cycles get compounded further.

A large problem for social theory has been figuring out the means to get from here to there. Just asking for men to do more around the house, or crying out for institutional answers like better part-time work, does not seem to be doing the trick. Mild legislative solutions, such as family leave laws, have been ineffective and may even be counterproductive. But tax just might do it. We have seen repeatedly that tax has a unique power to motivate. And, lo and behold, optimal tax theory is telling us that taxing men more is exactly what society ought to be doing, if it cares about utility or social wealth. It should so care, especially when justice and fairness go hand in hand with the economist's advice.

9

The Curious Nostalgia of
the Contracts

A CHANGE OF PACE?

It may seem like an abrupt change of pace to leave the field of economics theory and turn to the two *Contracts*, adding the Christian Coalition's *Contract with the American Family* to the more official *Contract with America*, authored by Newt Gingrich and other conservative congressional Republicans. But while I do intend that this chapter provide a break from economics, there are many ways in which a consideration of the *Contracts* fits nicely here. I am wrapping up the tax part of the story, and the *Contracts* complete the political and intellectual histories, or at least bring them down to the present.

By waiting until after the consideration of optimal tax for this discussion, we gain some advantages. First, we are able to see how the language and rhetoric of the *Contracts* pick up the part of optimal tax theory that recommends generally low tax rates in the interests of economic growth, but not the part that advocates lower rates on married women. This continues the principal theme of the intellectual history: Only the logic that favors traditional concerns gets heard. Optimal tax theory also helps us, in a surprising way, to understand the structure of the *Contracts'* principal tax reform proposal: to compensate mothers whether they work or not, leaving the price distortions against secondary earners in place. This is like giving the orange eaters a dollar while keeping in effect the tax that raised the price of oranges to two dollars. It is, in many ways, perverse.

Knowing what we now do about both the accountant's and the economist's tales does more: it allows us to see that the *Contracts* are wrong. A good deal of tax is political, and the *Contracts* obviously have a particular political agenda, in favor of traditional families and values. That much is fair game; reasonable people differ about politics and values. But where the *Contracts* do not play fair is in their particular invocation of tax. Tax is central to just about everything that goes on in the *Contracts*. But the use that these documents make of tax is not only insensitive to issues of gender justice; it is also factually inaccurate. The economist's and accountant's tales help us to see this.

Now we can make better sense of the title of this part, "Theory, Practice, and Rhetoric: On (Not) Getting It." Optimal tax helped to give us some relevant theory. The accountant's and political/historical tales have given us a good working sense of our social practices in regard to tax. The *Contracts* now give us a good look at rhetoric, and at not getting "it"—not getting the point of women's continuing legitimate complaints about gender bias. Our politics, writ large, are offensive to women's quest for equality. The more we know about tax and other socioeconomic systems, the deeper that offense becomes.

A CLOSER LOOK: FEAR OF TAX

Let's begin our investigations with a close look at some of the language in the *Contracts*. To keep matters simple, I'll call the *Contract with America* *"Contract I,"* and the *Contract with the American Family* *"Contract II."*

A pronounced fear of tax oozes from just about every one of the nearly two hundred pages in the popular paperback edition of *Contract I*. On page 4 we are introduced to the "five principles" of "American civilization": individual liberty, economic opportunity, limited government, personal responsibility, and security at home and abroad. The first three translate immediately and repeatedly throughout the text into an argument for lower taxes: We need to limit government by reducing taxes so that economic opportunity and individual liberty can once again flourish. The fourth principle, too, translates into lower taxes, for "personal responsibility" largely stands for a cutback on the welfare state, with the promise, however illusory, of smaller government and lower taxes. Only the fifth principle, "security at home and abroad"—and it is not insignificant that it is fifth and last—reflects any continued legitimate resource need. Even here, the fact that the cold war is over sends out an at least subliminal expectation of tax reduction.

The obsession with tax recurs throughout *Contract I*. On page 8 and throughout the text, we are promised what the new, Republican Congress will do on its very first day in office: eight steps, most of which involve the internal management of Congress (all federal laws are to apply to Congress itself; committee chairs are to have limited terms; meetings are to be open to the public; and so on) or accounting matters (auditing Congress itself for waste; changing federal budgetary procedures). But the odd man out on this list is a provision requiring a "three-fifths majority vote to pass a tax increase." This is an important, substantive provision that would effect a radical change in the way government works. By moving the threshold for approval from 50 percent to 60 percent of the votes cast, this proposal would make tax increases, already a difficult matter given their prominence and the public's obvious distaste for them, even harder to enact. At the same time, cutting benefits, which has the same effect on those who have been getting them as raising taxes does, would continue to require the bare minimum of 50 percent. Lumping this provision with essentially clerical changes that hardly require debate is disingenuous.

Pages 9 through 11 give us a list of major legislative acts that are to implement *Contract I*. These begin with the Fiscal Responsibility Act, which is a "balanced budget/tax limitation amendment." Aside from an anti-crime law (the Taking Back Our Streets Act); a defense-related bill (the National Security Restoration Act, largely designed to limit the service of United States troops under United Nations command); and a legal reform proposal (the Common Sense Legal Reforms Act, designed to limit personal-injury suits), each act has ramifications for tax policy. The Personal Responsibility Act would lower welfare payments and thus reduce taxes; the Family Reinforcement Act features tax incentives; the American Dream Restoration Act is exclusively about large-scale tax reduction; the Senior Citizens Fairness Act is concerned with the taxation of social security benefits; the Job Creation and Wage Enhancement Act turns on capital gains tax cuts, indexing, and other business tax provisions.

The final proposal is the Citizen Legislature Act, calling for a "first-ever vote on term limits to replace career politicians with citizen legislators." Lest anyone miss the connection here to tax, the point is drawn later in the text of *Contract I*, when term limits are discussed at length: "An entrenched body of politicians erodes Congress's accountability and responsiveness. An enormous national debt, deficit spending, and political scandals are but a few of the results." Term limits are needed as insurance that our politicians do not become "unaccountable." "Accountability," a word that resonates from the Richard Nixon era, has come largely to mean no new taxes.

Within the main body of *Contract I*, there is one consistent story. The text begins with the idea of balanced budgets and the "tax limitation" amendment. The dead center of *Contract I* is chapter 6, entitled "Tax Cuts for Families." The text ends with the extended call for term limits. The whole story fits together beautifully: An overly large government, full of unaccountable career politicians, has wantonly taxed the American people, destroying home, liberty, and freedom along the way. A perverse crimping of growth in the economic sector is precisely paralleled by an equally perverse distortion of nature in the home sector, as we'll come to see more fully. America must cut taxes, and thereby get back to the basics of morality and growth.

WHOSE DREAM IS THIS, ANYWAY?

Much of that would be interesting but hardly exceptional. Americans clearly hate taxes; they have ever since before the Revolutionary War. But what does all this have to do with taxing women? At this point, the answer should not surprise. The *Contracts* use the rhetoric of family to argue for massive tax reduction centered on traditional families. Conversely, but equally accurately, the *Contracts* use an aversion to tax to set the stage for reforms designed to foster and reward traditional families. The link between tax and morality runs deep. High taxes are immoral in and of themselves, and morality guides the specifics of tax reduction plans—it tells us how to cut taxes.

The Traditionals are knocking at the door again, as they did in 1939, 1948, 1986, and many times in between. Tax affords a nice, subtle opening for family values. For whatever reason—and just what this reason is is one of the motivating puzzles behind my writing of this book—it is a lot easier to convince Pete Stark and other politicians to incorporate family values into tax policy than to get Congress to change the Constitution to allow prayer in schools, or to prohibit abortion, say. We'll see later that the liberal Congresswoman Patricia Schroeder of Colorado supported a plan for increased personal and dependency exemptions. It turns out that this plan, which sounds innocent enough, would hurt secondary-earning wives within the current tax structure. This is why it drew the warm support of Mothers at Home and Gary Bauer, the president of the conservative Family Research Council. Unlike Stark, Schroeder was not making a political calculation to favor single-earner families; she simply failed to see, in the complex maze of tax, the deep biases against working wives.

Let's return to the language of *Contract I*, to see how rhetoric and reality blend together. Consider the beginning of the pivotal chapter 6:

DON'T YOU THINK your tax bill is too high—that you aren't getting what you pay for out of Washington? In 1992, America was promised tax relief for middle class families. However, the promise of a middle-class tax cut quickly turned into the largest tax increase in American history. In the first one hundred days of a Republican Congress, we will make good where others have failed by voting on the American Dream Restoration Act.

Our *Contract with America* recognizes families for what they are—the basic building block of society. Renewing the American Dream is our goal, and renewing that dream starts at home, with the family. To help families reach their American Dream, our *Contract* calls for [a] $500-per-child-tax-credit, to make raising children a little more affordable. With this tax cut, a family of four earning $28,000 a year would see their tax burden cut by a third.

Then we'll begin to repeal the marriage tax penalty. The government should reward, not punish, those who enter into the sacred bonds of marriage. And finally we will create American Dream Savings Accounts to make it easier for average Americans to save money, buy a home, pay for medical expenses, and send their kids to college.

Renewing the American Dream is what our *Contract* is all about. By strengthening families, we strengthen America.

There is an unmistakable conflation of familial, moralistic, and anti-tax rhetoric here. We'll explore shortly the three practical family-oriented planks of both *Contracts'* tax reform proposals: child, not child-care, credits; marriage penalty relief; and an expanded IRA. But first let's dwell on the language a bit more.

Note that the very institutional and political meaning of "renewing America" and "strengthening families" is tax relief. This whole central chapter is labeled and devoted to "tax cuts for families." Tax reduction is repeatedly linked to "dreams," "sacred bonds," families, and America itself. Marriage, home ownership, and providing for medical needs and children's education are all evoked as basic, moral activities that the presently perverse tax laws impede rather than support. "The government should reward, not punish, those who enter into the sacred bonds of marriage," we are told. The "American Dream" is eerily personified, made into an initial capital proper noun, in the singular, and repeated throughout: the phrase appears five times in the thirteen sentences. It is as though some specter had gained access to the corridors of power, demanding satisfaction via tax relief. But this American Dream is nothing more than a nightmare of patriarchy for many American women—a nightmare from which they cannot awake. *Contract II* emphasizes and deepens all of these themes, with a vengeance.

HAND IN HAND

Contract II parallels *Contract I* in many ways, not the least of which in its populist and popular style. The text is full of catchy phrases, italics, capital letters, lists of three or five or ten or twelve great principles, and so on, all repeated at length. *Contract II* stresses different issues at times, and it is more openly moralistic than is its more political predecessor. But tax and family once again take center stage.

Chapter 5 of *Contract II*, entitled "Family-Friendly Tax Relief," spells out practical proposals that mimic *Contract I's*—a per-child credit, marriage penalty relief, and expanded IRAs for homemakers. The *Contracts* are tightly coordinated, and they fit in with a conservative plan long in the works. For example, Gary Bauer, in testifying before the Select Committee chaired by Pat Schroeder in 1991, declared himself "pleased to announce today that the Family Research Council, in conjunction with the staff of the Heritage Foundation, has developed . . . a plan. Our proposal, the Tax Freedom for Families Plan, would offer a per-child tax credit worth

$1,800 for preschool children and $1,200 for children ages 6 and up."
Bauer, who emerges as a central player in the conservative tax and family
drama, occupied high-ranking positions under President Reagan. A *New
York Times* article comments that "even in the conservative Reagan White
House, Mr. Bauer was known for his archconservative outlook. As William
J. Bennett, the former Education Secretary, put it, 'Gary was usually a few
degrees to my right.'" After 1988, Bauer remained in Washington, leading the Family Research Council, maintaining close ties to the Christian
right wing, and vigorously lobbying for conservative social positions. He
also demonstrated a particular fondness for, and aptitude in, using tax to
advance the traditional conservative agenda.

It is apparent that the particular tax-related proposals of both *Contracts*
are the product of sophisticated conservative strategy. Bauer made clear
that his 1991 support for increased personal exemptions was an attempt
to get "something that can get through this Congress, and can get White
House support"; he was willing to wait for a "universal credit . . . down
the road." That road reached paydirt with the sweeping Republican victories in 1994, propelled by *Contract I* with its tax reduction revolving
around a per-child credit. The Tax Freedom for Families Plan—scaled
back from its ambitious but wildly unrealistic initial level of cost—became the American Dream Restoration Act. It is thus no coincidence that
the practical recommendations of the two *Contracts* converge. But it is
also notable that the rhetoric and the moralistic tone of *Contract II* are
stronger than in the more traditionally political document of *Contract I*.

ARE THESE GUYS SERIOUS?

Chapter 5 of *Contract II* begins with a ringing endorsement of the traditional family and a swipe at the government's purported substitute for it:
"IT HAS BEEN SAID that the intact family is the most successful Department of Health, Education, and Welfare ever created." The juxtaposition
of the traditional "intact" family with a large central bureaucracy is significant: the *Contracts* want to get us back to nature's basics, away from
liberal society's bureaucrats. The recurrent imagery links high taxes with
a bloated and bureaucratic government, drawing a sharp contrast with the
smaller, more intimate and more moral traditional family, which flour-
ishes in some kind of nontaxed state of nature. *Contract I* had similarly
stressed that the family is "the basic building block of society."

Unfortunately, the "intact" family is eroding, and *Contract II*, almost
stunningly, places the blame squarely on the tax code:

> It is hard to overestimate our tax code's damage to American fam-
> ilies. Many people look back to the 1950s and 1960s with nostalgia.
> At least with regard to the tax code, that nostalgia is understandable.

Those were the days when one income was often all that was needed to support a family. Today, many families need two incomes just to pay taxes and meet basic needs.

Over and over again, *Contract II* tells a consistent tale: the need to pay taxes is driving women out of the home and away from their children. Shockingly, given what we know of both taxes and the state of gender justice in America in the 1950s, *Contract II* yearns openly for a return to that era, tax laws and all. This was the height of phase 2, a time when life was grandest for the Traditionals. No attention whatsoever was then paid to working wives and mothers, except to discourage them or to concede, as in the grudging child-care provisions, that lower-income wives might have to work. This nearly obsessive commingling of tax, family, and moral rhetoric in *Contract II* would be almost comic—if it weren't so eerily serious and so effective.

In this chapter concerned exclusively with *tax* reform, we are told that "parents spend about 40 percent fewer hours with their children than parents did just a generation ago." We read "preeminent Harvard psychiatrist Robert Coles" lamenting that overworked, overtired parents are leaving their kids "with a Nintendo or a pair of Nikes." "What has caused this situation?" *Contract II* asks. "An overbearing tax system" is the immediate, entire, and unequivocal answer. This is a shocking statement, and only in part because it is completely untrue. How could tax be the *only* cause of the deterioration of the modern family? But there is a deeper puzzle. The tax system was set up in the 1930s, 1940s, and 1950s in part to *discourage* women from working outside the home. The accountant's tale told to Susan and Elizabeth confirms how effective these mechanisms were and still are.

This is not the story that *Contract II* would have us believe. *Contract II* identifies two-worker families, by which it obviously means—witness the nostalgic reference to the 1950s, among many other telltale signs— working wives, as the problem. Actually, *Contract II* consistently sees two problems, working wives and taxes. Seeing two problems, it links them in the most basic way possible, as cause and effect. High taxes force women to work. The policy recommendation then follows simply enough: Lower taxes, and wives can stay home and keep the kids away from Nikes and Nintendos.

But *Contract II's* facts are wrong. Among other things, lower taxes will *increase* married women's work; this is the precise point of the elasticity figures considered in chapter 7 of this book, confirmed by the work of Nada Eissa and others, on the effects of the Tax Reform Act of 1986. Thus, the *Contracts* have to come up with a way to lower taxes and to keep married women at home. This is *exactly* what a per-child credit can be expected to do.

Contract II, still in its chapter dealing exclusively with tax relief, repeatedly rues the loss of family time in America.

> Perhaps the most disturbing thing about this dramatic loss of family time is the fact that the second income does little to improve family financial well-being. In fact, approximately two-thirds of a working mother's income is consumed solely by the family's federal tax liability. Unless the tax burden on families is reduced, working-parent families will continue to see one of their two incomes supporting government, not the family.

This passage makes explicit the connections we've been discussing: high taxes are driving mothers out of the home. There are two evils, taxes and working mothers. Fortunately, these can be killed with a single stone: cleverly designed tax reduction. Or so the *Contracts* would have us believe.

A TRICK

The *Contracts* turn on a neat rhetorical trick. Let's take a closer look at how they pull off this particular act of legerdemain. These documents at least give a nod to many of the same accounting facts that we have seen, establishing that most married women with children are barely making any money by working outside the home: "the second income does little to improve family financial well-being." That much is the story of Susan and Elizabeth. Note, by the way, that the *Contracts* have no difficulty in identifying this "second income" as belonging to the "working mother." In our case, these facts, especially when supplemented with a bit of history and gender consciousness, led us to rethink how society should tax women, with the aim of alleviating the burden on working wives and mothers.

The *Contracts* note these same facts and also treat them as the occasion for fundamental tax reform—except that they would push things completely, perfectly, and perversely in the *opposite* direction. By a rhetorical sleight of hand, the *Contracts* give a different spin to the fact that "the second income does little to improve family financial well-being." This fact *correctly* means that many married women who try to work outside the home, like Susan and Elizabeth, will barely, if at all, break even after taxes and other work-related expenses. It does *not* mean that women are working *in order to pay* taxes—that high taxation has somehow compelled women to leave hearth and home.

Yet the story that the *Contracts* tell is indeed one of wives *having*, not *wanting*, to work. The conservative Bauer testified to this effect in 1991, in supporting an increased personal exemption:

> I think the fact that so many parents and so many households have been driven into the workforce—not necessarily because they

want to be but because they can't pay their bills without two incomes—you can see what some of the economic trends are and what the major argument is for passing this exemption.

Congressman J. Dennis Hastert, a high-ranking Republican from, in his own words, a "rather affluent community and district" in Illinois, agreed:

> Mothers are still forced to go into the workforce, not because they want to but because, economically, if they want to provide for the education of their children after they get out of high school, or if they want to take that family vacation, that's important to a lot of people's belief, or if they want to achieve more of the American dream by moving from a rental property to owning their own home, then they have no choice.

Ronald Reagan, in signing the Tax Reform Act of 1986—which lowered taxes for all married couples, especially the Traditionals, while repealing the secondary-earner deduction that had been designed for the Equals—accepted the same view of the matter. "With inflation and bracket creep also eroding incomes, many spouses who would rather stay home with their children have been forced to go looking for jobs," Reagan remarked. I'll get back to the 1986 act later in this chapter, for it turns out that Reagan was exactly wrong.

Heidi Brennan of Mothers at Home, Inc., testifying in the same 1991 hearing with Bauer, echoed these sentiments. Brennan also supplied poll results showing support of increased personal exemptions and a replacement of the child-care credit with a per-child one. Her data indicated that 73 percent of all two-parent families would have one parent stay home if "money were not an issue" (the statement does not say whose opinion this was—that of the husband, wife, or both); 88 percent of mothers who worked agreed that "if I could afford it, I would rather be home with my children"; two-thirds of all mothers who worked full time would like to work fewer hours and spend more time with their children; and 82 percent "of the American public" believe it is best for "young children to be cared for by one or more parents or by extended family members." The *Contracts* have simplified the evil force pushing married women to work against their will; they have made it taxation alone.

Let's take a closer look at this trick. *Contract II* claims that "approximately two-thirds of a working mother's income is consumed solely by the family's federal tax liability." This comes from allocating the total tax burden *exclusively* to the secondary-earning wife. But this is not a compelling way of doing marginal analysis. A married woman's tax is being occasioned by her work alone, not by her husband's.

To illustrate, if Tom Traditional makes $48,000, his work occasions $4,800 in income taxes under our standard illustrative rate table 3, and about $3,800 in social security taxes, for a total of $8,600. If Tina gets a job paying her $30,000, she enters the workforce at a 30 percent income tax rate, and thus will pay $9,000 in income taxes to go along with $2,400 in social security ones: $11,400, or 38 percent of her pretax salary, in total. This is how we have been looking at it: our concern has been that the tax on Tina, at a 38 percent average effective rate, is so much higher than that on Tom, at an 18 percent rate. The numbers are worse for both the poor and the rich, but that's the basic picture. We came to something like the 67 percent figure, or even to the case of losing money by working, like Elizabeth, when we added in state and local taxes and the work-related costs of the secondary earner, especially for child care, to which the tax system pays very little heed.

Contract II goes in another direction. It adds Tom's and Tina's federal taxes together, getting a family total of $20,000, and allocates all of it to the wife's salary, getting a figure of two-thirds ($20,000 out of $30,000). The implicit argument behind this allocation is that the wife is being forced to work to pay her *husband's* taxes, and, because her work is also being taxed, she has to work even harder than she otherwise might. To be perfectly fair to the *Contracts*, this story could be true, as a factual matter. There is a coherent story to tell that traditional, single-earner families were hit hard by taxes on the breadwinning male, and this drove the wife away from the noble pursuit of homemaking into the workforce to make up for the tax hit. There she faced high enough taxes herself that she ended up having to work full time. This is the conservative spin.

The problem with this story is in the facts. There is almost no reason to accept the conservative tale as a compelling account of the aggregate story. As the elasticity figures we looked at in chapter 7 show, married women are working *despite*, not *because of*, taxes. If a family just wanted more cash income, it makes far more sense to have the primary-earning male put in a few more hours or take a second job, as we saw with Mel Middle and Umberto Upper. Recall that the Uppers could net as much from Umberto's getting a $4,000 raise as they could from Ursula's taking a $30,000 job. There seems to be one major reason why participation rates for women of all sorts, including married mothers, have been steadily increasing over the last half of the century: Women really want to work outside the home.

The studies invoked by Heidi Brennan and others, which show that many mothers are unhappy working full time outside the home, indicate that many married mothers would prefer good, high-quality, part-time work. Some of these studies are ambiguous because they seem to reflect what men want or what people would want if "money were not an issue." Most Americans would say that they would not work if money were not an issue. But there is something else going on with married mothers. Many studies supplement our common experiences to confirm a basic truth in America today: Mothers of young children are not happy. Those who work full time wish they could work less so that they could spend more time with their children, and they wish that their husbands would help out a bit more with the children, and around the house, too. Those who work part time wish that they could be working full time because the part-time job market features bad jobs—ones that are low in pay, prestige, and possibilities. And those who stay at home full time wish that they could get out of the house more, to maintain job market skills, to share some of the joys of the working world, to experience more diversity in their lives, and to earn some money and independence—all of which can be critical in the case of divorce. It's all a matter of where, and how, one looks. The conservatives look at working women, and predicate a program on their unhappiness that seems scarcely responsive to what most women seem to want. It is, rather, what committed Traditionals really want.

A PUZZLE, AND A CLEVER SOLUTION

Conservatives face a quandary under the current facts. The status quo serves one part of the conservative agenda. The way things are *does* encourage married mothers to stay at home, largely because traditional family values have so heavily shaped the tax laws. If all that conservatives want is to get women back into the home, they could try to achieve their ends by funding accountants to go forth and spread the good word to the Susans and Elizabeths of this world that they should, in fact, stay home. But this is not all that the conservatives want. It never has been. As we've seen, ever since the 1930s, at least, Traditional-like families do indeed want women to stay home. But even more than this, they want tax reduction for themselves.

The elasticity figures from chapter 7 contradict the neat little story that women are willing participants in, or at least beneficiaries of, the conservative plan, and they create another quandary for the *Contracts'* planners. The accountant's tale shows that the *Contracts'* portrayal of the accounting reality is wrong; optimal tax helps to show that their portrayal of nature is, too. To say that women are pushed to work by taxes—a double perversion of taxation, to the conservative mind—would mean that women are led to work by *income* effects. That is, women are working to get money so as to pay tax, as the *Contracts* intimate; otherwise, women want to be home. A good response would be to give women income so that they can do what they really want to do and should do, stay home and keep the kids away from Nikes and Nintendos.

But the elasticity figures show that women have a high compensated as well as uncompensated elasticity; that is, even if we put aside the income effects of a tax, women as a group are ambivalent about work outside and inside the home. If women really were as wedded to the hearth as the conservative story would have them be, and as men are wedded to their work desks, their compensated elasticity would be zero: no change in wage rates could lure them out of the home, putting income aside. They would be inelastic homemakers. But they are not. The conservatives, presuming to speak for what women really want, are not listening.

Actually, the conservatives are listening, in a sense, but they are drawing perverse conclusions. An earlier generation of conservatives, under Ronald Reagan's leadership, had pushed for tax reduction and simplification, along the lines of the contemporary flat tax plans. This led to the massive Tax Reform Act of 1986, with its dramatic lowering of rates across the board. Recall that the top marginal income tax rate fell from 70 percent to 28 percent in the first five years of Reagan's presidency. One hope was to get women back in the home, as we saw above with Reagan's remarks on signing the law. (Reagan had proceeded to boast that "we're going to make it economical to raise children again.") But *this* kind of tax lowering—ironically, for Reagan and his conservative allies—led to *increased* participation by married women. This is just as the elasticity data would predict, and as Nada Eissa and others have shown.

The ultimate proof of the analysis I am advancing here lies in the pudding of the *Contracts'* precise tax-reduction mechanism. The *Contracts* would transfer a lump sum of money—$500 per child—to families, leaving in place all the distortions against secondary earners that have been present for decades. This proposal is brilliant in its fidelity to conservative ends. It also gives the lie to the *Contracts'* own story, of mothers being pushed out of the home by taxes. The *Contracts* are cleverly and consciously using tax to do the pushing—to push mothers back into the home.

LET'S BE HONEST

Even without the fact that women are not fully committed to the home with anywhere near the rigidity that men are to their work stations, the conservatives should come clean with the fact that they are making political arguments about tax, ones that just so happen to favor their own preferred family visions. We've seen that a seemingly neutral tax policy literature was legitimating a tax structure chosen on gendered grounds. Now we are encountering another neutral phantasmagoria. The conservative argument for tax reform, and a broader reshaping of government driven by tax reduction, has much of the trappings of a market-oriented, freedom- and liberty-loving laissez-faire. An overly big government fueled by a massive tax burden has distorted the true natures that would flourish under a free market. We must get back to nature and the basics, and get the government out of our lives, by reducing taxes and removing their distorting influences.

The animus to tax manifested in the *Contracts* is fine as far as it goes: taxes may indeed be too high, even for a liberal state. In any event, avowedly political arguments should be fair game in a democracy. There is nothing wrong, and a good deal right, about an open and honest dialogue among people holding different ideals about the size and role of good government. But there is a factual error playing a key role in the conservative rhetoric. The invocation of free market mechanisms is disingenuous. How should taxes be reduced in a way that would most effectively lessen the distorting influence of the taxes that remain? The answer comes by way of optimal tax theory. That is *exactly* what optimal tax does. It tells us, for a given level of taxation, what tax structure is least distorting. This is precisely the project that Frank Ramsey and his followers set for themselves: maximizing utility means minimizing price distortions. Far from the conservative recommendation to direct tax relief toward traditional families, the answer coming from optimal income tax theory is clear and consistent: Lower the taxes on married women. Michael Boskin recommended that married men be taxed at twice the rate of married women. How far can we get from where we are, and from where the *Contracts* would further take us?

Liberals and feminists who want equal concern and respect for women and who are willing to look at the tax laws as a locus for this concern are thus not out of line. They are doing the same thing as conservatives, making political arguments about tax, just for different ends. But it is also the case that the facts of the matter do not support the conservative argument that women really want to stay home or that freer markets would take us back to the 1950s. Conservatives are arguing against revealed preferences, against freedom, not in its cause. They are making a coercive argument that tax systems should be set up in a way that preserves traditional families, notwithstanding the large psychological and financial cost of so doing. Conservatives ought at least to be compelled to make better arguments, and to use fewer rhetorical tricks, to carry the day in an honest court of judgment. Well-meaning and well-informed liberals and feminists should put them to just that test.

THE PECULIAR YET PRECISE PERVERSION OF CHILD, NOT CHILD-CARE, CREDITS

The per-child credit is far and away the largest plank in the conservatives' platform. In the initial House bill that implemented the *Contracts*, the child credit accounted for $162.3 billion over the seven-year period of projections. This figure is well over one-half of the total tax reduction called for and is fully 86 percent of the so-called family-type tax breaks. The only provision within as much as $100 billion of the child credit in its projected cost was the break for capital gains, estimated to cost $63 billion. The supposed reduction in the marriage penalty came in at $12.4 billion—less than 8 percent of the cost of the child credit.

The child credit is also the provision that most reveals the underlying social aims of the *Contracts'* tax reform agenda. Helping children sounds like a good thing to do and, to be clear, I have no problem at all with helping children as a general matter. The problem is that the *Contracts'* child credit is not a general matter; it is a quite particular device to help the Traditionals. To make it perfectly plain what the motivation is, these child credits are not refundable. The independent Center on Budget and Policy Priorities, in line with other contemporary studies, estimates that 24 million, or 34 percent of all American children, will get *no* benefit from the per-child credit because they live in families too poor to pay positive income taxes; another 7 million will get a reduced benefit because they live in families that pay less than $500 per child in income taxes. These families do, of course, pay taxes under the 16 percent payroll tax system, and many of them are losing the earned-income tax credit or other welfare-like benefits on account of their earnings, but they do not pay positive income taxes. Recall the child-care credit, which is also non-refundable. Laura Lower could be in a 50 percent or higher marginal tax bracket—with the earned-income tax credit phaseout added to her income, social security, and state and local taxes—without qualifying for a single cent from the proposed child credit. I have noted throughout that the tax burden on families, as opposed to individuals, is of most concern at the lower-income levels; this is where the marriage penalty matters most and is also most severe. The *Contracts* would do nothing about this situation.

To show the lamentable state of American politics, and the utter lack of attention paid to concerns of gender justice, the only real debate over the child-credit proposal has been whether every rich, upper-income family should get it, or if it should be limited to families making less than $200,000, $110,000, $75,000, or some such figure—all decidedly upper-class sums, affecting a small percentage of the populace. The poor will not get any benefit from the credit at all. Under a proposal that would phase out the credit for a married couple with two children beginning at $110,000 of income, and eliminate it completely when the family reached $150,000, for example, only 5 percent of children would receive less than a full credit because their families were at the *upper* end of the income scale, as compared to 44 percent who would fail to gain full benefits because they were on the *lower* one.

Child credits are also very bad indeed from the perspective of gender justice. The child credit, as a matter of opportunity costs, *maintains* the high marginal tax rates that largely deter secondary-earning wives and makes their paid workforce roles difficult and unstable. Meanwhile it transfers income to all parents, thereby reducing the incentive to become two-earner families in the first place. By "opportunity cost," I refer to the accounting or economic analysis that looks to alternative means of spending money. The per-child credit is a tax reduction, or expenditure, of $162 billion over seven years. An opportunity cost analysis would ask how else we could spend this money. We could, for example, lower rates across the board. But this is exactly what the *Contracts* do not want to do; it would repeat the disappointment (to them) of the 1986 act.

Thus it is precisely as if society decided to raise taxes by taxing working wives particularly heavily, in order to get $162 billion to give money to all middle- and upper-income families—the more kids, the merrier. The proposal is in fact a tax reduction for breadwinning males, the Tom Traditionals. The family gets its money from the child credit whether Tina works or not, and without changing at all the disincentives facing her. Susan and Elizabeth face exactly the same set of facts as they did at the start of this book, except that an extra $500 per child would be on the kitchen table as they chatted with their accountants about whether to work outside the home. This extra cash, of course, would make it *more* likely for them to stay home.

The per-child credit is thus a brilliant way to get around the 1986 act's effect, wherein a general rate reduction increased married women's participation in the labor market. The credit solves that problem by lowering taxes in a way that does not lower them on secondary earners. It is exactly like the perverse apples-and-oranges example we considered in chapter 7, in which the government raised the price of apples by a tax, from $1 to $2, and then gave each person a dollar back. We saw that this giving and taking away had a lasting effect because it kept the price facing orange eaters at $2. Here the *Contracts* are keeping the tax rates for working wives and mothers in place, while giving money to all the parents in middle- and upper-income brackets. Just as the oranges example would lead to fewer oranges being purchased, so too will this real-world tax example lead to lessened labor market participation by women.

All of this should sound familiar. It is what the United States did in the social security system in the 1930s: impose a pure tax on working wives to subsidize breadwinning men in traditional families. It is how the structure of fringe benefits evolved: rewarding traditional, single-earner families, implicitly taxing two-earner ones. It is what Congress did when it repealed the secondary-earner deduction in 1986, in order to finance tax reduction for all married families—or, at least, all wealthy married families. And it is all, from an optimal tax perspective, *precisely* perverse.

The child credit is perfectly and ingeniously designed to unravel the alleged perversion of women's working to pay Uncle Sam, and to get mothers back in the home, with their kids, where they belong. It is an attempt to return to the 1950s and 1960s—a time, we are told, that "many people look back to . . . with nostalgia." Presumably, the women complaining about glass ceilings, inflexible labor markets, stressful child-care options, and so on, are not among these many people. The married men who continue to work full-time jobs with astounding rigidity, and who wish that their wives would simply stay home and take care of the kids and the house, are. The nonrefundability of the child credits means they will do nothing at all for the poorest third of American families, the ones under the greatest stress. For them, we suppose, there is not much point in getting back to the 1950s, a time no better for our poorest citizens. This is tax reform for the middle- and upper-class Traditionals, yet again ingeniously cloaked in the rhetoric of family values.

RHETORICAL MARRIAGE PENALTY RELIEF

Both *Contracts* contain, in addition to the child credits, two other tax reduction proposals as part of their "family-friendly tax relief." First, there is a provision to address the marriage penalty, which had been raised for upper-income couples under a Clinton administration tax increase. But the relief here is limited to no more than $145 per family per year. This is a little more than $10 a month, something less than 50¢ a day—enough, in some small towns, for a one-way bus fare.

Further, this marriage penalty relief is available to a good many families with widely disparate earnings between husband and wife. The *Contracts'* provision essentially works so that any couple who pays more than $145 as a married couple than as an unmarried one gets the full relief; thus, a couple with something like a $50,000/$15,000 split in relative earnings would qualify for the maximum benefit. This is hardly a concern for the true Equals. The provision is even outweighed, in its dollar magnitude, by a spousal IRA provision available *only* to Traditional-like families.

To make matters even worse, the *Contracts'* token nod toward two-earner families was apparently too much for the Republican-controlled Senate to swallow. In their version of the *Contract with America*, the marriage tax relief took the form of an increase in the standard exemption level for all married couples. That's a step which benefits *all* families, traditional single-earner ones included. It is, in effect, a move toward the 1948 rate schedule. We are back to the sophistic understanding of marriage penalties we saw in chapter 3.

Under the *Contracts* themselves, the marriage penalty relief pales in comparison to the $500 per-child credit, the obvious linchpin of the *Contracts'* tax reform plans. Having one child brings more than three times the tax relief of having two workers, while having three children is more than ten times as beneficial. If Susan and Elizabeth stay home, cultivate imputed income, and take care of their own children, the *Contracts* will give them $500 per child per year. If either Susan or Elizabeth tries to work outside the home, the *Contracts* insure that society will tax every penny she makes, at high tax rates dictated by her husband's salary, and a pure social security tax of 16 percent. Nothing in the accountant's tale will change at all, except that the law will throw the family with a working wife 50¢ a day to help out a bit.

There is no general rate reduction in the *Contracts*, just a transfer of money to families with children. The $145 token relief is another rhetorical trick designed to call attention to Clinton's tax increase, perhaps, and to be able to use the phrase "marriage penalty" repeatedly, so as to claim the cloak of morality. But it does no real good. It's an insult, or at least it ought to be. *Contract II* repeatedly rues the burden on women as secondary earners and laments their loss of time at home with their families. What it is really lamenting is the very fact of working wives at all, as its nostalgia for the 1950s makes clear. Its insultingly small "marriage penalty relief" is a cover for this agenda. Its strikingly large nonrefundable child (not child-care) credit is its proof. The *Contracts* put our money where their hearts are: with traditional families featuring stay-at-home wives.

ONE MORE INSULT

The final provision for "family-friendly tax relief" once more gives the lie to the marital penalty provision's ostensible concern for second earners—a lie already given by the Senate's subtle substitution away from it. Presently, working people not covered by company pension plans are entitled to put up to $2,000 a year into an IRA. If one spouse does not work outside the home, the couple gets to put in $2,250—obviously less than double the individual amount. The *Contracts* view this situation with alarm, as did Helen Coyne, of Mothers at Home, Inc., in 1985. This issue has become a rallying cry for those who would make the stay-at-home wife into a victim, and it has spawned more empty neutrality talk. In the absurdly named Mother's and Homemaker's Rights Act, *Contract II* proposes to reverse this "important inequity of IRA policy" by allowing couples with stay-at-home spouses to contribute a full $4,000.

It's a bit hard to get too worked up over all of this. Among other things, one wonders how many families who could afford to put $4,000 into an IRA are not already covered by an employer pension plan. Furthermore, there are plenty of other tax-favored ways for savvy investors to save: certain privately available annuities, for example, work in much the same way as IRAs. The House version of the *Contracts* was projected to cost $7.5 billion over seven years for its IRA expansion. This is hardly a major sum in a total package costing more than $300 billion, and there are reasons to doubt that the actual cost is even that high. It is, once again, the rhetoric of the *Contracts* that is so puzzling and offensive.

Structurally, the Mother's and Homemaker's Rights Act has much the same effect as the social security reforms of 1939 or the evolution of fringe benefit practices. It just enables a traditional breadwinner man to provide more easily for his retirement or premature death. There is no functional difference between the Mother's and Homemaker's Rights Act and a "Breadwinning Male Power Act," which would provide that any person married to a stay-at-home spouse could put twice as much money into an IRA as anyone not so married. That is what the *Contracts'* provision would do. Calling this a Rights Act is insulting to the word "rights."

The provision also works in exactly the opposite direction of the "marriage penalty relief"; it is a provision unequivocally aimed to favor and reward stay-at-home spouses. It would benefit traditional families in the 15 percent bracket up to $262.50 per year and those in the 30 percent bracket twice as much. It does no good at all for the Equals or, for that matter, for any couple in which the wife earns at least $2,000; such a family could get a full spousal IRA under current law. Since both the Equals and the Traditionals gain from the child (not child-care) provision—although Traditionals benefit more, as fertility rates are lower for working mothers—the relative benefits turn on these two provisions. The Equals get $145 from the marriage penalty relief, and the Traditionals get $262.50 from the IRA provision. Under the Senate bill, the Traditionals get the same benefit from the "marriage penalty relief" as the Equals do, so the relative victory of the Traditionals is even greater. The very fact that this is a major issue, a complaint of the Traditionals for a long time, shows the force of the concern for truly traditional families. Pete Stark would understand.

Given tax laws that were set up in the 1930s and 1940s to favor traditional households with stay-at-home spouses—biases that have steadily increased since then—conservatives have decided to shoot for the moon in documents like the *Contracts*. They have taken the offensive, complaining that *they* are being most hurt by taxes, and have brilliantly structured a tax reduction plan to help themselves, first and foremost. The biggest insult may be to all of us, in thinking that we could fall for this; the worst tragedy may be that we seem to be doing so. The *Contracts* ought to drive home once and for all the dangers of a broad ignorance of the tax laws. They ought to be a wake-up call to feminists, progressives, and liberals everywhere, to get out there and learn the facts of tax.

FLAT ISN'T THE ANSWER, EITHER

In addition to the tax reform proposals contained in the *Contracts*, the other prominent conservative proposals on the table as I write this book involve moves to a flat-rate tax system. These proposals, however, all feature a generous zero bracket and joint filing, so that they in fact continue the very large secondary-earner bias, and in some cases make it worse.

TABLE 11. Flat-Rate Tax Schedule

INCOME	MARGINAL TAX RATE
$0–$25,500	0%
$25,500 and up	20%

Considering them gives us one more look into practical politics and its failure to take into account the concerns of gender justice in tax.

I'll focus mainly on the proposal advanced by Robert Hall and Alvin Rabushka in their book *The Flat Tax*. Hall and Rabushka are both affiliated with the conservative Hoover Institution, and Hall is also associated with Stanford University. Their short, popularly oriented book first appeared in 1985, in the midst of the discussions over the Tax Reform Act of 1986; a second edition was released in 1995, in the midst of the tax reform/reduction fever in which the *Contracts* were playing a major role. The Hall-Rabushka plan features a $16,500 personal allowance for married couples and a further $4,500 allowance per child or other dependent. The proposal put forth by Congressman Richard Armey of Texas is essentially the same: this plan actually has a $21,400 exemption for married filing jointly and an additional $5,000 allowance per dependent. The Armey plan has no marriage penalty because the zero bracket for married couples is twice that for singles, like the 1948 rate schedule; the Hall-Rabushka plan looks more like the 1969 schedule, with a slight marriage penalty. But none of this affects the basic story.

Under Hall-Rabushka, a family of four has a zero bracket of $25,500 ($16,500 plus $9,000 for the two children). Above this, the flat tax kicks in. The tax rate must be higher than the lowest bracket now in effect, 15 percent, to accommodate for the lessened revenue generated at the top. Hall-Rabushka themselves use a 19 percent rate; the Armey plan has a 17 percent one; and some have questioned the accuracy of both sets of revenue projections. Using a 20 percent rate, to keep things simple, this looks like a two-bracket system, as shown in table 11 above. The rate schedule of table 11 still leaves in place the secondary-earner bias because it retains the joint filing feature. If a primary-earner husband makes $25,500 or more, his wife faces an initial marginal income tax rate of 20 percent, to go along with social security and state and local taxes. If she goes to work outside the home, despite this 38 percent total tax rate, she still has to make up for the loss of tax-free imputed income, now with *no* tax relief for work-related costs like child-care expenses. This would represent a tax *increase* on Molly Middle, for the flat rate means, as we have noted above, that the single rate is higher than the lowest one that Molly actually enters.

Like other flat tax proposals, Hall-Rabushka would simply abolish any special child-care provision, leaving no particular help in place for working mothers. Hall and Rabushka write:

Like many of the complicated, special provisions in the tax system, the child care credit fails to focus its benefits in an area of particular social need. It potentially lowers the taxes of a significant fraction of all taxpayers—families with two earners and one or more children. It is available at all income levels. In 1993, for example, even the very rich were able to claim a credit of $480 [*sic*]. . . . Higher tax rates are required to compensate for this lowering of the amount of taxes. Features like the child care credit are antithetical to the flat-tax philosophy, which favors the broadest possible tax base with the lowest tax rate. We think that the special problems of helping families with child care and other responsibilities should be attacked specifically within the welfare system, not with the scattergun of the tax system. The flat tax provides plenty of revenue for a generous welfare program.

This passage nicely illustrates several of the themes we've encountered thus far. Hall and Rabushka complain about what they see as a "special" benefit to a "significant fraction of all taxpayers—families with two earners and one or more children." They thus buy into the neutrality of a system that does nothing at all to help such families, à la the *Smith* case we looked at in chapter 5, or the repeated testimony to this effect from conservatives like Gary Bauer. Heidi Brennan of Mothers at Home felt in 1991 that the case was so clear that she did not have "to go into ideological or philosophical reasons at this point about why [the dependent-care tax credit] is currently discriminatory" for the House Select Committee. Hall and Rabushka also complain that "even the very rich" are able to get the child-care benefit, and would leave the "special problem" of child care to the "welfare system." This perpetuates the view that two earners are a lower-income problem and that we ought not to be doing anything at all for upper-income wives, on account of the fact that they are upper income. Finally, Hall-Rabushka pass the buck to a welfare system that their conservative allies, in other forums, are chafing at the bit to dismantle. This is like the ostensible concern for the poor manifested in such laws as the child-care credit, which was carefully set up to favor lower-income taxpayers—but which, in practice, such taxpayers cannot and do not use at all because of its nonrefundability. There is a very skillful us/them technique behind the current conservative positions: First lower our taxes, then we'll cut their benefits.

WATCHING THE COMPANY ONE KEEPS

More generally, flat taxes like the Hall-Rabushka plan reflect a strategy of increased personal exemptions and dependency allowances, advocated by Gary Bauer, Heidi Brennan, and other conservatives. Ronald Reagan had supported these reforms in 1986. Although raising the tax-free amount for individuals, couples, and dependents certainly sounds like a good idea—the 1991 hearings, chaired by Pat Schroeder, made frequent references to the effects of inflation and the erosion of the personal exemptions over time—such exemptions in fact lead to greater zero bracket amounts. Within a joint filing system, this is *not* a good idea along gender justice lines. Indeed, some 90 percent of all married taxpayers faced such a system before 1948 under table 5, with its double exemption or zero bracket amount for couples filing jointly. This system was clearly set up with lower- and middle-income Traditionals in mind, as its very brief modification during World War II proved. In short, primary earners benefit from these large zero bracket exemptions. Because the provisions lose revenue that has to be made up somewhere else, they raise or at least maintain the high tax rates on secondary earners.

Let me take a minute to clarify this last point, which relates again to what we might call the "opportunity costs" of any given tax decrease. These days, with Gramm-Rudman and other accounting mechanisms in the air, it often seems as if particular tax cuts are "linked" to particular spending cuts. If the $500 per-child credit, for example, is projected to cost $162 billion over a seven-year period, our political processes require a "matching" spending cut, say in Medicare spending. It then looks as if we have a neat package: a tax cut financed by a spending cut.

In fact, though, there is no such thing. What we have are two decisions: one to cut taxes, the other to cut spending. We can easily view the two decisions separately. The $162 billion Medicare cut means that we can afford a $162 billion tax cut without affecting the budget balance. The question then becomes how, if at all, do we want to cut taxes? (We could, of course, not cut taxes per se, using the money to reduce the deficit instead.) A per-child credit, as in the *Contracts*, can be seen as displacing other plans, such as a return to separate filing, secondary-earner relief, child-care credits, or, for that matter, across-the-board rate reductions. So, too, with personal exemptions. A decision to raise the zero bracket is a decision to cut taxes; the question is, then, Is it the best one? Since the cut flows almost exclusively to primary earners, who are overwhelmingly likely to be men, the answer, along gender lines, is a clear no.

The confusion over this point is nicely illustrated in an exchange between Gary Bauer and Pat Schroeder at the 1991 hearing. Speaking of increased exemption levels, which Schroeder had long supported, Bauer began his oral comments as follows:

> Madam Chairwoman, I have been in Washington now for about 20 years, and during the time we have both been in Washington, I have had a hard time recalling an issue where you and I agreed. As I realized that both of us agree on this issue, I assumed there were

only two explanations: one, that one of us had miscalculated, or that, second, this idea really has a lot of power to it and a lot of common sense to it.

I think you have concluded, as I have, that, in fact, it is a very powerful idea that has the potential to unite Republicans and Democrats, liberals and conservatives, and feminists and traditionalists. So I'm looking forward to working with you on it and trying to pass it in the months ahead.

When Bauer was finished speaking, Schroeder, a well-known and respected liberal and advocate of women's issues and the then highest-ranking Congresswoman, thanked him: "I'm glad we're all united fighting for this. As Congressman Wolf pointed out, there's a lot of 'Gucci shoes' outside the Ways and Means Committee that we're going to have to fight off, but I think it's very important that we do it."

It turns out that Bauer was actually right about at least one thing: Schroeder had "miscalculated." Liberals and feminists ought to be troubled by increased exemptions under a joint filing system, as we've just seen; Democrats, at least those like Pete Stark, present a more ambiguous case. The reason that Bauer and Mothers at Home, and Ronald Reagan before them, were lined up behind the proposal was that it would in fact benefit traditional families and do little to alleviate the secondary-earner bias. Indeed, it might make this bias worse, as for Molly Middle. Unless Schroeder's brand of liberal feminism also leads her to favor stay-at-home wives and a tax system set up to heavily discourage secondary-earning ones, she ought to recalculate her stand.

Bauer's true conservatism was barely hidden; in the open comments period, he noted, still referring to the raising of the exemption levels:

> While we've got an interesting coalition here supporting the idea, I think the coalition is in danger of unraveling fairly rapidly when you look at other ideas. For example, I had to restrain myself as I listened to the arguments about increasing the dependent care tax credit, which we already feel is unfair and discriminatory against those families who choose to have the mother or father stay home with their children instead of having two incomes.

Once again, any nod to two-worker families, however slight, is viewed as "unfair and discriminatory," and indeed is so violently opposed that self-restraint is needed on the congressional floor when the idea is floated by a committee. Any slight to single-earner families, such as the spousal IRA provisions, is likewise condemned in virulent terms. Bauer made clear that his heart lay more in the per-child credit idea, but tactics precluded this in 1991: "If you're looking for something that can get through this Congress, and can get White House support, I think you're probably better off in this round to stick with an exemption increase, even though it has some drawbacks." "Down the road," which turned out to be a short one, Bauer hoped for a universal, per-child credit.

Meanwhile, no one is complaining much about what we don't see— the deep biases of the tax system against working wives. Liberals and feminists like Pat Schroeder had best watch the company they, at least sometimes, keep—especially when it comes to taxation. It is a subject that the conservatives have long since mastered.

TWO BRANDS OF CONSERVATIVES

The discussion of the flat-rate tax proposals ties in nicely with the previous one of the *Contracts*. There is much overlap between the two camps: Richard Armey, for example, is both a named author of the *Contract with America* and the sponsor of one of the most prominent flat tax plans. The Armey plan would bring us right back to the 1948 rate schedule, with no marriage penalty but a persistent secondary-earner bias. Gary Bauer, testifying in 1991 in favor of the types of increased personal exemptions that get prominently picked up in all of the flat tax plans, announced the working project between the conservative Family Research Council and the Heritage Foundation in favor of the kind of child (not child-care) credits that were to become a linchpin for the *Contracts'* tax plans. The proposals for a flat tax, like the *Contracts*, reflect a deep resentment of any benefits directed toward two-earner couples, like the child-care credit.

Still, there are important differences in the two approaches. The flat tax plans, which have many of their intellectual roots in the early Ronald Reagan years of supply-side economics and the Laffer Curve, reflect an older version of conservatism, one more passive and market-oriented than its contemporary cousin. The flat tax plans hold out the allure of a simpler, less interventionist government and set of laws so that individuals can decide what is best for themselves in free markets. There can be little serious doubt that the flat tax plans would simplify matters: Hall and Rabushka are fond of describing their "postcard" tax return. Even if simplification in and of itself is overvalued as a virtue and even if the simplification gains are overstated, as they surely seem to be, it is hard to deny that a system with far fewer credits and deductions and with lower top marginal rate brackets would be simpler.

The *Contracts* are something else altogether. The child credit, as we have seen, is the main item of expense in the *Contracts'* tax proposals, accounting for more than one-half of its total tax reduction. Restoring a capital gains tax break is a distant second in terms of expense, but the two provisions, combined, are about 75 percent of the total. These two items would most definitely *not* simplify tax; a capital gains preference is notoriously complicated. The *Contracts* thus reflect a different brand of conservative—social conservatives, not necessarily market-oriented, ready, willing, and able to use the tax code and other laws as an active tool of social engineering in the service of conservative causes. The child credit represents a very large-scale attempt to return us affirmatively, as *Contract II* itself notes, to the 1950s. This is not simply preserving a status quo, or getting the government off our backs, as the saying goes. It is, rather, an attempt to turn back the clock; it is what is meant by a "reactionary" politics.

The *Contracts* would keep in place all the disincentives we have discussed and would mail a check to middle- and upper-class parents with children. This is a new, sophisticated, and aggressive form of conservatism. It is also one that has mastered the tool of tax as an instrument of social policy and construction. The *Contracts'* tax plan is a perfect renunciation of the teachings of optimal tax. Liberals, progressives, and feminists had best heed the implicit wake-up call: It is time to learn tax, too. What we don't know can most definitely hurt us.

One might think that conservative social forces, in the interests of increasing social wealth or of getting closer to free markets, would want to use the theory of optimal tax to minimize the net distortions of tax. But in America—after the extensive history and politics we've considered, from 1913 down to the *Contracts*—we should know better. The precepts of optimal tax are powerless in the face of the skilled rhetorical mixing of tax and family brilliantly captured in the *Contracts*—rhetoric that works even on liberal Democrats like Pete Stark. Other liberals, like Pat Schroeder, fail to detect the biases and perversion of a system set up in an era of deep patriarchy, and slanted against two-earner families, working wives, and mothers.

We are left, then, with a rather effete intellectual reason for needing to understand optimal tax theory: it shows us just how unfair the current system is for women in America and how much worse the *Contracts* would make it. Our political processes seem barely to have noticed any of this, and there is little hope for greater gender justice in tax in the immediate future. These are bad times—for women, for gender justice, and for all of us who care about fairness and decency. These are bad times, indeed: The 1950s are right around the corner.

PART FOUR

Beyond Tax: Getting Worse, Still

10 Not Just Tax

THE CURTAIN RISES

As the curtain rises on this, the final part, the tax story begun with the accountant's tale featuring Susan and Elizabeth is at an end. It has been enriched by the political, intellectual/historical, and economist's tales: The way America goes about taxing women is not only burdensome, it is wholly, completely, and perversely backward to the soundest recommendations of ostensibly neutral economic theory. Faceless accountants, with no axe to grind and no sense of history, feminist theory, or economics were able to present the facts of the matter to Susan and Elizabeth. These women got the point, and they decided to stay home. History reveals that this outcome was no accident. All along, conscious choices were made to tax married women's paid work, to keep them at home, and to set up a system meant to reward and entrench the dominant traditional model of family life.

Meanwhile, an intellectual history evolved to give cover to the political/historical developments, brandishing arguments turning on logic, neutrality, and common sense at every turn. But the economist's tale gave the lie to any sense of necessity, logic, or neutrality informing the status quo. Before we could get carried away with a hope that the depths of patriarchy were behind us and that economic theory was shedding much-needed light at the end of a too long tunnel, however, along came the *Contracts* to pull us back. These political documents returned to the substance and style of arguments seen in regard to the social security reforms in the 1930s and the joint filing reform in 1948. Once again, wealthy traditional forces are deliberately using the rhetoric of family to argue for tax reduction for themselves, at the expense of working wives and mothers. Nothing important has changed.

This alone makes for a fairly complete story, one that casts a harsh light on tax policy. Tax is deeply gendered. It does not have to be, and it should not be, if we care about justice, utility, fairness, or wealth. Joint filing; the structure of social security; the nontaxation of imputed income; the tax treatment of work-related expenses, child-care costs, and fringe benefits; state and local taxes—all conspire to tax unduly those married women with children who try to work outside the home. Tax burdens add a fiscal tax to the psychological toll in evidence to all who would look. These effects have dramatic impacts across the entire range of income classes, as lower-income families are made unstable, middle-class married women are stressed, and upper-class wives are rendered marginal. That's enough for a pretty good book right there.

But it would be wrong to end here. Stopping at the conclusion of the tax tale would contribute to a sense that tax is a discrete set of issues, isolated from the rest of our lives. So we may be taxing two-earner families a bit heavily; so what? Tax is all about winners and losers, anyway. The Traditionals have by and large won and the Equals have by and large lost, but that's the way the votes fell in this round—and things may change. Pete Stark and his congressional colleagues understand this political calculus. It's all just one more tale in the "ever changing but never ending drama entitled 'Victims of Tax Injustice,' " as Boris Bittker put it. That's life, as they say.

Nothing could be further from my own view of the matter. I believe that tax is big and deeply gendered, and its gender biases cannot help having large effects throughout the entire socioeconomic system. Confining tax to a set of political questions about who pays what amount lets the forces of patriarchy off the hook too easily. It would be another example of a static and distributive focus blinding us to the deeper, richer, more significant questions of behavior over time. We have a tendency, perhaps most keenly felt in academia, to compartmentalize, to break matters up into small units for analysis and understanding. Thus we often miss bigger stories that transpire at the intersections of different spheres of activities. What is most wrong with the story of taxing women has little to do with tax per se: it has to do with the equality of concern and respect we are not showing to working wives and mothers—with the quality of life for women today.

We need to look at tax in context to see that the burdens of tax extend well beyond tax itself. America's means of taxing married women and mothers contribute to the major stresses and problems that all women face all the time in labor markets and in contemporary society generally. Part 4 goes beyond tax, without ever forgetting its grounding in a richer understanding of tax and its gendered structure, to consider more generally how we are treating women in America today.

THE BASIC STORY

The basic story gets played out every day, in ordinary lives all across America. Look around. Think of the modern image of women, especially working mothers. Countless magazines, newspapers, popular books, movies, and television shows supplement our individual, personal experiences, all painting a consistent picture. The working wife is harried and stressed, juggling the often competing demands of work and family. She remains the primary parent. Working mothers in two-worker households in fact spend more time with their children and much more time working around the house than do their husbands. Working mothers bear the brunt of the logistical and psychological stresses of dealing with child care; working mothers take time off to deal with sick children, and on and on. There is a recurrent theme of gendered vicious cycles, from Nancy Chodorow's psychoanalytic perspective on the social reproduction of mothering to Arlie Hochschild's portrait of the "second shift"—whereby women continue to work when they get home from work, while men rest and recharge for the next day's battles. Many working mothers are single parents, and many of these are poor; such mothers have all of the stresses of working wives, and then some.

These burdens play themselves out, but only in a one-way fashion, at work. Working mothers bear the stigma at work of *being* working mothers. Colleagues and superiors come to expect that their loyalties, time, and attention will be divided. Coworkers often resent working mothers, superiors often isolate them from managerial jobs or other avenues for upward mobility. Studies continue to show discrimination against women at the promotion stage. The working mother is also confronted with feelings of guilt, aggravated by the facts that her mother was far less likely to have been a full-time working mother than she is and that, even today, when much is made of the growing participation rates of women and mothers in the workforce, more than 40 percent of married women with young children are full-time mothers. Yet while the working mother is hurt by her status in the workforce, she is not helped by it in any meaningful way. A more dynamic workplace has not emerged to offer her satisfactory options. Part-time work is generally unattractive; flexible-time arrangements are rare; child care, which remains by and large the mother's responsibility, is limited, costly, and deeply unsatisfying on many levels. There is, for working mothers, no time, no help, no way out. This is a picture that reeks of stress and pain.

And what of men? The story of working fathers stands in stark contrast to that of working mothers. To return to popular images, the working father sometimes plays a light comic motif in television shows and movies. How cute it is to see Daddy struggle to change diapers while answering the phone! Isn't he adorably incompetent? We chuckle at the image of "Mr. Mom," delighting in an oxymoron that need not obviously be one at all. The facts of the matter are that husbands continue to hold full-time jobs with astounding regularity—95 percent of fathers of young children seem to be full-time workers. Fathers do far less housekeeping than their wives. They earn much more outside of the house. As we have seen with Connie and David and the nameless husbands of Susan and Elizabeth, a father's work outside the home comes first—first compared to his domestic responsibilities, and first compared to his wife's paid work. The gender gap is most acute—around 40 percent—when dealing with married persons; as of 1987, in married couple families in which both husband and wife worked full time, year round, wives earned 63 percent, on average, of what their husbands did. Men, in short, continue to do what they have done for most of the century: work full time in the paid workforce, playing the breadwinner role around the house and leaving the domestic details to their wives, whether or not these women also work outside the home.

None of this is to say that men do not suffer, too, from the lack of flexibility in the prevalent social models of work and family. They do. The burdens we've been considering on women go hand in hand with certain definite expectations on men. Men are pushed to play the primary-earning breadwinner role in the traditional families toward which the laws are skewed, even if they don't want to.

In a scene from the popular movie *Parenthood*, Gil, the character played by Steve Martin, has finally worked up the nerve to quit his job, where his boss has passed him over for promotion in favor of a less talented but harder working single man, Phil Richardson. Gil's boss holds against him the divided loyalties that Gil shows to his work and family; earlier, he had explained: "We get and keep clients because my partners and I work 25 hours a day, 8 days a week, 53 weeks a year. Phil Richardson works nights. He works weekends. He wears a beeper for whenever I need him. I can't even get you in on a Saturday." But Gil's liberation from his oppressive workplace is short-lived. He finds out that his wife, Karen, is pregnant again. After a brief but painful argument and discussion, Gil concludes that he must go back to the dreaded office, and make up with his boss:

> KAREN: Maybe this isn't the best time for you to be out of work or starting a new job. . . . You know this puts a minor crimp in *my* life, too. I was thinking about going back to work this fall. Now I can't.
>
> GIL: Well, you know, that's the difference between men and women. Women have choices, men have responsibilities.
>
> KAREN: Oh really? Okay. I choose for *you* to have the baby. Okay? That's my choice. *You* have the baby. *You* get fat, *you* breast-feed till your nipples are sore. *I'll* go back to work.
>
> GIL: All right. Let's return from La-La Land. That ain't gonna happen. And whether I crawl back to Steve or get another job; it's obvious now I've gotta put in more hours 'cause I ain't getting anywhere. So *whatever* happens you have to count on less help from me.

Because Gil is trying to do something more modern and creative than his fellow men at work, he finds that he shares something in common with his wife: he has no choice. He must play out a role created for other men, in other eras.

The fictional Gil's experience easily resonates with those American men and women in the middle 1990s who are trying to break out of a mold set decades before, whose constraining effects are barely visible but powerful nonetheless. The basic picture of the labor market in America today, when viewed with gender in mind, is one of inflexibility, discrimination, and particular stress on working women. Life has remained pretty much the same for men—itself a problem for those men, like Gil, who want something else—as women have borne the pressures of adapting to a new environment, one barely bending to accommodate them. The main theme I want to highlight in these final chapters is this lack of flexibility in terms of work-family balances.

A THOUGHT EXPERIMENT, AND A REALITY CHECK

To drive home this point, consider a basic mental experiment. Imagine knowing only limited facts about two periods in time. In 1940, on the eve of World War II, traditional, single-earner families were the norm, with an overwhelmingly high percentage of men working full time outside the home and women full time inside it. Fewer than 9 percent of all married mothers worked in the paid workforce, mostly among the lower classes. Claudia Goldin's work reminds us that most women left the workforce on getting married, and only a small minority returned; marriage bars were still in place. Fifty years later, by 1990, nearly 60 percent of married women with young children worked; 17 million married mothers were in the workforce in 1993. Marriage bars had disappeared and were now in fact illegal in most states. The gender wage gap had narrowed dramatically, almost disappearing in some categories. Now ask yourself, What else changed between 1940 and 1990?

Two possible answers spring to mind. One possibility is that traditional, single-earner families remain the norm, but now sometimes it is the man who stays home. A second possibility is that the workplace evolved different work-family balances, by featuring more and better part-time or flexible-hour jobs, to accommodate the massive influx of married working women and the new model of two-earner families.

Neither answer is correct. There are almost no traditional, single-earner families in which the man stays home and the woman works outside the home. An overwhelming majority—around 95 percent—of married men with young children work full time, whereas more than 40 percent of married women with young children are staying home full time. Men are four to five times more likely to be the single earner in traditional households, and in those relatively rare cases where women are the single earners, the families earn one-half as much as when the men are.

Nor has a more dynamic workplace evolved for the 60 percent of married women with children who do work outside the home, or for the millions of families headed by single-parent working women, most of them poor. Most jobs, even for married women, remain full-time ones; part-time labor is generally low in pay and prestige. Almost no families feature two part-time workers. Married mothers, even when they work outside the home, do two or three times as much work inside the home as do their husbands. Over and over again, the same story emerges to anyone who cares to listen: We are taxing women. Women simply bear far more of the stresses of modern life than men do. And we offer them few and limited ways to lighten their burdens.

That's the story I am going to be grappling with from now on. Many measures of women's lives in the paid workforce, like the gender wage gap and labor market participation rates, have been showing "improvement." But we'll come to see in chapter 11 that such facts as the narrowing of the wage gap are not at all inconsistent with the basic tale of deep and continuing gender injustice. In this chapter, meanwhile, I plan to sketch out how basic economic theory would have free labor markets work, and then to look at some things that make the world a very different place from the economist's chalkboard.

A CAUTIONARY NOTE OR TWO

I want to be clear at the beginning about what I am and am not doing. I include the analysis that follows, not to set out a final, definitive explanation of the causes or nature of gender bias in the workforce—a task that has eluded many highly skilled labor market theorists—but for three far more humble reasons, connected to the primary tale of taxing women.

One, I want to emphasize that the problems of taxing women cannot meaningfully be confined to tax alone, whatever that would mean. The deep skew of the tax system against working wives must affect labor markets, family models, and other important domains of modern life. Two, I want to establish that a genuine equality for women, one that shows them equal concern and respect, cannot just be about such objective indexes as the gender wage gap or labor market participation rates; I want to show how the gender gap might narrow, without undermining any of the gender injustice we have already seen. Three, I want to lay the foundations for an argument against doing nothing at all. We have heard from the social conservatives of the *Contracts*, who would turn back the clock and point us toward the 1950s. But there is another conservative chimera in the air: an argument that equality of the right sort has been obtained, such that we can dismantle affirmative action laws and turn things over to the free market, come what may. I shall end by saying a few words against this seductive notion.

These three goals are closely related. Since the gender wage gap is closing and since labor market participation rates for women are increasing, there is a temptation both to declare an end to the quest for equality for women and to denigrate any continuing complaints about tax or other socioeconomic systems along gendered lines. Can things really be that bad if women's pay is increasing? Or if women are working more than ever, and attending professional schools more, and so on? A large motivation in this part is negative: I intend to argue against the case that we need not worry about gender justice in tax or anywhere else any more.

The structure of the argument in this part runs as follows. I am going to assume certain "best case" facts for the conservative, laissez-faire, do-nothing position—such as that individuals and firms operating in labor markets are all rational and have no particular distaste for women—in order to show that, even on these facts, the case for doing nothing is very weak. In doing so, I am not taking any kind of stand on the reality of these facts. This part simply argues against those who would discount the evidence we have already encountered, who would have us believe that we are, indeed, approaching a promised land of equality for women, such that any lingering complaints of gender injustice are beside the political point.

There is a puzzle that has so many signs of unhappiness and yet so few signs of flexible, dynamic workplaces or work-family balances. Most families with children in America fall into one of three groups: a working man with a stay-at-home wife; two full-time working parents; or a single mother. In 1993, there were 65 million American children under the age of 18. Of these, 24 percent lived with their mother alone (compared with 3.5 percent with their father alone); 40 percent in households where both parents worked, the vast majority featuring two full-time workers; and 23 percent in dual-parent, single-earner families, mostly with the father working. The tax system, set up with a traditional single-earner family in mind, plays a large role in all this. These are the Lowers, Middles, and Uppers again.

Where are the families with two part-time workers? In 1987, the last year for which I could find specific statistics on this point, 637,000 of the 43,450,000 married-couple families with earnings fit the two part-time worker model—that is less than 1.5 percent, and even this number presumably includes a good many elderly couples without children at home. Where are the families in which it is the *husband* who takes time off to raise the children? The Census Bureau simply does not maintain tables listing the work experience of fathers, but well over 95 percent of all married men between the ages of 20 and 44 are in the paid workforce, and most are working full time. Why does such a big, diverse, rich, and dynamic market economy as we see in the United States offer such astoundingly limited work-family choices, especially when so many individuals want something else, and more?

THE BASIC EXPLANATION

My basic explanation for the paradox before us has five steps. One, the tax system is very heavily slanted, in its practical effects, against working wives and mothers. This is the accountant's tale. Two, women—at least *some* women, like Susan and Elizabeth—act on the basis of these biases and decide to stay home, at least for awhile, and care for their children. Other women see their households break up, as the economics of two workers among the lower-income classes results in unstable families.

Three, as women act in the face of these barriers, the basis on which rational employers calculate statistical probabilities changes. Firms conclude that married women are apt to be less dedicated, less persistent workers than men are. Employment, salary, and promotion decisions follow, constrained only by the fairly weak limitations against outright gender discrimination imposed by law. This third step sets in motion a certain "feedback loop," or self-fulfilling prophecy. Concluding that married women are less stable long-term employees, firms offer them lower wages and fewer promotions. Many women, in view of their prospects, see the handwriting on the wall and have even greater reason to stay home. These women are now even more likely to be the secondary earner in two-worker families, and we have seen that the tax system's bias is precisely against secondary earners. The circle closes in on itself.

It is chiefly at this third step that I am simplifying the complex labor market story. In my model, this stage relies on rational firms engaging in what economists call statistical discrimination. Statistical discrimination theories have long been a staple of explanations of the interaction between labor markets and gender, but they have failed to explain all of the gender wage gap or other evidence of employment discrimination against women. Within such theories, it bears noting that statistical discrimination is neither necessarily socially efficient—indeed, the optimal tax literature gives good reason to doubt statistical discrimination's efficiency, precisely because of the greater elasticity of married women workers— nor free of disturbing elements on other social grounds. I have several reasons for invoking statistical discrimination notwithstanding these qualifications. I want to keep the exposition simple; to make assumptions that paint the conservative arguments in their best possible light; to show that, even in that light, in the face of deep market imperfections like the tax system, the case for doing nothing is weak.

To be quite clear, however, I am not ruling out other explanations of gender bias in the workforce: what the literature on gender and work calls "human capital" models, misogyny, socialized discrimination, tastes for discrimination, and so on. The deep biases of the tax system add to and work with all of those explanations, as well, so our story can just be multiplied at this third stage. Tax is biased against working wives; people act on the bases of these biases; these actions set the stage for human capital decisions, tastes for discrimination, misogyny, and so on. Each cause adds to and compounds every other cause, and all contribute to an overall environment in which there are large collective action problems, the next step in the analysis. Gender discrimination, like many social phenomena, is overdetermined by a series of individually underdeterminative causes: no one explanation captures everything, but all the explanations, taken together, are more than enough.

Four, all parties—men, women, and firms—face what is called a "collective action problem" in addressing the resultant situation. Individual women have a hard time convincing firms that they will be different from their statistically dictated peer group. Men, offered higher salaries as husbands while their wives are offered lower ones, are hard-pressed to sacrifice real income for symbolic equality. Firms, faced with a societywide syndrome, are limited in their abilities to buck the trends. Many people will be unhappy but will see no way out of their personal dilemmas.

So much, perhaps, is at least dimly familiar. It captures a certain understanding of the reality of life in America today. Married women and mothers are in fact discriminated against, however rational this discrimination may be, and individual husbands, wives, and firms are unable to change things on their own. What is not as commonly seen is the role of our social systems in shaping and confirming the patterns. This observed reality is often written off to the "choices" men and women make, as if women would somehow freely choose a world in which they were disproportionately poor, marginal, unhappy, overworked, underappreciated, and stressed. So this story, somewhat familiar, takes on a different hue after our extended investigation into taxing women. Society is responsible, and perversely so, for the patterns that have emerged.

But now I want to add a fifth step, one rarely taken in our thinking about gender injustice in the workplace. Women with children, faced with a high hurdle on their way to paid work in the labor market, separate into three groups. One group, the mothers of one-quarter of all the children in the United States, are trying to do it all on their own. These are the single-women parents, most of them poor.

A second group, presently about 40 percent of all married mothers, decides to stay home. This group bears the stigma of this decision: women who ever take time off from the paid workforce are termed "gappers," and their pay and status level remain lower than those of non-gappers. Recall that when Susan reentered the workforce after a spell at home with her children, she had to accept a lower-paying position. A *Wall Street*

Journal article in 1996, entitled "After the Kids," describes some of the attitudes that Susan and Elizabeth may one day confront:

> All too often, employers feel that taking time away shows you're not competitive enough in the corporate workplace. They fear mixing older, more mellow employees with youthful, aggressive ones, thinking they might have trouble relating to each other. And they worry that homemaking experience could make an employee too nurturing in a fast-paced workplace.

There is some factual dispute among labor market economists about how long the lower status of gappers persists and when, if ever, it ends. But there seems little doubt that women pay at least some penalties, of various sorts, for having ever taken time off from the paid workforce.

A third group, encompassing about 60 percent of all married mothers and 40 percent of all American households with children, decides to leap over the hurdles facing them and work outside the home. These women still must deal with the collective action problem sketched above. They cannot, by themselves, will that there be attractive part-time or flexible-time options, for example, or that their husbands join them in a bold search for a creative, two-spouse, work-family balance. Instead, they must convince potential employers that they will be stable, productive, and successful workers—that is, that they will fit the only image firms have of such model employees. They will attempt to convince employers that they will work as men have always worked, throughout this century: full time and with full commitment. So working mothers will marry later, educate themselves more, have fewer children, remain on their jobs longer (to prove their commitment to the workplace), and stay in the workforce just as men do. In fact, the data bear this story out.

All we need to do to close the story out is to turn to men. The explanation predicts that they will not have changed much at all, because their pattern of work remains the model toward which women who work outside the home have had to aspire. In fact, married fathers continue to work full time with astounding regularity, and to do rather little around the home, even when their wives also work full time.

By pushing the story out to this fifth stage we can begin to see that society has been looking for equality in all the wrong places. Participation rates for married women might increase, and the gender wage gap may shrink, but nothing truly important has changed. We have simply said that we will "allow" women to be paid more or less like men—if they work like men, continue to bear primary responsibility around the home, put no pressure on men to change *their* ways, and pay a large fiscal tax for the privilege, to boot. No wonder many feminists have begun to despair of "equality" talk altogether. With equality like that, maybe justice isn't all it's been cracked up to be.

HOW LABOR MARKETS ARE SUPPOSED TO WORK

Let's consider now how labor markets are supposed to work in a free market. Then we'll look at a variety of market failures—tax will be a major one—that keep the simple story from prevailing and that make the real world a much more gendered place than the economist's blackboard is.

At least since the days of Adam Smith, free markets have held a tremendous attraction for liberal, democratic societies. Some of that attraction lies in the promise of aggregate betterment: following free market policies generally leads to an increase in the size of the social pie, as it were. So free market advocates, the alleged heirs to Smith, argue for competition, free trade, and open markets, to help the whole of society to grow richer and more productive.

But to Smith himself, his contemporaries, like David Hume, and most modern philosopher-economists, as diverse as the libertarian Friedrich Hayek and the liberal Amartya Sen, much of the appeal of free markets lies in their solicitude for individual liberty and happiness. Under free markets, individuals are free to do whatever they want to do, consistent only with certain rules against harming others, the brute facts of scarcity, and other human limitations. By each specializing in what he or she does best and trading freely with others, everyone can be made wealthier and happier without anyone's being made worse off. There is no coercion. Free markets and a minimal government presence are all that is needed—human nature, driven by self-interest and perhaps "confined generosity," to use Hume's phrase for the altruism individuals feel toward a small band of connected others, will do the rest.

Free markets for labor suppliers mean that individuals can do whatever they want and get paid their "marginal physical product of labor," in technical economic jargon, or what they are worth, in plain English. Suppose Jane is an excellent candlemaker. By looking at the demand side of the labor market to see what the demand for candles is, we can determine a price or wage schedule for Jane's work. If Jane were to decide, notwithstanding her talents and society's demands, that she would rather be a poet, nothing would stop her in our mythical free market state—she would make less money, presumably, but the choice would be hers. Jane could, for instance, spend her mornings making candles for $10 an hour and spend her afternoons writing poetry. Perhaps not devoting all her time to candlemaking might make Jane a lesser candlemaker than others, but that is no real bother: Jane might get just $8 an hour for her candlemaking skills, whereas more devoted candlemakers could reap $10. One can see, in this simple example, the attraction of free markets. There is no need for any centralized, coercive authority. The price system takes care of all that, and individuals decide to do what they want to do in the face of it.

Abstractly free and perfect markets feature what are called "spot markets" in goods and services. We are all familiar with this concept when it comes to goods: free markets like those in America lead to a rich and diverse marketplace, where consumers can buy a wide range of goods of different qualities, quantities, and prices at nearly any time of day or night. Think of the choices one has in buying bread or breakfast cereal in supermarkets. When it comes to services, spot markets mean that individuals sell their own skills, as individuals, however much they want, given only the constraints put on by demand, directly to the parties who want such services. Jane is, in other words, on her own. She can spend eight or ten or two hours a day making candles; she can work weekends or not; she can take months off at a time. How many candles she makes might affect the price of candles, although this is unlikely given a suitably large demand for candles, and it certainly might affect how good a candlemaker she is. But it's all up to her.

HOW LABOR MARKETS REALLY DO WORK

Perfectly free markets are nearly perfectly good things. But the world is not perfect, and this simple fact sets the stage for the rest of this chapter. Almost all of modern applied public economics deals with *market failures*, or situations where real markets do not work as perfectly free ones would. I will explore five such market failures: imperfect contracts, imperfect information leading to statistical discrimination, taxes, incomplete markets, and collective action problems. The point is to see how real-world labor markets affect women.

Imperfect Contracts

The first market failure arises simply from the need for cooperation in an imperfect world. Ronald Coase, who won a Nobel Prize in economics for a handful of surprisingly rich insights, wrote his first major article in 1937, "The Nature of the Firm." Coase pointed out that most individuals did not function as the self-sufficient atoms that pure free market theory depicted. Rather, people came together and formed firms. The reason for this coming together was to save on transaction costs—the first and, in many ways, classic example of a market failure:

> The main reason why it is profitable to establish a firm would seem to be that there is a cost of using the price mechanism. The most obvious cost of "organizing" production through the price mechanism is that of discovering what the relevant prices are. . . . The costs of negotiating and concluding a separate contract for each exchange transaction which takes place on a market must also be taken into account.

What Coase means here is that in a world without transaction costs, everyone would simply know the price of everything, including one's own labor. Coase is describing how various transaction costs move us away from the atomistic universe of Adam Smith and ideal, costless markets and into the real world of institutions, firms, and long-term contracts.

Imagine that Jane's best talent lies in making tires for automobiles. Pam decides that her best skill is in assembling cars. In the simple free market model, Pam would contract with a whole series of individuals—Jane for tires, Bob for steering wheels, Cathleen for engines, and so on—on the spot market. Obviously, these individual contracting sessions would get costly, as would the need to check up on each subcontractor and coordinate his or her activities. At some point, Pam decides that it is better to form a firm, and bring together under one roof all the individuals needed to manufacture cars. The institutional firm becomes the employer, and Jane and other individual workers become the employees. The presence of firms and employment contracts is, in itself, a deviation from free market theory; spot markets give way to institutions and longer-term contractual arrangements. Surprisingly, this deviation is going to have dramatic impacts that are disparate along gendered lines.

How can this be? Recall that Jane could work as much or as little as she wanted; she was paid only for what she produced. Free labor markets parallel free consumer ones in their wide range of choice for individuals. But once we have brought firms and employment contracts into the picture, we introduce processes that have their own imperfections. Instead of just getting paid for what she does, when and as she does it, Jane is going to sign a contract that will spell out various rights and duties in advance. Pam will not want to negotiate highly individualized contracts. She is also going to have the problem of figuring out exactly what Jane does. This latter effect is called a monitoring problem, and it is made difficult by the fact that most work represents the joint product of several individuals. It is hard, sometimes impossible, to figure out the value of any one person's work. Pam and Jane will sign some kind of contract with crude specifications: the number of hours per week Jane is to work, what is expected of her, when and how much time she can take off, salary and fringe benefits, and so on. In entering into this contract, Pam will have to make certain estimates. This leads us to a second market failure, imperfect information leading to statistical discrimination.

Statistical Discrimination

In the simple story, Jane has no accountability except to herself. She is paid on the spot market for the candles or automobile tires she makes. But the real world does not work that way. Individuals get together to form firms, and relatively standardized employment contracts soon result. In this setting, the employer has to sit down and figure out what to pay

Jane. Pam is likely to come up with a salary that is relatively constant over time, one that may feature annual raises and fringe benefits. In devising this employment contract, Pam, as we saw before, has to make some estimates.

Among the most important of Pam's guesses will be those that concern Jane's expected tenure with the firm. It takes time and money to find a good worker and enter into an employment contract—in the lingo of the day, these are search costs—so that Pam is unlikely to be enthusiastic about contracting with Jane unless she expects Jane to stay around and work for a while. For some jobs, search costs may be low, so the need for the employer to guess expected tenure is also low—but so is the pay. For skilled jobs, the employer has more need to estimate the likely tenure or "staying power" of the employee. Jane will need time to learn the ropes, and such training costs Pam and her firm time and money; finding new workers is also a time-consuming and costly process, and losing workers and having a high turnover can be demoralizing. As between two equally qualified potential employees, Pam is going to hire the one that she expects to stick around longer.

There is good evidence that firms think this way. Indeed, common sense alone confirms it. The importance of stability or tenure is the reason young workers are counseled against changing jobs too often. Almost anyone who has ever been in a job interview knows the importance of attempting to convince the interviewer about her desire to stay on that job for a while. A *Wall Street Journal* article from 1996, entitled "What You Should Say about Family Duties in a Job Interview," perfectly captures the problem:

> What do you say about family in a job interview? The issue poses a dilemma for job seekers and employers alike. Unless you explore an employer's expectations for face time and night and weekend work, you might end up working for the wrong company. Yet if you raise the issue in the first place, you may never get in the door.

This phenomenon of the stressful interview points to a major problem the employer has: she cannot completely trust the job candidate. Every decent candidate is going to try to convince the interviewer of her desire to stay in that job forever. How can the employer figure out the truth? This is the problem of *imperfect* or *incomplete information*. The employer does not know a key variable affecting the employment contract, expected tenure; the employee herself will generally not know exactly what her likely tenure is going to be; in any event, the employer cannot trust the employee in regard to this issue.

What does a rational employer do in the face of these problems? The answer is, of course, to guess—to play by the odds. Unable simply to take a potential employee's word for it, an employer will resort to some formal or informal mechanism of guessing. This is called *statistical discrimination*. Economists like the Nobel laureate Kenneth Arrow have long noted this tendency and its particular and pernicious influence on women and other groups that are discriminated against. From the employer's point of view, statistical discrimination is "rational" or efficient and profit-maximizing. This means only that the private benefits of statistical discrimination outweigh its private costs. Businesses regularly make decisions on the basis of information about probabilities, as in deciding what products to offer, and where and when and how to price them. Firms that are not capable statistical discriminators soon find themselves out of business in a competitive market, having lost out to their more efficient peers.

Statistical discrimination is not necessarily efficient or wealth-maximizing from society's point of view, but that is not my concern right now. Nor are the various psychological and symbolic harms that flow from statistical discrimination. What is my concern is the fact that the statistical discrimination in which firms engage relative to expected tenure is overwhelmingly likely to affect women adversely. At least in an early stage of the story, say in the 1950s or 1960s, firms were going to "guess" that young women would get married if they were not yet married, have children when they did get married, and leave the workforce for at least a while after giving birth. There is nothing necessarily sexist about the firms' motives here; they were just looking at the facts. And those facts still say that most women get married and have children. About 90 percent of all women marry at least once in their lives, and some 85 percent of women bear at least one child. A good many mothers take at least some time off after childbirth; even today, 40 percent of married mothers of young children stay home full time. Meanwhile, back to the men, the statistics suggest an opposite story: married fathers are *less* likely to move or take time off. They are the most committed of all employees.

There is good evidence that firms think this way or, at least, that other variables—such as individual human capital accumulations—take this effect into account. For one thing, the gender wage gap occurs mostly among married persons; single men and women get paid about the same. Why? In part it is because single women may be trying to convince potential employers that they will place their jobs first: that is, they will act as men traditionally have acted. It is also partly because the planning time frame of the firms may be short enough—firms are estimating only one or two years in advance—that a firm can ignore the risk of a maternity leave for the time being. Employment antidiscrimination laws also have some teeth, and firms may be trying hard to get more women employees for a variety of legal and public relations reasons. But employers are still going to try to get the women most likely to be committed first, and this means single women are more attractive to them. It is also the case that singles of both sexes get paid less than married men do—single men pose some risks, too. Marriage has a dramatic effect on all this: men see their pay go up on marriage, and women see theirs go down.

Firms thus discriminate against married women and in favor of married men. One of my favorite pieces of evidence, though of an anecdotal nature, is the tale told by Felice Schwartz in *Breaking with Tradition: Women and Work, The New Facts of Life*. Schwartz relates what she terms the "riddle of the rings": young women business students hide their wedding rings on the way to interviews so that firms will not know they are married. I was amazed by this story, enough to mention it one day to one of my large law-school classes. After class, many of the students came up to me and confirmed Schwartz's tale with their own life experiences. This is just one more of the strange but true ways we tax women.

Back to Tax

The statistical calculations disfavoring married women that rational firms perform are not just based on purely private preferences or on sociobiology, as is often presumed more offensively. These are not somehow "pre-market" choices—ones formed before entering into the economic spheres of life. Quite to the contrary, women's decisions are being made in the face of patriarchal social policies long in place. That's a major reason why the way we tax women is so offensive and also why the optimal tax story is so central: Women are making second-best decisions in an environment stacked against their working outside the home in stable two-parent households. The tax system was designed to foster and reward single-earner families, in which men could play the role of breadwinners, and women's work outside the home remained marginal and discretionary. This is what firms see today: individuals acting in the face of these incentives. It is not "life," in any abstract and general sense, that forces women to bear the brunt of statistical discrimination, to make difficult human capital decisions, or to face "tastes for discrimination" against them. It is *our* life—one we have chosen and constructed all along, at least in part with this outcome in mind.

Statistical discrimination used to be easy. As late as the 1950s, there were marriage bars in the workplace, so it was a pretty straightforward assumption that married women would leave the workforce. Susan and Elizabeth were not facing any official marriage bars, nor was there any inkling in their particular stories that they were dealing with women-hating employers. Rather, they were dealing only with the supposedly neutral tax system and the facts of life for working mothers today. But this was easily enough to tell them to stay home, and they did. As the stories of Susan and Elizabeth are replayed in millions of American homes, rational firms making statistical estimations of the likely tenure of potential employees have all the data they need. They, too, will tax working married women precisely because the tax system does, and life will get worse, still, in a viciously downward spiral. We will end up, at the bottom of that spiral, a long way from the calm logic of the neutral principles that rest at the top.

Tax is part of the incentive structure facing women, leading to decisions that enter into the statistical bases of employers' rational calculations. Susan and Elizabeth listened to their family accountants, and stayed home. They were acting perfectly rationally. Firms across America observe that the Susans and Elizabeths are likely to call it quits, at least for a while, after giving birth. Such firms then become reluctant to hire young married women in the first place. They are acting perfectly rationally, too. Men pick up the slack by working more, like Gil in *Parenthood*, or David, the Washington lawyer married to Connie, another Washington lawyer. Everything and everybody is being perfectly rational.

But what is *not* rational is what is hidden in all of this: the tax and other socioeconomic factors leading to household decisions to revert to traditional households after childbirth. There is nothing "rational" about this; it simply reflects political choices that society has made in decades past and that have grown in magnitude over the years. Tax plays a large role in this vicious cycle set in motion by informational failures—failures themselves set in motion by the fact that firms in real labor markets are sitting around thinking about employees' likely tenure in the first place. Tax is an input, as it were, in other market failures.

Tax is also a direct market failure. Classical free market theory takes no account of taxes; public economists have long known that taxes destroy the ideal properties of free markets. When taxes are added to otherwise free markets, strange things happen, as a variety of distortions to the price mechanism are introduced. This is exactly why economists developed the theory of optimal tax. The precise point of optimal tax, its founding inspiration, is to make taxes the least distorting they can be. We have already seen that the precepts of optimal income tax have been precisely and perversely rejected when it comes to taxing women.

Michael Boskin and other economists tell us we ought to be taxing married men twice as much as married women, in the interest of minimizing the distortions of tax. Politicians like Pete Stark, in stark contrast, tell us that we ought to be taxing families where the wives work more than those where they stay home, and the *Contracts* would simply pay women to stay home and care for their kids, maintaining all of the biases against working wives. Our actual policy is consciously and precisely backward to ideal economic theory. Society is deliberately exacerbating free market failures to get a social result it wants, at a high cost in terms of happiness and social wealth. This is what is known—or what should be known—as "social engineering."

Incomplete Markets

Another market failure, which until recently has been little studied in formal economic theory and which remains rarely noted in more public discussions of free market policies, is that of *incomplete markets*. Ideal market theory would have spot markets in goods and services, with everyone doing and getting what he or she wants, subject only to the constraints imposed by scarcity and the inexorable laws of supply and demand. If Dick wants bell-bottom pants, he should be able to buy them; if Allegra wants a lime green Volkswagen Beetle, she should be able to buy that. Anyone willing to pay the marginal cost of producing a good should be rewarded with the good.

Life does not, however, work that way. We seem, typically, to get much closer to ideal theory in practice on the consumer demand side—it is, in fact, possible to buy an astounding range of goods in America—than we do on the labor supply side. In the ideal free market world, it is up to Jane how and when to work: how to divide her time up among various jobs, when to take a vacation, and so on. Jane just makes her candles or automobile tires and sells them for what the market will bear. The rest is up to her.

In reality, the labor market moves away from spot markets and individuals and into firms and long-term contracts. To make matters worse, the choices of style of working are narrowly limited. In the case of Adam and Eve, in chapter 7, we saw that women were more elastic, and thus likely to react differently—and far more strongly—to labor taxes, such as the income or social security tax system. Figure 8, reprinted here, showed this graphically. This picture illustrated what happened when a 50 percent wage tax was imposed: Men, who were inelastically committed to a 40-

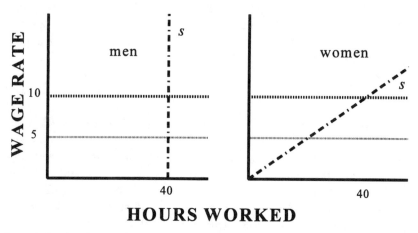

Figure 8. Men's and Women's Labor Supply, with Taxes

hour workweek, continued to work as before, but women, who had a wage elasticity of 1, preferred to work 20-hour workweeks.

The problem women face in the real world is the absence of good choices at that level. Part-time work remains low in pay, prestige, and opportunities for advancement, and flexible work patterns have been slow to develop. We have seen reasons for this on both the supply and the demand side of labor markets. As a result, women like Molly Middle must make second-best, all-or-nothing choices. Although something like 20–30 percent of married women who work do so part time—anything less than 35 hours per week, as the government defines it—the dominance of the full-time work model, for most married women and just about all married men, is striking. A good many part-time workers are involuntary ones, individuals who wish they could work full-time. Economist Chris Tilly points out that 17.5 percent of married women who work part time do so involuntarily, in the precise and obviously limited sense that they report themselves as "involuntary." Most part-timers are also what Tilly calls secondary, working in jobs "marked by low skill, low pay and few fringe benefits." Only a small fraction—less than a third—of part-time workers have what Tilly calls "retention" jobs, that is, "work schedules created to retain . . . valued employees whose life circumstances prevent them from working full-time."

A strong impression that emerges from surveys and other studies of working mothers is that nearly all are unhappy. Full-time workers wish they could work part time, to have more time with their children; part-time ones wish they could work full time, to get better, perhaps more dignified jobs. This is exactly what figure 8 would predict; if married women and mothers really want to work 20 hours a week, a market giving them their best options at zero or 40 hours a week is not going to satisfy them, and they will be left unhappy and struggling. That's a market set up for traditional households.

Labor markets are badly—sadly—incomplete, because there are individuals who would like to work, are willing to work for their efficient wage, but cannot find work arrangements to fit their needs and desires. In and of itself, that's a market failure. Something is wrong when people cannot do what they want to do and get paid just what they're worth for doing it. We can buy what we want, if we are willing to pay its social cost. Why can't we sell our labor as we want, if we are willing to accept its social value? Once again, the story is gendered. Too often it is women who are faced with options ill-suited to their preferences. This is exactly the point of the optimal tax findings: Women are disproportionately unhappy because the market does not offer them what they want. The fixity of the male preference for full-time work is also a part of the problem. This rigidity keeps firms from having to offer a broader range of choices, and it sets in motion the statistical discrimination discussed above. This fixity in male behavior is also part of the social script, for the tax laws were set up to reward and entrench this primary breadwinning role, as we saw most clearly in the social security and fringe benefit aspects of the tale. Primary earners meet the family's needs for medical and life insurance and retirement savings; secondary earners undervalue part of their pay; and employers look for either highly committed, full-time workers or low quality, part-time ones. Men like the fictional Gil from *Parenthood* get caught up in cycles, too. We all do, whether we notice it or not.

Collective Action Problems

There is one final market failure to put on the table: the idea of collective action problems. These result when a single individual or actor is powerless to pursue her own best interests because these interests depend on the actions of others, with whom it is too difficult and costly to coordinate. Women face this problem in spades. So do firms. So do men looking for some model other than that of being full-time, fully committed breadwinners.

What many women like Susan and Elizabeth want would seem to be more choice and more flexibility. They do not want to have to quit their jobs after giving birth. Recall Elizabeth's frustrated lament: "I had to quit because I could not afford my job." Women like Susan and Elizabeth might prefer to cut back a bit on their hours, at least for a while, while their husbands do, too. Or they might want other sharing arrangements with their husbands. Perhaps each might work full time for three-month intervals, while the other stays home with the children. But how can they do this on their own? How can they convince their employers to make an exception for them, and then go to their husbands' employers and argue for another exception?

Much of the literature on women's search for equal concern and respect in the workplace has taken place in the teeth of this kind of collective action problem. Thus, many books and articles argue for government policies to break the cycle, mandating better part-time work, maternity and paternity leaves, better child care, and so forth. But such centrally mandated regulations suffer from some well-noted problems. Rent control often springs to mind, where the suppression of the free market price system has led to a depressed supply of rental units, fewer landlords, lessened upkeep, and a byzantine black market among renters attempting to get the windfall benefit of submarket prices. Minimum wage laws also can have bad effects, and so on. The failures of regulation repeatedly make free markets, by contrast, look good. More generally, conservative academics and politicians have been able to look good in contrast to liberal and progressive ones because market interventions so often fail. The former communist regimes of Russia and Eastern Europe played out this story on a broad scale.

But there is a deeper perversion at work in the case of gender in the workplace. Society *is* regulating things, via tax and other socioeconomic systems, and doing so against working wives and mothers. The *Contracts* perfectly illustrate this theme. These documents went out of their way to find a particular means of reducing taxes that would leave in place all the adverse incentives to market work that Susan and Elizabeth and other married mothers face, and they celebrated just this fact. It is highly unlikely that other regulations are going to work, if they ever will, until we right that ship. The basic distortions of tax are compounded by statistical discrimination and incomplete markets, and they leave individuals and firms with a very big collective action problem.

Other books and articles take a different approach, arguing for individual empowerment on the part of women or changed behavior on the part of men. But these techniques, however wise and commendable they may be, also fly in the face of the social system and its collective action problems. Suppose Emma and Earl Equal decide that they are each going to work thirty hours a week, overlapping for perhaps ten hours while little Emily and Eddie get cared for in the neighbors' house—their neighbors having struck a similar deal—and each caring for the kids during the rest of the week. How will the Equals get their employers to listen to their fine plan? A small margin of progressive employers, in jobs that can lend themselves to this kind of thing easily enough, and for employees skilled and valued enough to make it worth their while, may go along. Other employers might just laugh at Earl and Emma, or say no, or even fire them. The deeper problem is that Earl and Emma are trying to write a modern and creative script on top of a social structure that is anything but modern and creative.

When we turn to real-world labor markets, which are flawed in any event, the deep gender biases of the tax laws make things at least doubly worse. Indirectly, tax enters into a cycle of statistical discrimination stacked against married women or into any of the other causes of gender bias. Directly, tax falls most heavily on such women, keeping them from being able to achieve as much happiness as other individuals. Tax is big, and it sets up a big collective action problem for all of us. In the face of this very large set of problems, ad hoc institutional reform or exhortatory rhetoric is not going to do the trick. We have a good deal more to do than that.

11 Not Just the Gender Gap

CHANGING THE TUNE

Chapter 10 sketched out a dynamic in which the already severe discriminations of the tax system against working wives and mothers were worsened by the rational and predictable actions of firms in the "free" labor market. Ideal markets hold out the promise of flexibility, freedom, and respect for individuals and their choices. In the real world, however, things go awry. Firms quickly replace individual actors, and standard employment contracts replace the spot markets of the economist's chalkboard. In this setting, statistical discrimination compounds the distortions of tax; other factors, such as decisions affecting human capital, or investments in education and training, follow suit, working interactively in a giant feedback loop. Women bear the brunt of market failures—of imperfect contracts, incomplete information, statistical discrimination, tax, and incomplete markets. Collective action problems make things worse, as individual women, men, and firms stand almost powerless in the face of large social forces, often little understood.

At this point in the story, many married women with children are throwing up their hands. Why bother swimming upstream forever? They might as well listen to what Pete Stark, Ronald Reagan, Newt Gingrich, the Christian Coalition, accountants everywhere, and the tax and social security systems are all trying to tell them: stay home with the kids, at least for a few years. They can always get back into the labor market later—at lower pay, to be sure, and stigmatized by the fact that they have breaks in their employment histories. But at least that's better than the absurdity of working full time outside and inside the home, struggling to make ends meet, and having insult added to the considerable injuries of it all when the family accountant tells them that they are actually costing the family money. Employers simply presume that mothers will not be fully committed workers, anyway, so that such women face daily barriers at work and at home, and all for a few dollars at best.

A good many married women with children do stay home full time. This strong tendency drives the statistical discrimination considered in the last chapter: firms know that the odds are good that young married women will leave the workplace after giving birth. The high elasticity of women at the participation stage suggests that many women who stay home are conflicted, as are many of the married mothers who are working full time outside the home. The Traditionals and the Christian Coalition want mothers to stay married and stay home; they want to get back to that golden age of the 1950s. But statistics and common experience confirm that many women want something else, something more deeply respectful of them and their autonomy. Women want their children to be loved and well cared for, and to grow up happy, healthy, and successful. But why should it be that the only or best way to do this is for women, alone, to stay home? Society ought to be disturbed by the facts that so few married fathers stay home; that so many working wives would like to have more flexible jobs; that a good many stay-at-home mothers would like to work at least part time; that many lower-income households are single-parent, female-headed ones; that divorce has left many women with underdeveloped job market skills. Over and over again, a story emerges of limited and unhappy choices facing women, matched by monotony in the male sphere of work and family.

WHAT ABOUT THE GOOD NEWS?

The bleak picture just sketched is not all of the story. What about the other 60 percent of married mothers, the ones who do work outside the home? Participation rates for married women with children have been steadily escalating for decades, as figure 9 shows. This figure indicates the enormous growth in participation by married mothers, from 8.6 percent in 1940, at the outset of World War II, to 66.3 percent in 1990, a steady escalation of approximately 10 percent per decade, or 1 percent a year, over the entire period. June O'Neill, in a 1994 article in the *Wall Street Journal*, noted that "close to 60% of married women with children under age six are now in the labor force; in 1960, the proportion was only 19%."

A similar, if more complicated, picture could be shown for the gender wage gap. Although the difference between men's and women's wages goes through periods of stagnation, it has been moving toward elimination over a long period of time. Claudia Goldin, who has traced the gender wage gap from the early nineteenth century down to the present, reports that women's earnings as a percentage of men's have gone from around 30 percent to more than 70 percent in that span. By 1993, white working women had median weekly earnings of about 76 percent of white men; African American women had median weekly earnings of 89 percent of their male brethren. Figure 10 presents some of this data.

Figure 10 illustrates the stagnation in the gender wage gap during the 1960s and 1970s, which understandably drew a good deal of scholarly and public attention and concern. But the figure continues to show the dramatic narrowing of the gender gap since 1980.

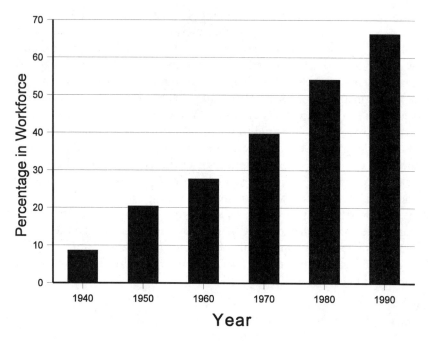

Figure 9. Participation Rates for Married Mothers, 1940–1990

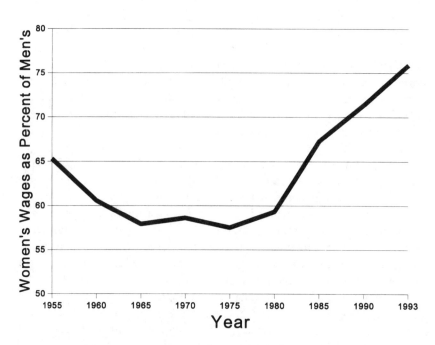

Figure 10. Gender Wage Gap, Full-Time White Workers, 1955–1993

Of course, there is no way to be certain that the positive trend will continue, but Goldin's work and other data give us reason to believe that it may well. By 1990, younger women made nearly 80 percent of what men the same age did. June O'Neill, in the article mentioned above, writes that even the 80 percent figure "overstates the gender gap between men and women with similar skills and training"; she points out that "at ages 25 to 34, where women's skills have increased the most, the ratio is 87%." A 1996 salary survey in the popular magazine *Working Woman* found that "in the 28 fields for which salary information was available by gender, women typically earn 85% to 95% of what men in similar jobs take home—far better than the 74 cents-on-the-dollar figure cited by the Bureau of Labor Statistics as the difference between women's and men's wages." There is reason to think that the gender wage gap may soon become a thing of the past, although we still, as these figures indicate, have some way to go, and the last steps may be the hardest.

The reaction to these objective signs of improvement for working women has been predictable enough. They have been used to buttress a conservative call to dismantle any affirmative action programs, to stop having any special preferences for women, and to get back to a "neutral" status quo. Don't the numbers tell the story? Women asked for equality in the workplace, and now they are getting it; any lingering shortfall is due to free choices that reflect, rather than disprove, the attainment of a promised land of equal rights. It isn't fair to change the rules of the game now and to start asking for something else, and more. Then leading Republican Presidential candidate Bob Dole cosponsored a bill, strategically named "The Equal Opportunity Act of 1995," to get rid of federal affirmative action programs for women and racial minorities, and moves are afoot on many state levels to do the same. It is time, these conservatives are saying, to move on.

SAME OLD SONG

But the objective numbers of "improvement" are not harbingers of a promised land of full, rich equality for women. How could they be? Marriage bars continued into the 1950s; federal laws prohibiting discrimination against women in the workplace were not enacted until the 1960s; the ERA, attempting to guarantee full equality for women, was defeated in 1982. How could a single generation of formal equality wipe out the biases deeply entrenched during centuries of patriarchy? Those who would declare an end to the special problems of women are looking, conveniently enough, in all the wrong places. If we look better, and harder, we will indeed see the persistent signs of taxing women in abundance. The fact that married women have been flocking into the workplace should not cast doubt on the basic tale. This story of bias against working wives is too well grounded in accounting, economic, and historical facts to crumble in the face of some merely potentially inconsistent data.

A closer look tells a truer tale. The signs of improvement noted above are taking place in the face of, and in many ways despite, the barriers to a richer, deeper equality for women. Women are succeeding in the still male-dominated workplace because of the force of their talents and the intensity of their desires to work outside the home—and not because that workplace is changing to accommodate them. Society is still taxing women, in part by forcing them to work, if they stubbornly continue to insist on working outside the home at all, under terms and conditions set in a patriarchal period.

I now present an explanation of the objective signs of improvement— the narrowing of the gender gap and the rising labor market participation rates for married women—that is consistent with both our tentative conclusion and the omnipresent subjective signs of women's stress. Such an explanation is not hard to come by. All we have to do is to look at *how* the gender gap is narrowing, and not just the fact that it is. Women are beginning to get paid like men because they have separated into two groups: one that stays home, the other that works the way men in traditional households have long worked. This should not be taken as a completely happy tale or as a mark that the need to address gender issues has ended. We have taken only the easiest first steps on what will no doubt be a long journey.

WOMEN'S CHOICES: BETWEEN ROCKS
AND HARD PLACES

Many women want to do something other than stay home full time or work full time outside it. This is confirmed by countless sources: surveys of working and nonworking mothers, magazine articles, popular television shows, untold family discussions transpiring in relative anonymity every day. Married mothers, at least a good many of them, would like a world of deeper equality and partnership with their husbands. Women would like the men to help out more and better in the home and with the kids; they themselves would like to get out of the home on a regular basis, maintaining workplace skills and contributing to the financial well-being of the household; and they would *also* like to have ample time to raise and nurture their children personally. Sharon Nickols, a professor of family economics, wrote in 1994 that "the growing literature on balancing the demands of work and family indicates that what employees most need and desire is greater flexibility, as one employee put it, 'to get more control over my life.' " The elasticity figures showing the conflicted nature of women's desires testify to this pattern of preferences.

It is not a crazy set of preferences. Nothing in nature alone would prevent these three sets of circumstances from coming to be—men helping out, women getting out, and both parents mutually engaging in parenting their children. Much of the appeal of free labor markets lies in their ability to accommodate just such desires. Given spot markets, no one cares if Emma Equal works outside the home in the mornings, while Earl works inside it, and the two trade places in the afternoons, leaving some days for family getaways, or if instead they alternate entire months at work. These desires point to an institutional order in which husbands and wives each work inside and outside the home, equal in both spheres. This would mean that both spouses could work part or reduced time or on flexible schedules. This is far from a crazy set of preferences; it is also one that is hardly available to most American families today.

I'll return to the male side of this picture, featuring the astounding rigidity of husbands' work patterns. Here I take a deeper look at married mothers. I speculated above that such women, in the face of labor market options not accommodating their preferred choices and a tax system heavily skewed against them, would make all-or-nothing choices, as Molly Middle did. In fact, they have. The more than 40 percent of married mothers of young children who stay home full time is obviously a large group of women. We tend to neglect this segment of the population, in part because it is a pool that has been shrinking. No politicians are writing documents like the *Contracts*, regretting the fact that so many mothers are still staying home full time. An occasional feminist, like Rolande Cuvillier, does indeed rail against housewives, but most feminists have come to appreciate and respect women's choices to stay home and nurture their families—as long as these are choices freely and fairly made. That's the rub I'm getting at here; women's choices are far more constrained than men's are.

What about the 60 percent of married mothers of young children who do work outside the home? Although statistics are hard to come by, only a small part of these working mothers seem to be working part time. In 1993, for example, about 25 percent of all women who worked did so part time, but less than 20 percent of all working women between ages 25 and 54 did so. (This age range is annoyingly large, but it is how the Census Bureau tracks women's work.) The proportion of 25- to 54-year-old working women employed part time had dropped from 22 percent in 1980 to 19.6 percent by 1993. We need to look at the overall number with some care, because working women are a very large group. Figure 11 presents the percentage of women working part time in 1993, broken down by age group. This figure demonstrates that contrary to what our expectations might have been, part-time work is least likely to be found among women in the prime parenting years. Part-time work is far more common among teenage and senior women. It has not emerged as a major solution to the stresses facing working wives and mothers.

Other more casually obtained statistics often put the percentage of

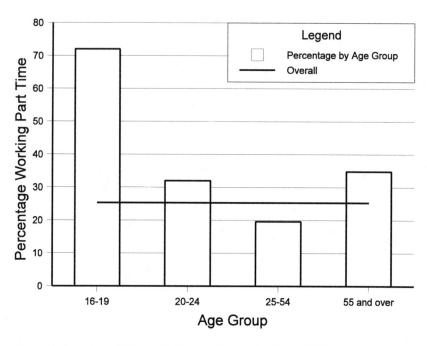

Figure 11. Percentage of Women Working Part Time by Age Group, 1993

working mothers who work part time between 20 and 30. All of these figures are in some ways overstated, though, because they count involuntarily part-time workers, women who report that they are working part time while looking for full-time work. Chris Tilly points out that almost all of the increase in part-time workers since 1979 has been among these involuntary part timers. The particular percentage of mothers voluntarily working part time in 1989 was actually lower than it had been twenty years before, in 1969. Meantime, to complete the picture, very few fathers seem to be working part time. Less than 5 percent of all working men between ages 25 and 54 worked part time in 1993, and this again would include some involuntary part-time workers.

Even if we put the proportion of working mothers of young children who work part time at 20 percent—probably too high a figure—it means that, of all married women with young children, roughly 48 percent work full time, 40 percent stay home full time, and 12 percent work part time, many of the latter unhappy and wishing to work full time. And these figures are based on a definition of part time as including anything less than thirty-five hours a week. It all hardly fits the ideal story sketched above, of women working part- and flexible-time schedules, inside and outside the home, while their husbands do, too. But the pattern does fit the all-or-nothing effect we saw when taxes and other costs of being a working mother were considered in chapter 6, and the sense of incomplete labor markets discussed in chapter 10.

Note just how far away we have gotten from the mythical free market system, where individuals could call all the shots. Now we see that tax and other factors affect the choices individuals are making on the supply side. Many women, once they are given the facts of tax, child care, and other socioeconomic realities, including statistical discrimination and collective action problems, decide either to work full time outside the home or to stay at home full time. Among the lower-income classes, the burdens impede stable family structures, and many of the poor female heads of households are also pushed to look for full-time work.

Meanwhile, on the demand side, employers face little pressure from women and no pressure at all from men to change their ways, to offer more or better part-time options. Employers do use part- and flexible-time labor, increasingly, but this is for their own reasons: to skirt fringe benefit requirements, to save on overtime pay, to have more flexibility to hire and fire along with the business cycle. This leads to the depressed state of the part-time labor market, where individuals are involuntarily part-time workers. It is crucial in our thinking about part-time work to differentiate two broad sectors—one of low pay, prestige, benefits, and mobility, dictated by demand side pressures, and the other of meaningful, decent work done for fewer hours than the full-time model. The latter sector, which is clearly what most individuals who yearn for part-time work want, is by far the smaller part of the bigger picture.

All this means that the workplace gets set up on the old model of full-time, fully committed workers—what we had around 1950. In a deeply flawed market, made especially bad by taxes, aggravated by imperfect contracts, statistical discrimination, and collective action problems, married women with children are offered starkly limited choices. The fact that the women who are working full time and with full commitment are getting paid almost the same as men who work that way hardly gives us, all by itself, equality of the right sort.

Women as a class seem unhappy with this state of affairs, as both optimal tax theory and empathetic common sense readily show. That the women who are working full time have managed to succeed as well as they have, both at work and at home, is a tribute to their resilience, intelligence, strength, and courage. It has nothing to do with how society has helped women, for, by and large, it has not.

GIVING SIGNALS

Economics has become increasingly sophisticated in its analysis of human behaviors in the presence of market failures in general and informational shortcomings in particular. In many situations, parties do not have all of the information that they would like to have to make a decision. Very often, one side of a transaction has better information than the other; this is known as a problem of *asymmetric* information. Reactions to asymmetric and other informational problems turn out to play an interesting role in gender discrimination.

Michael Spence first and most lucidly pointed out the important role that signaling plays in real-world markets. Spence's prime example of signaling was education; his insight was that a degree from a prestigious institution serves as an excellent signal of a potential employee's abilities. This is one reason why résumés are so important and why graduates of the best schools so often get the best jobs. Employers want to know about an employee's intellect, work habits, and general aptitudes. But how do they find this out in short interviews? Giving an intelligence test would often be seen as clumsy. A university degree gives a nice signal.

Signaling helps to continue the tale I've been telling, in a way that highlights both the burdens that women disproportionately face and how the gender wage gap could be closing without the real sting of these burdens going away. We have seen that rational employers in actual labor markets are concerned with the likely tenure of their potential hires. Firms want workers who will stick with it, learn the ropes, and become long-term productive "players," as they say. This minimizes the firm's search, training, and disruption costs. But how is the firm going to figure out which potential employees will stay a long time and which will not? It cannot gain much by asking a job candidate how long he or she expects to stick around. The answer to that—something like "Forever, sir" or "As long as you'll keep me"—is neither surprising nor particularly helpful. Firms have a problem, and potential employees do, too. Individuals are going to fish around for signals of their likely persistence or staying power with the firms so that they can get the job in the first place.

Men have it pretty easy. Men, especially married men, are more or less presumed to be stable, long-term players. Just as automobile insurance rates for men go down on marriage, so do their employment prospects look up. Employers rationally conclude that young married men are going to be productive full-time workers. For men, having children is even viewed as a positive thing at work. It increases the family's need for income and makes it far more likely that the wife will stay home, even further increasing the need for income. Gil from *Parenthood* knows this. The best way for young men to signal their commitment to the workforce is to be young men, although getting married is not a bad idea, either.

What about women? Yet once again, the story gets more complicated, and decidedly worse for women. For all the reasons that men have it pretty good and easy in the signaling game, women have it hard and bad. Firms that are drawn by market failures to discriminate statistically are overwhelmingly likely to do so against women, especially young women, and especially young married women. The gender wage gap increases steeply among married persons and as we move from the youngest cohort, ages 25–34, into the prime parenting years, 35–44.

How do women who take the "working" side of the stay-at-home-or-work-full-time coin attempt to convince potential employers of their seriousness about work? They will try to signal. How? One way is to attempt to hide the fact of their marriage: to take their wedding rings off on the way to job interviews, quite literally. This might paradoxically hurt all women, as employers begin to just assume that women are married: the "signal" of being ringless gets weakened. What else might they do? Women who want to work at good full-time jobs might marry later and have fewer children, for one thing. An excellent way to show commitment is also to be committed; this is a large reason why gappers like Susan forever bear the stigma of having interrupted their working career. So working women would be expected to stay in the job market longer, and maybe even stick it out in particular jobs longer—longer than they otherwise might and longer even than similarly situated men.

Here is more gender irony. Men can change jobs, because the presumption is that they are "moving up," and all rational employers want talented, ambitious workers, even if they sometimes lose them. At least the initial employer will have some chance, some option, to retain the worker, by offering to match the terms of the newer, better job. Losing good men is a cost of success that firms prefer to the option of not hiring good men in the first place. Women, in contrast, are less mobile. If they move, the inference might be not so much that they were talented and ambitious, like men, but rather that they had to follow their husband around. A rational firm would be wary of hiring someone who might move for reasons it could not know or control. How is a firm to see a *husband's* relocation coming? or to match *his* better job offer? This is yet one more cost of being secondary, on the margin.

Back to signals, another excellent possibility is education, Spence's own example. By pursuing education—say, getting an advanced degree in law, medicine, business, nursing, accountancy, engineering—a woman is doing at least two things to address her need to signal commitment, over and above the general signaling of ability and the actual training that both men and women obtain from schooling. Women are further showing potential employers that they are serious about work. Why would anyone work her way through law or business school just to quit as soon as she has a baby? Women are also typically putting themselves in debt, committing themselves to a need for money income that imputed income from housework won't satisfy. This also helps to convince potential employers that the woman is serious about working outside the home.

THE GENDERED FACTS OF THE MATTER

We've seen that married women face large barriers in labor markets, aggravated and set in motion in many ways by the large discriminations of the tax system. This system was set up to entrench and perpetuate single-earner families, where women stay home. Faced with these and collective action problems, women face an all-or-nothing choice—to stay home or to work full time outside the home. There is excellent evidence that most women have chosen one of these two routes; working wives and mothers are not turning to part-time work. The women who choose to work still face problems, however, of convincing potential employers of their likely persistence, as rational firms continue to engage in statistical discrimination. Our simple discussion of signaling predicted that such women would marry later; have fewer children and have them later in life; stay on particular jobs longer—longer than they might otherwise, but also longer even than men, who don't especially need to signal commitment in this way; stay in the workforce over their lifetimes; and educate themselves more—once again, more than they might otherwise, and more than men.

Statistics bear out all of these predictions. Working women have been marrying later, having fewer children, staying on their jobs longer, and educating themselves more. Many studies, such as Elaine Sorensen's *Exploring the Reasons behind the Narrowing Gender Gap in Earnings*, have shown that a large factor in the narrowing of the gender wage gap has been the increasing advanced professional education of women. Women are making gains in law, accountancy, and medical fields, for example. Francine Blau and Marianne Ferber present particularly interesting data showing that in 1970, 64.2 percent of women ages 20 to 24 had been married at least once; by 1989, this figure had plummeted to 37.5 percent—a remarkable social change in less than twenty years. Claudia Goldin, Sorensen, and others have demonstrated that these two decades were a period of especial acceleration in the narrowing of the gender gap, as figure 10 showed. Fertility rates until very recently had been steadily dropping since the 1950s, more or less in lockstep with the rising participation rates for married women and mothers and with the increase in women's earnings. As women work and earn more, they are also having children later in life. Although significantly less than 10 percent of women say that they plan on never having children, and although statistics indicate that 85 percent or more of all women will become mothers at some point, the likelihood of becoming a parent is lower for the best educated and highest paid. June O'Neill, in the *Wall Street Journal* article mentioned above, notes: "Through delayed marriage, low fertility, and an increasing tendency for mothers of young children to work, women have acquired many more years of continuous work experience than was true in the past."

Of course, there are varying explanations for all these trends. Higher pay, for example, increases the "opportunity costs" of having children or leaving the workforce—what a woman gives up when she stays home. Explaining large-scale social movements is a delicate business. I do not aim to give a single, definitive explanation for the observed changes in women's behavior. Instead, I want to indicate the consistency of the observed data with the predictions sketched above. This should at least cast some doubt on the meaning of objective measures like the gender wage gap and women's labor participation rates.

Blau and Ferber present data on the "labor force turnover" rates of men and women. This statistic measures how much individuals move into and out of the paid workforce in any given year. It is, a bit more technically, the difference between the labor force experience rate—the percentage of a group's members in the workforce at some point in time during a year—and the labor force participation rate, which is the average percentage of the group in the workforce at any one point in time, as a percentage of the latter. In 1957, for example, 47 percent of women worked at some time during the year, but only some 36 percent were working at any one typical time. The labor force turnover rate in that year was thus nearly one-third (47 minus 36 divided by 36). This meant that many women who sometimes worked did not always do so. If, to take another example, 95 percent of a given group was working at some time throughout the year, and 95 percent were also working on any average workweek, that group would have no turnover at all—no member of it would ever have taken time off.

The labor force turnover statistic thus gives a sense of the relative attachment of workers to the workforce. Figure 12 shows the labor force turnover rates for men and women at five-year intervals, from 1957 to 1989 (the last period is a seven-year one). This figure dramatically illustrates the central point. Women who work are beginning to work as men do and always have, and men have not changed very much at all. Whereas male turnover rates have remained rather steady at the 8 percent range, dropping a bit to 5 percent in the 1980s, women's turnover rates have steadily plummeted, from 33 percent as recently as 1962 to 9.9 percent just twenty-seven years later.

Similarly, the elasticity of working women is approaching that of working men, as Robert Triest, James Heckman, and others have observed. The continued high elasticity of married women is at the participation stage, when it comes to deciding whether to work at all, although upper-class women seem also to have some flexibility in decisions about hours of work. Once they are working, though, women stay on their jobs just as men do, even in the face of tax increases. This is related to the turnover story captured in figure 12: women who work are sticking with it, just as men who work always have.

Once again, it is not clear what to make of these facts. As to the labor

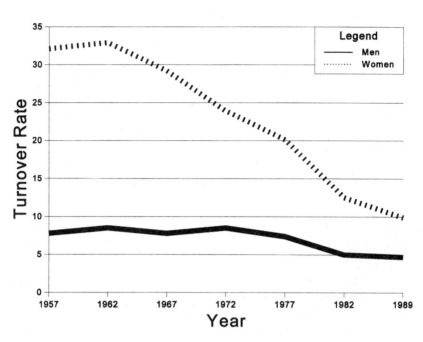

Figure 12. Labor Force Turnover Rates of Men and Women, 1957–1989

force turnover and elasticity data, one could tell a story that working breeds a "taste for work," and that women, just like men, quickly get socialized into a full-time workweek model. But one could tell quite a different story, equally well, consistent with the general tenor of our analysis to this point. Women of all sorts are holding on for dear life. Working wives continue to be unhappy and frustrated; they miss their children, and feel a bit guilty, but they also desperately want to work in a dignified fashion and preserve their career skills and options. Such women know full well what statistics and common experience verify: if they ever give into the temptation to leave the workforce, even for a brief spell, as Susan and Elizabeth did, they may spend the rest of their careers in lower paying, less prestigious jobs. Many of these working mothers are not really much different from the stay-at-home ones: they are deeply conflicted about work and family. They behave like men at work have always behaved—working full time, come hell or high water—because they have no real choice.

PAYING THE PRICE

One way to understand the central point of this discussion is to see that signaling has its costs. Some social theorists miss this point because signaling is always, from an individual's point of view, *rational*; one would signal only if the personal benefits of doing so outweighed the personal costs. But this does not mean that signaling, any more than statistical discrimination, which is also a rational act for its perpetrators, is a good thing. Signaling, like all reactions to market failures, has its costs, and justice dictates that we look to see where those costs fall before we just sign off on the market, failures and all.

In the real world, people have to signal—and women have to signal more things, more often, than men do. In order for women to get good and dignified jobs in a culture set up for men to work full time, with full commitment, they have had to prove to potential employers that they can and will act as men do. Women are being perfectly rational when they stay home, when they work, or when they go to great lengths to show that they will work like men. They are being perfectly rational in the face of deeply and disturbingly limited choices. It is precisely this lack of choice that is the big structural underlying problem, not the rationality of the choices made in the face of that lack of choice.

Meanwhile men, who as a class never wanted these choices, have kept up business as usual, while society at large continues to place barriers, sometimes insurmountable, in the way of working women. Psychological and other studies, like the elasticity and labor force turnover data for working men, repeatedly show both that men are generally comfortable with their role as full-time working breadwinners and that they are uncomfortable when women encroach on that role—when women start to work and earn as much as men do, and even exercise authority over them. We are not going to get more and better choices until we redistribute the burdens of modern life, until we make it a little bit easier for women to do what they want and a little bit harder for men to do what they want. That's what a true equality of concern and respect suggests.

The gender wage gap is not a complete measure of equality because it looks only to the visible, static index of paid wages. There is a grave danger in dwelling too much, too exclusively, on the obvious—especially when so much of gender bias is obscure and invisible. "Equal wages for equal work" cannot be all that women want. It is a good thing, and something that women clearly and rightfully deserve, and they ought to get it. But the bigger picture is one of gender justice, of equal concern and respect for women. This is a more abstract set of goals, and, on that account alone, a more difficult one to obtain. There is a nearly exact parallel to what we saw in the history of the income tax. Handy, seemingly neutral slogans like "equal tax for equal-earning couples" stood in the way of the deeper, richer, more important yet more difficult and abstract quest for gender justice in tax. This is a mission that would take into account behaviors, time, and diverse values.

Many women seem to want more choices and more respect for their preferences, needs, and desires. They want flexibility and options, and they want men and the workplace to shoulder some of the stresses of change, too. Women want to stop being singled out and taxed—taxed literally, by seeing so much of their earnings disappear, and metaphorically, by bearing so many of the burdens of market failures and limitations, and of modern life generally. Once again, optimal tax theory confirms this tale: Women's choices are being distorted by the real world, far more than men's choices are. Women have had to bend and twist and contort their desires to fit into a world that continues to burden them at every turn. It is not fair, and even the total elimination of the gender wage gap will not make it fair. Gender injustice will not disappear when women have made the marginal value of their labor equal to men's and when rational firms recognize that fact. It is a lot harder than that, and it is going to take a lot more time and effort.

WHAT ABOUT THE MEN?

The tax system was set up at a time when Traditionals ruled; most married women did not work outside the home, and most married men did. Further, men worked in a particular way—full time with full commitment. Men liked things this way, as the elasticity and numerous surveys have confirmed, and they did not want change. Individual men like Gil from *Parenthood* who might now want to opt out of their expected roles face collective action problems: they, too, are trapped by the rigidity of the social structure.

Figure 12 gave us a pretty good sense of male persistence. Men have always had rather low labor force turnover, and the trend of this statistic has been pretty flat over the past four decades at least, a time when women's turnover has changed dramatically. The elasticity figures presented above also underscored the monotony of male patterns of work. It is rare for married fathers to do much other than work full time. Although the Census Bureau does not track the labor market status of men and fathers nearly as much or as well as it tracks that of women and mothers—itself, of course, a tale of some interest—more than 95 percent of fathers seem to work, and almost all of them do so full time. That number has not changed much at all as the participation rate for married women has escalated dramatically. It is still clear, when the *Contracts* or Pete Stark or Ronald Reagan talk about one-worker families, whom they mean.

Let's look at two more pictures to drive home this point of male inflexibility, while noting an oddity in our intellectual understanding of matters. It is sometimes said that things are changing for men, too, and that one reason for the narrowing of the gender wage gap has, in fact, been the decline of male labor market participation rates. An article by Howard Hayghe and Steven Haugen, then economists in the Division of Labor

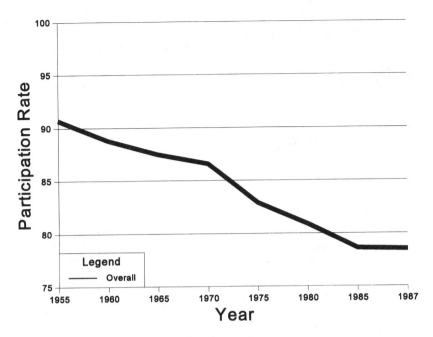

Figure 13. Labor Force Participation of Husbands, 1955–1987

Force Statistics for the Bureau of Labor Statistics, is often cited on this point. Hayghe and Haugen include a diagram, like figure 13 (which is slightly altered), graphically showing the decline in the labor force participation rate of husbands.

At first glance, figure 13 seems to show a story of some dynamic change among married men: a labor force participation rate for husbands that dropped significantly, from 90.7 percent in 1955 to 78.5 percent in 1987. This is not as dramatic as it sounds, given the far more than tripling of married mothers' participation rates over this same period. But at least it shows some movement in the male sphere. Yet we need, once again, to look more closely at the numbers and break them down by different age cohorts or groups to get a more accurate picture of what is going on. Figure 14 superimposes onto figure 13 the particular participation rates for husbands in the age groups 25 to 34 and 35 to 44, prime parenting years.

Figure 14 shows the real story of what has been going on. Husbands between the ages of 25 and 44 have been working with astounding regularity, so much so that these age cohorts crowd each other out in the very top of the chart. In the age group 25 to 34, for example, 98.8 percent of husbands worked in 1955, and 97.1 percent of them did in 1987. These are astonishing numbers. In how many elective, voluntary ways are 97 or

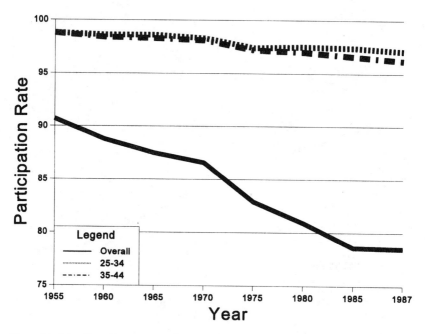

Figure 14. Labor Force Participation of Husbands, Take 2

98 percent of all people in any very large group the same? The story is quite similar in the adjacent age cohorts, 16 to 24 and 45 to 54, at a slightly lower level of participation rates.

This amplified picture illustrates that the Hayghe-Haugen finding—the overall pattern from figure 13—is driven by what is happening among *older* husbands. These men are living longer, retiring earlier, and becoming a larger percentage of the population. In fact, 44.2 percent of all husbands 65 and older worked in 1955; that number had dropped dramatically, to 17.5 percent, by 1987. This is what is pulling the overall trend down, not any change in the behavior of fathers of young children. And so the trend doesn't have much to do with the challenges young mothers face. Their husbands are overwhelmingly unlikely to be home helping out—now, then, or ever. Men have not changed, except to reap a few more benefits of the good life, like early retirement. Once the kids have left, home becomes a nice place to be.

12 On Doing Nothing, and Some Things to Do

BRINGING IT ALL BACK HOME

In this final chapter, I'll take a last look at what is by far the most commonly advocated response to the problems we've been considering: Nothing. Doing nothing is always the easiest and most tempting thing to do. At present, powerful voices are indeed arguing that nothing is exactly what society should be doing for and about women. Unwilling to end our project on such a bleak and unpromising note, I'll then set forth a variety of things we can do, readily enough, if we have the will to change. I hope this book has helped to foster that will, but it is at just that point that I must leave it up to others.

As a person who makes his living teaching and writing about tax, I am aware of how distant and alienating the facts of tax seem to most people. Americans have trouble filling out their own tax forms; understanding the deep, complex, and pervasive gender bias of our tax system, writ large, is a formidable task. But we've seen, I hope, that it is a task worth the effort, for the tax system is indeed deeply gendered, and its gendered effects cannot plausibly be confined to tax alone. Getting across that latter point has been the central purpose of my admittedly quick overview of labor markets generally.

The tax system was set up in the 1930s, 1940s, and 1950s with a traditional family model in mind. We had to work a bit hard to see this, for our intellectual processes, helped along considerably by the tax policy academy and various political forces, have covered the deeply gendered status quo in a veneer of logic, neutrality, and common sense. But close attention to tax in context shows that the system pushes against two-worker marriages at all income levels. This bias translates into unstable families among the lower-income classes, where the need for two incomes is strong; stress among middle-class wives; and strong pressures on upper-class mothers to follow the traditional route and stay home with their children. All these effects have grown significantly in intensity as the breadth and depth of the tax system have increased in the postwar era. Susan and Elizabeth have been our living proof of these facts, as captured in the accountant's tale.

But things could not and did not stop there, with tax alone. When we take the tax system and add it into real and already flawed labor markets, things quickly go from bad to worse. In their attempts to work outside the home, married women already have an anchor tied to them by the tax system. Firms saw this easily enough, or at least saw that married women were less committed to the workforce than married men were. The market failures that led away from a mythical free market of atomistic individuals and spot markets generated a need for statistical discrimination. So rational firms did just that—against women. This led to lower wages and less prestigious, less important job offers, which in turn led to a downward spiral. Offered less pay and less prestige, women were all the more likely to become secondary and marginal earners in their families; like Susan and Elizabeth, such earners are easily led to stay home after giving birth; the employer's rational prediction is confirmed. This whole process had been rigged, of course, by the often unnoticed presence of a socioeconomic system put in place with just this result in mind. The story perpetuated itself, and individual women, men, and firms seemed powerless to buck the relentless logic of profit-maximizing rationality.

But our story did not end here, either. Many women really do want to work outside as well as inside the home—they want the satisfaction, stimulation, prestige, engagement, and financial rewards of paid work, and they don't want to spend all of their time in the often exhausting, frustrating, underappreciated, and unpaid domestic sphere. The facts of rising labor market participation by married mothers, notwithstanding the undeniable reality of the accountant's tale and other evidence of large burdens on them; the statistics of labor supply elasticities; and, perhaps most important, our common experiences—all underscore this basic truth. Among the lower-income classes, there is less choice not to work; the "choices" here are whether to marry or to stay married, and many poor women do indeed find themselves heading families by themselves. Faced with strong pressures not to work outside the home, many mothers have decided not to. But many others—the majority of mothers today— have not accepted the implicit command to stay home and raise their children full time. Women are not the ones, by and large, pining for a return to the 1950s.

The facts of women's commitment to work outside the home and their resilience in the face of socioeconomic barriers against such work do not mean that the forces of patriarchy have been defeated. Far from it. There is no escaping the relentless logic of the accountant's tale. Women cannot simply will it away. The tax system in context is deeply biased against working wives and mothers, and this bias becomes a part of the lived experience for women of all income classes, regardless of how much they consciously understand tax. The tax system, and other socioeconomic institutions for which tax stands here as a model, operates like a deep, dark, subliminal secret, exerting a brooding and inescapable force on the quality of life today.

Many women give up the fight, for it is tiring to swim upstream all the time. Those women who do decide to fight and to work outside the home, notwithstanding tax and other barriers against such work, must pay another price: they must work on terms and conditions shaped by the forces of a patriarchal society. Working women must by and large work full time. But they must do more. To have a decent shot at the benefits and rewards of decent work, they must go to considerable lengths to signal that they are going to act as men have long acted, and work not just full time but with full commitment as well. They will educate themselves more, marry later, have fewer children and have them later in life, and stick it out on their jobs.

While women are bending and twisting their preferences to fit into an institutional structure that is surprisingly inflexible—especially given the general tenets and principles of ideal democratic market theory—men march along. Men haven't changed; the workforce hasn't changed. Women have, and there is plenty of evidence that women have paid, and continued to pay, a price for their enforced compromises. The point of every chapter in this book has really been the same: We are taxing women.

THE SIREN CALL OF NOTHINGNESS

The tale of taxing women stands in stark relief to the most common proposals to deal with the problems of taxing women. We have seen the answer that the *Contracts* would give: these deeply conservative documents would take us back to the 1950s, both in terms of tax and family life. But there is perhaps a greater enemy to the quest for gender justice lurking around the corner. This is an older technique of conservatives: the call to do nothing at all. Nothing is always the easiest thing to do. Conservatives always have this advantage, this final trump. Contemporary cognitive psychology teaches us that we all think in ways that are deeply wedded to the way things are. People evaluate life from the perspective of the status quo. We don't like change, and we especially don't like losses. Such cognitive biases operate across nearly every sphere of our intellectual life.

We see life as we know it as neutral; whatever the status quo is at the moment is taken to be our baseline. We've seen the seductive allure of a neutral baseline throughout the book. The *Smith* case in chapter 5, for example, established the principle that child-care expenses of two-earner families are personal, nondeductible costs. The opinion itself noted that this was the first time the issue had come up in the courts—and we saw that the reasoning of the court was, quite plainly, bad. Still, the *Smith* logic became an accepted part of our tax consciousness. Ever since then, we have viewed child-care provisions as special deviations from some neutral income norm. Congress has thus sought to limit any benefits to the lower and middle classes, in a conscious act of social engineering reflecting the bias that only poorer wives need to work. Gary Bauer, Mothers at Home, Ronald Reagan, and flat tax advocates like Hall-Rabushka all view child-care provisions as discriminatory, non-neutral, and unfair. But if the *Smith* case had gone the other way, and we had come to accept reasonable child-care expenses of two earner families as being the same kind of deductible business expenses that the cost of goods sold are to a retailer, or travel and entertainment expenses are to a salesperson, we could easily imagine that their abolition or abridgment by Congress would be seen as the unfair and discriminatory act. Why should we single out one class of business expenses, ones that happen to go along with being a working mother, as nondeductible? What we take to be the baseline shapes our subsequent questions—and our answers.

I encountered this problem firsthand when I gave a talk on taxation and the family before a group of economists, academics, and government tax officials. I centered my brief comments on the biases of the tax system against women, especially working women with children, and I talked about the wisdom of separate filing, provisions for child care, and a secondary-earner exemption under the social security system. I met with question after question challenging my particular form of "social engineering," and the lack of neutrality of my recommendations. Participants questioned my "using" tax to advance "social" purposes. There was a clear resistance to doing anything at all, except possibly moving to a flat tax, the one thing which the audience seemed to believe was even more neutral than the status quo. But as we saw in chapter 9, the flat tax proposals would do nothing about the gender biases in tax, and might make them worse. Simple solutions don't always fix complex problems.

I must confess, after all the work I've done on this book and its underlying ideas, to getting a bit exasperated by this kind of response. What is it that these people think that we have already done? In 1948, 1969, 1986, the *Contracts*, and numerous points in between? One way to read this book is as a long paean to *restore* some neutrality to laws that are deeply and often intentionally gender-biased. This is why the history, economics, social commentary, and accountant's tales are all so important and integrally related. I personally would prefer to drop the talk of neutrality and social engineering altogether, for I don't think that it is especially helpful. I would substitute core concepts like fairness and justice, which are more honestly open-ended, and more fundamental. These concepts seem to invite reasonable political dialogue and discussion, just as arguments turning on logic, neutrality, and common sense seem to preclude it, to silence opposition. If we are going to use the idea of neutrality, we should at least step up and realize that we have been social engineering all along. The *Contracts*, to take a ready example, are engineering in spades.

We seem especially averse to losses. Politicians like Pete Stark have a good sense of this. Stark saw that, given the fact that there are preferences built into the tax laws, those who lose benefits are apt to scream. He could have added something that the cognitive psychologists know: the screaming of the losers is going to be louder than the joy of the winners. Modern economic theory, when it moves to being prescriptive—to giving advice about what we should do—has unwittingly helped to entrench this bias. Most economists work with the goal of "Pareto superiority" in mind. This is a norm that only recommends actions where there are no losers. Only win-win deals go forward.

But this no-loser bias means that it would be nearly impossible to change the deeply gendered ways of tax. Taxing women less means taxing men more—at least, there is a good argument to be made that it should mean that—and we can predict that men and traditionalists will scream quite loudly, as they did about the limited secondary-earner deduction in place from 1981 to 1986 and over the absence of a full spousal IRA benefit. People writing about social security, for example, often point out that under a move to earnings-sharing, men would "lose." This particular complaint is a bit odd, for what men would "lose" is the windfall they were given in the 1930s—a windfall that was ostensibly put in place to help women. The complaint against social security reform is simply symptomatic of a more general problem: if we can make only those social changes that do not adversely affect anyone, we are apt to make few changes at all. Conservatives have a number of tools at their disposal for convincing us of what we want to believe anyway—that there is no point in doing anything.

MARKET RHETORIC AND INERTIA

The crowning glory of do-nothingism is laissez-faire, free market theory. The theory is eloquently, seductively, simple. It runs as follows: Governments can only muck things up. We do better—in terms of individual freedom and social wealth—when we leave things to free, unregulated markets. Advocates of this view can draw on a long line of philosopher-economists, from Adam Smith to Friedrich Hayek and Milton Friedman. But even better proof comes from the lessons we learn just about every day, from observing modern governments in action. Bureaucracies often do not work, as a matter of fact.

Richard Epstein, in his 1992 book, *Forbidden Grounds: The Case against Employment Discrimination Laws*, takes this logic about as far as it can seriously be taken. Epstein argues for the total elimination of all laws against employment discrimination. Although the book runs over five hundred pages, its basic point is very simple: Markets work. Why would any firm discriminate? If it did so irrationally, it would lose out to more rational, profit-maximizing actors. But if firms only engage in rational discrimination, what's wrong with that? Rationality is good. Epstein points out the fact that women who want to work can rationally signal their intentions, without alluding to any of the deep social and normative costs of signaling. In the end, he is left with a simple solution to the problems of employment discrimination: Do nothing. The market will take care of things.

Epstein's lengthy volume makes no reference to tax, let alone to its deep gender biases. More generally, there is not an extended discussion of *any* market failure: like the authors of the *Contracts* and other conservative rhetoricians, Epstein juxtaposes a perfect, natural free market with an imperfect, artificial, coercive central government. Here is how Epstein prefaces his case against the gender discrimination laws:

> The differences in sex roles are so important that no one can ignore them, and their effects are not cordoned off into any limited domain of human experience. What goes on outside the workplace heavily influences what takes place within it. Thus, the large percentage of women who plan to devote a substantial proportion of their adult lives to raising children and managing a family should be expected on average to make relatively low levels of investment in skills that would yield high returns on the job. . . .
>
> The pervasive importance of sex roles can be stated even more strongly: durable marriages often depend on a conscious division of labor within the family whereby both partners realize gains from specialization and trade, just as people do in ordinary economic markets. Decisions about marriage and child rearing thus create very different incentives for men and women (or at least some men and some women), and these incentives influence enormously the patterns of interaction and the job decisions of men and women in the workplace. Historically these forces were quite strong, especially when women's work was needed to raise children and run a household in the days before laborsaving devices and improved contraception. But even today many asymmetries still remain in the form of male and female work patterns, and there is no question that choices in the job market differ much more by sex than they do by race. . . .
>
> [This] conventional wisdom and the traditional practices on sex differences have come under heavy assault in recent years. It has become fashionable to assert that historical accident and cultural conditioning explain much, perhaps all, of this differentiation in

sex roles. Some radical feminists have even taken the view that androgyny—the elimination of all sex-specific roles—is appropriate not only for the workplace but for the greater society at large. In so doing they commit the sin of hubris by insisting that they can, through law and coercion, transform the behavior and preferences of ordinary women and men.

Epstein goes on to note that he "incline[s] to the view that the biology of sex differences is profound," but he concludes that we need not take a position on the debate about culture versus biology as root cause. All that matters is that individuals are expressing their free choices in free markets, and these desires should be respected. "No market can operate on the assumption that it should be organized *as if* the tastes and preferences of the work force were wholly uncorrelated with sex, when the correlations are there."

Epstein provides us with a masterly example of the logic and rhetoric of a skilled free market advocate. He insists on relying on individual "tastes and preferences," and he castigates "radical feminists" and others for their "sin of hubris by insisting that they can, through law and coercion, transform the behavior and preferences of ordinary women and men." But now we can turn the tables on Epstein and like-minded critics. For this is *exactly* what we've been seeing throughout this book, through the facts of the accountant's tale, history, and economic theory, that a patriarchal society has been doing to women. When Epstein leaves out tax, he leaves out a powerful tool of social engineering, designed precisely to use "law and coercion" to shape the behavior and preferences of married women. Men were committing the sin of hubris long before women even had the opportunity to try.

Further, the actual data on the "tastes and preferences" of women is contained in the elasticity measures we looked at in chapter 7. As a matter of fact, women really do want to work outside the home, although they are conflicted about it. Epstein wants to tell a tale of "pre-market" choices, in which women are different from men and happily accept a gendered division of labor in the interests of efficiency, "just as people do in ordinary economic markets." The problem with this argument lies in the facts: it's not true. We are not seeing "pre-market" choices—ones somehow formed before economic markets have influenced behavior—but instead we are seeing after-tax ones. The technical recommendation of market-oriented public finance economists like Michael Boskin is that society should dramatically reverse its course in the way that it taxes men and women, precisely because the status quo is distorting and coercive toward women. Optimal tax is about minimizing the distorting effects of "law and coercion"; it tells us that changing the way we tax women is a move in the direction of mitigating social pressures on individual choices. Presumably, this is what libertarians like Epstein would want. When Epstein misses all of this, he misses his own free market boat.

To Epstein, rational behavior is both explanatory and justificatory. He repeatedly fails to make use of the basic insight that private rationality can lead to bad social outcomes. It was to counter this kind of reasoning that I have gone to some lengths to include only rational actors in my analysis of labor markets. Even with the best intentioned of employers and firms, with no misogyny in the story, life ended up treating women pretty harshly. Rationality is a fact of life, not a social program.

Some years ago, it might have been possible to dismiss academics like Epstein, an extreme libertarian or believer in minimal governments, as fringe players. No more. The attraction for markets and against government action of any kind is spreading, propelled, I believe, by its seductive simplicity. Epstein has more books out, including a recent one entitled *Simple Rules for a Complex World*. How can doing nothing do harm? This fits in with our basic predisposition to do nothing anyway. There is a strong intellectual, moral, emotional, and aesthetic appeal to the case for minimal government. The case is also quite clearly buttressed by the failures of most market interventions. Many liberals, with their stubborn devotion to big government as the solution to many—too many—social ills, have become their own worst enemies. Liberals should be committed to the *ends* of liberal social theory, such as greater autonomy, freedom, and equal concern and respect for all individuals, but not to any of the *means* chosen to these ends, like big governments or particular regulatory policies. Life is too complicated for that kind of dogma.

The real problem with the happy tale of laissez-faire or free market ideology is that society *has* done things—many things, for many years— slanted against women. Calling it quits now is not fair, and it is certainly not "neutral," whatever that would mean. It would seem only to mean that we would bury the sins of the past, by fiat, and leave them in place, unchallenged and unacknowledged, forever. It turns out that tax is not only the locus of many of our greatest sins, it is also an excellent place to look for change. Following the lead of optimal tax by taxing women less is quite an effective way to lessen the harms being done and to get the government off our backs, without any characteristically liberal big government, centrally mandated set of policies. It is also, apparently, the last thing that some people want.

WHAT ARE THEY THINKING?

Let's continue for a moment with the puzzle before us, in a slightly different guise. It is now increasingly said, thought, or hoped that the feminist movement or women's liberation has run its course. Women are working more than ever, being paid better than ever, closing the wage gap with men. Professional school enrollments are approaching parity, and women are increasingly occupying positions of prominence and power. What more can be done? A new dawn has arisen, so this story goes. Now that we have the formal equality of opportunity that was the only legitimate end of the antidiscrimination crusade in the first place, it is time to stop paying special attention to women. Society can dismantle affirmative action programs and move on to other concerns, like tax reduction, pro-growth policies, immigration, welfare reform, and fighting crime. It is time, perhaps, for "angry white males," as the somewhat offensive slogan goes, to come out of their closet and start asserting, or reasserting, *their* rights. As the *Contracts* tell it, it is time to get back to the 1950s.

This book has aimed to cast severe doubt on that tidy story. Even if women obtain equal wages in the workforce and equal representation in certain important sectors, such as professional school enrollments, why should we count the feminist movement as no longer needed? How could we think that centuries of patriarchy, discrimination, and repression could be wiped clear with a generation of nominal, formal equality? How could we think that meaningful equality could be had simply by opening the doors to the all-men's club that the workplace had been for centuries, and "letting" women do what men had come to do within a highly patriarchal society? How could we think that laws enacted by overwhelmingly male Congresses, and signed by male presidents, all in a time of deeply entrenched patriarchy, could not, somehow, reflect the gendered structure of that society, and come to serve as an anchor against the emergence of more respectful, more fully equal treatment? How could we think that money alone, in the form of nearly equal wages for nearly equal work, could give women all that they really want, need, and deserve?

We have to think more, better, and harder than that. Gender bias has been a fact of life for eons, and, as we have seen in our extended consideration of the tax system, it has reached into deep, dark, and distant corners of the social space. It gets hard, indeed impossible, to tell what our "true" preferences are, or what our "true" natures might want. Everything has become so deeply colored by a social world that entrenches prejudices in one generation to haunt the next. We need a more active, creative, political theory to help us see our way through to better days. A good place to start is by asking ourselves just what we mean, or should mean, by "equality."

WHAT IS EQUALITY?

It is not clear just what equality for women ought to mean. Equal rights to participate in the paid workforce, in and of themselves, seem necessary but hardly sufficient. Women now have equal rights to participate, but only under terms and conditions set up for men in traditional, single-earner families. This is not attentive to, and respectful of, the preferences of most women, or to the needs of changing times. It is like Anatole France's famous observation that "the majestic egalitarianism of the law . . . forbids rich and poor alike to sleep under bridges." Everyone in America is now free to work, but only in ways inherited from a patriarchal past. Similarly, equal pay for equal work—although this, too, is an important goal—ought not to be all that we seek. "Equal tax for equal-earning couples," the linchpin of the neutrality norm in tax, is perhaps the emptiest definition of equality of all.

My focus throughout this book has been on something more abstract, deeper yet harder to measure: equality of concern and respect. This stems from the classically liberal belief that all citizens, men and women alike, should share equally in the benefits and burdens of modern life, including taxation. Men and women should equally be able to pursue their life's plans and projects and should be equal in the degree to which market failures impede them. This is, once again, why optimal tax theory is so relevant: it moves away from the observed space of participation rates and earnings levels, toward the invisible, psychologically oriented space of choice and autonomy. Optimal tax shows that we are accommodating men's choices but distorting women's. That's not fair.

But optimal tax is, in the end, only a part of our tale. It mainly adds some color, perspective, and grounding. The kind of liberal political theory that aims for equal concern and respect for all citizens, whatever their race, gender, or creed, can hardly rest satisfied turning the affairs of state over to some utility-maximizing social scientists. Getting to a decent and respectful political life is harder than that and less certain. There are some procedural devices available for thinking about all this, such as the "original position" technique of the political philosopher John Rawls, set out most famously in his classic work, *A Theory of Justice*. Under this device, individuals imagine and debate a system of fair rules for social cooperation under conditions of relative anonymity and obscurity, behind what Rawls calls a "veil of ignorance." Since these parties don't know what their particular positions or places within society will be, they come up with fair rules of generality and reciprocity. Using this or related techniques, we could reason our way through to a fairer tax and socioeconomic system. What kind of tax system would any one of us want to set up if we didn't know whether we would be a man or a woman, a husband or a wife?

None of this would be easy or free of controversy. Rawls and his "original position," for example, have been criticized, most notably by Susan Moller Okin, as being insufficiently attentive to the concerns of women and families. It is too late in the day for me to pursue these musings to their end, necessarily uncertain in any event. But we should at least be able to see our way through to the general direction and shape of reform. Right now we are taxing women far more than men, entrenching and rewarding one particular model of the family above all others, and looking at the wrong things when we declare that an end is at hand. It is high time to stop this bad and unfair reasoning. Whatever else we ought to do, we are not going to get to a deeper, more meaningful equality and sense of gender justice until we realize that we are burdening women far more, and far more unfairly, than men.

DOING THINGS

I never intended this book to be a specific, practical program for change. The problems of taxing women are deep, and I want mainly to shed some light on them, to serve as a bit of a wake-up call to those interested in gender justice in America to pay more attention to tax. My main aim was to do a bit of what used to be called consciousness raising.

Nonetheless, as I hope should be clear by now, there are some pretty good responses to the central issues of taxing women. We have seen these at many junctures along the way. There are also good reasons to wind down our project by setting out these responses. They show that nongendered answers to our questions are available and feasible. This both offers some hope and confirms the deliberateness of, and even the culpability in, society's choices of other, more gendered answers all along.

It also turns out that tax is a good place to look for social change in pursuit of gender justice. Changing tax avoids many of the problems of a more heavy-handed, "top down" style of regulatory intervention. Centrally mandated proposals for better part-time work or for maternity and paternity leaves interfere with the rational planning of firms and can often and easily backfire. Changing tax, in contrast, changes the predicates on which rational individual and firm actions are based. It can be a just, fair, and efficient thing to do.

The different answers that have emerged from the long journey we've made together fall into three categories. The first consists of an ideal legislative change. We should tax married men more, and married women less. This is what developed out of the theory of optimal tax. Actually, the recommendation can, and indeed should—at least in part for Constitutional reasons—be couched in gender-neutral terms. We should tax primary earners more, and secondary earners less. We could do this easily enough by moving toward separate filing with a more generous rate schedule, or greater deductions, for the lesser-earning spouse. Mostly this will mean, at least in the near term, taxing men more and women less, as we should all know by now. This solution will strike many, probably most, citizens as counterintuitive: they will object that such a proposal reeks of "social engineering," that it is unfair and "non-neutral," that it is disrespectful of family values, possibly even sexist, some kind of tyrannical act of liberalism.

The theory of optimal tax shows that we do not have to answer these concerns with a polemic. This is not an instance of "male bashing." The case for taxing married women less than married men rests on a solid and respectable logical, economic, and ethical base. We saw Michael Boskin, a conservative economist and former high-ranking Bush administration official, endorsing just this proposal. Right now, we are taxing women far more than men; the tax system is not at all neutral or fair or ungendered. Quite the contrary. Optimal tax, resting on the neutral principles of economics and objective data, counsels that what we should do is exactly the opposite of what we are doing. Among the reasons to look seriously at the optimal tax solution is to come to see that the received tax wisdom has evolved in a decidedly gendered fashion.

Some Specific Things

The optimal tax answer nonetheless has little chance of being enacted into law anytime soon, if ever. It may not even be a good idea to enact it. It is far from clear that we should publicly turn our political processes over to a quasi-scientific, utilitarian social theory. There are also technical problems involved with making at least somewhat permanent features of our tax system depend on transient measurements, like elasticities; there are questions about whose elasticities should count, and when and how to measure them. This then leads to a second category of answers, narrower, more specific and ad hoc, and therefore more politically palatable.

Of these, the most important perhaps is for a system of separate filing under the income tax. The failure to have such a system was the subject of part 1. Other ideas emerged in part 2: reforming the social security system, as by allowing an exemption level for secondary earners over the range in which they are paying a pure tax, or moving to a system of "earnings sharing"; instituting greater secondary-earner relief; expanding and rethinking child-care deductions or credits and the entire panoply of fringe benefit laws. Note, by the way, that the seemingly impractical solution of optimal tax, to tax married women less than married men, is largely met by a practical system that features (1) separate filing for spouses; (2) a more generous child-care deduction or credit, allocated to the lesser-earning spouse; (3) a secondary-earner exemption level under social security. That optimal tax supports these commonsensical recommendations, which seem independently fair and just anyway, only strengthens their appeal.

In any event, each factor that we discussed in the first half of the book has a less gendered solution. All of these ideas have existed in the public domain for some time, and the failure to adopt them or, in most cases, to give them any extended discussion or thought at all, forms a big part of our intellectual history. Something was missing; some things were wrong.

A General Thing

Even these sensible, practical answers—all of which will inevitably be politically controversial—are in some sense not enough; they miss a certain essence of the bigger picture. Coming to terms with the deeply gendered structure of contemporary American life, on the one hand, and jockeying for votes to muster a legislative majority for an increased child-care deduction, on the other, are two very different tasks. I am enough of an academic to care more about the former. I am enough of an optimist to hope that the resulting deeper understanding one day motivates the latter. Thus, the first two categories of solutions—the ideal and the practical legislative changes—lead naturally to a third. This concerns the practice of social theory.

A close and careful look at the tax system should help us to see the depths of the gendered structure of society, and the often hidden, obscure, and unintended ways that it perpetuates itself. Once we come to see this, we can learn to talk about things differently, and better. A principal lesson of contemporary social theory is that dialogue, and the conditions of dialogue, is often the most important political mechanism. Sometimes it is the only thing. Our discussion of gender and equality has been hampered by the obscurity of many of the gendered forces at work. We need to shed light on these, as a first step toward having a more enlightened dialogue; we need to put society on the couch, so to speak. We need to understand that the most important principles and norms are rarely specific or static, rarely capable of being reduced to readily observed metrics such as wage scales. We need to think more about what equality and respect mean.

MORE PUZZLES OF TIME

One of the things that makes reforming the tax system so complicated and controversial is the puzzle of time. What are we to do *now*, at a time when many families have grown up in the face of the incentive structure put in place during the patriarchal period of the 1930s, 1940s, and 1950s? This brings up the question of transitional rules, which have bred a fair amount of controversy in legal academic thought and have contributed to much of the inertia in our political life. The problem of changing a system on which some persons have relied is one of the several reasons why I am reluctant to get highly specific with any narrow legislative agenda.

But this does not mean that there is nothing we can say. One easy thing to note is that the type of tax *reform* presently being advocated, as I write this, would effect a change that would make the problems of taxing women *worse*. This is, of course, the central theory behind the *Contracts*. Moving to a flat tax without doing more—as by also moving to separate filing—would be an opportunity lost. We are often changing the tax system, and the least we can do is to avoid changes that make for greater gender injustice. The child (not child-care) credits of the *Contracts* are especially perverse on this score, but even the kind of increased personal exemptions in the flat-rate tax proposals, which once drew the support of Pat Schroeder, are not a step in the right direction. There is no reason to make things worse.

In terms of broader issues of transition, it strikes me that all the principal, practical recommendations for changing course seem to be workable. Instituting a thoroughly optimal tax plan might indeed be disruptive, and this is one of several reasons to back off from that ideal change, but I never took that answer as especially realistic. It is worth pointing out that we did have separate filing, at least for the upper-income classes, until 1948, less than fifty years ago, and that a number of other countries have made the transition back to separate filing; England did, in 1990, for example. Changing social security to create a secondary-earner exemption or to institute an earnings-sharing system would not seem to unsettle people's reasonable expectations. Note again that benefiting widows need not be paid for out of taxing working wives; the contribution and benefit decisions are distinct. If society concluded that it was unfair to withdraw support for wives in traditional families, it could still institute a second-earner exemption, to get rid of that bias. The Equals need not foot the bill for the Traditionals' largesse. Rethinking fringe benefits is long overdue, and could well involve efficient changes that make a large number of people happy. Allowing better provision for child care might be a "pie expanding" move, one that increases social wealth—this is part of what optimal tax is telling us—and, in any event, could be done less expensively than the per-child credit of the *Contracts*.

Most important, though, we ought to firm up our resolve to do something. The state of taxing women reflects deep gender biases and continues to contribute, on an ongoing basis, to the disproportionate stress and unhappiness borne by American wives and mothers every day. It is unconscionable to leave this system in place, simply because it is now the status quo. No law, or logic, should allow thieves to keep their gains or the abusers of power to maintain the abuse. At some point, we have to reverse course against the forces of patriarchy. It is time for the Traditionals to return some of their winnings to the common pool.

STILL HOPEFUL, AFTER ALL THESE YEARS

Much of this book has been pessimistic about the state of politics in America today. We've seen a deeply gendered socioeconomic system come into being and grow, all but ignored by academics and politicians. Traditional forces have seized on every opportunity to paint the status quo in neutral terms and to resist any accommodation whatsoever for emergent family models. The *Contracts* evidence a new brand of conservatism, sophisticated and aggressive, eager to turn back the clock to the 1950s, and ready and able to use tax, in a brilliant manner, in their cause. Other conservatives call, seductively and simply, for doing nothing at all. Meanwhile, liberals and progressives seem asleep at the switch, failing to comprehend what is happening all around them, and unable to see themselves and their tired, traditional, big-government solutions as part of the problem. We are taxing women—badly and unfairly—and we cannot even bring ourselves to see this fact, let alone to correct it. I often think that these are bad times, indeed.

But I cannot bring myself to end on such a sour note. Hope is as much a cause of action as it is its consequence, and we need hope aplenty in these complex and troubled times. I'll take just a few more pages, to articulate my final hope, however ill-founded it may seem.

As I have alluded to at several points along the way, I have lived with the project of this book for many years, through two lengthy law review articles, numerous academic seminars, discussions, and conferences across the country, and the writing of this book itself. It has not always been a smooth and easy process, although I continue to have my basic belief in the fact of the deep gender bias of tax confirmed. Opposition has come from all quarters. Friends on the left have seen the story as just one more piece of evidence—as if one were needed—of the corruption of liberal democratic capitalism: our present society is hopelessly gendered, materialistic, and selfish. Why not just abandon liberal, market-oriented social theory altogether? Friends on the right have argued against what they see as my social engineering and overly liberal slant, and they point to the current state of politics as proof that what Americans really want is a return to core conservative values; I am writing in the wrong decade. Why don't I just abandon the project of liberal social theory altogether? Friends in the vast middle of the political spectrum, or with no particular political leanings, have raised other doubts: no one will take the time to understand tax; the subject matter is too complicated and controversial; ultimately, it is all political, and people will just disagree; tax is nothing but a matter of selfish, special interest politics; in any case, no one in his right mind would try to explain optimal tax theory to the people. Why don't I just abandon the project of merging tax and liberal social theory altogether?

I have listened to all of this, more or less patiently. I have indeed had my days of wondering just why it was I was working so hard to write this book—motivated, from the start, by a desire to reach a large audience, the people at large. While I heard and understood the various doubts, I could not, in the end, rid myself of two faiths. The first was in the story. The tax system is indeed gendered, and deeply so. It was deliberately set up to be that way, and its biases cannot plausibly be confined to tax alone. I know these truths. More generally, something is wrong with the state of gender justice in America today, something that is not being captured in the narrowing gender wage gap or rising labor market participation rates for married women. We need more dynamism, more choice, more room for creative work-family balances. We need more gender justice, too, and more and better thinking about just what this means. I felt these truths. The more I looked at the whole story, or set of stories, the more I believed in it.

I had a second faith that got me through the long trip: a faith in liberal democracy itself, and in the American people. There are always arguments against any social theory or reform. There are always those who argue that the world we have made is the best of all possible worlds. If the tax system has any biases, they are the result of democratic forces, so there is no point complaining about them. After all, the *Contracts* were enormously successful political documents. Who can argue, in a democracy, with electoral success? But this inertial, passive approach flies in the face of what I see as the slow but steady progress of America toward a better, more just, more fair society—one that established a great democratic Republic, abolished slavery, steadily extended the franchise, developed sophisticated and rich civil rights and feminist movements and that, at its best, still speaks powerfully to universal human rights around the world.

I know of course that we are not a perfect, or a perfectly fair, society, but I believe that our enduring greatness as a culture lies precisely in our ability and commitment to learn and grow and become more fair, more just. Many of the problems of taxing women flow from the complexity and obscurity of the tax system, and the failure of the tax policy academy to understand and communicate the gendered structure of tax to the people. Perhaps this sounds like a liberal's apology for the people, and there are some who would, indeed, blame popular ignorance—we don't see what we don't want to see. But modern life has gotten more and more complicated, and tax is enormously so. The points I have made in this book, although they have mostly been available in some form for years, have not always been understood even by professors of tax law. We have seen liberals like Pat Schroeder, obviously sincere in her commitment to women's equality, make mistakes such as supporting increased personal exemptions under a joint filing system. Other prominent liberals, such as Hubert Humphrey or Pete Stark, have feared to tread on the hallowed grounds of tax and family. How can we expect the average American to rise up against the gendered structure of tax?

We can indeed have that expectation, though, or at least the hope, in some sense because we must have it. Tax is too important to leave to the narrowly political people who write such documents as the *Contracts*. The great American experiment in democracy faces two large and related challenges. On the one hand, we must fight off the reactionary forces that would turn the project back on itself, and make us a smaller-hearted, meaner-spirited people. On the other hand, we must come up with a deeper, richer understanding of equality, of what it is we are striving for. There are tempters all about us, whispering that equality of the proper sort has now been obtained, that we can now dismantle the liberal welfare state, and turn back to the 1950s or whenever. But we have not yet arrived at a satisfactory equality of concern and respect for all of our citizens. A detailed exploration of the tax system confirms what an empathetic understanding of daily life suggests. Mothers in America, to take one rather large group of persons, are particularly and unfairly burdened and unhappy. Pushing them back into the homes they left in the 1950s is not a fair response to their unhappiness. It is, in any event, not what they seem to want.

At the same time, there is little point in foolishly denying that something is wrong, that government per se is not the answer to all our problems. Indeed, there is this dark warning for big-government advocates in what we have learned: government was and still is a large part of the problem in taxing women. Yet the manifest failure of big government as an answer to all of our concerns does not mean that we ought not to have those concerns. We need to go back to the roots of our democratic project and our settled commitment to the ends of liberalism—to a basic right of all individuals to pursue happiness on fair and equal terms, guided by their own personal lights. We need to come up with new and better means to our deepest and most cherished ends. We need to keep trying.

Notes

References are to page numbers.

INTRODUCTION

2.   "Nearly 90 percent of women will get married, and 85 percent will have children": Statistical Abstract Tables 105 and 142; Schwartz 1992b, 111.

CHAPTER 1: WOMEN ON THE MARGIN

The stories in this chapter are drawn from Johnson 1991 and Lewin 1991.

17.   Feenberg and Rosen 1995, 99.

21–22.   The history is from Goldin 1990 and Jones 1988.

22.   ERA references are from Mansbridge 1986, 20–22. See also Whitney 1984.

23–24.   McIntyre 1980, 483–84.

27.   Oldman and Temple 1960, 597, 602.

27–28.   Pechman and Englehardt 1990, 9, 10.

CHAPTER 2: A BIT OF HISTORY, 1913 TO 1948

36.   Bittker 1975, 1394.

37.   *Lucas v. Earl,* 281 U.S. 111 (1930).

40.   *Poe v. Seaborn,* 282 U.S. 101 (1930).

42.   *Hoeper v. Tax Commission of Washington,* 284 U.S. 206 (1931).

44.   Holmes 1897, 469.

49–50.   Paul 1954, 273, 275.

52.   U.S. House 1947, 751, 752.

53.   U.S. House 1947, 760–61.

54.   Paul 1954, 494.

57.   Surrey 1948, 1111.

CHAPTER 3: STILL HIS STORY, 1948 TO THE PRESENT

59.   The Humphrey anecdote is related in Paul 1954, 611–13.

60.   Groves 1963, 83, 93n., 106–7.

61.   Thorson 1965, 116, 128; Pechman 1966, 81–84; Bittker 1975, 1438.

63.   Groves 1963, 106.

69.   Barton 1950, 111–13.

70.   Pechman 1966, 89.

71–72.   Bittker 1975, 1431.

72–73.   Bittker 1975, 1432 note 123, 1435, 1436.

73–74.   Bittker 1975, 1437, 1442.

76. McIntyre and Oldman 1977, 1596.
76–77. Stark quotations are from U.S. House 1980, 25–26, 218–19.
78. Gann 1983, 487.
79. Table 8 is from U.S. Congress 1987, 19.
80. Coyne quotation is from U.S. House 1985, 3065.
83. Feenberg and Rosen 1995, 94.

CHAPTER 4: SOCIAL SECURITY ISN'T WHAT IT LOOKS TO BE

96. Steuerle and Bakija 1994, 208.
97. Table 10 is based on Steuerle and Bakija 1994, 211, table 9.1.
99–100. Kessler-Harris 1995, 101.

CHAPTER 5: PILING IT ON THE MARGIN

106–7. Shellenbarger, Moffet, and Chen 1995.
108. Bittker 1975, 1435.
109–10. The *USA Today* article is Belton and Wark 1995. The *New York Times* article is Lewin 1991.
111. Representative Griffiths' quotation is from U.S. Congress 1973, 274. The court case is *Smith v. Commissioner*, 40 B.T.A. 1038 (1939), *affirmed without opinion*, 113 F.2d 114 (2d Cir. 1940).
114. See Blumberg 1972; Klein 1973.
116. The data in figures 2 and 3 are from U.S. House 1993, 1067.
119. U.S. House 1991, 73.
122. Simons 1938, 42–43.
122–24. McIntyre and Oldman 1977, 1611, 1614, 1616. McIntyre and Oldman later discuss child care, but assert that they "can find no predictable difference between one- and two-job couples in the consumption of self-performed child-care services" (1614–15).
125. Hochschild 1989, 254; Hersch and Stratton 1994, 124.
127. Figure 4 is from McCaffery 1994a, 1908.
128. *United States v. Drescher*, 179 F.2d 863 (2d Cir. 1950).
130. Langbein and Wolk 1990, 433–34.

CHAPTER 6: TAXING FAMILIES

138. The survey of executives is set out in Trapp, Hermanson, and Carcello 1991.
139. The 5 percent figure is from U.S. Congress 1988, 81. For a debate on the practical consequences of marriage penalties, compare Alms and Whittington 1995 and Sjoquist and Walker 1995. Scheffler 1988 has a good discussion of consequentialism.
146–47. See Steuerle 1995a,b,c for a discussion of marginal tax rates facing AFDC and other welfare recipients.
147. Feenberg and Rosen 1995, 94.

CHAPTER 7: SOME TAXING HOPE

180–81. Atkinson 1995, 147–48; Boskin and Sheshinski 1983, 293, 296; Killingsworth and Heckman 1986, 185; Pencavel 1986, 82, 94; Triest 1990, 492.

181.	Leuthold 1983, 154; Leuthold 1984, 103; Hunt, DeLorme, and Hill 1981, 431, 432.
183.	Triest 1990; Heckman 1993, 118. For good evidence of the trend toward lower elasticities in general, and for women in particular, see Atkinson 1995; Heckman 1993; MaCurdy 1992; MaCurdy, Green, and Paarsch 1990; Mroz 1987; and Zodrow 1992. Goldin 1990, 119–58 has a good, reasonably general discussion of some of the data and trends affecting women's labor supply elasticities. Piggott and Whalley 1996 appeared while this book was in press. They argue that under certain plausible assumptions, joint or household filing might be efficient. This result follows from the possibility—long noted in the literature on the economics of the family (see, for example, Becker 1991)—that there can be efficiency gains to a specialized division of labor within the family. If these gains outweigh the efficiency costs of deterring secondary-earner participation in the paid workforce, joint filing may be efficient. If the result were generally valid—there are good reasons to doubt that it is—then feminists supporting separate filing would indeed have to argue against efficiency. But there would be perfectly good reasons and weapons to wage that battle, as the text of this book repeatedly argues. Piggott and Whalley do not dispute, for example, that joint filing would perpetuate a gendered division of labor; their central finding is that such a division might be efficient.

CHAPTER 8: NOT JUST THE FACTS

190.	Discussion of relevant psychological studies can be found in Hunt and Hunt 1987 and in Nickols 1994; the central point that men are not as flexible as women in the face of changing roles is a major theme in Hochschild 1989 and at least a background one in Faludi 1991 and Mahony 1995.
191.	Scanlon 1975.
200.	See Pollitt 1995 for an example of a mildly satiric proposal to tax men.

CHAPTER 9: THE CURIOUS NOSTALGIA OF THE *CONTRACTS*

The *Contracts* are Republican National Committee 1994 (Contract I) and Christian Coalition 1995 (Contract II).

203–4.	Contract I, 8, 9–11, 159.
205–6.	Contract I, 85.
206–7.	Kolbert 1995; U.S. House 1991, 59, 106.
207–8.	Contract II, 1, 52, 53.
209.	Contract II, 54.
209–10.	U.S. House 1991, 49, 113, 79; Reagan 1986, 1424.
213.	Reagan 1986, 1424.
214–15.	Estimates are from Center on Budget and Policy Priorities 1995; Citizens for Tax Justice 1996; Greenstein, Shapiro, and Parrott 1995; and Shapiro 1995.
221.	Hall and Rabushka 1995, 114–15; U.S. House 1991, 102.
222–23.	U.S. House 1991, 49, 61.
223–24.	U.S. House 1991, 102, 106.

CHAPTER 10: NOT JUST TAX

232.   *Parenthood* 1989.
238.   Quintanilla 1996. For the factual dispute among labor market economists as to the extent of the shortfall that "gappers" experience, compare Jacobsen and Levin 1995 with Stratton 1994; for an anecdotal confirmation of the problem, see Quintanilla 1996.
239.   Hume 1978, 351–57.
240.   Coase [1937] 1988, 38–39.
242.   Shellenbarger 1996.
244.   Schwartz 1992a, 9–26.
247.   Tilly 1990, 1, 7.

CHAPTER 11: NOT JUST THE GENDER GAP

251.   O'Neill 1994.
251–53.   Goldin 1990, 58–62, supplemented with Statistical Abstract and Statistical History; O'Neill 1994; *Working Woman* article is Harris 1996.
254.   Nickols 1994, 82.
260–62.   Blau and Ferber 1992, 260; O'Neill 1994. Figure 12 is derived from Blau and Ferber 1992, 79.
265.   See Hayghe and Haugen 1987.

CHAPTER 12: ON DOING NOTHING, AND SOME THINGS TO DO

272–73.   Epstein 1992, 270–72.

Bibliography

This book grew out of McCaffery 1993a and 1993b, the two articles I refer to from time to time. McCaffery 1996 was written for a symposium when the book was nearly complete and summarizes part of its argument structure. McCaffery 1994a explores social and psychological understandings of tax, and McCaffery 1994b contains reflections on tax theory of a more political/philosophical sort; both contain some historical and descriptive material related to my concerns in this book. All five of these articles contain many footnotes, and the dedicated scholar may turn to them for more detail.

For general background on taxation and the family, Blumberg 1972 is the seminal source. Helpful discussions can also be found in Gann 1980 and 1983, Kornhauser 1993, and Zelenak 1994a and 1994b. See also Munnell 1980 and Rosen 1977 and 1987. The classic sources, of which I am often critical but which still contain much helpful background material, are Bittker 1975 and McIntyre and Oldman 1977. Groves 1963 and Pechman 1966 are useful for deeper historic perspective. Cain 1991 is a good treatment of the tax issues confronting same-sex couples.

The statistics I use throughout are largely drawn from government sources, mainly the U.S. Department of Commerce 1994 (herein Statistical Abstract) or, in some cases, earlier. I also draw on the Budget of the United States 1995, Fleenor 1995, United States Bureau of the Census 1976 (herein Statistical History), United States Treasury Department, 1921–54 (herein Statistics of Income), and assorted other government publications and materials, such as U.S. Congress 1988 and issues of the *Monthly Labor Review* published by the U.S. Department of Labor. Hanson and Ooms 1991 has been a main source on the costs of two-earner households; Lewin 1991 was a useful supplement. Hofferth, Brayfield, Deich, and Holcomb 1991 was helpful on child-care costs, as were Casper 1995 and Veum and Gleason 1991. Particular statistics on women in the labor markets came from Bergmann 1986, Blau and Ferber 1992, Dowd 1989 and 1990, Fuchs 1988, Goldin 1990, and Sorensen 1991, although I regularly updated these secondary sources with current government statistics. Dowd 1995 is very helpful on single-parent households; I also used

Usdansky 1996 and U.S. Congress 1988. Gordon 1994 is a wonderfully interesting, comprehensive historical source. My inflation adjustment figures—for example, bringing 1916 dollars roughly into 1995 dollars—were done using indices for the price of consumer goods in the Statistical Abstract and Statistical History.

General sources on the stresses women face in the labor market and in juggling two domains of work include Berry 1993, Czapanskiy 1991, Dowd 1989, 1990, and 1995, Faludi 1991, Gerstel and Gross 1987, Goldin 1995, Hochschild 1989, Mahony 1995, McKenry and Price 1994, Quintanilla 1996, Schwartz 1992a and 1992b. I found Hanson and Pratt 1995 to be very useful and interesting.

Much of my discussion of the part-time labor market draws on Tilly 1990 and 1996. Other sources include Chamallas 1986, Owen 1989, Stratton 1994, and the Statistical Abstract.

Jones 1988, 1989, and 1994 were indispensable sources for the historical discussions. Siegel 1994a and 1994b give a fine account of the history of marital property. Kessler-Harris 1995 was the main source for social security history. Paul 1954, Stanley 1993, Webber and Wildavsky 1986, and Witte 1985 are good sources on the history of the income tax in general. Goldin 1990 gives a comprehensive survey of general labor market history, and so do Kessler-Harris 1981 and 1982. Abramovitz 1988, Bergmann 1986, Fuchs 1988, and Matthaei 1982 are also helpful. Besides these I used a variety of primary sources, such as the Statistics of Income, legal decisions and official records of Supreme Court cases, and many transcripts of government hearings. I frequently had recourse to various historically annotated versions of the Internal Revenue Code, 26 U.S.C. §1 and following, and other laws and regulations.

The earned-income tax credit is discussed in Alstott 1995, Yin 1994, Yin, Scholz, Forman, and Mazur 1994.

Good discussions of community property can be found in Blumberg 1993 and DeFuniak 1971. McKay 1925 provides some historical perspective.

Becker 1989, Blumberg 1980, Boskin and Puffert 1987, Kessler-Harris 1995, and Steuerle and Bakija 1994 were my major sources for the discussion of social security in chapter 4. More general background can be found in Myers 1993 and in Nash, Pugach, and Tomasson 1988. Contemporary reform ideas are discussed in Ferber 1993 as well as in Steuerle and Bakija 1994.

Good general sources for the type of liberal social and political theory I employ throughout are Rawls 1971 and 1993, Scheffler 1988, Sen 1992, and Sen and Williams 1982. A feminist perspective on the liberal tradition is set out in Okin 1989. Lloyd 1994 is a helpful essay integrating contemporary social and political theory with feminism. I discuss much of this in McCaffery 1996. For more general feminist theory, I have profited from

Chodorow 1978, Friedan 1963, Grant 1993, Lerner 1986, MacKinnon 1987, Olsen 1983, Shultz 1990, the essays in Weisberg 1993, and Williams 1989. Ferber and Nelson 1993 is an interesting volume that attempts to combine feminist and economic perspectives.

Optimal tax is discussed in both McCaffery 1993a and 1993b. Good, fairly general introductions can be found in Bankman and Griffith 1987, Bradford and Rosen 1976, and Slemrod 1990a. More advanced general discussion can be found in Atkinson 1995 and Atkinson and Stiglitz 1980. The classic sources are Mirrlees 1971 and Ramsey 1927. Boskin and Sheshinski 1983 is a prime source on the application to the family and married women. Goldin 1990 has a good general discussion of elasticities for married women over time. I have also used Eissa 1996, Feenberg and Rosen 1983, Hausman 1981 and 1985, Hausman and Poterba 1987, Heckman 1993, Hunt, DeLorme, and Hill 1981, Killingsworth and Heckman 1986, Leuthold 1983 and 1984, MaCurdy 1992, MaCurdy, Green, and Paarsch 1990, Mroz 1987, Pencavel 1986, Rosen 1976, and Triest 1990. Piggott and Whalley 1996 appeared while this book was in press; I comment on the article briefly in the preceding notes.

The labor markets are a more diffuse topic that I treat rather summarily. Much of my discussion is drawn from general microeconomic principles, which can be found in texts such as Kreps 1990, Nicholson 1989, and Varian 1992. Coase [1937] 1988, Smith [1776] 1981, and Spence 1974 are classics. Arrow 1973 contains a good general discussion of statistical discrimination, as do Phelps 1972 and Schwab 1986. A neoclassical view of the family is famously set forth in Becker 1991; Becker 1971 is a related analysis of theories of discrimination, prominently featuring human capital models. Blau and Ferber 1992 and Goldin 1990 are important sources on women's roles in labor markets; Blau and Ferber 1992 is helpfully arranged around different theories of labor market discrimination and contains many useful citations. I have also drawn on Cohen and Haberfeld 1991, Hersch and Reagan 1990, Hersch and Stratton 1994, Hill 1979, Jacobsen and Levin 1995, Lazear and Rosen 1990, Light and Ureta 1992, Loprest 1992, Lundberg and Startz 1983, Maume 1991, Rubery 1987, Sorensen 1991, and Stratton 1994 and 1995. Legal perspectives of a laissez-faire bent can be found in Epstein 1992, Fischel and Lazear 1986, and Posner 1987, 1989a, and 1989b; good responses are set forth in Becker 1986; Donohue 1986, 1989, and 1992; Rutherglen 1992; and Verkerke 1992.

Abramovitz, Mimi. 1988. *Regulating the Lives of Women: Social Welfare Policy from Colonial Times to the Present.* Boston: South End Press.

Alm, James, and Leslie A. Whittington. 1995. Does the Income Tax Affect Marital Decisions? *National Tax Journal* 48:565–72.

Alstott, Anne L. 1995. The Earned Income Tax Credit and the Limitations of Tax-Based Welfare Reform. *Harvard Law Review* 108:533–92.

Altshuler, Rosanne, and Amy Ellen Schwartz. 1996. On the Progressivity of the Child Care Tax Credit: Snapshot versus Time-Exposure Incidence. *National Tax Journal* 49:55–71.

Arrow, Kenneth J. 1973. The Theory of Discrimination. In *Discrimination in Labor Markets*, edited by Orley Ashenfelter and Albert Rees. Princeton: Princeton University Press.

Atkinson, Anthony B. 1995. *Public Economics in Action: The Basic Income/Flat Tax Proposal.* Oxford: Clarendon Press.

Atkinson, Anthony B., and Joseph E. Stiglitz. 1980. *Lectures on Public Finance.* New York: McGraw-Hill.

Bankman, Joseph, and Thomas Griffith. 1987. Social Welfare and the Rate Structure: A New Look at Progressive Taxation. *California Law Review* 75:1905–67.

Barton, Walter E. 1950. *Federal Income, Estate, and Gift Tax Laws Correlated.* 10th ed. Washington, D.C.: Tax Law Publishing Co.

Becker, Gary S. 1971. *The Economics of Discrimination.* 2d ed. Chicago: University of Chicago Press.

———. 1991. *A Treatise on the Family.* Enl. ed. Cambridge: Harvard University Press.

Becker, Mary E. 1986. Barriers Facing Women in the Wage-Labor Market and the Need for Additional Remedies: A Reply to Fischel and Lazear. *University of Chicago Law Review* 53:934–49.

———. 1989. Obscuring the Struggle: Sex Discrimination, Social Security, and Stone, Seidman, Sunstein, and Tushnet's *Constitutional Law. Columbia Law Review* 89:264–89.

Belton, Beth, and Tammi Wark. 1995. Economics of Child Care: Problems of Supply, Demand Defy Logic. *USA Today,* 13 October, sec. B, p. 1.

Bergmann, Barbara R. 1986. *The Economic Emergence of Women.* New York: Basic Books.

Berry, Mary Frances. 1993. *The Politics of Parenthood: Child Care, Women's Rights, and the Myth of the Good Mother.* New York: Penguin Books.

Bittker, Boris I. 1975. Federal Income Taxation and the Family. *Stanford Law Review* 27:1389–1463.

Blau, David M., ed. 1991. *The Economics of Child Care.* New York: Russell Sage Foundation.

Blau, Francine D., and Marianne A. Ferber. 1992. *The Economics of Women, Men, and Work.* 2d ed. Englewood Cliffs, N.J.: Prentice-Hall.

Block, Caryn J., Madeline E. Heilman, Richard F. Martell, and Michael C. Simon. 1989. Has Anything Changed? Current Characterizations of Men, Women, and Managers. *Journal of Applied Psychology* 74:935–42.

Blumberg, Grace Ganz. 1972. Sexism in the Code: A Comparative Study of Income Taxation of Working Wives and Mothers. *Buffalo Law Review* 21:49–98.

———. 1980. Adult Derivative Benefits in Social Security. *Stanford Law Review* 32:233–92.

———. 1993. *Community Property in California.* 2d ed. Boston: Little, Brown and Company.

Boskin, Michael J., and Douglas J. Puffert. 1987. Social Security and the American Family. In *Tax Policy and the Economy,* vol. 1, edited by Lawrence H. Summers. Cambridge, Mass.: National Bureau of Economic Research and MIT Press.

Boskin, Michael J., and Eytan Sheshinski. 1983. Optimal Tax Treatment of the Family: Married Couples. *Journal of Public Economics* 20:281–97.

Bradford, David F., and Harvey S. Rosen. 1976. The Optimal Taxation of Commodities and Income. *American Economic Association Papers and Proceedings* 66:94–101.

Budget of the United States Government. 1995. *Historical Tables: Fiscal Year 1996.* Washington, D.C.: GPO.

Cain, Patricia A. 1991. Same-Sex Couples and the Federal Tax Laws. *Law and Sexuality* 1:97–131.

Campbell, Donald J., Kathleen M. Campbell, and Daniel Kennard. 1994. The Effects of Family Responsibilities on the Work Commitment and Job Performance of Non-Professional Women. *Journal of Occupational and Organizational Psychology* 67:283–96.

Casper, Lynne M. 1995. *What Does It Cost to Mind Our Preschoolers?* U.S. Department of Commerce. *Current Population Reports* P70–92, September.

Center on Budget and Policy Priorities. 1995. Only about Half of Children Receive Full Child Tax Credit: Those Denied Credit Heavily Concentrated on Low-Income Families. 21 November.

Chamallas, Martha. 1986. Women and Part-Time Work: The Case for Pay Equity and Equal Access. *North Carolina Law Review* 64:709–75.

Chodorow, Nancy. 1978. *The Reproduction of Mothering: Psychoanalysis and the Sociology of Gender.* Berkeley: University of California Press.

Christian Coalition. 1995. *Contract with the American Family: A Bold Plan by Christian Coalition to Strengthen the Family and Restore Common-Sense Values.* Nashville: Moorings.

Citizens for Tax Justice. 1996. Table: The Cost of Congress's Pending 1995 Tax Bill.

Coase, Ronald H. [1937] 1988. The Nature of the Firm. In *The Firm, the Market, and the Law.* Chicago: University of Chicago Press.

Cohen, Yinon, and Yitchak Haberfeld. 1991. Why Do Married Men Earn More than Unmarried Men? *Social Science Research* 20:29–44.

Cuvillier, Rolande. 1979. The Housewife: An Unjustified Financial Burden on the Community. *Journal of Social Policy* 8:1–26.

Czapanskiy, Karen. 1991. Volunteers and Draftees: The Struggle for Parental Equality. *UCLA Law Review* 38:1415–81.

DeFuniak, William Q., and Michael J. Vaughn. 1971. *Principles of Community Property.* 2d ed. Tucson: University of Arizona Press.

Donohue, John J. III. 1986. Is Title VII Efficient? *University of Pennsylvania Law Review* 134:1411–31.

———. 1989. Prohibiting Sex Discrimination in the Workplace: An Economic Perspective. *University of Chicago Law Review* 56:1337–68.

———. 1992. Advocacy versus Analysis in Assessing Employment Discrimination Law. *Stanford Law Review* 44:1583–1614.

Dowd, Nancy E. 1989. Work and Family: The Gender Paradox and the Limitations of Discrimination Analysis in Restructuring the Workplace. *Harvard Civil Rights–Civil Liberties Law Review* 24:79–172.

———. 1990. Work and Family: Restructuring the Workplace. *Arizona Law Review* 32:431–500.

———. 1995. Stigmatizing Single Parents. *Harvard Women's Law Journal* 18:19–82.

Eissa, Nada. 1996. Tax Reforms and Labor Supply. In *Tax Policy and the Economy*, vol. 16, edited by James M. Poterba. Cambridge, Mass.: National Bureau of Economic Research.

Epstein, Richard A. 1992. *Forbidden Grounds: The Case against Employment Discrimination Laws*. Cambridge: Harvard University Press.

Evetts, Julia. 1988. Managing Childcare and Work Responsibilities: The Strategies of Married Women Primary and Infant Headteachers. *Sociological Review* 36:503–31.

Faludi, Susan. 1991. *Backlash: The Undeclared War against American Women*. New York: Crown Publishers.

Feenberg, Daniel R., and Harvey S. Rosen. 1983. Alternative Tax Treatments of the Family: Simulation Methodology and Results. In *Behavioral Simulation Methods in Tax Policy Analysis*, edited by Martin Feldstein. Chicago: University of Chicago Press.

———. 1995. Recent Developments in the Marriage Tax. *National Tax Journal* 48: 91–101.

Ferber, Marianne A. 1993. Women's Employment and the Social Security System. *Social Security Bulletin* 56:33–55.

Ferber, Marianne A., and Julie A. Nelson, eds. 1993. *Beyond Economic Man: Feminist Theory and Economics*. Chicago: University of Chicago Press.

Fields, Judith, and Edward N. Wolff. 1991. The Decline of Sex Segregation and the Wage Gap, 1970–80. *Journal of Human Resources* 26:608–22.

Fischel, Daniel R. and Edward P. Lazear. 1986. Comparable Worth and Discrimination in Labor Markets. *University of Chicago Law Review* 53:891–918.

Fleenor, Patrick, ed. 1995. *Facts and Figures on Government Finance*. 30th ed. Washington, D.C.: Tax Foundation.

Friedan, Betty. 1963. *The Feminine Mystique*. New York: W. W. Norton and Company.

Fuchs, Victor R. 1988. *Women's Quest for Economic Equality*. Cambridge: Harvard University Press.

Gann, Pamela B. 1980. Abandoning Marital Status as a Factor in Allocating Income Tax Burdens. *Texas Law Review* 59:1–69.

———. 1983. The Earned Income Deduction: Congress's 1981 Response to the "Marriage Penalty" Tax. *Cornell Law Review* 68:468–87.

Gerstel, Naomi, and Harriet Engel Gross, eds. 1987. *Families and Work*. Philadelphia: Temple University Press.

Goldin, Claudia. 1990. *Understanding the Gender Gap: An Economic History of American Women*. Cambridge: Harvard University Press.

———. 1995. *Career and Family: College Women Look to the Past*. Working Paper No. 5188. Cambridge, Mass.: National Bureau of Economic Research.

Gordon, Linda. 1994. *Pitied but Not Entitled: Single Mothers and the History of Welfare 1890–1935*. Cambridge: Harvard University Press.

Grant, Judith. 1993. *Fundamental Feminism: Contesting the Core Concepts of Feminist Theory*. New York: Routledge.

Greenstein, Robert, Isaac Shapiro, and Sharon Parrott. 1995. Senate Child Tax Credit Proposals Would Raise Taxes for Low-Income Working Families and Reduce Them for Wealthy Families. *Center on Budget and Policy Priorities*, 27 September.

Groves, Harold M. 1963. *Federal Tax Treatment of the Family*. Washington, D.C.: Brookings Institution.

Hall, Kermit L., ed. 1992. *The Oxford Companion to the Supreme Court of the United States.* New York: Oxford University Press.

Hall, Robert E., and Alvin Rabushka. 1995. *The Flat Tax.* 2d ed. Stanford: Hoover Institution Press.

Hanson, Sandra L., and Theodora Ooms. 1991. The Economic Costs and Rewards of Two-Earner, Two-Parent Families. *Journal of Marriage and the Family* 53:622–34.

Hanson, Susan, and Geraldine Pratt. 1995. *Gender, Work, and Space.* New York: Routledge.

Harris, Diane. 1996. How Does Your Pay Stack Up? Salary Survey 1996. *Working Woman*, February, 27–37.

Hausman, Jerry A. 1981. Labor Supply. In *How Taxes Affect Economic Behavior*, edited by Henry J. Aaron and Joseph A. Pechman. Washington, D.C.: Brookings Institution.

————. 1985. Taxes and Labor Supply. In *Handbook of Public Economics*, vol. 1, edited by Alan J. Auerbach and Martin Feldstein. Amsterdam: Elsevier Science Publishers.

Hausman, Jerry A., and James M. Poterba. 1987. Household Behavior and the Tax Reform Act of 1986. *Journal of Economic Perspectives* 1:101–19.

Hayghe, Howard V., and Steven E. Haugen. 1987. A Profile of Husbands in Today's Labor Market. *Monthly Labor Review* 110 (10):12–17.

Heckman, James J. 1993. What Has Been Learned about Labor Supply in the Past Twenty Years? *American Economic Review Papers and Proceedings* 83:116–21.

Hersch, Joni, and Patricia Reagan. 1990. Job Match, Tenure, and Wages Paid by Firms. *Economic Inquiry* 28:488–507.

Hersch, Joni, and Leslie S. Stratton. 1994. Housework, Wages, and the Division of Housework Time for Employed Spouses. *American Economic Review* 84:120–25.

Hill, Martha S. 1979. The Wage Effects of Marital Status and Children. *Journal of Human Resources* 14:579–93.

Hochschild, Arlie. 1989. *The Second Shift: Working Parents and the Revolution at Home.* New York: Viking Penguin.

Hofferth, Sandra L., April Brayfield, Sharon Deich, and Pamela Holcomb. 1991. *National Child Care Survey, 1990.* Urban Institute Report 91-5. Washington, D.C.: Urban Institute Press.

Holmes, Oliver Wendell. 1897. The Path of the Law. *Harvard Law Review* 10:457–78.

Hume, David. 1978. *A Treatise of Human Nature.* 2d ed. Edited by L. A. Selby-Bigge and P. H. Nidditch. Oxford: Oxford University Press.

Hunt, Janet C., Charles D. DeLorme, Jr., and R. Carter Hill. 1981. Taxation and the Wife's Use of Time. *Industrial and Labor Relations Review* 34:426–32.

Hunt, Janet G., and Larry L. Hunt. 1987. Male Resistance to Role Symmetry in Dual-Earner Households: Three Alternative Explanations. In *Families and Work*, edited by Naomi Gerstel and Harriet Engel Gross. Philadelphia: Temple University Press.

Jacobsen, Joyce P., and Laurence M. Levin. 1995. Effects of Intermittent Labor Force Attachment on Women's Earnings. *Monthly Labor Review* 118 (9): 14–19.

Johnson, Elizabeth. 1991. I Couldn't Afford My Job. *Redbook*, April, 89.

Jones, Carolyn C. 1988. Split Income and Separate Spheres: Tax Law and Gender Roles in the 1940s. *Law and History Review* 6:259–310.

————. 1989. Class Tax to Mass Tax: The Role of Propaganda in the Expansion of the Income Tax during World War II. *Buffalo Law Review* 37:685–737.

———. 1994. Dollars and Selves: Women's Tax Criticism and Resistance in the 1870s. *University of Illinois Law Review* 1994:265–309.

Kessler-Harris, Alice. 1981. *Women Have Always Worked: A Historical Overview*. Old Westbury, N.Y.: Feminist Press.

———. 1982. *Out to Work: A History of Wage-Earning Women in the United States*. New York: Oxford University Press.

———. 1995. Designing Women and Old Fools: The Construction of the Social Security Amendments of 1939. In *U.S. History as Women's History: New Feminist Essays*, edited by Linda K. Kerber, Alice Kessler-Harris, and Kathryn Kish Sklar. Chapel Hill: University of North Carolina Press.

Keynes, John Maynard. [1936] 1964. *The General Theory of Employment, Interest, and Money*. New York: Harcourt Brace Jovanovich.

Killingsworth, Mark, and James J. Heckman. 1986. Female Labor Supply: A Survey. In *Handbook of Labor Economics*, vol. 1, edited by Orley Ashenfelter and Richard Layard. Amsterdam: Elsevier Science Publishers.

Kim, Chankon. 1989. Working Wives' Time-Saving Tendencies: Durable Ownership, Convenience Food Consumption, and Meal Purchases. *Journal of Economic Psychology* 10:391–409.

Klein, William A. 1973. Tax Deductions for Family Care Expenses. *Boston College Industrial and Commercial Law Review* 14:917–41.

Kolbert, Elizabeth. 1995. Politicians Find a Window Into the Heart of the Christian Right. *New York Times*, 1 November, sec. A, p. 14, late edition.

Kornhauser, Marjorie E. 1993. Love, Money, and the IRS: Family, Income-Sharing, and the Joint Income Tax Return. *Hastings Law Journal* 45:63–111.

Kreps, David M. 1990. *A Course in Microeconomic Theory*. Princeton: Princeton University Press.

Langbein, John H., and Bruce A. Wolk. 1990. *Pension and Employee Benefit Law*. Old Westbury, N.Y.: Foundation Press.

Lazear, Edward P., and Sherwin Rosen. 1990. Male-Female Wage Differentials in Job Ladders. *Journal of Labor Economics* 8:S106–S123.

Lerner, Gerda. 1986. *The Creation of Patriarchy*. New York: Oxford University Press.

Leuthold, Jane H. 1983. Home Production and the Tax System. *Journal of Economic Psychology* 3:145–57.

———. 1984. Income Splitting and Women's Labor-Force Participation. *Industrial and Labor Relations Review* 38:98–105.

Lewin, Tamar. 1991. For Some Two-Paycheck Families, the Economics Don't Add Up. *New York Times*, 21 April, sec. E, p. 18.

Light, Audrey, and Manuelita Ureta. 1992. Panel Estimates of Male and Female Job Turnover Behavior: Can Female Nonquitters Be Identified? *Journal of Labor Economics* 10:156–81.

Lloyd, S. A. 1994. Family Justice and Social Justice. *Pacific Philosophical Quarterly* 75: 353–71.

Loprest, Pamela J. 1992. Gender Differences in Wage Growth and Job Mobility. *American Economic Review* 82:526–32.

Lundberg, Shelly J., and Richard Startz. 1983. Private Discrimination and Social Intervention in Competitive Labor Markets. *American Economic Review* 73:340–47.

MacKinnon, Catharine A. 1987. *Feminism Unmodified: Discourses on Life and Law*. Cambridge: Harvard University Press.

MaCurdy, Thomas. 1992. Work Disincentive Effects of Taxes: A Reexamination of Some Evidence. *American Economic Review Papers and Proceedings* 82:243–49.

MaCurdy, Thomas, David Green, and Harry Paarsch. 1990. Assessing Empirical Approaches for Analyzing Taxes and Labor Supply. *Journal of Human Resources* 25 (3):415–90.

Mahony, Rhona. 1995. *Kidding Ourselves: Breadwinning, Babies, and Bargaining Power.* New York: Basic Books.

Mansbridge, Jane J. 1986. *Why We Lost the ERA.* Chicago: University of Chicago Press.

Matthaei, Julie A. 1982. *An Economic History of Women in America: Women's Work, the Sexual Division of Labor, and the Development of Capitalism.* New York: Schocken Books.

Maume, David J. Jr. 1991. Child-Care Expenditures and Women's Employment Turnover. *Social Forces* 70:495–508.

McCaffery, Edward J. 1993a. Slouching towards Equality: Gender Discrimination, Market Efficiency, and Social Change. *Yale Law Journal* 103:595–675.

———. 1993b. Taxation and the Family: A Fresh Look at Behavioral Gender Bias in the Code. *UCLA Law Review* 40:983–1060.

———. 1994a. Cognitive Theory and Tax. *UCLA Law Review* 41:1861–1947.

———. 1994b. The Political Liberal Case against the Estate Tax. *Philosophy and Public Affairs* 23:281–312.

———. 1996. Equality, Of the Right Sort. *UCLA Women's Law Journal* 6:289–320.

McIntyre, Michael J. 1980. Individual Filing in the Personal Income Tax: Prolegomena to Future Discussion. *North Carolina Law Review* 58:469–89.

McIntyre, Michael J., and Oliver Oldman. 1977. Taxation of the Family in a Comprehensive and Simplified Income Tax. *Harvard Law Review* 90:1573–1630.

McKay, George. 1925. *A Treatise on the Law of Community Property.* 2d ed. Indianapolis: Bobbs-Merrill Company.

McKenry, Patrick C., and Sharon J. Price, eds. 1994. *Families and Change: Coping with Stressful Events.* Thousand Oaks, Calif.: Sage Publications.

Mirrlees, James A. 1971. An Exploration in the Theory of Optimum Income Taxation. *Review of Economic Studies* 38:175–208.

Mroz, Thomas A. 1987. The Sensitivity of an Empirical Model of Married Women's Hours of Work to Economic and Statistical Assumptions. *Econometrica* 55:765–99.

Munnell, Alicia H. 1980. The Couple versus the Individual under the Federal Personal Income Tax. In *The Economics of Taxation,* edited by Henry J. Aaron and Michael J. Boskin. Washington, D.C.: Brookings Institution.

Myers, Robert J. 1993. *Social Security.* 4th ed. Philadelphia: Pension Research Council and University of Pennsylvania Press.

Nasar, Sylvia. 1992. Women's Progress Stalled? Just Not So. *New York Times,* 18 October, sec. 3, p. 1, late edition.

Nash, Gerald D., Noel H. Pugach, and Richard F. Tomasson, eds. 1988. *Social Security: The First Half-Century.* Albuquerque: University of New Mexico Press.

Newbery, David M. 1989. Missing Markets: Consequences and Remedies. In *The Economics of Missing Markets, Information, and Games,* edited by Frank Hahn. Oxford: Oxford University Press.

Nicholson, Walter. 1989. *Microeconomic Theory: Basic Principles and Extensions.* 4th ed. Chicago: Dryden Press.

Nickols, Sharon Y. 1994. Work/Family Stresses. In *Families and Change: Coping with Stressful Events*, edited by Patrick C. McKenry and Sharon J. Price. Thousand Oaks, Calif: Sage Publications.

Nickols, Sharon Y., and Karen D. Fox. 1983. Buying time and Saving Time: Strategies for Managing Household Production. *Journal of Consumer Research* 10:197–208.

Okin, Susan Moller. 1989. *Justice, Gender, and the Family.* New York: Basic Books.

Oldman, Oliver, and Ralph Temple. 1960. Comparative Analysis of the Taxation of Married Persons. *Stanford Law Review* 12:585–605.

Olsen, Frances E. 1983. The Family and the Market: A Study of Ideology and Legal Reform. *Harvard Law Review* 96:1497–1578.

O'Neill, June Elenoff. 1994. The Shrinking Pay Gap. *Wall Street Journal*, 7 October, sec. A, p. 10.

Owen, John D. 1989. *Reduced Working Hours: Cure for Unemployment or Economic Burden?* Baltimore: Johns Hopkins University Press.

Parenthood. 1989. Orlando, Fla.: Universal. Film.

Paul, Randolph E. 1954. *Taxation in the United States.* Boston: Little, Brown and Company.

Pechman, Joseph A. 1966. *Federal Tax Policy.* Washington, D.C.: Brookings Institution.

Pechman, Joseph A., and Gary V. Englehardt. 1990. The Income Tax Treatment of the Family: An International Perspective. *National Tax Journal* 43:1–22.

Pencavel, John. 1986. Labor Supply of Men: A Survey. In *Handbook of Labor Economics*, vol. 1, edited by Orley Ashenfelter and Richard Layard. Amsterdam: Elsevier Science Publishers.

Phelps, Edmund S. 1972. The Statistical Theory of Racism and Sexism. *American Economic Review* 62:659–61.

Piggott, John, and John Whalley. 1996. The Tax Unit and Household Production. *Journal of Political Economy* 104:398–418.

Pollitt, Katha. 1995. Subject to Debate; Political Ramifications of Children out of Wedlock. *The Nation* 260:120.

Posner, Richard A. 1987. The Efficiency and Efficacy of Title VII. *University of Pennsylvania Law Review* 136:513–21.

———. 1989a. An Economic Analysis of Sex Discrimination Laws. *University of Chicago Law Review* 56:1311–35.

———. 1989b. Conservative Feminism. *University of Chicago Legal Forum* 191–217.

Quintanilla, Carl. 1996. After the Kids: For Parents Re-Entering the Job Market, Getting a Career Back on Track Requires Overcoming a Lot of Misconceptions. *Wall Street Journal*, 26 February, sec. R, p. 10.

Ramsey, Frank P. 1927. A Contribution to the Theory of Taxation. *Economic Journal* 37:47–61.

Rawls, John. 1971. *A Theory of Justice.* Cambridge: Harvard University Press.

———. 1993. *Political Liberalism.* New York: Columbia University Press.

Reagan, Ronald. 1986. Remarks on Signing H.R. 3838 into Law. *Weekly Compilation of Presidential Documents* 22:1423–25.

Republican National Committee. 1994. *Contract with America: The Bold Plan by Rep. Newt Gingrich, Rep. Dick Armey, and the House Republicans to Change the Nation.* New York: Times Books.

Rosen, Harvey S. 1976. Tax Illusion and the Labor Supply of Married Women. *Review of Economics and Statistics* 58:167–72.

———. 1977. Is It Time to Abandon Joint Filing? *National Tax Journal* 30:423–28.

———. 1987. The Marriage Tax Is Down but Not Out. *National Tax Journal* 40:567–75.

Rubery, J. 1987. Women's Wages. In *The New Palgrave: Social Economics*, edited by John Eatwell, Murray Milgate, and Peter Newman. London: Macmillan Press.

Rutherglen, George. 1992. Abolition in a Different Voice. Review of *Forbidden Grounds: The Case against Employment Discrimination Laws*, by Richard A. Epstein. *Virginia Law Review* 78:1463–80.

Scanlon, T. M. 1975. Preference and Urgency. *Journal of Philosophy* 72:655–69.

Scheffler, Samuel, ed. 1988. *Consequentialism and Its Critics*. Oxford: Oxford University Press.

Schwab, Stewart. 1986. Is Statistical Discrimination Efficient? *American Economic Review* 76:228–34.

Schwartz, Felice N. 1992a. *Breaking with Tradition: Women and Work, The New Facts of Life*. New York: Warner Books.

———. 1992b. Women as a Business Imperative. *Harvard Business Review* 70:105–13.

Sen, Amartya. 1992. *Inequality Reexamined*. New York: Russell Sage Foundation.

Sen, Amartya, and Bernard Williams, eds. 1982. *Utilitarianism and Beyond*. Cambridge: Cambridge University Press.

Shapiro, Isaac. 1995. The House Child Income Tax Credit: Who Would Be Helped? *Center on Budget and Policy Priorities*, 30 October.

Shellenbarger, Sue. 1996. Work & Family: What You Should Say about Family Duties in a Job Interview. *Wall Street Journal*, 10 April, sec. B, p. 1.

Shellenbarger, Sue, Matt Moffett, and Kathy Chen. 1995. Universal Concerns: Around the World, Women are United by Child-Care Woes. *Wall Street Journal*, 25 August, sec. A, p. 1.

Schultz, Vicki. 1990. Telling Stories about Women and Work: Judicial Interpretations of Sex Segregation in the Workplace in Title VII Cases Raising the Lack of Interest Argument. *Harvard Law Review* 103:1750–1843.

Siegel, Reva B. 1994a. Home as Work: The First Woman's Rights Claims Concerning Wives' Household Labor, 1850–1880. *Yale Law Journal* 103:1073–1217.

———. 1994b. The Modernization of Marital Status Law: Adjudicating Wives' Rights to Earnings, 1860–1930. *Georgetown Law Journal* 82:2127–2211.

Simons, Henry C. 1938. *Personal Income Taxation: The Definition of Income as a Problem of Fiscal Policy*. Chicago: University of Chicago Press.

Sjoquist, David L., and Mary Beth Walker. 1995. The Marriage Tax and the Rate and Timing of Marriage. *National Tax Journal* 48:547–58.

Slemrod, Joel. 1990a. Optimal Taxation and Optimal Tax Systems. *Journal of Economic Perspectives* 4 (1):157–78.

Slemrod, Joel, ed. 1990b. *Do Taxes Matter? The Impact of the Tax Reform Act of 1986*. Cambridge: MIT Press.

Smith, Adam. [1776] 1981. *An Inquiry into the Nature and Causes of the Wealth of Nations*. 2 vols. Edited by R. H. Campbell and A. S. Skinner. Reprint, Indianapolis: Liberty Classics.

Sorensen, Elaine. 1991. *Exploring the Reasons behind the Narrowing Gender Gap in Earnings.* Washington, D.C.: Urban Institute Press.

Spence, A. Michael. 1974. *Market Signaling: Informational Transfer in Hiring and Related Screening Processes.* Cambridge: Harvard University Press.

Stanley, Robert. 1993. *Dimensions of Law in the Service of Order: Origins of the Federal Income Tax, 1861–1913.* New York: Oxford University Press.

Staudt, Nancy C. 1996. Taxing Housework. *Georgetown Law Journal* 84:1571–1647.

Steuerle, Gene. 1995a. The True Tax Rate Structure. *Tax Notes* 69:371–72.

———. 1995b. Combined Tax Rates and AFDC Recipients. *Tax Notes* 69:501–3.

———. 1995c. Giving Jobs to Welfare Recipients: The Tax Rates They Face. *Tax Notes* 69:641–44.

Steuerle, C. Eugene, and Jon M. Bakija. 1994. *Retooling Social Security for the 21st Century: Right and Wrong Approaches to Reform.* Washington, D.C.: Urban Institute Press.

Stiglitz, Joseph E. 1987. Pareto Efficient and Optimal Taxation and the New New Welfare Economics. In *Handbook of Public Economics*, vol. 2, edited by Alan J. Auerbach and Martin Feldstein. Amsterdam: Elsevier Science Publishers.

Stratton, Leslie S. 1994. Reexamining Involuntary Part-Time Employment. *Journal of Economic and Social Measurement* 20:95–115.

———. 1995. The Effect Interruptions in Work Have on Wages. *Southern Economic Journal* 61:955–70.

Surrey, Stanley S. 1948. Federal Taxation of the Family—The Revenue Act of 1948. *Harvard Law Review* 61:1097–1164.

Thorson, Douglas Y. 1965. An Analysis of the Sources of Continued Controversy over the Tax Treatment of Family Income. *National Tax Journal* 18:113–32.

Tilly, Chris. 1990. *Short Hours, Short Shrift: Cause and Consequences of Part-Time Work.* Washington, D.C.: Economic Policy Institute.

———. 1996. *Half a Job: Bad and Good Part-Time Jobs in a Changing Labor Market.* Philadelphia: Temple University Press.

Tolman, Audrey E., Kristina A. Diekmann, and Kathleen McCartney. 1989. Social Connectedness and Mothering: Effects of Maternal Employment and Maternal Absence. *Journal of Personality and Social Psychology* 56:942–49.

Trapp, Michael W., Roger H. Hermanson, and Joseph V. Carcello. 1991. Characteristics of Chief Financial Officers. *Corporate Growth Report* 9:17–20.

Triest, Robert K. 1990. The Effect of Income Taxation on Labor Supply in the United States. *Journal of Human Resources* 25:491–515.

U.S. Bureau of the Census. 1976. *The Statistical History of the United States: From Colonial Times to the Present*, with an introduction by Ben J. Wattenberg. New York: Basic Books.

U.S. Congress. 1973. Joint Economic Committee. *Economic Problems of Women: Hearings before the Joint Economic Committee.* 93d Cong., 1st sess.

U.S. Congress. 1987. Staff of the Joint Committee on Taxation. *General Explanation of the Tax Reform Act of 1986 (Public Law 99–514).* 100th Cong., 1st sess. H. Rep. No. 3838.

U.S. Congress. Congressional Budget Office. 1988. *Trends in Family Income, 1970–1986.* Washington, D.C.: GPO.

U.S. Department of Commerce. U.S. Bureau of the Census. 1994. *Statistical Abstract of the United States.* 114th ed. Washington, D.C.: GPO.

U.S. House. 1947. Committee on Ways and Means. *Revenue Revisions, 1947–48: Hearings before the Committee on Ways and Means.* 80th Cong., 1st sess.

U.S. House. 1980. Committee on Ways and Means. *Tax Treatment of Married, Head of Household, and Single Taxpayers: Hearings before the Committee on Ways and Means.* 96th Cong., 2d sess. Serial 96–93.

U.S. House. 1985. Committee on Ways and Means. *Comprehensive Tax Reform: Hearings before the Committee on Ways and Means,* vols. 1 and 4. 99th Cong., 1st sess. Serial 99–41, 99–44.

U.S. House, 1991. Select Committee on Children, Youth, and Families. *Reclaiming the Tax Code for American Families: Hearings before the Select Committee on Children, Youth, and Families.* 102d Cong., 1st sess.

U.S. House. 1993. Committee on Ways and Means. *Background Material and Data on Programs within the Jurisdiction of the Committee on Ways and Means.* 103d Cong., 1st sess.

U.S. Senate. 1986. Committee on Finance. *Tax Reform Act of 1986: Hearings before the Committee on Finance, Parts I, II, III.* 99th Cong., 2d sess.

U.S. Treasury Department. Internal Revenue Service. 1921–1954. *Statistics of Income: Compiled from the Returns for 1918–1949.* 31 vols. Washington, D.C.: GPO.

Usdansky, Margaret L. 1996. Single Motherhood: Stereotypes vs. Statistics. *New York Times,* 11 February, sec. 4, p. 4, late edition.

Varian, Hal R. 1992. *Microeconomic Analysis.* 3d ed. New York: W. W. Norton and Company.

Verkerke, J. Hoult. 1992. Free to Search. Review of *Forbidden Grounds: The Case against Employment Discrimination Laws,* by Richard A. Epstein. *Harvard Law Review* 105:2080–97.

Veum, Jonathan R., and Philip M. Gleason. 1991. Child Care: Arrangements and Costs. *Monthly Labor Review* 114(10):10–17.

Webber, Carolyn, and Aaron Wildavsky. 1986. *A History of Taxation and Expenditure in the Western World.* New York: Simon and Schuster.

Weiler, Paul C. 1990. *Governing the Workplace: The Future of Labor and Employment Law.* Cambridge: Harvard University Press.

Weisberg, D. Kelly, ed. 1993. *Feminist Legal Theory Foundations.* Philadelphia: Temple University Press.

Wethington, Elaine, and Ronald C. Kessler. 1989. Employment, Parental Responsibility, and Psychological Stress: A Longitudinal Study of Married Women. *Journal of Family Issues* 10:527–46.

Whitney, Sharon. 1984. *The Equal Rights Amendment: The History and the Movement.* New York: Franklin Watts.

Williams, Joan C. 1989. Deconstructing Gender. *Michigan Law Review* 87:797–845.

Witte, John F. 1985. *The Politics and Development of the Federal Income Tax.* Madison: University of Wisconsin Press.

Yin, George K. 1994. Summary of EITC Conference Proceedings. *American Journal of Tax Policy* 11:299–315.

Yin, George K., John K. Scholz, Jonathan B. Forman, and Mark J. Mazur. 1994. Improving the Delivery of Benefits to the Working Poor: Proposals to Reform the Earned Income Tax Credit. *American Journal of Tax Policy* 11:225–98.

Zax, Jeffrey S. 1988. Fringe Benefits, Income Tax Exemptions, and Implicit Subsidies. *Journal of Public Economics* 37:171–83.

Zelenak, Lawrence. 1994a. Children and the Income Tax. *Tax Law Review* 49:349–418.

———. 1994b. Marriage and the Income Tax. *Southern California Law Review* 67:339–405.

Zodrow, George R. 1992. Review of *Do Taxes Matter? The Impact of the Tax Reform Act of 1986*, edited by Joel Slemrod. *Journal of Economic Literature* 30:916–18.

Index